OMNIBUS MAGISTRIS MEIS
QUI IN ME A TENERA AETATE
STUDIUM ANTIQUITATIS FOVERUNT
A.H. †R.S.B. A.G.D.
A.G.H. C.H.B. I.B.F. C.R.B.E.
R.W.B.B. R.R. P.A.B. †I.A.R.

PREFACE

It is now well over thirty years since Syme's account of the Northern Frontiers under Augustus appeared in volume X of the *Cambridge Ancient History*. In this time, and especially in the last few years, archaeologists have greatly increased our knowledge of Roman military operations in this sector. Much new evidence has come to light in the course of road-building and other construction work, often revealing Roman sites whose existence was unsuspected thirty years ago. In this way Drusus' supply base at Rödgen was found during the levelling of a site for a new school; the Augustan and Tiberian bases at Neuss were discovered during the construction of an autobahn and a housing estate; and other chance finds have revealed the bases at Anreppen and Dangstetten. Techniques of excavation have become increasingly refined, and a better knowledge of pottery (Appendix I) and coinage (Appendix II) permits us to date these new sites more accurately, and requires us to re-examine the accepted conclusions about the old ones. It is one of the aims of this present work to bring together all relevant evidence and to see what conclusions we may draw from it.

It is now also thirty years since the publication of Syme's *The Roman Revolution*, written by a man who had just watched the rise of Hitler and the Spanish Civil War, a work which showed us Augustus as the ruthless party boss out for power, and not too nice about his methods and his henchmen. Thirty years on, we have still more experience of what it all really meant, the spontaneous acclamation by 'tota Italia', 'respublica restituta', the dictatorship behind the façade of propaganda. And yet this new realization that Augustus was not an English gentleman has not led to a corresponding attempt to see his frontier policy in the contemporary Roman context. The traditional view that his aims were basically defensive still holds the field, although the discussion by Brunt in *JRS* liii (1963) of Meyer's *Die Aussenpolitik des Augustus und die augusteische Dichtung*, published in 1961, should have forced the

traditionalists to re-examine their assumptions. It is therefore
another of the aims of the present work to place Augustus'
German campaigns, as known to us from archaeological and
literary evidence, in the context of Roman imperialism and of
Augustus' own overriding ambition. I do not myself believe
that the conventional theory of a basically defensive frontier
policy can be sustained.

Syme found in European politics of the 1930s the key to the
understanding of Augustus' rise to power. Nothing in contemporary politics helps us to make the effort of historical
imagination required to appreciate his frontier policy. To
understand how the Romans felt about their empire in Late
Republican and Augustan times, we must go back to an
earlier generation than our own. Open and unashamed
imperialists, such as the Romans were (below, Chapter 1),
are nowadays virtually extinct, at least in the English-speaking
world. Imperialism must be veiled in the decent hypocrisy
of talk about 'liberation' and 'democracy'. But when James
Morris in his recent book *Pax Britannica*, writing of the British
Empire in the last years of the nineteenth century, speaks of
'a conviction, common among imperialists of diverse kinds,
that a spiritual destiny had called the British to their pre-
eminence' (p. 502), do we not recognize this as the same
conviction about Rome's destiny which we find in those two
noted imperialists, Livy and Virgil? Destiny has a habit of
leading ever onwards. When Morris records that 'the search
for a "scientific frontier" was endless' (p. 277), should this not
lead us to reflect upon the inherent unlikelihood of an Elbe–
Danube frontier proving satisfactory for long? What could
be more Roman in spirit than this passage: 'What enterprise
. . . is more noble and more profitable than the reclamation
from barbarism of fertile regions and large populations? To
give peace to warring tribes, to administer justice where all
was violence, . . . to draw richness from the soil, to plant the
earliest seeds of commerce and learning, to increase in whole
peoples their capacities for pleasure and diminish their chances
of pain—what more beautiful ideal or more valuable reward
can inspire human effort?' The author is not however Cicero
or Livy, but the young Winston Churchill (*The River War*, p. 9).

We, their grandchildren, are now often embarrassed by

the attitudes which the British of the 1890s and early 1900s displayed towards their subject peoples, or the barbarians on their borders. These attitudes are however very Roman. Read Cicero and the Augustan writers, or the panegyrists of Rome in later centuries, like Aelius Aristides or Rutilius, and compare them with Lord Curzon on the British mission in India; read Curzon's 1907 Romanes Lecture on 'Frontiers'; read Morris on the belief that the natives had to be ruled for their own good (p. 132), or on the attitude of Lord Cromer in Egypt (p. 245); read Lord Bryce on *The Ancient Roman Empire and the British Empire in India*, published in 1914; read Kipling, Newbolt, and a host of lesser writers; or study the history of British dealings with the native potentates in Southern Africa. What Alföldi has called 'the Moral Barrier on Rhine and Danube' had its late-nineteenth-century parallel.

Churchill himself picks out 'parcere subiectis et debellare superbos' as his ideal of policy, commenting: 'The Romans have often forestalled many of my best ideas, and I must concede to them the patent rights in this maxim' (*My Early Life*, p. 346). British methods of warring down the proud can put us uncomfortably in mind of Germanicus' raid on the Marsi in A.D. 14, when 'non sexus, non aetas miserationem attulit' (Tac., *Ann.* i. 51). What about this passage, again from Churchill, describing operations in which he took part on the North-West Frontier? 'Sir Bindon sent orders that we were to stay in the Mamund valley and lay it waste with fire and sword in vengeance. This we accordingly did. . . . Whether it was worth it, I cannot tell. At any rate, at the end of a fortnight the valley was a desert, and honour was satisfied' (*My Early Life*, p. 162). What unites British and Roman is the common conviction of being supremely in the right. We had God, or the gods, on our side, and a civilizing mission to perform. It is hard now to recapture this boundless confidence. Britain of course knew limits to her power, where Rome had a clearer field. As Brunt has written: 'Generals were ambitious for triumphs, and the Romans came to believe that they were destined by providence to rule the world. Cecil Rhodes entertained not much dissimilar ambitions for Britain, but sober statesmen like Salisbury hardly gave such dreams a thought' (*Comparative Studies in Society and History* vii (1965), pp. 267–88). Augustus may not

have thought that he could rule the whole world; but he had
no thought of renouncing fresh conquests. And it is the ultimate
aim of this book to demonstrate it.

It is perhaps an early diet of Kipling and others which
predisposed me to the study of Roman arms. The present work
however had its more immediate origin in an Oxford D. Phil.
thesis, 'The Frontiers of the Roman Empire under Augustus',
submitted and accepted in 1965. The thesis dealt with all the
frontiers of the Empire, and the omission from this book of
the chapters dealing with the Danube lands, the East, Egypt
and Africa, has entailed the complete rearrangement and
extensive rewriting of the other chapters. The archaeological
evidence has of course been brought up to date, and a wholly
new chapter on the Celts and Germans (Chapter 2) has been
added. Of the inadequacies of this chapter I am uncomfortably
aware; the subject could not be passed over in silence, but to
give it the treatment it deserves would require a whole book,
which many scholars are more competent to write than I am.
The conclusions put forward in Chapter 2 should be regarded
as highly tentative; the best I can hope is that they will serve to
stimulate the book that is needed.

This manuscript was closed in September 1969, immediately
after the Eighth International Congress of Roman Frontier
Studies and the Pilgrimage of Hadrian's Wall. New material
which has come to my notice since that date is included in the
Addenda, and the symbol [ADD.] in the notes indicates that the
Addenda should be consulted. By the kindness of the Clarendon Press, however, I was able to insert references in the
text itself before printing began to Professor Schönberger's
article on the German frontier in *JRS* lix (1969), which
recorded for the first time various items of information which
I had otherwise had to note down as 'unpublished'. For those
errors and omissions which persist I can only beg my readers'
indulgence, but the time has come to make an end. The
benefits of further revision or expansion would be outweighed
by the disadvantages of further delay. The die is cast: 'fuge
quo descendere gestis; non erit emisso reditus tibi'.

Certain peculiarities of arrangement and limitations in the
scope of this work should be indicated. The main narrative

thread is carried through the chapters with simple numbers (Chapters 1, 2, 3, etc.). The subdivisions (Chapter 3. 1, 3. 2, etc.) summarize the archaeological evidence from each specific site. Appendix I and Appendix II contain the explanation of what is taken for granted in the preceding chapters about the history and typology of Augustan pottery and coinage. Since this book deals only with the German frontier, it can have no pretensions to being the definitive military history of Augustus' reign, and certain topics are therefore merely touched upon in passing, which deserve fuller treatment. One of these is the development of the Augustan army and the movements of the individual units. The picture drawn by Ritterling (*RE* xii, s.v. 'legio') and corrected by Syme (*JRS* xxiii (1933), pp. 14–33) is however still basically sound, though possibly somewhat rigid. The archaeological evidence tends to show that the legions changed their bases more frequently than in later times (below, Chapter 5). The size of the garrison of Africa after 19 B.C. and the vexed question of the Homonadensian War need to be re-examined, together with the detailed history of the Revolt of A.D. 6–9 in Illyricum, but they lie outside the scope of the present work.

The bibliography at the end of the work lists all the books referred to in the notes, together with all articles except those dealing with one specific site only, references to which will be found in the notes on the chapter devoted to that site, and can be tracked down through the index. It has not been my intention to trace in detail the *Forschungsgeschichte* of all the sites discussed. Full bibliographies for each site are to be found in Forni's article 'limes' in the *Dizionario Epigrafico*; I have cited only those articles necessary for an understanding of the site, and they will usually be found to contain references to previous articles, particularly where a series of preliminary or interim reports had led up to the definitive report on a site.

In the matter of nomenclature, I have encountered two problems. The first is that noted by Cary in his preface to *The Geographic Background of Greek and Roman History*: 'A writer describing geographic features which remain discernible at the present day, but doing so in reference to past history, will almost inevitably find his pen slipping to and fro between the present and past tenses.' I have resolved this dilemma by adopting Cary's rule, 'to select in each instance whichever tense is most appropriate to the particular context'. In the second place, I have found it hard to be consistent in using the modern or the Latin name of places and geographical features. Sometimes we do not know what the Latin name was, sometimes the site is now unoccupied and nameless. Vetera is often equated with Xanten and Carnuntum with Petronell, but this is only an approximation. I have not therefore sought to be consistent, but have used in every case the name which I judged would be most familiar to English readers. The important thing is to have as clearly and vividly before our eyes as possible the actual geography of the area with which we are concerned. So I speak of Nijmegen, Cologne, and Zürich, but retain the Latin name for Vindonissa, Poetovio, and Burnum. If they are unfamiliar, it does not improve matters to write instead Windisch, Ptuj, and Šuplja Crkva.

On two points, however, I have abandoned traditional English usage. Measurements are given in metres and hectares (1 ha. $= 2 \cdot 471$ acres); and I have preferred to speak of 'legionary bases' rather than 'fortresses'. This is deliberate. I do not think that the *castra hiberna* of Augustus' reign can possibly be called 'fortress' without grave terminological inexactitude. As I have argued below in Chapter 5, these *hiberna* were bases from which the army operated, not strong-points which it planned to defend, and they were thus less permanent than the later 'fortresses'. Only with Claudius indeed can we begin to speak of 'fortresses', when the bases along the Rhine and Danube were rebuilt in stone as part of a permanent frontier system, and I have in fact retained the term when speaking of Claudian and Flavian installations. But for the Augustan period it is better to use the neutral term, 'base'.

In writing this book and the thesis which preceded it I have been helped most generously by various institutions and, in a different way, by innumerable scholars. The University of Ottawa granted me two years' leave from 1962 to 1964, during which most of the basic research for my thesis was completed. My special thanks are due to the Revd. Etienne Gareau, O.M.I., at that time Chairman of the Department of Greek and Latin at the University of Ottawa, but for whose initiative and support I should never have had this opportunity. During those two years I enjoyed the hospitality of my own college, Oriel, and also benefited from a Canada Council Doctoral Fellowship. My gratitude to the Canada Council has since been deepened by its generosity with travel and research grants, but for which I should not have been able to complete this work. Among libraries, my greatest debt is of course to the Haverfield Library in Oxford. I have however also enjoyed the hospitality of the libraries of Harvard and Yale, of the British School at Rome, and of the Institut für Vor- und Frühgeschichte at Munich.

Among Oxford scholars, my thanks for help and counsel are due especially to Professor Sir Ronald Syme, whose advice on the reshaping of the thesis into a book, as well as on specific points of scholarship, has been invaluable. My debt to his successor in the Camden Chair, P. A. Brunt, goes back still further, since the seed from which this whole book grew was an essay which I wrote for him when I was an undergraduate. His comments on my thesis have enabled me to expunge numerous errors in revising the thesis material for this book. I am also grateful to the examiners of the thesis, Mr. E. W. Gray and Mr. A. N. Sherwin-White, for their comments and encouragement. Two other Oxford scholars guided me in their own specialized fields: Dr. C. M. Kraay devoted much time to advising me on matters concerning the Augustan coinage, while it was a stimulating and scintillating paper, still unpublished, by Professor C. F. C. Hawkes which first drew my attention to the problem of Celts and Germans (below, Chapter 2). Professor Hawkes has since increased my debt to him by advice, information, and encouragement.

Among scholars elsewhere, Professor H. Comfort (Haverford) and Dr. Elizabeth Ettlinger (Zürich) have both shared their enormous knowledge of Augustan pottery far more generously than either the brotherhood of scholars or the claims of friendship would require. Professor H. Schönberger (Römisch-Germanische Kommission) and Professor G. Ulbert (Munich) have shown me round sites and museums, made me free of all the information they possessed, provided me with offprints, and made me feel always that I could rely on their help in any way it might be required.

Others who have freely communicated information, often before it was published, or have generously discussed with me matters of common interest include Dr. G. Alföldy (formerly of Budapest, now Bonn), Dr. H. Aschemeyer (Münster), Dr. D. Baatz (Saalburg-Museum), Dr. H. Beck (Münster), Dr. J. E. Bogaers (Nijmegen), Dr. H. Brunsting (Leiden), Dr. R. Fellmann (Basle), Dr. G. Fingerlin (Freiburg i. Br.), Dr. A. V. M. Hubrecht (Nijmegen), Dr. W. A. Jorns (Darmstadt), Dr. R. Nierhaus (Freiburg i. Br.), Dr. H. von Petrikovits (Bonn), Dr. A. Radnóti, (Frankfurt-am-Main), Dr. O. Roller (Speyer), Dr. C. Rüger (Xanten), Dr. H.-G. Simon (Bad Nauheim), Dr. Grace Simpson (Oxford), Mr. C. E. Stevens (Oxford), the late Dr. N. Walke (Augsburg), Dr. C. Weissgerber (Dortmund), Dr. Edith Wightman (McMaster University, Canada), and the late Dr. H. R. Wiedemer (Brugg). The list might well be extended further; certain specific debts are recorded in the notes. If anyone has been forgotten, I beg forgiveness.

I should also like to thank colleagues and students at the University of Ottawa, and others who have heard me expound some of the views contained in this work at meetings of learned societies or in the classroom, and whose comments and criticisms have been invaluable. Mr. E. C. Marquis patiently checked innumerable bibliographical details. Mrs. R. Zimmerman typed both thesis and book with unfailing efficiency and interest. The debt I owe to all those under whom I have studied the classics and the ancient world since I first began over twenty years ago is acknowledged in my dedication of this book to them. I cannot express the debt I owe to my wife for her unfailing encouragement and enthusiasm, for at first enduring and afterwards abetting my talk of pots and ditches, and simply for being all that she is.

It need hardly be said, when so many have had a hand in helping me shape this book, that not one of them necessarily agrees with all that is in it, and that possibly some of them will agree with nothing that is in it. In any case, the responsibility is wholly mine.

I have left to the last the late Professor Sir Ian Richmond, who directed my research for the D. Phil., and who unfortunately died without even having read the thesis that resulted. Nevertheless every chapter of that thesis and of this book owes something to him. Not only did he open my eyes to the importance of archaeology, but his vast knowledge of Roman life and classical literature again and again illuminated problems that seemed wholly obscure. Despite his own scholarly activity and his enormous expenditure of time on committees and enterprises of far greater importance, he always brought to his students' problems apparently unlimited time and unruffled concentration. His reputation abroad was awe-inspiring; to be able to introduce oneself as his pupil was a great privilege. Had he lived, his wise advice would have made this book far better than it is. His death was an incalculable loss to scholarship, and the personal loss of those who knew him is still unabated. Of him it can truly be said, in Hazlitt's words: 'When a person dies, who does any one thing better than anyone else in the world, which so many others are trying to do well, it leaves a gap in society.'

Ottawa, Canada C. M. WELLS
June, 1971

CONTENTS

INTRODUCTION
THE BACKGROUND TO THE GERMAN CAMPAIGNS

PART I
THE CONQUEST OF THE ALPS

CONTENTS

PART II
THE PERIOD OF CONFIDENT EXPANSION

PART III
EPILOGUE

APPENDICES

LIST OF FIGURES, TABLES, AND MAP

TABLES

MAP

LIST OF ABBREVIATIONS

THIS list includes abbreviations of titles of standard works and periodicals, where these are not readily obvious. A complete list of periodicals cited in this book, with titles in full, is included in the Bibliography (pp. 307–10). Conventional abbreviations have also been used for classical authors and their works; these should cause no trouble, and do not need explaining here. The symbol [ADD.] at the end of a footnote indicates that there is further information on that point in the Addenda.

AArchKöb.	*Acta Archaeologica* (Copenhagen)
AArchHung.	*Acta Archaeologica Academiae Scientiarum Hungaricae*
AE	*Année Épigraphique*
AEA	*Archivo Español de Arqueologia*
AErt.	*Archaeologiai Értesítö*
AJA	*American Journal of Archaeology*
AJP	*American Journal of Philology*
BerRGK	*Bericht der Römisch-Germanischen Kommission*
BJ	*Bonner Jahrbücher*
BMC	Mattingly, *Coins of the Roman Empire in the British Museum*
Bod. Westf.	*Bodenaltertümer Westfalens*
CAH	*Cambridge Ancient History*
CIL	*Corpus Inscriptionum Latinarum*
CQ	*Classical Quarterly*
Diz. Epig.	De Ruggiero, *Dizionario Epigrafico di Antichità Romane*
EE	*Ephemeris Epigraphica*
FITA	Grant, *From Imperium to Auctoritas*
FMRD	Gebhart–Kraft, *Fundmünzen der römischer Zeit in Deutschland*
GJ	*Geographical Journal*
HSCP	*Harvard Studies in Classical Philology*
ILS	Dessau, *Inscriptiones Latinae Selectae*
JDAI	*Jb. des Deutschen Archäologischen Instituts*
JGPV	*Jber. der Gesellschaft Pro Vindonissa*
JNG	*Jb. für Numismatik und Geldgeschichte*
JÖAI	*Jahreshefte des Österreichischen Archäologischen Instituts*
JRGZ	*Jb. des Römisch-Germanischen Zentralmuseums*
JRS	*Journal of Roman Studies*
JSGU	*Jb. der Schweizerische Gesellschaft für Urgeschichte*
MAKW	*Mitt. der Altertums-Kommission für Westfalen*
MEFR	*Mélanges d'archéologie et d'histoire de l'École française de Rome*
MH	*Museum Helveticum*
MZ	*Mainzer Ztschr.*

Nass. Ann.	*Annalen des Vereins für nassauische Altertumskunde und Geschichtsforschung*
NC	*Numismatic Chronicle*
OMRL	*Oudheidkundige Meded. uit het Rijksmuseum van Oudheiden te Leiden*
ORL	Fabricius et al., *Der obergermanisch-raetische Limes der Römerreich*
PBA	*Proceedings of the British Academy*
PIR²	Groag–Stein, *Prosopographia Imperii Romani, saec. I–III*, editio altera
PZ	*Prähistorische Ztschr.*
RBPh.	*Revue Belge de Philologie*
RCRFA	*Rei Cretariae Romanae Fautorum Acta*
RCRFComm.	*Rei Cretariae Romanae Fautorum Communicationes*
RE	Pauly–Wissowa, *Realencyclopädie der classischen Altertumswissenschaft*
REA	*Revue des études anciennes*
REL	*Revue des études latines*
RGKbl.	*Römisch-Germanisches Korrespondenzblatt*
Rh. Mus.	*Rheinisches Museum*
RIC	Mattingly–Sydenham, *Roman Imperial Coinage*
RLÖ	*Römische Limes in Österreich*
SJ	*Saalburg-Jahrbuch*
SMACA	Grant, *Six Main Aes Coinages of Augustus*
SZG	*Schweizerische Ztschr. für Geschichte*
TAPA	*Trans. and Proc. American Philological Association*
TKNAG	*Tijdschrift Kon. Nederlandsch Aardrijkskundig Genootschap*
TZ	*Trierer Ztschr.*
VAHD	*Vjesnik za Arheologiju i Historiju Dalmatinsku*

INTRODUCTION

THE BACKGROUND TO
THE GERMAN CAMPAIGNS

1

AUGUSTUS IN THE TRADITION OF ROMAN IMPERIALISM

'RERUM gestarum divi Augusti quibus orbem terrarum imperio populi Romani subiecit'[1]—this then is how Augustus wished to be remembered, the world-conqueror, the greatest and most successful of Rome's generals. 'Rei militaris gloria praestat ceteris omnibus', said Cicero; 'haec nomen populo Romano, haec huic urbi aeternam gloriam peperit, haec orbem parere huic imperio coegit.' In the Republican tradition this was indisputable: 'qui potest dubitare quin ad consulatum adipiscendum multo plus adferat dignitatis rei militaris quam iuris civilis gloria?'[2] and he goes on to point out that there was more glory to be gained 'in propagandis finibus' than 'in regendis'. Did not Augustus himself set up in his forum statues of the great Roman conquerors, his own among them, 'ut ad illorum vitam velut ad exemplar et ipse, dum viveret, et insequentium aetatum principes exigerentur a civibus'?[3]

It has, however, been argued that the idea of Rome's destiny to rule the world is an anachronistic legacy from the Republic, when it could indeed already be spoken of as almost accomplished.[4] But the Augustan writers continued to emphasize Rome's divine mission; only later in the course of the first century A.D., recognizing the disparity between what

---

[1] RG, introd.

[2] Cicero, pro Murena ix. 22, though admittedly in a context which requires him to emphasize and perhaps exaggerate the importance of military as against forensic success. The great model was, of course, Alexander the Great, both for late Republican generals and for Augustus himself, Sattler, Augustus und der Senat, p. 67, n. 164; also Bruhl, MEFR xlvii (1930), pp. 205-8; Balsdon, JRS xxvi (1936), pp. 159-60; La Penna, Orazio e l'ideologia del principato, pp. 93-4; Kienast, Gymnasium lxxvi (1969), pp. 430-56.

[3] Suet., Aug. 31; Vell. ii. 39; cf. Cic., de rep. iii. 24, that such statues bore the inscription 'fines imperii propagavit'.

[4] Cf. Cicero, de prov. cons. xiii. 31, pro Sestio, xxiii. 51, pro Balbo vi. 16, etc.; see also Meyer, Die Aussenpolitik des Augustus und die augusteische Dichtung, esp. pp. 102-4.

Rome actually ruled and the extent of the world as shown, for instance, on Agrippa's map, did writers abandon the idea that Rome's power was to be coterminous with the *orbis terrarum*.[1] Virgil, however, writes: 'His ego nec metas rerum nec tempora pono; imperium sine fine dedi'.[2] So too Livy: 'Abi, nuntia, inquit, Romanis, caelestes ita velle ut mea Roma caput orbis terrarum sit; proinde rem militarem colant scientque et ita posteris tradant nullas opes humanas armis Romanis resistere posse.'[3] It is a constant theme in the Augustan poets.[4] And Augustus was designated to fulfil the mission: 'Praesens divus habebitur Augustus adiectis Britannis imperio gravibusque Persis.'[5] Most explicitly of all, again in the *Aeneid*, in the prophecy of Anchises, we find:

> Augustus Caesar, divi genus, aurea condet
> saecula qui rursus Latio regnata per arva
> Saturno quondam, super et Garamantas et Indos
> proferet imperium . . .

a speech which ends with the quintessential statement of Roman imperialist doctrine:

> tu regere imperio populos, Romane, memento
> (hae tibi erunt artes), pacisque imponere morem,
> parcere subiectis et debellare superbos.[6]

The last line embraces the whole of non-Roman mankind: all who were not *subiecti*, and who did not want to be, were automatically *superbi*.

Should we find it strange that Augustus, especially in the 20s B.C., was seen in this light? Should we even find it strange if he saw himself in this light? The author of the *Res Gestae* was not indifferent to the opinion of posterity, and the boy who set out at the age of eighteen to make himself master of the Roman world was not lacking in ambition. The conquests of Caesar and Pompey had been celebrated by Cicero, to whose eloquence Augustus was not unreceptive.[7] Would he not

---

[1] Vogt, *Orbis Romanus zur Terminologie des römischen Imperialismus*, esp. pp. 23–7; cf. also below, p. 6, n. 6.

[2] Virg., *Aen.* i. 278–9. [3] Livy I. xvi. 7.

[4] Passages conveniently collated by Meyer, op. cit.

[5] Hor., *od.* III. v. 2–4.

[6] Virg., *Aen.* vi. 792–5, 851–3; see also above, p. ix.

[7] Plut., *Cicero* 49.

feel it incumbent upon him to match, if not surpass, their achievements? Military success was an immediate practical necessity, if he was to establish his regime;[1] it was also the surest way to lasting glory.

And yet generations of scholars have seen Augustus' policy as basically defensive. 'The first seven centuries (of Rome's existence) were filled with a rapid succession of triumphs; but it was reserved for Augustus to relinquish the ambitious design of subduing the whole earth and to introduce a spirit of moderation into the public councils . . . He bequeathed, as a valuable legacy to his successors, the advice of confining the empire within those limits which nature seemed to have placed as its permanent bulwarks and boundaries.' So wrote Gibbon in the opening chapter of his *Decline and Fall*, characteristically trenchant and assured, and his opinion has been generally echoed. Augustus' conquests were intended merely to stabilize the frontier on the best defensive line.[2] And the usual corollary to this is the belief that his intended frontier in Europe was the line of the Elbe and Danube. This is thought to explain the attempt to conquer Germany. Gibbon, it is true, ignores the campaigns across the Rhine, which he lists among the 'permanent bulwarks and boundaries', but almost all scholars have accepted the theory of an Elbe frontier policy,[3] despite the absence of any direct evidence in the ancient sources for this view. Augustus designates the North Sea coast as far as the mouth of the Elbe as the boundary of the Empire at the end of his life, and at one time he forbade his generals to cross the river, but for purely prudential reasons, so as not to unite the

[1] Cf. Schmitthenner, *Historia* xi (1962), pp. 29–85, on the importance of the Spanish campaigns in establishing Augustus' position at Rome. Hammond, *HSCP* lxix (1965), p. 145, suggests that Augustus' 'portrayal as a great general' was influenced by what public opinion expected; no doubt, but I cannot follow him when he discerns in Augustus' acts 'a real avoidance of grandiose military undertakings'. Really?

[2] Cf. Meyer, op. cit., p. 3: 'Augustus hat mit Entschiedenheit die Aussenpolitik auf eine grundsätzliche Defensive umgestellte; eine grundsätzliche Defensive, denn Expansionen, die gerade wegen der defensive Haltung an manchen Stellen um der Abrundung willen geboten schienen, waren nicht ausgeschlossen.'

[3] Cf. list of names in Oldfather and Canter, *The Defeat of Varus and the German Frontier Policy of Augustus*, pp. 9–10; enshrined by Syme, in *CAH* x, pp. 351–4, the view still appears in, e.g., Levi, *Il tempo di Augusto*, pp. 390–1; Koestermann, *Historia* vi (1957), p. 466; von Petrikovits, *Das römische Rheinland*, p. 15; Scullard, *From the Gracchi to Nero*, p. 265; *et multi alii*.

tribes on both banks in common hostility to Rome; Drusus certainly tried to cross, and Ahenobarbus actually did so.[1] An Elbe frontier may look neat on a modern map; strategically though, it would have left much to be desired.[2]

Others, not professional classical scholars, have seen Augustus' policy differently. Creasy in his *The Fifteen Decisive Battles of the World* (one of which was the defeat of Varus) wrote: 'It is a great fallacy, though apparently sanctioned by great authorities, to suppose that the foreign policy of Augustus was pacific. He certainly recommended such a policy to his successors . . . but he himself, until Arminius broke his spirit, had followed a very different course.'[3] Von Ranke believed that Augustus' plans for the conquest of Germany displayed 'das ideale Ziel der Welteroberung, welches aus einem ungeheuren geographischen Irrtum entsprang', on which Oldfather and Canter comment: 'There is at least consistency in von Ranke's position. The only conceivable reason for the conquest of Germany would be precisely such a fantastic dream of universal empire.'[4] Was this in fact what Augustus dreamed of?

Brunt has recently expressed very cogently the case for thinking that Augustus aimed at world empire,[5] emphasizing the magnitude of the geographical error on which this ambition was based.[6] It was apparently thought that the distance from the Rhine to the Ocean beyond China was only three and a half times as great as the distance across Gaul, and most of the area sparsely inhabited, if at all. Caesar achieved the conquest of Gaul in less than ten years with only limited resources. What might not Augustus do with the whole power of Rome at his command? The doctrine of 'manifest destiny', which in the middle of the last century swept Texas and California and

---

[1] *RG* 26, on which Wells, *Phoenix* xxiii (1969), pp. 323–4; Strabo vii. 291; see also below, pp. 158–9.

[2] Even scholars who believe that Augustus aimed only at a defensible frontier have concluded that this would ultimately have led him on, after the conquest of Bohemia, to that of Dacia, e.g. Buchan, *Augustus*, p. 304; Alföldi, *JGPV* 1948/9, p. 7; Wilkes, *Univ. of Birmingham Hist. Journ.* x (1965), p. 25. On rivers as frontiers, see below, p. 24.

[3] Creasy, op. cit., pp. 121–2.

[4] Oldfather and Canter, op. cit., p. 59 and n.

[5] Brunt, *JRS* liii (1963), pp. 170–6.

[6] Ibid., p. 175, following Klotz, *Klio* xxiv (1931), pp. 38–58, 386–466. Cf. also Dion in *Mélanges Carcopino*, pp. 249–69. [ADD.]

Oregon into the Union on a wave of imperialism and expansionism, which the European powers invoked in the scramble for Asian and African territory, is implicit in the writings of Livy and the Augustan poets.[1] The fates were driving Rome on to world conquest: 'nullas opes humanas armis Romanis resistere posse'. In the flood-tide of Augustus' conquests, the period of confident expansion, as I have called it below, this must have seemed literally true.

The geographical error could, moreover, be corrected only by experience. Caesar tells us how impossible he found it to get satisfactory information about Britain from merchants, so that he was obliged to cross over and gather it himself.[2] Even if we suppose that the traders may not have wished to reveal more than they need (though nothing that we know of Roman methods suggests that they would lack the skill and the means to extract information even from the unwilling), this incident reminds us that, while information gathered from traders was an important part of the Roman army commanders' knowledge of what lay beyond their frontiers, this information was likely to be vague, imprecise, and lacunose on the very points where the soldier would most desire full and accurate intelligence; and that this information was in any case no substitute for that to be derived from military reconnaissance. For the interior of Central Europe however traders must have been one of the main sources, if not *the* main source of Roman knowledge. When after the rebellion in Illyricum and the subsequent loss of Varus' army in Germany the policy of expansion was abandoned and Augustus left to his successor 'consilium coercendi intra terminos imperii', thus posthumously preaching what all his life he had so conspicuously failed to practise, it

---

[1] See above, Preface, pp. viii–ix, and cf. also Lord Bryce, *The Ancient Roman Empire and the British Empire in India*, pp. 18–19, with elaborate comparison of Armenia's position between Rome and Parthia to that of Afghanistan between British India and Russia, and much talk of 'spheres of influence' and 'manifest destiny'.

[2] Caesar, *BG* iv. 20: 'itaque vocatis ad se undique mercatoribus, neque quanta esset insulae magnitudo, neque quae aut quantae nationes incolerent, neque quem usum belli haberent aut quibus institutis uterentur, neque qui essent ad maiorem navium multitudinem idonei portus reperire poterat'; cf. Collingwood in Collingwood and Myres, *Roman Britain and the English Settlements*, p. 35. On army maps as a source of geographical information (in this case, misinformation), cf. Pliny, *NH* vi. 40. Value of soldiers' and traders' reports discussed in detail by Norden, *Die germanische Urgeschichte in Tacitus Germania*, pp. 428–50.

may have been largely because the Romans now for the first time began to appreciate what wellnigh inexhaustible reservoirs of manpower Central and Northern Europe held. Had Augustus died eight or nine years earlier, let us suppose in the winter of A.D. 5/6, with his armies assembled to strike into Bohemia, and Illyricum and Germany to all appearances pacified, can we imagine that his 'consilium' would still have been the same?

'Pacified' is of course a word to be understood in the Roman sense. Scholars who believe that Augustus was a man of peace, and his frontier policy basically defensive, lay great stress on the triple closure during his reign of the Temple of Janus, closed only twice before in the whole of Rome's history, under Numa and after the First Punic War.[1] This bogus antiquarian revival (for in the circumstances it can scarcely be regarded as a living tradition) served Augustus' propaganda, it is true; but the terms in which he himself defines the conditions on which the ceremony was performed, 'cum per totum imperium populi Romani terra marique esset parta victoriis pax',[2] make it a symbol as much of victory as of peace. *Pax, pacare* always have these overtones of conquest.[3] When Virgil prophesies of the child of the Fourth Eclogue, 'pacatumque reget patriis virtutibus orbem',[4] he foresees the pacification, not as a blessing from the gods, but as the result of Roman conquest. It will be a Roman world.

Augustus claimed to have fought only when he had to, and with justice on his side.[5] But then the Romans always did.[6] Alföldi has rightly emphasized that Rome recognized no obligations to barbarians, quoting Mommsen: 'Beyond the frontiers, in the territory of states which broke their allegiance

---

[1] e.g. Meyer, op. cit., pp. 3, 30–1.

[2] *RG* 13. This is not of course to deny the emphasis which Augustus' propaganda laid on peace in Italy, cf. for instance Kähler, *JDAI* lxix (1954), pp. 67–100, on the Ara Pacis, which has much the same message as the fourth book of Horace's *Odes*, cf. Benario, *TAPA* xci (1960), pp. 339–52.

[3] Fuchs, *Augustin und der antike Friedensgedanke*, pp. 182–205; cf. also the remarks of Haverfield, *Some Roman Conceptions of Empire*, pp. 5–6. On the ancients' attitude to peace and war compared to ours, see Nestle, *Der Friedensgedanke in der antiken Welt*; peace was generally something attained and preserved only by force.

[4] Virg., *Ecl.* iv. 17; cf. also Cic., *de prov. cons.* xii. 31: 'nulla gens est quae non . . . ita pacata, ut victoria nostra imperioque laetetur.'

[5] Suet., *Aug.* 21. 2; cf. *RG* 26, on the Alpine tribes.

[6] Cicero, *de off.* i. 35–8.

to Rome or had never concluded a pact with her, or are at war/ with Rome, i.e. in the *ager hosticus*, there is no law, but only the implications of the situation'.[1] A succession of frontier wars was not incompatible with stability and peace in Italy and the provinces out of the front line. The *aurea saecula* which Augustus in Anchises' prophecy is to restore do not exclude wars of conquest in Africa and Asia. The barbarians against whom the wars of pacification on the frontiers were directed had, as we have seen above, no rights in the matter. It was inconceivable that they might prefer their own freedom to the Roman peace. The nomadic Sarmatians did not stay to be conquered: 'tanta barbaria est, ut nec intellegant pacem'.[2]

The only ancient writer who does in fact state openly that Augustus' whole policy was defensive is Dio.[3] As Brunt however has pointed out: 'Dio's fictitious speeches have little authority . . . Dio was always opposed to expansion; he would have been very ready to make Augustus, the exemplar for later emperors, more pacific than he really was.'[4] Nor is Suetonius to be cited in support of the view that Augustus' aims were basically defensive when he lists his conquests at full length, and then goes on: 'Nec ulli genti sine iustis et necessariis causis bellum intulit, tantumque afuit a cupiditate quoquo modo imperium vel bellicam gloriam augendi, ut quorundam barbarorum principes in aede Martis Ultoris iurare coegerit mansuros se in fide ac pace quam peterent.'[5] The claim to have fought only from necessity and in a just cause is a familiar one, as we have seen, and the Romans always made it, while the second half of the statement says no more than that Augustus never made war for its own sake: not that he was indifferent to territorial

---

[1] Alföldi in *Congress of Roman Frontier Studies, 1949* (1952), p. 5. On Roman attitude to war guilt, Collins, 'Propaganda, Ethics and Psychological Assumptions in Caesar's Writings', p. 37; cf. also Strasburger, *Caesar im Urteil seiner Zeitgenossen*, pp. 21-3. Further, Saddington, *Acta Classica* iv (1961), pp. 90–102; Weiler, *Carn. Jb.* 1963/4, pp. 34-9, largely however dealing with post-Augustan period.

[2] Florus ii. 29.

[3] Dio liii. 10. 4-5, liv. 9. 1, lvi. 41. 7.

[4] Brunt, op. cit., p. 172. Although Jameson, *JRS* lviii (1968), p. 83, still takes Dio seriously, I cannot follow her in believing that Augustus' policy *became* defensive around 20 B.C., despite Dio's assertion (liv. 9. 1) that in this year Augustus announced to the Senate that Rome was now a satisfied power intent on no further annexations. The context suggests that, if the story is true, it in any case refers only to the East, where indeed no further annexations *were* planned—for the time being.

[5] Suet., loc. cit.

C

expansion or military glory, but that he did not pursue them
by any and every means, with the emphasis on the words
'quoquo modo'. The barbarian chieftains, in the case which
Suetonius cites, were being sworn into the circle of Roman
pax. Henceforward *subiecti*, they might now be justly and
necessarily warred upon, if they rebelled. As Brunt points out
in a similar connection: 'The most aggressive rulers seldom
desire war for its own sake, when they can take the fruits of
victory without it.'[1] Gibbon in his journal speaks of 'la politique
d'Auguste, qui dans toutes les affaires préféroit aux voyes de
violence les moyens doux et lents'.[2] This is true, so far as it
refers to means, to what Brunt calls his 'steady and subtle
procedures', but the most painstaking care in choosing one's
means is not incompatible with the greatest audacity in
conceiving one's ends, and Augustus' ends, in foreign policy,
as in the struggle for power at Rome, were neither limited nor
narrow.

It is instructive in this context to consider Augustus' campaigns of the 20s and 30s B.C. The emphasis placed on Britain
by Horace ahd others is significant. Britain could be regarded
as *de iure* Roman as a result of Caesar's campaigns, even if *de
facto* Rome had not yet taken possession of its property.[3]
Horace, as we have seen, links Parthia with Britain as the
twin goals of Augustus' expansion, whose conquest will seal his
godhead manifest. Already in 34 Augustus, then still Octavian,
had been credited with plans to invade Britain in emulation
of Caesar,[4] just as his wanton attack on the Segestani in the previous year was attributed in part to a mere desire to train and
feed his army at someone else's expense, and in part to a plan
to seize their capital, Siscia, as a base for a future attack on the
Dacians and Bastarnae, another of Caesar's unfinished projects.[5] The campaigns in Illyricum in these years were very

---

[1] Brunt, op. cit., p. 174.

[2] G. Bonnard (ed.), *Le Journal de Gibbon à Lausanne. 17 août 1763–19 avril 1764*,
p. 92.

[3] Stevens in *Aspects of Archaeology*, pp. 332–44; Britain was in everyone's mind,
the place where glory was to be won, cf. *Paneg. Mess.* 150: 'te manet invictus
Romano Marte Britannus.'

[4] Dio xlix. 38. 2. Britain drops out of sight after 23 B.C., cf. Momigliano, *JRS* xl
(1950), pp. 39–41.

[5] Motive alleged by Appian, *Illyrice* 22, 23; cf. Strabo vii. 313, where Siscia is
again described as a good base against the Dacians; on Octavian's Illyrian

limited in extent,[1] and it is not likely that Octavian was in fact contemplating full-scale expeditions across the Danube or the English Channel in 35–34, but it is significant that he could be credited with this intention, and still more significant that during the next decade writers close to him could go on committing him to designs of widespread conquest, if Augustus himself knew that he had no intention of fulfilling the expectations which were thus being so publicly aroused.

The main military effort of the twenties was of course in Spain, where a large army was tied up and where losses were heavy.[2] This did not exclude frontier warfare elsewhere in Europe, nor local thrusts and advances, such as those of M. Licinius Crassus and the unfortunate M. Primus in Macedonia,[3] or the conquest of the Salassi in the Val d'Aosta (see below, Chapter 3), so important in Augustus' later strategy. The twenties also saw campaigning in Africa and Egypt, until the limits of direct Roman control had been pushed as far south as was deemed practicable.[4] More important still was the campaign against Arabia in 25–24, surely a stumbling-block for all those who believe that Augustus eschewed aggressive, imperialistic designs. Strabo indeed states frankly that the motive for the expedition was simply to get hold of the Arabians' wealth.[5] This objective was not achieved, and the moderation of Augustus' reference to the expedition in the *Res Gestae* tells its own tale, but the Sabaeans do at least appear to have

campaigns, see esp. Appian, op. cit., 16–28 and Dio xlix. 34–8; also Strabo iv. 207, vii. 313–15; Livy, *epit.* 131–2; Vell. ii. 78. 2; Suet., *Aug.* 20; Florus ii. 23; Oros. vi. 19. 3. According to Dio, Octavian wished to exercise his army and feed it at someone else's expense (xlix. 36. 1); so too Vell. ii. 78. 2. On Caesar's plans in this direction, Plut., *Caesar* 58.

[1] Schmitthenner, *Historia* vii (1958), pp. 189–236, to my mind conclusive, with refs. to earlier discussion.

[2] Heavy losses, Dio liv. 11. 5; Florus ii. 33; Oros. vi. 21. 10; at least 7 legions in Spain, see Ritterling, *RE* xii, cols. 1221–3, cf. also García y Bellido, *AEA* xxxiv (1961), pp. 114–32.

[3] Dio li. 23–7; Florus ii. 22. 3; Livy, *epit.* 134; Dio liv. 3; on Augustus' reaction to the success of Crassus, see Mócsy, *Historia* xv (1966), pp. 511–14. In the controversy surrounding the trial of Primus, I follow those who accept Dio's date, see esp. Balsdon, *Gnomon* xxxiii (1961), pp. 393–6; Bauman, *Historia* xv (1966), pp. 420–32.

[4] Cagnat, *L'Armée romaine d'Afrique*, pp. 3–9; Romanelli, *Storia delle province romane dell'Africa*, pp. 175–87. Strategic factors governing choice of frontier in Egypt, Kirwan, *GJ* cxxiii (1957), p. 15.

[5] Strabo xvi. 780.

accepted Roman *amicitia* and opened their ports to Roman ships.[1]

Augustus' dealings with Parthia in these years show how cautious he could be in his means, and what capital his propaganda could make even of a bloodless victory. There could be no major war in the East while Europe remained unsettled. The year 20 saw the vindication of his eastern policy with the recovery of the lost standards from Parthia and the crowning of Tigranes as client king of Armenia by Tiberius.[2] Armenia was 'conquered', and coins celebrated the fact with the legend ARMENIA CAPTA. Dio's detailed account of Augustus' doings in 20 shows the way in which he was accustomed to exercise control over the Roman provinces and the client kingdoms alike.[3] The only difference between Armenia and any other client state was that it proved harder to hold.

By 19 then there was peace, 'parta victoriis pax', in Egypt, Africa, and especially in Spain, which need now no longer pre-empt the services of so many troops and of Rome's best generals, who thus were freed for campaigns on other fronts. Where the thirty years following Caesar's death had seen only defensive actions or limited advances, the period 15–9 B.C. was one of expansion, of large-scale operations and large-scale conquests, beginning with the conquest of the Raeti and Vindelici of the Central Alps and the Voralpenland and the peaceful absorption of Noricum, and going on to the simultaneous offensive across the Rhine and down the Sava which the control of the Alpine regions lying at the hinge of the two armies made possible. In the years 12 and 11 the Roman army was fully extended, with fighting along the whole European front, in Germany, Illyricum, and Thrace, and the newly-conquered

---

[1] *RG* 26; Strabo xvi. 779; *Peripl. maris Eryth.* 23. On the effects, cf. Holmes, *Architect of the Roman Empire* ii, p. 20; *CAH* x, pp. 252, 389. Their inadequacy stressed by Jameson, op. cit., p. 82.

[2] Dio liv. 8. 1–3; *RG* 27, 29, 32; Vell. ii. 94. 4, 104. 5; Tac., *Ann.* ii. 3–4; Suet., *Tib.* 9. 1, 14. 3. Note esp. *RG* 27: 'Armeniam maiorem . . . cum possem facere provinciam, malui maiorum nostrorum exemplo regnum id Tigrani regis Artavasdis filio . . . tradere', and so on, in the same vein; cf. Brunt, *JRS* liii (1963), p. 174.

[3] Dio liv. 7. 5–6, 9; on the Augustan dispositions see Magie, *Roman Rule in Asia Minor*, pp. 443–95, with nn., pp. 1349 ff.

Raetia and Vindelicia to be garrisoned.[1] So large an enterprise would not have been possible ten years earlier, when so many troops were tied up in Spain, nor would it have been possible without the long and careful planning which we shall endeavour to retrace in subsequent chapters. Almost unbroken success was to attend this policy of aggression until the rebellion of Illyricum in A.D. 6 demonstrated the shakiness of its foundation and the loss of Varus' legions three years later put an end to it (below, Chapter 7).

Augustus did not leave to his successors all the territory he had planned to. Germany was irretrievably lost, Bohemia remained unattempted. His conquests were still impressive, however, and the *Res Gestae* made the most of them. Among the propagators of the Empire, whose claim to *rei militaris gloria* was greater than Augustus'? 'From the beginning, his sense for realities was unerring, his ambition implacable . . . He was only eighteen years of age: but he resolved to acquire the power and the glory along with the name of Caesar.'[2] He inherited Caesar's projects, the planned wars of conquest as well as the duty of avenging his death. 'Qui parentem meum trucidaverunt, eos in exilium expuli, iudiciis legitimis ultus eorum facinus, et postea bellum inferentis rei publicae vici bis acie. Bella terra marique civilia externaque toto in orbe saepe gessi.'[3] The external wars could not be avoided, if he wished to succeed and surpass his adoptive father. Nor did he wish to avoid them: 'Summa dignitas est in iis qui militari laude antecellunt.'[4] He aimed at no less, and in supreme confidence. Was there any limit to Rome's expansion, to her divine mission? 'Imperium sine fine dedi'? Augustus himself may well have believed it.

[1] Nothing more vividly illustrates the absence of adequate reserves than the events of 13 B.C. and A.D. 6, when reinforcements had to be taken from the Eastern provinces to suppress rebellion in the Balkans, see Dio liv. 34. 6; Vell. ii. 92. 4; cf. Dio lv. 28. 2–3, on which see Syme, *Klio* xxvii (1934), pp. 139–43; Vell. ii. 112. 4, cf. Atkinson, *Historia* vii (1958), p. 328.

[2] Syme, *The Roman Revolution*, p. 113.

[3] *RG* 2–3.   [4] Cicero, *pro Murena* xi. 2

2

CELTS AND GERMANS

'GERMANI qui trans Rhenum incolunt': thus Caesar intro-
duces the Germans, and throughout the first book of his *Gallic
War* we find this same emphasis on the Rhine as the boundary
between the Germans and those 'qui ipsorum lingua Celtae,
nostra Galli appellantur'.[1] At the same time he insists on the
terror which the Germans inspire and the danger they present:
'ingenti magnitudine corporum, incredibili virtute atque
exercitatione in armis', used to a country and a way of life
incomparably ruder than that of the Gauls, the Germans are
on the move.[2] The Suebi, 'gens . . . longe maxima et belli-
cosissima Germanorum omnium', are massed on the Rhine
ready to cross, and a hundred and twenty thousand Germans
are reported to be already settled in Gaul under Ariovistus,
'rex Germanorum', himself apparently of Suebic origin.[3]
If the German invasion is not checked, Caesar suggests, the
Germans may overrun all of Gaul and then turn their attention
to Italy, 'ut ante Cimbri Teutonique fecissent'. There were
men still alive at Rome who could remember the panic which
the Cimbri and Teutoni had caused, and the Cimbri and
Teutoni are duly paraded before us four times in the first two
books of the *Gallic War* to mark the parallel.[4] We are to understand that only Caesar's success in holding the Rhine against

---

[1] Caesar, *BG* i. 1. 1. [ADD.]

[2] *BG* i. 29. 1, 26. 7, 31. 11, etc.

[3] Description of Suebi, *BG* iv. 1. 3; 120,000 Germans, i. 31. 5; Ariovistus 'rex
Germanorum', i. 31. 10; Suebic origin inferred from i. 53. 4, that one of his wives
was 'Sueba natione, quam domo secum duxerat', cf. Pliny, *NH* ii. 170, vindicated
by Kraft, *Germania* xlii (1964), p. 317, against Hachmann's scepticism in Hachmann, Kossack, and Kuhn, *Völker zwischen Germanen und Kelten*, p. 48. The name
Ariovistus however appears to be Celtic, cf. Florus i. 20. 4, where it belongs to a
chieftain of the Insubrian Gauls, and again *CIL* vii. 1320, from Kenchester
(Herefordshire), apparently a doctor. The etymology of the name in Evans, *Gaulish
Personal Names*, pp. 54–5, 141–2. Cf. below, p. 28, n. 3.

[4] *BG* i. 33. 4, 40. 5; ii. 4. 2, 29. 4.

them has stopped the Suebi and the other Germans this time from threatening Italy just as the Cimbri and Teutoni had done before.

Now one difference between Celts and Germans should be that of language.[1] But if the differences in other respects are as great as Caesar suggests, and if the Rhine is the boundary, we should expect there to be a corresponding difference in material culture, so that the archaeological evidence from the right bank should be quite different from that which we find on the left bank. Such however, as we shall see, is not the case. If on the other hand we examine the evidence from Gaul on the one side and from North Germany and the Baltic regions on the other, leaving aside for the moment the area along the Rhine, then we do find for the first century B.C. two totally different cultures such as Caesar leads us to expect. On the one side, in the interior of Gaul, excavation reveals *oppida* such as Bibracte (Mont Beuvray), Alesia (Alise-Sainte-Reine), and Avaricum (Bourges), precisely as Caesar describes them, identical with those we find in other regions of the Celtic world, as at Tarodunum (Zarten) in the Black Forest area, the Engehalbinsel at Bern in Helvetia, Manching and Kelheim on the Upper Danube, the Hradischt at Stradonitz in Bohemia, the Magdalensberg in Noricum, Židovar in the Sava valley, and numerous others.[2] In Gaul particularly, they may have the *murus Gallicus* defences so accurately described by Caesar, although this is less common outside Gaul.[3] The material culture which is characteristic of all these *oppida*, from Gaul eastwards to the

---

[1] Ariovistus spoke Celtic 'longinqua consuetudine' only, *BG* i. 47. 4; cf. Tac., *Germ.* 43. 1: 'Cotinos Gallica, Osos Pannonica lingua coarguit non esse Germanos.'

[2] General accounts of the *oppida* and other aspects of Celtic life by Powell, *The Celts*, esp. ch. 2; Piggott, *Ancient Europe*, ch. 6; Moreau, *Die Welt der Kelten*; Eggers in Eggers et al., *Kelten und Germanen in heidnischer Zeit*. Survey of recent work by Hawkes in *Le Rayonnement des civilisations grecque et romaine*, pp. 61–79, esp. on *oppida* pp. 73–5. Further in Déchelette, *Manuel d'archéologie* iv, esp. pp. 452–91; Vetters, *Carinthia I* cxli (1951), pp. 677–716. Also Christ, *Historia* vi (1957), pp. 229–35, pointing out how importance and precise function of *oppida* in different areas depend upon local economic conditions and position relative to other main centres of the Celtic world.

[3] On the construction of the *murus Gallicus* (Caesar, *BG* vii. 23) and the range of its occurrence, see Cotton in Wheeler and Richardson, *Hill Forts of Northern France*, pp. 159–216; on *muri Gallici* outside Gaul, pp. 210–16; scarce in Germany, von Uslar, *Studien zu frühgeschichtlichen Befestigungen*, pp. 8–10. See further Dehn, *Germania* xxxviii (1960), pp. 43–55.

Carpathians, and which is named after the village of La Tène in Switzerland, is remarkably homogeneous, and the typological development of La Tène artefacts and the relative chronology of the La Tène period are well established.

It has been suggested that the La Tène *oppida* may be considered as indicating the minimum area of Celtic settlement in the Late La Tène period, although we shall see later in the chapter that there is some reason to doubt whether the most northerly participants in this culture were by strict linguistic criteria true Celts; however that may be, it is clear that the northern limit of the *oppida*-culture is the River Lippe, except for outliers along the Mittelgebirge, the most northerly of all being the Babilonie near Lübbecke in the Wiehengebirge (fig. 1).[1] More restricted in distribution than the *oppida*, but belonging to the same Late La Tène culture and period, are the so-called *Viereckschanzen*, which are very numerous between the Alps and the Upper Danube, extending also northwards to the Main.[2]

North of the area in which the *oppida* are found, however, and thus in those regions which beyond all doubt lie outside the area of La Tène settlement, such as the Lower Elbe and the Jutland peninsula, whence the Cimbri themselves originally came, we find a totally different culture.[3] Instead of the well-organized and firmly established La Tène *oppida*, with their

[1] Hachmann, op. cit., pp. 31–4, with map 2. Cf. also von Uslar, *Westgermanische Bodenfunde*, pp. 158–9; id., *Studien zu frühgeschichtlichen Befestigungen*, pp. 11–15. On *oppida* as hallmark of Celtic occupation, Eggers, op. cit., p. 12: 'Sicher ist aber, dass die Oppida der Spät-La Tène-Zeit nur keltisch sein können, also ein Minimum des Territoriums darstellen, das den Kelten zugesprochen werden darf'; cf. also p. 16, and map of known *oppida*, ibid., p. 14. Cf. also Piggott, op. cit., pp. 216–20.

[2] Schwarz, *Atlas der spätkelt. Viereckschanzen Bayerns*, map 2; cf. id. in *Neue Ausgrabungen in Deutschland*, pp. 205–14, and id., *Jber. Bay. Bodendenkmalpflege* 1962, pp. 22–73, on the function of these controversial structures, with further maps; also Paret in *Ur- und Frühgeschichte als hist. Wissenschaft*, pp. 154–62. The only other area where they are found in any quantity is on the Lower Seine. Further maps in Kimmig and Hell, *Vorzeit am Rhein und Donau*, p. 97, fig. 111 (cemeteries), and p. 99, fig. 112 (*oppida* and *Viereckschanzen*), with text, pp. 99–100 [Add].

[3] This view of the Cimbri has been challenged, and it is true that all their personal names as transmitted are Celtic in form, but see below, p. 28, n. 3; also Waller, *Hammaburg* vii (1961), pp. 67–92, in answer to Hachmann, *Gnomon* xxxiv (1962), pp. 56–65, reviewing Melin, *Der Heimat der Kimbern*. Still valuable is Marcks, *Jb. Altfr. Rh.* xcv (1894), pp. 29–45. Further, Jacoby, *Die Fragmente des griechischen Historiker* iic, pp. 179–84, commenting on iiA, pp. 240–2, Posidonius, fr. 31); also Norden, *Die germanische Urgeschichte bei Tacitus Germania*, pp. 67–84.

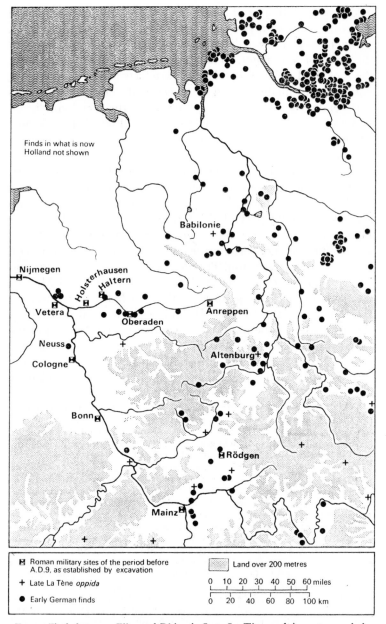

Finds in what is now
Holland not shown

Babilonie
+

Nijmegen
Holsterhausen
Haltern
Vetera
Oberaden
Anreppen
Neuss
Cologne
Altenburg +

Bonn
Rödgen
Mainz

Roman military sites of the period before
A.D.9, as established by excavation

+ Late La Tène *oppida*

● Early German finds

Land over 200 metres

0 10 20 30 40 50 60 miles

0   20   40   60   80   100 km

FIG. 1. Finds between Elbe and Rhine in Late La Tène and Augustan periods
(finds in Holland not shown)

settled population and their specialized trades and social structure, we find a people whose way of life is semi-nomadic, living in a country still largely covered with forest, even in the areas of settlement.[1] Their burial rites differ entirely from those of the La Tène world; their artefacts are primitive, their pottery hand-made instead of wheel-made, and conscious artistic endeavour altogether lacking, since the social conditions necessary to its development were also absent.[2] This is how we should expect the Germans to be, from Caesar's description of them.

Beginning in the first century B.C., such German elements (using 'German' conventionally to refer to the northerners described in the preceding paragraph) begin to intrude into regions originally part of the Celtic La Tène world, such as Bohemia. Here there were originally two main areas of Celtic settlement, the one, perhaps the territory of the Boii, centred on the Vltava valley, around Prague and Pilsen, the other around Bratislava between the Rivers Vah (Cusus-Doria) and Morava (Marus) and extending up the valleys of both rivers, perhaps the territory of the Volcae.[3] In both areas we find evidence of the overthrow of the main Celtic centres around the end of the first century B.C., linked with the arrival of strong German elements, whose material culture has strong affinities with that of the Elbe region, and whose domination leads to the steady

---

[1] On the nature of the country, Jankuhn, *Archaeologia geographica* x/xi (1961/3), pp. 19–38, with maps.

[2] Eggers, op. cit., p. 7: 'Einen germanischen Handwerkstand hat es also in der vorrömischen Eisenzeit noch nicht gegeben. Es konnte ihn noch nicht geben, weil die soziologischen Voraussetzungen dazu fehlten.' Cf. distribution map of wheel-made pottery in Hachmann, Kossack, and Kuhn, op. cit., map 4. General account of archaeology of area at this time in Klindt-Jensen, *Denmark before the Vikings*, pp. 81–131. Conventional picture of the Germans, primarily from literary sources, in Thompson, *The Early Germans*, esp. ch. 1. Brief survey of technological and economic factors involved by Rowlett, *Science* clxi (1968), pp. 123–34.

[3] Evidence of coin finds, Nohejlová-Prátová, *Nálezy mincí v Čechách, na Moravě a ve Slezsku*, map 1, and Ondrouch, *Nálezy keltských, antických a byzantských mincí na Slovensku*, map 1. Settlement and grave finds in Motyková-Sneidrová, *Die Anfänge der römischen Kaiserzeit in Böhmen*, esp. p. 3. See also Benadík et al., *Keltské pohrebiská na juhozápadnom Slovensku*. On Boii and Volcae, Preidel, *Die vor- und frühgeschichtlichen Siedlungsräume in Böhmen und Mähren*, pp. 144–51. The major work on this area in the Celtic period is Filip, *Keltové ve střední Evropě* (with German summary); see also Dobiaš, *Dějiny československého území před vystoupením Slovanů* (with English summary), with extensive bibliographies, and in English Neustupný, *Czechoslovakia before the Slavs*.

Germanization of the whole area during the succeeding century.[1] This would appear to reflect the invasion of the area by the Marcomanni and Quadi, Suebic tribes which were driven out of the Upper Main region by Drusus' successful campaigns, leaving vacant their old lands, on which Ahenobarbus was to settle the migrant Hermunduri a few years later.[2] Literary and archaeological evidence agree in identifying the Elbe–German culture with that of the Suebi, as has long been generally recognized.[3]

Not only in Bohemia, but in the Main valley and in Thuringia also, there is no doubt that German finds represent a new and intrusive element in an area where, before the coming of the Germans, the whole archaeological picture, *oppida*, pottery, coinage, iron-working, and all, is the same as that of Gaul in the Late La Tène period.[4] The German take-over of the area can be dated to approximately the period of Augustus, the finds seeming to link it to the period after the destruction of Manching but not so late as the reign of Tiberius.[5] The same picture is repeated in the Wetterau region, north of the Lower Main, and in the Taunus and the adjacent hill-country along the right bank of the Rhine, where the culture is again of the La Tène type, although with certain differences, and poorer, as if the inhabitants did not wholly belong to the world of their neighbours south of the Main, however strongly influenced by them.[6] They may be of different stock, for there are also

[1] Filip, op. cit., pp. 550–1 (German summary); Preidel, op. cit., pp. 131–66; Dobiaš, op. cit., pp. 354–68; Neustupný, op. cit., pp. 145–80. Cf. also Bóna, *AArchHung.* xv (1963), pp. 249–63.

[2] See below, p. 158. Evidence for Marcomanni on Upper Main cogently presented by Nierhaus, *Das swebische Gräberfeld von Diersheim*, pp. 228–30. Glüsing has also tried to show that there was Suebic settlement south of the Danube, *Offa* xxi/xxii (1964/5), pp. 7–20, but the finds which he cites do not seem conclusive.

[3] See also below, pp. 30–1.

[4] Kossack, op. cit., pp. 77–86, cf. Kuhn, ibid., pp. 119–20. In some detail, Pescheck, *Bay. Vorgbl.* xv (1960), pp. 75–89. On Thuringia, Werner, *Germania* xxvi (1942), pp. 148–54; also von Uslar, *Germania* xliii (1965), p. 146, commenting on Wenskus, *Stammesbildung und Verfassung*; cf. Voigt, *Alt-Thüringen* vi (1962/3), pp. 383–402. Also Pescheck, *Ber. des Hist. Ver. des ehem. Fürstbistums Bamberg* cii (1966), pp. 7–23.

[5] Kossack, op. cit., accepts 15 B.C. as the date of the destruction of Manching, erroneously, see below, pp. 72–4.

[6] Schönberger, *SJ* xi (1952), pp. 21–130, cf. p. 71: 'In dieser Zeit unterscheidet sich unser Gebiet in zahlreichen Formen durch nichts vom geläufigen Spätlatène Rheinhessens, Starkenburgs und der Rheinprovinz. Doch wirkt es in Gegensatz zu

linguistic differences between the area between the Main and
the Lippe and the heartland of the La Tène region to the south.[1]
It should however be emphasized that there is on the other
hand no difference between the left and right banks of the
Rhine. Archaeologically speaking, the river here is not a border
between two different cultures, and the culture of the La Tène
period develops without a break from the earlier so-called
Hunsrück–Eifel culture. Neither side of the river has any
archaeological trace of Germans, in the conventional sense
of that name, despite what our reading of Caesar would lead
us to expect.[2]

The Wetterau region is of special interest, because here we
have evidence linking native and Roman sites and permitting
us to see something of the interaction between the two. There
was a native settlement around the salt springs of Bad Nauheim
when the Romans under Drusus established a supply base at
Rödgen nearby (see below, Chapter 6. 8, 6. 9). Its culture was
of the La Tène type, and its people were on friendly terms with
the Romans. The Bad Nauheim settlement continued into the
first decade of our era, after Rödgen was given up, but had
already been abandoned by its La Tène inhabitants before
Germanicus fortified the strong defensive position of Friedberg
(see below, Chapter 6. 8), which blocks the exit southwards
from the Wetterau and which the Romans had not thought it
necessary to occupy earlier. By this time typically German
finds occur in the area,[3] and it is a reasonable hypothesis that
it is the taking-over of the area by hostile Germans, replacing
the friendly La Tène occupants, that caused the Romans to
fortify the Friedberg position.

Now the original inhabitants of this area appear to have been
the Mattiaci. Their name is apparently Celtic, although Mattium appears as the name of an *oppidum* which Tacitus ascribes
in A.D. 15 to the Chatti, who are undoubtedly Germans.[4]
The Mattiaci therefore are commonly taken for Germans also,

den dortigen Fundreichtum eigentlich arm, ja geradezu als Randgebiet.' Cf.
Kossack, op. cit., pp. 94–100, Hachmann, ibid., p. 62.
    [1] Cf. Hachmann, Kossack, and Kuhn, op. cit., p. 134. North of this the popula-
tion genuinely spoke German, Kuhn, op. cit., p. 121.
    [2] Tackenberg, *Fundkarten zur Vorgeschichte der Rheinprovinz* (1954), p. 105, cf.
Kossack, op. cit., pp. 97–8. [ADD.]
    [3] Schönberger, op. cit., p. 72.   [4] Tac., *Ann.* i. 56. 6.

'a strongly Celticized tribe, . . . a subdivision of the Chatti, as is proved by their name',[1] while Mattium itself is commonly identified with the Altenburg at Niedenstein, north of the Wetterau. This site the excavator assumed to be German, and went to some pains to explain away the undoubted similarities between the Altenburg finds and those from indubitably La Tène sites.[2] Re-examination of his report makes it clear however that in fact the Altenburg is a genuine La Tène *oppidum*, although impoverished by comparison with the great centres of La Tène culture.[3]

The Altenburg indeed, like the rest of the area between the Main and the Lippe, shows all the characteristics of a border zone. Hand-made pottery, for instance, is found alongside the normal wheel-made La Tène varieties; but just as in the Hunsrück–Eifel region, there is no question of a change of population before La Tène times, the culture of the La Tène period in this region also developing without a break from that which we find here in earlier periods. The archaeological evidence would support the theory that this border zone, originally on the frontier of and associated with the La Tène world, was subsequently overrun by the Chatti, thrusting down from their original lands north of the Lippe,[4] and driving the indigenous inhabitants before them. The pressure of the Chatti will have been relieved for a time by Roman intervention, but renewed as soon as the stabilizing influence of the Roman army was removed by the Varian Disaster. It was perhaps fear of this that made the Mattiaci Rome's allies, and with reason; having already lost their northern lands, including the Altenburg, if this really is Mattium, they were now, when Roman protection was removed, pushed out of the Wetterau as well and right back on to the Rhine.

The Rhine was no more a cultural boundary in its upper

---

[1] Anderson (ed.), *Cornelii Taciti de origine et situ Germanorum*, p. 146.

[2] Hofmeister, *Die Chatten* i: *Mattium*, e.g., pp. 76–7, explaining pottery sherds as 'ärmere Verwandte der keltischen Keramik', weapons and equipment as imports etc., and concluding triumphantly: 'Für die Kelten bleibt kein Platz mehr.' Kossack, op. cit., p. 95, describes it more accurately as 'nichts anderes als ein Oppidum in Böhmen oder in Gallien'. Similarly Nierhaus, op. cit., p. 227; von Uslar, *JRGZ* viii (1961), p. 62; Hachmann, op. cit., p. 32.

[3] Hachmann, op. cit., p. 36; cf. Nierhaus, op. cit., p. 211. [ADD.]

[4] Hachmann, op. cit., pp. 51–2, 60; it is noteworthy that there is no mention of the Chatti in Caesar.

or lower course than it was in its middle reaches. South of the Main, between Main and Upper Danube, there is no doubt that the indigenous population both east and west of the Rhine was Celtic. The Black Forest area has its *oppida*, like Tarodunum mentioned above, and Tacitus still describes the inhabitants of the *agri decumates* specifically as Celtic.[1] The Germans whom Caesar speaks of in this area, who were engaged in continuous warfare with the Helvetii, may have been migrating Suebi, like those we hear of elsewhere; if so, they moved on and left no archaeological trace.[2] Three Suebic settlements are indeed known from the Upper Rhine area, south of the Main, but they do not go back to Caesar's time, and the settlers seem to have been clients of the Romans, deliberately established here as a sort of frontier militia. Those on the Neckar around Lopodunum (Ladenburg), and those in Starkenburg around Gross-Gerau go back to late Augustan or early Tiberian times, those at Diersheim, north-east of Strasbourg, to the middle of the first century A.D. only.[3]

Ariovistus' men west of the Rhine leave no trace either, as a survey of possible German finds from Alsace, Pfalz, and Rheinhessen shows.[4] This was the area where under the Empire three tribes dwelt which Caesar records amongst the members of Ariovistus' host, the Nemetes, the Triboci, and the Vangiones.[5] Of these only the last have a name which is not obviously Celtic in form, and even a scholar who is passionately defending the thesis that all three tribes really are Germans is nevertheless constrained to admit that from the archaeological evidence one would suppose even the Vangiones to be Celtic.[6]

---

[1] Bittel, *Die Kelten in Württemburg*, esp. p. 191: 'Ganz fehlen bis jetzt auch noch die germanischen Funde, die wir aus dem 1. Jahrh. v. Chr. auf Grund der Schriftstellernachrichten im Lande erwarten dürften'; finds show 'dass sich keltisches Volkstum ungestört bis in die römische Zeit gehalten hat'. Cf. Fischer, *Bad. Fundber.* xxii (1962), pp. 37–49, on the *oppidum* at Tarodunum. Tacitus speaks of these people as 'levissimus quisque Gallorum', *Germ.* 29. 4.

[2] Caesar, *BG* i. 1. 4, cf. Nierhaus, op. cit., p. 220, n. 140.

[3] Nierhaus, op. cit., pp. 182–98, 230–4 (date of Neckar and Starkenburg groups given as second or third decade A.D., p. 194, as Augustan, p. 231); cf. Schönberger, op. cit., pp. 72, 74.

[4] Nierhaus, op. cit., pp. 199–207, cf. pp. 2–3, commenting on Behrens, *Denkmäler des Wangionengebietes*. German graves could be those of Roman auxiliaries, and the Niedermodern brooch, which is something of an oddity, might be an 'heirloom'.

[5] Caesar, *BG* i. 51. 2; cf. Pliny, *NH* iv. 106.

[6] Koepp, *Götting. Gel. Anz.* cxc (1928), pp. 210–13; on the names of these tribes,

They must, he suggests, have been very rapidly Celticized. It has on the other hand been suggested that none of the three was there right through from Ariovistus' time on, but that all were driven out with the rest of his forces, only to be allowed to return later.[1] More probably these three tribes, like those of the area from which they probably originate, the Wetterau and the regions between the Main and the Lippe, of whom we spoke above, are in the strict linguistic sense neither true Germans nor true Celts, but a border people who have however assimilated the La Tène culture of their Celtic neighbours.[2]

The situation on the Lower Rhine is different from that farther south, although here again the one sure fact is that the Rhine, before the Romans came, was not a boundary between two distinct cultures: 'Both the middle and lower reaches of the river show a well-defined civilization of the Late La Tène type . . . The material civilization of the Ubii and the Sugambri, prior to their transplantation, in no way differed from that of the Treveri and other Celtic peoples, except that they were a little poorer.'[3] Although the evidence from the area of what is now Holland for the period before the coming of the Romans is extremely scarce and hard to interpret, it is clear that in the pre-Roman period the western part of Northern and Middle Germany was not, on the basis of either linguistic or archaeological evidence, German. We are again brought to the conclusion that neither the Belgae west of the river nor the tribes east of it were fully German or Celtic in the normal sense.[4]

The discrepancy between Caesar's evidence and that of

Feist, *Germanen und Kelten in der antiken Überlieferung*, pp. 19–22; Much, *Ztschr. für deutsches Altertum und deutsche Litteratur* lxv (1928), p. 18. Cf. also Schönberger, op. cit., p. 74; Kahrstedt, *BJ* cl/cli (1950/1), p. 64; Schumacher, *Siedlungs- und Kulturgeschichte der Rheinland* ii, pp. 269–77; Nierhaus, op. cit., pp. 221–2.

[1] Nierhaus, loc. cit., following Nesselhauf.

[2] Hachmann, op. cit., p. 62.

[3] Kahrstedt in *Congress of Roman Frontier Studies, 1949*, p. 44; cf. id., *BJ* cl/cli (1950/1), pp. 63–80. Also, emphatically, Tackenberg, op. cit., p. 106, noting also, p. 104, that on Lower Rhine original inhabitants neither German nor Celt, on which Hachmann, Kossack, and Kuhn, op. cit., *passim*, esp. Kuhn, pp. 110–13, 126–8, and jointly pp. 129–33. Further data on present-day Belgium and Holland in de Laet's review, *Helinium* iv (1964), pp. 265–71. Cf. also Kraft, *Germania* xlii (1964), pp. 313–20, suggesting valuable corrections on points of detail, but not confuting the basic thesis.

[4] Hachmann, Kossack, and Kuhn, summarizing their joint conclusions, op. cit., pp. 129–33, cf. Kuhn, ibid., on linguistic evidence in particular, pp. 110–13, 126–8.

archaeology is marked, and the problem of how to resolve it has given rise to much discussion.[1] At one extreme are those who take all remains east of the Rhine for German, because Caesar says so; at the other is the view most clearly expressed by Feist, that all tribes referred to as Germans down to the time of the great migrations are in fact Celts.[2] There can however be no doubt that two separate linguistic groups exist, nor is it easy to follow those who suggest that Celts and Germans are simply archaeologically indistinguishable at this period.[3] To disprove this it is only necessary to go back beyond the zone of contact and compare the archaeology of Denmark with that of South Germany or Central Gaul. It is the identification of the tribes within the zone of contact which provides the problem.

The identity of culture on both banks of the Rhine may conflict with Caesar's evidence, but it is not otherwise to be wondered at. Historically, rivers are not natural frontiers; they join rather than separate, and serve more readily as highways than as barriers.[4] They are convenient lines of demarcation, if two powers wish to negotiate a frontier, but the Romans did not negotiate with barbarians as with equals.[5] It was only when the Romans themselves had stabilized their frontier along the Rhine and Danube, and had set up forts and fortresses, with customs posts and artificial restrictions on natural freedom of movement along and across the river, that a real cultural gap was created between the provincial on the one side and the barbarian on the other, although even so there

[1] On the *Forschungsgeschichte* of the question, see Nierhaus, op. cit., pp. 1–12; further, esp. on early controversies between Schuchhardt and Kossinna, Eggers, *Die Einführung in die Vorgeschichte*, pp. 199–254. Of particular importance for methodology are the contributions of Wahle, *Zur ethnischen Deutung vorgeschichtlicher Kulturprovinzen*, and von Uslar, *JRGZ* viii (1961), pp. 38–65, 'Germanische Bodenaltertümer um Christi Geburt als Interpretationsbeispiel'. Modern parallels by Kahrstedt in *Ur- und Frühgeschichte als historiche Wissenschaft*, pp. 60–2.

[2] Feist, op. cit., pp. 28–9, concluding that German is a 'Spezialisierung' of Celtae, like Galli, Galatae, Gaesatae, etc.

[3] Cf. Piggott, *Ancient Europe*, pp. 223–4: 'The archaeology involved, it has been remarked, "is easy to misconstrue because so drab"; nevertheless it does seem impossible to make any meaningful division before the end of the first millenium B.C.' [ADD.]

[4] Cf. Lord Curzon, *Frontiers*, pp. 20–1, on unsuitability of rivers as frontiers. Cf. also Salmon, *A History of the Roman World 30 B.C. to A.D. 138*, p. 275. Only exceptionally is a river a military barrier either, as below, p. 69.

[5] See above, pp. 8–9.

extended beyond the river a zone of Roman influence, if not in fact actual political control.[1] The evidence of post-Augustan times is therefore misleading as a guide to the cultural situation along the Rhine as it was before the campaigns of Drusus and his successors completely altered the position. An attempt to work out the situation which Augustus found must therefore go back once more to the evidence of Caesar.

We began by noting the emphasis which Caesar in Book I lays on the Rhine as the boundary between Celts and Germans and on the basic difference between them. This appears to be his own innovation; earlier writers, such as Posidonius, know of people called Germans on the Lower Rhine, but do not distinguish them from the Celts.[2] Caesar himself moreover in later books blurs the distinction he has set up in Book I, recognizing that there had once been Gauls east of the Rhine, such as the Boii, and the Volcae Tectosages were still there, a remnant now reduced to the same wretched standard of living as the Germans, their neighbours.[3]

Still more surprisingly we learn in Book II that there are also well-established German tribes west of the river. We hear first of 'Germanos qui cis Rhenum incolant'.[4] We then learn that the Belgae in general are reputed to be of German origin: 'plerosque Belgas esse ortos ab Germanis Rhenumque antiquitus traductos propter loci fertilitatem ibi consedisse'.[5] Tacitus similarly notes that, 'qui primi Rhenum transgressi Gallos expulerint ac nunc Tungri, tunc Germani vocati sint'.[6]

---

[1] On trade and contacts, Eggers, *Der römische Import im freien Germanien*, pp. 66–70, distinguishing *Grenzhandel* and *Fernhandel*. On political control, Klose, *Roms Klientel-Randstaaten*. On Romanization of Rhineland, see Rüger, *Germania Inferior*, pp. 11–14, esp. p. 14: 'Aus dem archäologischen Material wird der Beginn der Romanisierung erst mit der Ankunft der römischen Truppen am Rhein angezeigt. Die Einwanderung rechtsrheinischer Gruppen hat die spätlatènezeitliche linksrheinische Tradition Ostgalliens ebensowenig geändert wie die faktische Zugehörigkeit zum römischen Reich seit etwa 50 v. Chr.'

[2] Cf. Jacoby, *Die Fragmente der griechischen Historiker* iic, pp. 169–70, commenting on iiA, p. 232 (Posidonius, fr. 22); also Hachmann, op. cit., esp. pp. 43–4. On persistence of 'Celtae' and 'Celtice' in later Greek writers, see Norden, *Die germanische Urgeschichtein Tacitus Germania*, pp. 101–2.

[3] Caesar, *BG* vi. 24. There were other Volcae in Gaul, vii. 7, vii. 64.

[4] Caesar, *BG* ii. 3. 4. Norden's discusssion of this whole subject, op. cit., chapter 6, esp. pp. 353–405, remains of prime importance, and is of great value for its bringing together of the relevant source-material, even if, as will be clear, I cannot accept his conclusions.

[5] Caesar, *BG* ii. 4. 1.   [6] Tacitus, *Germ.* 2. 5.

Caesar also mentions four small tribes, the Condrusi, Eburones, Caeroesi, and Paemani, 'qui uno nomine Germani appellantur', and in a later passage we hear of a fifth, the Segni.[1] The Aduatuci moreover are named as the descendants of the Cimbri and Teutoni, who stayed behind when the main body went on.[2]

The early part of Book IV is equally instructive.[3] We learn that at least one Belgic tribe, the Menapii, occupied and cultivated land on both banks of the river. They are invaded in the winter of 56/55 by two tribes whom Caesar specifically describes as German, the Usipetes and Tencteri: 'causa transeundi fuit quod ab Suebis compluris annos exagitati bello premebantur et agri cultura prohibebantur.' The invaders are invited to settle amongst the Condrusi and Eburones, two of the tribes known collectively as 'Germani', clients of the Treveri, but Caesar refuses permission and instead offers to let them settle among the Ubii, back on the right bank, who are also under pressure from the Suebi and asking Caesar's help. When they do not agree, they are attacked and massacred; a remnant escapes across the river and takes refuge with the Sugambri, who will not give them up, so that Caesar builds a bridge and crosses the river in pursuit, but in vain, for the Sugambri take to the woods, avoiding battle. Caesar is however welcomed by the Ubii, who inform him that the Suebi are preparing to join battle in full strength, whereupon he returns to Gaul.

Now one reason why the Condrusi and Eburones were willing to accept the Usipetes and Tencteri may have been their common German origin. A more potent reason will have been that they saw them as potential allies against the common foe, the Suebi. Caesar records the fear which the latter inspired in the Treveri and their clients. The Treveri too claimed a German origin, in which they took pride, and Hirtius found them to differ very little from the Germans 'cultu et feritate'.[4] Later they were to seek and get German help against Caesar himself;[5] it is improbable, to say the least, that it was to the Suebi that they turned.

In their concern for their agriculture, the Usipetes and

[1] Caesar, BG ii. 4. 10, vi. 32. 1.   [2] Caesar, BG ii. 29. 4.
[3] Caesar, BG iv. 1–19.   [4] Hirtius, BG viii. 25. 2.
[5] Caesar, BG v. 2. 4, etc., vi. 2. 1, 7. 3, viii. 45. 1. Cf. Hachmann, op. cit., p. 64.

Tencteri differ strikingly from what Caesar has to say elsewhere on this subject about the Germans; they resemble in this the Ubii, who were also noted farmers.[1] The Usipetes and Tencteri are also notable for their cavalry; so too the Sugambri, with whom their survivors take refuge after the massacre by Caesar's troops, can put 2,000 cavalry into the field, when Caesar gives the word for a general plundering of the Eburones; the Treveri also are strong in cavalry, with reputedly the best cavalry in Gaul.[2] Again we see a common bond between these tribes, and when Caesar came to recruit the German cavalry which stood him in such good stead later, it will have been from such German tribes as these that he recruited it, not from the Suebi.[3] Even more significant is the fact that only the Suebi are represented as in a state of perpetual migration; the tribes along the Rhine, such as the Usipetes, Tencteri, Ubii, and Sugambri, are all represented as migrating only under pressure, in the first three cases from the Suebi, in the latter from the Romans.[4] Von Uslar has also drawn attention to the difference between the *oppida* of the Ubii, which are refuges in time of danger, and those of the Suebi, which are abandoned.[5] In all these respects, the Suebi stand out as unlike the other German tribes, and the latter resemble the tribes on the left bank more closely than they do the Suebi. It is in fact the Suebi who are at the stage of social development which Caesar wishes us to regard as typically German.[6]

Now Pliny and Tacitus state that the Suebi belonged to the branch of the German race known as the Hermiones; other tribes mentioned as belonging to this branch are the Hermunduri, who are in fact themselves a Suebic tribe, the Chatti, and the Cherusci. It is significant that the tribes along the Rhine, of whom the Sugambri are specifically mentioned by name, belong to a different group, that of the Istiaeones,

---

[1] Pliny, *NH* xvii. 42. The Ubii are said to be 'Gallicis moribus assuefacti', Caesar, *BG* iv. 3. 3.

[2] Caesar, *BG* ii. 24. 4, iv. 12. 2, vi. 35. 5.

[3] Caesar, *BG* vii. 13. 1, 65. 5, and many subsequent refs. in *BG* and *BC*.

[4] Noted by Hachmann, op. cit., p. 65; cf. Feist, op. cit., pp. 32–3.

[5] Von Uslar, *Studien zu frühgeschichtlichen Befestigungen*, p. 10, n. 42, cf. *BG* vi. 10, v. 19.

[6] Cf. *BG* iv. 1–3 (description of Suebi) with vi. 21–3 (description of Germans), see Kraner–Dittenberger–Meusel, *C. Iulii Caesaris Commentarii de Bello Gallico* ii, p. 179.

while yet a third group, the Inguaeones, includes the tribes around the mouths of the Rhine and Elbe, such as the Cimbri, the Teutoni, and the tribes of the Chauci.[1] What then is the common denominator of all three groups? When Caesar applies the name 'German' to tribes from each group, implying that in some way all three groups are alike, and to be distinguished from the Celts, what is his criterion? At first sight we might suppose it to be language, as it was apparently for Tacitus; Ariovistus is, as we have seen, said to speak the Celtic language 'longinqua consuetudine', implying that it is not his own.[2] Many of the names, however, which we find attributed to 'Germans', even, as we have seen, to Ariovistus himself, are Celtic in form, although it may be argued that true German names have perhaps become Celticized in transmission through Gallic intermediaries.[3] But even the etymology of the name 'German' itself has aroused a fierce controversy, without anyone having been able to show conclusively that it was either Celtic or German; one thing that is certain, however, is that there is no evidence for its use among the right-bank Germans as a name for themselves in the Roman period.[4] Only on the left bank do we hear specifically of people calling themselves, or called by their neighbours, 'Germani'.[5] What links them to the right-bank tribes? Is it simply that they themselves once crossed the river? We have seen how much emphasis Caesar places on the Rhine as the boundary. Perhaps the only common

---

[1] Pliny, *NH* iv. 96, 99–100; Tac., *Germ.* 3, cf. Much, *Die Germania des Tacitus*, pp. 53–5. Pliny notes two other groups which do not concern us here, Vandili, and Peucini and Bastarnae, the latter being identical in Tac., *Germ.* 46. By the time Pliny and Tacitus wrote, the Sugambri were no longer on the right bank, as in Caesar's time, but on the left, having been transported in 8 B.C. and resettled to the north of the Ubii, where they went by the name of Guberni or Cuberni, Pliny, *NH* iv. 106, cf. Much, op. cit., p. 58, and Pliny recognizes as Germans living within the Empire these two tribes, together with the Batavi and other tribes of the Lower Rhine on the one side, and three tribes mentioned also in connection with Ariovistus' host on the other, the Nemetes, the Triboci, and the Vangiones.

[2] See above, p. 15, n. 1.

[3] Argued at some length by Much in his attacks on Feist in *Wiener Präh. Ztschr.* xv (1928), pp. 1–19, and in *Ztschr. für deutsches Altertum und deutsche Litteratur* lxv (1928), pp. 1–50, esp. pp. 11–13, 30–2; also Neckel, *Germanen und Kelten*, p. 24. Cf. also Koepp's review of Feist, *Götting. Gel. Anz.* cxc (1928), pp. 201–17. This is better than supposing that German leaders actually adopted Celtic names, see Nierhaus, op. cit., p. 218, n. 133, with refs.

[4] Schmidt, *Geschichte der deutschen Stämme* i, pp. 42–5; cf. Kuhn, op. cit., p. 124.

[5] So, emphatically, Hachmann, op. cit., p. 46.

denominator of his Germans is the geographical one, that all live, or until recently lived, east of the Rhine.

Now it has been pointed out that the five tribes known collectively as Germani Cisrhenani all have Celtic names, and no archaeological evidence of German settlement, in the conventional sense, has been found in their territory. Hence the suggestion that they were in fact Celts, the last Celtic tribes who crossed the Rhine, and that they then held the river against the Usipetes, Tencteri, Ubii, and Sugambri, who were pressing closely upon their heels. These Cisrhenani were on this interpretation the real Germans, who had now moved to the left bank, and their name will have been transferred by Caesar to the tribes which replaced them, so that paradoxically it is these latter who have come down to history as the archetypal Germans.[1] Caesar's application of the word to the right-bank tribes would not however be plausible, unless there were similar tribes, also known as Germani, still left behind on the right bank in his time.[2] This then leads us to see the Usipetes, Tencteri, Ubii, and Sugambri also as 'Germani' of the same type as the Germani Cisrhenani, rather than as 'Germans' in the sense which the word was later to acquire, in which sense it is typified by the Suebi.[3] They need not however be for that reason Celts. Rather should we see them as belonging to the people of whom we spoke earlier, the border folk between Main and Lippe, neither true Celts nor true Germans in the usually accepted sense, participants however in the culture of the La Tène world, though with local differences. The Suebi are just as clearly not 'Germani' in this, the original sense of the word; Caesar has wrongly transferred to them, whence it also passes to other invaders from the north and east, such as the Chatti and Cherusci, a name to which they have no right.[4]

[1] Moreau, *Die Welt der Kelten*, p. 41; cf. also Powell, *The Celts*, p. 164.

[2] Hachmann, op. cit., pp. 46–8; but cf. Kuhn, pp. 124–5, begging however the question of Caesar's possible deliberate intention to confuse the issue and shift the meaning.

[3] On 'German' traces among the Ubii (but in which sense?), see Wild, *Germania* xlvi (1968), pp. 67–73. Their original home was in the Neuwieder Becken area, Nierhaus, op. cit., pp. 224–5. The Ubian cult of the Matronae has often been considered 'German' in the conventional sense, Much, op. cit., pp. 43–8, against Feist, op. cit., pp. 41–4, 65–6, whereas Hachmann, Kossack, and Kuhn, op. cit., pp. 134–5, see it as characteristic of the original Germani. [ADD.]

[4] So Hawkes in *Celticum* xii, pp. 1–7. My debt to Professor Hawkes has already been acknowledged, though inadequately, in the Preface, p. xiii.

He may well have done this deliberately, of course. He needed a generic name for all the transrhenan peoples, especially once he had decided to make the Rhine the boundary of his conquests. By representing it also as a boundary between two different races, he was also seeking to justify his 'thus far and no farther' decision.[1] And because of Caesar's own immense authority, and because the new usage of the term 'German' filled a need for a designation of the geographical entity that Germany became once the Romans on the Rhine had split it off from Gaul, the new usage stuck. Caesar will not have worried about strict accuracy. He was writing not so much history, and not at all a textbook of ethnography, but 'political journalism directed at his contemporaries'; and in writing political journalism, as in composing lapidary inscriptions, a man is not upon oath.[2] Germany became an ethnic as well as a geographical entity, however, only after the Rhine became stabilized as a permanent frontier early in Tiberius' reign; and it was the presence of the frontier itself which brought this about, crystallizing the provincial–Roman culture on the one side and what we can regard, in the new, post-Caesarean sense of the word, as 'German' culture on the other.[3]

The old La Tène world was now split. Gaul, Raetia, Noricum became Roman provinces. The Taunus, the Wetterau, the Black Forest became the military zone along the frontier. The Upper Main, Thuringia, Bohemia, and Moravia were abandoned to the Germans. Archaeology reveals the Suebi, with their culture characteristic of the Elbe region, moving into north-west Germany towards the end of the first century B.C., taking over all the land between the Lower Rhine and the

---

[1] e.g. Hachmann, op. cit., p. 45: 'Caesar die *ethnische Gliederung* der Bevölkerung am Rhein in Einzelheiten *erst* fixierte, nachdem er schon *vorher* den Rhein als Grenzlinie festgelegt hatte' (his italics); cf. also the joint conclusion of all three scholars, op. cit., p. 133: 'Bodenfunde und Namen sagen einheitlich aus, dass der Rhein, ehe die Römer dazwischen kamen, keine Völkerscheide gewesen ist.'

[2] Gelzer, *Caesar*, pp. 102–5, moderate in comparison with Rambaud, *L'Art de la déformation historique dans les commentaires de César*, who suggests that in the Commentaries we have 'la pensée de César . . . (transmise) à son public, à la postérité, sous la forme d'une image des faits. Dans cette représentation, conçue selon ses intérêts et pour sa gloire, tout contribue à l'apologie du grand homme' (p. 243, and similarly *passim*).

[3] Cf. Kossack in Millar, *The Roman Empire and its Neighbours*, pp. 307–17, on social developments in Germany.

Rivers Werra and Leine.[1] By the second half of the first century A.D. there has developed in the western part of this area a distinct culture, that of the so-called 'Weser–Rhine Germans,' which can be distinguished from the Elbe–German culture, and which is clearly influenced by La Tène forms and techniques taken over from the original inhabitants.[2] The Romans, by destroying the power of the indigenous La Tène inhabitants in the area between the Main and the Lippe, opened up this area for the invading Suebi, whose lines of penetration were the same as those used by the Romans, in the opposite direction (fig. 1); the defeat of Varus did not in fact so much liberate the Germans, if we use the word in the new sense which it had by now acquired, as create a vacuum into which they were able to move in increasing numbers.[3] Roman policy had engineered its own defeat.[4]

Centuries later, when the Empire crumbled, the Germans moved across the frontier that had for so long excluded them and checked their march to the south. Not until later still, in the eleventh century or thereabouts, did the people whom others called Germans feel the need to apply to themselves one collective name; and when they did, the name they took was 'Deutsch', from their language, 'vernacular', as opposed to Latin.[5] The influence of the Roman frontier continued to make itself felt, centuries after it had ceased to exist.

[1] Hachmann, op. cit., pp. 36–7, 39–42, 56, with further refs.

[2] Von Uslar, *Westgermanische Bodenfunde*, p. 3; cf. Hachmann, Kossack, Kuhn, op. cit., map 8.

[3] Kossack, op. cit., pp. 100–4, with map 7.

[4] See below, pp. 244–5: Caesar, wiser in this than his successors, had foreseen the danger of such a vacuum, see below, p. 35.

[5] Feist, op. cit., pp. 69–70.

PART I

THE CONQUEST OF THE ALPS

3

THE ROMANS IN HELVETIA

ONCE the Roman armies reached the Rhine, the territory of the Helvetii became strategically vital to them. Caesar's treatment of the Helvetii demonstrates this. On the eastern borders of Gaul, shut in by the Rhine, the Jura Mountains, Lac Léman, and the Rhône,[1] Helvetia was a buffer between Gaul proper and the raiding Alpine tribes; it could also become a base for the future suppression of these tribes; and, not least, it lay on the direct route from Italy over the Great St. Bernard Pass to the Rhine, a circumstance of little importance to the Romans as long as their interests and their armies were confined to Provence, but a different matter once Caesar had reached the Rhine.

In this area the Helvetii, before setting out in 58 B.C. on their abortive migration through Gaul, had some twelve *oppida* and four hundred *vici*, all of which they burnt themselves before leaving.[2] After their defeat, Caesar required them to return to their old lands and rebuild their settlements, including the fortified *oppida,* and arranged for them to be supplied with corn by the Allobroges, because, he says, he was afraid that if their lands were left unoccupied, the Germans from across the Rhine might move in.[3]

Even when the Helvetii sent a small contingent to join in Vercingetorix's revolt,[4] Caesar did not punish them, except for planting a colony at Nyon (Noviodunum, Colonia Julia Equestris) in the southern part of their territory, on the north shore of Lac Léman, about 15 miles north of Geneva, with

---

[1] Caesar, *BG* i. 2. 3.   [2] Ibid. i. 5. 2.
[3] Ibid. i. 28. 3–4; Christ, *SZG* v (1955), p. 459, n. 30, has denied that they would have been able to withstand the Germans after their defeat by Caesar, and urges that Caesar was concerned only to fill a 'Siedlungsvacuum'; cf. also van Berchem, *SZG* v (1955), p. 145; Caesar, however, helped the Helvetii to recover, and a 'Siedlungsvacuum' is dangerous only if there are undesirables at hand to fill it.
[4] Caesar, *BG* vii. 75. 3.

settlers drawn from the Roman citizen cavalry in Caesar's army.[1] The Helvetii were particularly strong in cavalry, in which capacity they are often found in the Roman army in the Early Empire,[2] and the immediate purpose of the colony at Nyon was to watch the Helvetii and to prevent them from raiding down the Rhône into Narbonensis, which Caesar's advance into north and west Gaul had left exposed. The northern route from Helvetia into Gaul was similarly blocked in 44–43, when L. Munatius Plancus founded another colony, complementing Nyon, at Augst (Colonia Raurica, later Augusta Raurica), on the Rhine just east of the great Rhine bend at Basle, guarding both the route round the north end of the Jura between the Jura and the Rhine, and also the most northerly passes of the Jura.[3]

Augst, however, was probably designed as an outpost directed less against the Helvetii than against the Raeti, whose Alpine haunts looked down upon the plains of Helvetia, which they made a habit of raiding.[4] The havoc which they might create is exemplified by the destruction of the native settlement on the Gasfabrik site at Basle (below, Chapter 3. 1), perhaps in the very raid in which Plancus earned his triumph. Caesar designates the Germans as the danger against which the Helvetii were intended to act as a buffer. If so, as we have seen in the previous chapter, these will have been war-bands like

---

[1] Kraft, *JRGZ* iv (1957), pp. 81–107, on date and composition of colony; on Nyon itself, see further Stähelin, *Die Schweiz in römischer Zeit*, pp. 91–5; Howald and Meyer, *Die römische Schweiz*, pp. 235–6. Pelichet in *Atti del 1° convegno preistorico italo-svizzero 1947*, pp. 96–103, tries to show that Helvetian territory extended only to the R. Aubonne, and that Nyon was built in the territory of the Sequani, but his arguments are not convincing, so again id., *Revue historique vaudoise* lxvi (1958), pp. 49–60.

[2] Kraft, op. cit., pp. 100–6.

[3] *CIL* x. 6087 (= *ILS* 886 = Howald and Meyer, op. cit., no. 334), Plancus' gravestone: *triump(h)avit ex Raetis . . . in Gallia colonias deduxit Lugdunum et Rauricam.* On the purpose of these colonies, besides Kraft, loc. cit., cf. also Meyer, *MH* xix (1962), pp. 145–6; van Berchem, *JSGU* xlvi (1957), p. 15. There is no reason to suppose that Lyons, Nyon, and Augst guarded a road from Lyons to the Rhine; Helvetia was not a thoroughfare until later, with the opening-up of the Great St. Bernard Pass, described below, and the question of what might have happened if Galba had succeeded in opening it up is irrelevant; cf. however Berger in *Provincialia: Festschrift für Rudolf Laur-Belart*, pp. 15–24, reviewing previous discussion and suggesting that Augst was also originally conceived as a base for operations across the Rhine.

[4] Strabo iv. 206.

those of Ariovistus.[1] Caesar had his own reasons for emphasizing the German danger. The danger from the Alpine tribes was no less real.

The importance of Helvetia increased with the conquest of the Salassi and the opening up of the Great St. Bernard Pass in 25, and it may have been now that Helvetia came under direct Roman administration. The Salassi had long been a nuisance to Rome. Occupying the Val d'Aosta, they prevented the Romans from using freely either the Great or the Little St. Bernard, since the way up from Italy to both these passes lies through that valley.[2] At Aosta the road forks, the right fork leading northwards over the Great St. Bernard into the Vallis Poenina, and the left going first west and then south-west over the Little St. Bernard, the most northerly of the passes which lead from Italy into Gaul. In the angle between the two passes stands the impenetrable barrier of the Mont Blanc massif. Of these two passes, the Little St. Bernard was practicable for waggons over most of its length by Strabo's day, the Great St. Bernard not, though Strabo recognizes it as a good short-cut.[3] It was however paved at the latest by Claudius, and thereafter, as Freshfield says, 'for centuries the (Great) St. Bernard found no rival among the possible passes of the Pennines'.[4]

Anyone using these passes under the Republic did so at his own risk and to the profit of the Salassi and their neighbours across the divide. The passage of an army through the Val d'Aosta could be a humiliating and expensive business. Sertorius paid for the privilege of going that way.[5] Decimus Brutus after Mutina was mulcted of one drachma a head for his troops.[6] Even Caesar himself was once plundered by the Salassi, who threw boulders down upon his legions on the

[1] See above, p. 14.
[2] It has been suggested that C. Gracchus built 'a road with military posts' through the Val d'Aosta and over the Little St. Bernard in 122 B.C.; so Hyde, *Roman Alpine Routes*, p. 61, citing Plut., *C. Gracchus* 7, which does not however support so improbable a theory.
[3] Strabo iv. 205, 208.
[4] Freshfield, *GJ* xlix (1917), p. 17. Paved at latest by Claudius, Howald and Meyer, op. cit., no. 377, cf. pp. 196–7; see also Stähelin, op. cit., pp. 163–4; thereafter passable even 'hibernis adhuc Alpibus', Tac., *Hist.* i. 69. Chilver, *Cisalpine Gaul*, p. 40, suggests that it was in fact paved under Augustus, though not by Agrippa, 'of whose work Strabo was aware'. On this pass see also Bouffard, *Ur-Schweiz* x (1946), pp. 48–52 and Blondel in *Hommages Grenier* i, pp. 308–15.
[5] Plut., *Sert.* 6. 5. [6] Strabo iv. 205.

delightfully improbable pretext that they were building roads and bridges.[1] Nor were the depredations of the Salassi confined to their own valley, for Ivrea (Eporedia), founded in 100 B.C. to hold them in check, failed of its purpose,[2] and the special attention they received from Augustus is a mark at once of their contumacity and of the value of the passes which they controlled.

Caesar had tried to open up the Great St. Bernard in 57, sending Servius Galba to attack it from the north, 'quod iter per Alpes, quo magno cum periculo magnisque cum portoriis mercatores ire consuerant, patefieri volebat'.[3] The attempt is significant. It failed, but had it succeeded, Caesar would doubtless have made more of it. Nor should we suppose that his only motive was an altruistic concern to save the merchants *portoria*. The pass was, as we have seen, of great strategic value.

Octavian was prepared to move against the Salassi in 35 B.C.[4] In that or the following year C. Antistius Vetus brought about a short-lived submission; when he retired, they reasserted their independence and mocked at Octavian's punitive measures.[5] Valerius Messalla subsequently defeated them,[6] but it was left for Terentius Varro to complete the conquest, conclusively enough, in 25 B.C.[7] Aosta (Augusta Praetoria) was founded on the actual site of Varro's camp;[8] and although Strabo says that all the tribe was sold into slavery, in fact the new colony included 'Salassi incolae', who 'ab initio se in coloniam contulerunt'.[9] Probably Dio is right to say that only the men of military age were sold off; as we shall see in Chapter 4, among the Raeti and Vindelici also the Romans took the same precaution.

---

[1] Strabo, loc. cit.   [2] Ibid.
[3] Caesar, *BG* iii. 1. 2.   [4] Dio xlix. 34.
[5] Appian, *Ill.* 17; Schmitthenner, *Historia* vii (1958), pp. 207–11, demonstrates that this refers to the Salassi of the Val d'Aosta, which some scholars have doubted.
[6] Messalla's campaign is recorded by Dio under 34 B.C. (xlix. 38), but wrongly; cf. Schmitthenner, op. cit., pp. 210–11, 234–6; Chilver, op. cit., p. 11, assigns the campaign, perhaps rightly, to Messalla's governorship of Gaul (28–27), rather than to any time before Actium.
[7] Dio liii. 25. 3–5; Strabo iv. 205–6.
[8] On Aosta, Barocelli, *Forma Italiae* xi. 1, *Augusta Praetoria*; a trace of what may be the actual ditch of Varro's camp has been found beneath the town wall, col. 92, with fig. a, cols. 93–4; see also id., *La romanizzazione della Valle d'Aosta*, pp. 20–47.
[9] *ILS* 6753, on which see Chilver, op. cit., p. 16, and esp. Beretta, *Acme* v (1952), pp. 493–508.

Since Strabo says that the Little St. Bernard was paved and the Great St. Bernard was not, some scholars have assumed that the Little St. Bernard was the more important of the twin passes to Augustus.[1] The Col du Mont Cénis however provides an alternative to the Little St. Bernard, and in later times was certainly by far the more important and frequented of the two, whereas the Great St. Bernard is the only route giving direct access to the Vallis Poenina and Helvetia and thence to the Rhine, and was in constant use by armies after the Augustan period throughout Roman and medieval times.[2] Archaeological evidence moreover suggests that it was after the opening up of the Great St. Bernard that an important trading station or supply depot developed at Vidy, now a suburb of Lausanne, a natural centre which could receive goods from Italy over the Great St. Bernard or from Gaul up the Rhône and along the lake, and distribute them throughout Helvetia and on to the Rhine.[3] We have already seen that the Great St. Bernard was a frequented trade-route, even under the Republic, when merchants paid heavy tolls. Its conquest by the Romans must have stimulated this trade, while there is evidence for water-borne trade between Lausanne and Geneva, which was at this time merely an unwalled Allobrogan *vicus* at the exit from the lake into the Rhône.[4] Throughout Helvetia Romanization

[1] So, e.g., Scullard, *From the Gracchi to Nero*, p. 263: 'To guard the road over the Little St. Bernard a military colony was established at Augusta Praetoria', with no mention of the Great St. Bernard. It used to be urged in support of this view that Aosta had at first no gate facing the Great St. Bernard: Promis, *Mem. d. R. Accad. d. Scienze di Torino*, 2nd ser., xxi (1864), p. 130; Mommsen, *CIL* v. 2, p. 761; Hyde, op. cit., p. 67; and still Goessler, *RE* xxi, col. 1162. Barocelli however, *Forma Italiae* xi. 1, col. 130–1, cf. 73, points out that the *porta praetoria* faced down the valley towards Rome, the *decumana* therefore giving access to the Little St. Bernard and the *principalis sinistra* to the Great St. Bernard. Cf. also Walser, *Die römischen Straßen in der Schweiz* i, p. 23.

[2] Hyde, op. cit., pp. 66, 68–70; but he denies that the Romans used the Mont Cénis at all, pp. 55–7, wrongly however: Caesar used it in 58 B.C., see Freshfield, *Hannibal Once More*, pp. 110–17, and now Meyer, *MH* xxi (1964), pp. 99–102; cf. also Philipp, *RE* iiA, col. 1107.

[3] Ettlinger in *Limes-Studien*, pp. 45–7; Bögli, *Ur-Schweiz* xxiv (1960), pp. 48–50; ibid. xxv (1961), pp. 19, 58; Sitterding, *Ur-Schweiz* xxvi (1962), pp. 53–4. [ADD.]

[4] On Geneva, see Stähelin, op. cit., pp. 91, 126, n. 1, 150–1, and Howald and Meyer, op. cit., pp. 219–20; some pottery published by Deonna, *Pro Alesia* N.S. xi (1925), pp. 1–81; cf. also Ettlinger, loc. cit. An inscription from Geneva dated to before A.D. 40 mentions the *nautae lacus Lemanni*, Howald and Meyer, no. 92, with note on date, while another inscription attests *nautae Leuson(nenses)*, ibid., no. 154, cf. 152, 153. Italian sigillata will have come this way up the Rhône.

proceeded apace: excavations in the Helvetian *oppidum* on the Engehalbinsel at Bern have revealed not only its destruction by the Helvetii themselves in 58 and the subsequent rebuilding, but also the transformation of the native *oppidum* into a Romanized *vicus*.[1] Augustan sigillata has been found here and at several other Helvetian sites, a sign perhaps of trade rather than necessarily, as once was thought, of the presence of Roman troops.[2]

Roman control of the Great St. Bernard also gave access to the Vallis Poenina, the Valais. The tribes of the Valais had to be overcome by force; their names appear on the Tropaeum Alpium, discussed in Chapter 4. But they were quickly reconciled,[3] and the fighting capacity which had so disconcerted Galba was enlisted in the service of Rome. Few records bring more vividly before our eyes the vastness of the Empire and the use to which Rome put her 'new-caught, sullen peoples' than the gravestone of one Scaurus, son of Ambitontus, born in the Vallis Poenina, 'domo Nantuas', who died far from his native Alps at Tell-el-Ghanime on the Euphrates.[4]

If there is no direct evidence for Roman garrisons in Central Helvetia and the Valais, this is not the case further north. Here the Romans set out to consolidate their newly won control

---

[1] Müller-Beck and Ettlinger, *BerRGK* xliii/xliv (1962/3), pp. 107–53; Müller-Beck, *JSGU* l (1963), pp. 47–50; id., *Jb. des Bern. Hist. Mus.* xli/xlii (1961/2), pp. 488–503; Wiedemer, *Germania* xli (1963), pp. 275–7; some criticism of Müller-Beck's methodology in Ulbert, *Der Lorenzberg bei Epfach*, pp. 105–6, n. 153. It is suggested that there was also a Roman garrison here, cf. Ettlinger, op. cit., pp. 148, 153, on the grounds of 11 pieces of what might be cavalry equipment, a strigil, and about 100 *stili*; the latter however need not be specifically military (we might think of Roman merchants), while the horse-gear may belong to native riders, perhaps even native militia.

[2] Kasser, *Ur-Schweiz* xix (1955), pp. 51–9, cf. Wiedemer, op. cit., p. 275 (Yverdon); Ettlinger, *JSGU* l (1963), pp. 83–4 (Nyon); Fellmann, *Basler Ztschr. für Gesch. und Altertumskunde* lx (1960), p. 34, n. 25 (Solothurn); Ettlinger, *Jb. des Bern. Hist. Mus.* xxxix/xl (1959/60), p. 328, cf. *JSGU* xlix (1962), p. 84 (Uetendorf); Schönberger, *JRS* lix (1969), p. 188, no. 34, citing Wiedemer (Olten). [ADD.]

[3] Howald and Meyer, nos. 37–40 (= *CIL* xii. 136, 145, 146, 141); cf. Stähelin, op. cit., pp. 125–8, and Howald and Meyer, pp. 195–7; for a contrary interpretation, van Berchem, *REL* xl (1962), p. 233, suggesting that the Valais was so isolated and unimportant as to be scarcely touched by the conquest, and that these inscriptions were merely set up by 'ses cités traditionnelles, heureuses de survivre'; see further id., *MH* xiii (1956), pp. 200–1; the Valais tribes later become 'civitates quattuor vallis Poeninae' (Howald and Meyer, nos. 41–2).

[4] Howald and Meyer, no. 461 (= *CIL* iii, Supp. 6707), pre-Claudian, see note ad. loc.

of the direct route to the Rhine, and to prepare for the next stage of conquest, that of the Alps themselves. Helvetia was no longer a buffer territory, but an artery of empire. A Roman garrison was established at Zürich (Chapter 3. 3), with watch-towers ahead of it along the Walensee, to guard against Raetian raids; the date, as shown below, appears to be between 25 and 20 B.C., contemporary with the rise of Vidy as a trade and supply depot. It was occupied for a few years only, perhaps abandoned after the success of the 15 B.C. campaign. Basle, Vindonissa, and Oberwinterthur (below, Chapter 3. 1, 3. 2, 3. 4) received military garrisons soon afterwards, probably around 20, guarding the route across the northern edge of the Alps which was to be used by Tiberius in his advance against the Raeti and Vindelici in 15. Basle was probably given up in the latter years of the century, although reoccupied later. Vindonissa became a legionary base, perhaps after the Varian disaster. Oberwinterthur may well have been occupied throughout the Augustan period, although the evidence is not very clear.

The dating of the first occupation of these sites depends upon the evidence of the sigillata finds. Vidy has yielded quan-tities of sigillata, still largely unpublished, including some very early pieces which find their only parallels at Zürich, Neuss (Chapter 5. 4), on the Magdalensberg in Noricum, and in Italy itself.[1] The earliest pieces so far found at Basle, Augst, Nyon, and Geneva appear to be contemporary with one another, slightly later than the earliest from Vidy and Zürich.[2] But even at Basle, Augst, Nyon, and Geneva, sigillata has been found earlier than any from Oberaden (Chapter 6. 3), founded *c.* 11–10 B.C. We have then three rungs of a ladder: the earliest finds are those from Vidy, Zürich, Neuss, the Magdalensberg, and Italy; then come those from Basle, Augst, Geneva, and Nyon; and then those from Oberaden.

In the days before the bulk of the Vidy finds were known,

[1] For the excavations at Vidy, see above, p. 39; on the earliest sigillata, Ettlinger, *RCRFComm.* iii. 3/4 (1962), p. 3; cf. id. and Laufer, *JSGU* li (1964), p. 116. On Augst, below, p. 43, n. 5; a fragment of Campanian ware (*Ur-Schweiz* xxiii (1959), p. 11, pointed out by Dr. Ettlinger) is earlier than any of the sigillata. See further below, pp. 260–1. [ADD.]

[2] Cf. Ettlinger, *Limes-Studien*, p. 46; the Trier–Petrisberg sigillata commonly in-voked in this context should probably be explained differently, Loeschcke, *TZ* xiv (1939), pp. 93–112, discussed more fully below, Appendix I, p. 265, n. 1.

Vogt and Fellman set the foundation of Zürich and Basle around 15 B.C.[1] Kenner on the other hand has dated to around 30–20 B.C. sigillata from the Magdalensberg which is parallel to the early sigillata from Basle, while Goudineau has suggested that the earliest pieces from Zürich can have been made little, if any, later than 30.[2] In the light of our present knowledge it seems reasonable to suppose that Basle and the sites contemporary with it go back to around 20 B.C., with Zürich to be dated somewhat earlier. The presence of very early pieces here is particularly significant in view of the very small number of finds in all. A foundation-date of 25–20 for the Zürich fort and for the first influx of sigillata to Vidy would not only suit the sigillata evidence, but would also go well with the presumption that Vidy owed its rise to the opening up of the Great St. Bernard.

Further north still, on the right bank of the Rhine, another Augustan site is known, perhaps a legionary base, at Dangstetten (Chapter 3. 5), just opposite Zurzach, at the mouth of the Wutach valley. Zurzach (Tenedo) was already in pre-Roman times an important Rhine-crossing, and was later the site of at least two successive Roman bridges, so that an Augustan–Tiberian fort was long ago conjectured here, though with no conclusive evidence.[3] The subsequent discovery of the Dangstetten site however vindicates the claims made for the importance of this river-crossing. We know already that Tiberius in 15 fought a naval battle with the Vindelici on the Bodensee and pushed on to the sources of the Danube.[4] It is probably safe to assume that the Zurzach–Dangstetten crossing will have been one of those which his army used. How Dangstetten itself fits into Roman strategy, and subsequently into the pattern of Roman occupation and administration, it is not possible to say, until further excavation has revealed when the site was first occupied and for how long, whether as a marching-

[1] Vogt, *Der Lindenhof in Zürich*, p. 35; Fellmann, *Basel in römischer Zeit*, p. 89.

[2] Kenner, *Carinthia I* cliii (1963), pp. 49–52; Goudineau, *Bolsena* iv: *La Céramique arétine lisse*, p. 284.

[3] Stähelin, op. cit., pp. 168–70, 182–4; map in *Ur-Schweiz* xxv (1961), p. 41; cf. *JSGU* 1 (1963), pp. 89–91. Late Arretine sherds reported by Wiedemer, cf. Schönberger, op. cit., p. 188, no. 36. On the importance of the Wutach valley as a link with the Upper Danube, see Schönberger, ibid., p. 154.

[4] Strabo vii. 292.

camp or on a permanent basis, by how many men, and so on.

There is no clear evidence of any other Augustan sites along this stretch of the Rhine, despite claims that have been made. Augustan sigillata has been found on the island of Werd, near Stein-am-Rhein,[1] and an early fort and harbour conjectured at Konstanz, but more precise information and more investigation are clearly needed.[2] Eschenz (Tasgaetium), like Zurzach an important crossing-point later in the first century A.D., has yielded early finds, but a supposedly Augustan pottery oven cannot be so accurately dated and need not be so early.[3] Bregenz, at the east end of the Bodensee, is better considered in connection with the other sites in the Voralpenland (Chapter 4). Finally, though somewhat removed from the Rhine itself, there is a coin-hoard from Haggen near Bruggen, not far from St. Gallen, the latest coin in which is a *denarius* of 15 B.C.; attempts to link it with the events of that year are however misconceived; it may have been buried at any time thereafter.[4]

It may seem strange that Augst does not have sigillata even earlier than that from Vidy and Zürich, since, as we have seen, it was founded some twenty years earlier. The bulk of the early sigillata so far discovered here is in fact considerably later, contemporary with that from Haltern, and the majority of the stamps on Italian sigillata belong to the Ateius group.[5] The suggested explanation of the gap between the foundation of the colony and the first arrival of sigillata was that the sigillata entered the area with the Roman army, and that a fort was established at Augst, as at Basle, alongside the colony, in preparation for the campaign of 15 B.C. We may accept the

[1] Stähelin, op. cit., p. 125, n. 4; Wiedemer, *Germania* xli (1963), p. 272; cf. Strabo vii. 292.

[2] Beck, *Vorzeit am Bodensee* 1961/2, pp. 27–40.

[3] Urner-Astholz, *Thurgauische Beiträge zur vaterländ. Gesch.* lxxviii (1942), pp. 15–18 (the oven), cf. pp. 19–21 (South Gaulish sigillata, no Italian); cf. Stähelin, op. cit., pp. 184–6.

[4] Vogt, *Neue Zürcher Zeitung*, no. 819, 13 May 1936; Stähelin, op. cit., p. 107, n. 4; Wiedemer, loc. cit., pp. 279–80; id. in *Helvetia Antiqua*, p. 168.

[5] Ettlinger, *Die Keramik der Augster Thermen*, p. 6; the earliest pieces are probably pl. 1. nos. 2, 14, 16; also early radial stamps of A. TITI FIGULI, PHILOG. A. SESTI, L. TETTI CRITO; slightly later, MENOPH./L. TETTI, A. TITI, M. TITI, L. SEMPR./ L. GELLI, RUFIO/UMRIC., CERDO/C. ANNI, SENTI: all mostly found in fill of the Flavian period.

first part of the explanation without also postulating the
fort. Once sigillata was available, the civilians at Augst, as at
the sites in Central Helvetia, could obtain it, but it became
available only when the opening of the Great St. Bernard and
the guaranteed market provided by the military occupation of
sites in Northern Helvetia made the export of Arretine to this
area economically possible.

Ettlinger has demonstrated how the distribution pattern of
early sigillata stamps in Helvetia shows the importance of Vidy
as an entrepôt in this trade.[1] Of twenty-five different early
Arretine potters' stamps from Swiss sites, only eight do not
occur at Vidy, and seven of these are found exclusively at one
or other of the sites, Basle, Augst, and Zürich (the eighth is
known at three sites, Augst, Vindonissa, and Geneva). No
other site contains so great a number of the known stamps as
Vidy (though we should not forget how numerous are the finds
from Vidy), and Ettlinger is right to associate this with Vidy's
position on the regular trade-route. Perhaps, as she suggests,
the seven stamps found only in Northern Helvetia got there,
not via Vidy, but direct from Gaul, whether in the baggage of
the soldiers themselves or by some other means. In support of this
theory, two of the seven stamps, although very rare, are also
found in the interior of Gaul.[2] The permanent importance of
Vidy in the distribution of sigillata is however indisputable,
and supports our previous conclusion that the beginning of
sigillata imports into Helvetia and the foundation of Vidy and
Zürich date from immediately after the opening-up of the
Great St. Bernard in 25 B.C., although at Vidy of course there
may already have been a settlement of sorts before the new
possibilities for trade brought it expansion and prosperity.

At the same time as Roman garrisons were being established
in Helvetia, Roman control was being extended over the
Alpine valleys leading out of Cisalpine Gaul. We shall discuss
the operations by which this was achieved in Chapter 4. The
ground was already being prepared for the campaign of 15 B.C.,
when Roman armies from Helvetia under the command of
Tiberius and from Cisalpina under the command of Drusus

---

[1] Ettlinger in *Limes-Studien*, pp. 45–8.
[2] Those of C. Sertorius and LTC, both from Basle, also at Paris and Saintes and
at Bibracte respectively (Fellmann, op. cit., pp. 122, 93).

were to complete the conquest of the Alps. But the conquest of the Alps was itself preparatory to still wider conquests. Although certain scholars have tried to interpret it as nothing more than a defensive measure to protect Italy,[1] it in fact makes sense, as Kraft has pointed out, only if deliberately intended to lead on to the conquest of Germany. For had such a step been necessary to ensure the safety of Italy, it would surely have been attempted before; nor does the extension of the zone of occupation beyond the Alps northwards towards the Danube have any point if defence were the only aim; and moreover the building of roads through the Alps actually increased the possibility of a successful invasion of Italy from the north.[2]

The initial conquest of the Salassi, the Romanization of Helvetia, the establishment of the fort at Zürich, and the linked system of watch-towers, all of these can be explained as designed only to safeguard Roman communications with the Rhine. Even if no forward movement had been planned, and the Rhine had been destined to remain the frontier, as Caesar left it, it would still have made sense to open up the Great St. Bernard and the road through Helvetia. But the subsequent concentration of troops in Northern Helvetia is more naturally to be interpreted as being in preparation for the campaign of 15 B.C. The indications we have that Roman garrisons were occupying such strategic points as Basle, Oberwinterthur, and probably Vindonissa in or soon after 20 B.C. are the more significant when we consider that neither Basle nor Oberwinterthur has been thoroughly excavated, and that at Vindonissa, which has, subsequent occupation has largely destroyed the evidence for the earliest period of occupation. Dangstetten offers possibilities for the extensive excavation of an unspoiled site. This is one reason why we may hope much from it.

Our investigation of Helvetia does not enable us to state categorically that in such or such a year the Romans took a definite decision or began definite preparations to proceed to the conquest of the whole Alpine area. Such a decision would, as we have argued earlier, imply a prior or simultaneous

[1] So, e.g., Stähelin, op. cit., pp. 104-5, starting from the premiss that 'auch neuen Eroberungen war Augustus grundsätzlich abgeneigt'.

[2] Kraft, *JRGZ* iv (1957), pp. 90-1.

decision to proceed thereafter to the conquest of Germany also. But it seems likely that such preparations were afoot by 20 B.C. or soon after; and the ultimate aim of advancing beyond the Rhine and the Alps to conquest and glory in Germany may already have been in Augustus' mind even before the conquest of the Salassi in 25.

3. I. BASLE

The cathedral hill, the Münsterhügel, at Basle (Basilia), on the left bank of the Rhine, dominates the great bend of the river. It is very steep on the landward side, with a huff-puff climb up zig-zag cobbled alleys, and on the other side it now falls sheer to the river, a retaining wall having been built in the sixteenth century. Excavations at various times in the open Münsterplatz in front of the cathedral and in the gardens and cellars of the buildings round about have revealed three or four periods of Roman occupation of the site under Augustus and during the first century A.D., as well as later Roman occupation.[1] The quantity of military finds from the site leaves no doubt that it was a military site, and traces of buildings have been found going back to the earliest period of Roman occupation.[2] There was no previous native occupation of the site,[3] such as has been observed nearby in the Birsig valley[4] and on the important Gasfabrik site beside the Rhine below the Münsterhügel, where stood a Raurican settlement and harbour, which were violently destroyed, probably in a Raetian raid, perhaps even, as has been conjectured, in the very year in which Munatius Plancus earned his triumph *ex Raetis*.[5]

[1] The evidence is collected by Fellmann, *Basel in römischer Zeit*, supplemented by account of more recent excavations in *Basler Ztschr. für Geschichte und Altertumskunde* lx (1960), pp. 7–46 (hereinafter cited as Fellmann I and Fellmann II respectively); also *JSGU* xlix (1962), pp. 69–70, 74–5; xl (1963), p. 80.

[2] Fellmann I, pp. 118, 121–2 (sigillata); I, p. 124, II, pp. 21, 41 (military finds); II, p. 17 (building foundations of earliest period).

[3] Laur-Belart, *JSGU* xxxv (1944), p. 74, cf. Fellmann I, p. 27. [ADD.]

[4] Berger, *Die Ausgrabungen am Petersberg in Basel*.

[5] Laur-Belart, *Über die Colonia Raurica und den Ursprung von Basel*, pp. 16–24; full reports by Major, *Gallische Ansiedlung mit Gräberfeld bei Basel*; further Laur-Belart, *Ur-Schweiz* iv (1940), pp. 34–42; vi (1942), p. 51; Schwarz, *JSGU* xxxi (1939), pp. 145–6; Laur-Belart, *JSGU* xxxii (1940/1), pp. 96–8; xxxiii (1942), pp. 62–3. On Plancus, see above, p. 36.

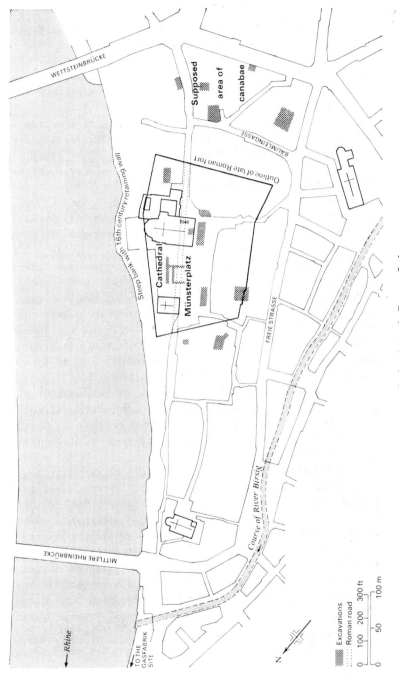

Fig. 2. Basle: the early Roman finds

The Münsterhügel finds come from two distinct areas, one centred round the Münsterplatz itself, the other further south on or near the Bäumleingasse (fig. 2). About half-way between the two areas runs the south wall of the Late Roman fort, whose foundations stand on mixed rubble, perhaps the debris of the earlier defences, no trace of which has otherwise been found. It seems probable that the Bäumleingasse area is that of the *canabae*. It has produced no specifically military finds, whereas it has yielded far more finds of the late first century A.D. and of the second and third centuries than the Münsterplatz area, which appears to have been very scantily occupied at this period, perhaps because the troops had been withdrawn to man the *limes*.[1] Laur-Belart suggests, perhaps rightly, that the old *canabae* continued to be inhabited even after the fort itself was given up.

The pottery finds from both areas are otherwise homogeneous. Fellmann described the earliest finds as being contemporary with the earliest from Zürich,[2] but this judgement can no longer be substantiated, since no piece from Basle is as primitive in form as the earliest from Zürich,[3] although otherwise the early sigillata from the two sites is very similar. But the presence of the *very* early sigillata at Zürich suggests that it was founded slightly before Basle, a conclusion acceptable on general historical grounds. If Zürich is to be dated to the period 25–20 B.C., as argued above, the foundation of Basle should be dated soon after. But whereas the fort at Zürich was soon given up, at Basle the pottery goes on throughout the first century A.D.

Laur-Belart from his excavations in the Münsterplatz area distinguished four separate occupation layers within this period, which Fellmann, drawing on the unpublished daybooks of the excavations, as well as on the published account, accepted: two early Augustan, a third from about the end of Augustus' reign to the middle of the first century, and a fourth from about 50–100.[4] Vogt however in his earlier excavations in the Bäumleingasse area observed only three periods, not dividing the early Augustan occupation into two.[5] Subsequent

[1] Laur-Belart, op. cit., p. 78.   [2] Fellmann I, pp. 30, 118, 123.
[3] i.e. Vogt, *Der Lindenhof in Zürich*, fig. 30, nos. 14, 15.
[4] Fellmann I, pp. 21–31.   [5] Ibid.

excavations in the Münsterplatz area again revealed only three
main periods, of the second decade B.C., the second decade
A.D. onwards, and the Flavian period; and from the earliest
period two separate subsidiary periods of building could be
distinguished.[1]

It would seem then that instead of trying to distinguish two
separate periods of occupation B.C., we ought perhaps rather
to talk of one period of occupation, which lasted long enough
for repairs or rebuilding to take place. On Laur-Belart's
original hypothesis of two distinct periods he and Fellmann
associated the first with the Alpine campaign of Tiberius and
Drusus in 15 B.C. and the second with Drusus' supposed
establishment of 'quinquaginta amplius castella' all along the
Rhine in 12–9 B.C., *castella* which, as we shall show in Chapter
5, modern scholarship is reluctant to accept.[2] It is in any case
difficult to accept so nice a distinction without overwhelming
evidence, and Fellmann's latest finds certainly cast doubt on
its validity. We could not hope to identify a break of only
three years in the sigillata, which in fact begins with pieces
earlier than any from Oberaden but includes others identical
with the Oberaden and Haltern finds.[3] It seems probable that
the earliest occupation of the Münsterhügel, beginning around
20 B.C. or soon after, lasted until the latter years of the century,
and that the site was reoccupied about the time when the
legionary base at Vindonissa was established.

3. 2. VINDONISSA (WINDISCH)

The legionary base at Vindonissa, most commonly supposed
by modern scholars to have been established in A.D. 17,[4]
lies in the angle formed by the Rivers Reuss and Aare, where
the village of Windisch now stands, above the town of Brugg.
The modern road from Basle to Zürich and Winterthur

---

[1] Fellmann II, pp. 22–3, cf. p. 17.
[2] See below, p. 97 n. 1.   [3] Fellmann I, p. 123.
[4] On dating, with refs. to history of discussion up to and including 1958, see
Ettlinger, *RE* ixA, cols. 83–7; also Wiedemer, *JSGU* liii (1966/7), pp. 63–70; the
date of Vindonissa is taken as a fixed point on which to hang the chronology of
Roman sites on the Rhine and Upper Danube, e.g. Kraft, *BJ* clv/clvi (1955/6),
pp. 95–111, esp. p. 105; Kellner in Krämer, *Cambodunumforschungen 1953* i, pp. 54–
9; Ulbert, *Die römischen Donaukastellen Aislingen und Burghöfe*, pp. 30–1.

actually goes across the site. Vindonissa commanded the only crossing of the lower Aare, a natural nodal point of communications, whence a legion might march out east or west, to cover the Great St. Bernard or the Upper Rhine passes to Italy, to drive out the invader or repress the rebel in Helvetia or the Voralpenland.[1] Directly in front of Vindonissa, however, lie only the sparsely populated and inhospitable hills of the Black Forest. It is not a base for offensive operations across the Rhine, nor for an attack on Bohemia. It has a basically defensive position, in which respect it resembles Strasbourg (Chapter 5. 9), where the legionary base also appears to be an early Tiberian foundation.[2]

The date A.D. 17 for the establishment of a legionary base at Vindonissa is generally accepted on three grounds: first because Vindonissa is supposed to have replaced Augsburg–Oberhausen (Chapter 4. 7) as a legionary headquarters, so that the date of the abandonment of Oberhausen is thought to be a *terminus post quem* for the foundation of Vindonissa; secondly on general historical grounds, that a permanent legionary base on so defensive a site is unthinkable before the Varian Disaster in 9 and most natural after Germanicus' recall; and thirdly on the evidence of the pottery. The first argument is worthless, since not only is there no reason to suppose that there ever was a legion at Oberhausen,[3] but even if there had been the site might still have been occupied by a smaller force after the legion was withdrawn. The second argument is strong, though the first half is stronger than the second, and it cannot be pressed to support 17 rather than 10. The precise dating therefore depends upon the pottery supported by the coin evidence. The pottery, unfortunately, has never been studied as a whole, and the sheer quantity of the finds would

---

[1] Laur-Belart, *Vindonissa* (1935), p. 1, describing it as 'eine von Natur geschaffene Festung gegen das in unbekannter Ferne sich verlierende Germanien in Norden', with its garrison resembling 'ein sprungbereites Raubtier in seiner Höhle'.

[2] Kraft, *JNG* ii (1950/1), p. 34, refers to its 'ausgesprochenen defensive Position'; cf. Laur-Belart, op. cit., p. 2, pointing out how sparsely populated the Black Forest area was, requiring no special attention as long as the Romans hoped to conquer the rest of Germany, and destined to fall as 'selbstverständliche Beute' once the rest of Germany was conquered. Cf. further Syme, *JRS* xxiii (1933), p. 96, cogently pointing out that until the Varian Disaster the legions were stationed offensively not defensively.

[3] Wells, *SJ* xxviii (1970), pp. 63–72.

now make such a study as arduous as it would be enlightening. It does however appear that the pottery found in the lowest level of occupation at Vindonissa, taken as a whole, is later than the mass of pottery from Haltern, and in particular it is significant that South Gaulish ware, in the true Gaulish fabric which is not found at Haltern, is found at Vindonissa mixed with Italian even in the very lowest levels.[1] Perhaps if we simply said that the base was established at the beginning of or during the second decade A.D., this is as close as we can get at the moment.

It has long been conjectured that a smaller fort may have stood on the site before the legionary base was built.[2] The chief objection to this view is that despite extensive excavation no trace of the defences of such a fort has ever been found. The earliest traces of occupation yet found are those of a tented camp, extending for at least 300 m. in one direction, whose date is uncertain.[3] Wiedemer wished to link it with certain pits whose contents establish them as early Tiberian, which would thus date the tented camp to this period also. This cannot be proved. The earliest buildings were of wood and three periods of wooden buildings are known, before stone came in under Claudius. The earlier wooden buildings were on a different orientation from the later ones, but we have no evidence to enable us to fix an absolute date for any of the three wooden periods. These levels as a whole however have yielded pottery typical of the period A.D. 10–40, between Haltern and Hofheim.[4] Whether the tented camp also fits into this period, or earlier, is not known. That there was some occupation before Tiberian times is suggested most strongly by the presence of a number of very early pieces of sigillata, comparable with those from the indisputably Augustan sites in Switzerland. Ettlinger's table of early sigillata stamps from

[1] Ettlinger, *JGPV* 1963, p. 48; Wiedemer, loc. cit.; the whole central area of the site has now been completely excavated, id., *RE* ixA, col. 86.

[2] Laur-Belart, op. cit., pp. 2–4; id., *JSGU* xxxvi (1945), pp. 65–9; Fellmann, *JGPV* 1953/4, p. 38; *JGPV* 1954/5, p. 37.

[3] Wiedemer, *JGPV* 1962, p. 19.

[4] Ettlinger, *JGPV* 1960/1, pp. 20–8; id., ibid. 1962, p. 48; Wiedemer, *JGPV* 1962, p. 24; cf. pp. 20–6 and *JGPV* 1963, pp. 16–18, on the two different orientations of the so-called 'schräge' and 'gerade' wooden buildings. Excavation continues to cast light on this question, see now Lüdin, *JGPV* 1966, pp. 24–31; *JGPV* 1967, pp. 31–4.

Swiss sites, other than stamps of the Ateius-group, specifically includes eight from Vindonissa, which however she suggests may be explained either as late products of the potters in question or as 'survivals', earlier pieces which were still in use and which were brought to Vindonissa in Tiberian times.[1] She specifically disclaims, however, Oxé's opinion that all stamps found at Vindonissa are *ipso facto* shown to be Tiberian.

One might however think that there were too many pieces of too early a date for all of them to be explained as 'survivals'. A complete re-examination of the sigillata to determine just how many pieces there are of this sort and where they were found might provide further information. Coin evidence unfortunately does not help. Augustan and early Tiberian issues preponderate and among these the later issues of each series outnumber the earlier (i.e. Lugdunum II exceeds Lugdunum I, and *tresviri* IV exceeds I–II).[2] This however is not surprising, since the fortress continued to be occupied throughout the first century, and it tells us nothing about the foundation date.

If then on the one hand there was no occupation of the site before the legionary base was established there, the early sigillata strengthens the case for dating the establishment of this base to 10 rather than 17; on the other hand, an earlier fort could have existed and its defences escaped notice, just as the evidence for the existence of tents escaped notice until very recently. A fort at Vindonissa dating from the years just before 15 B.C., contemporary with those at Basle and Oberwinterthur, which would explain the early sigillata perfectly, is also extremely likely on general historical grounds. The road linking Basle and Augst to Zürich and Oberwinterthur must have crossed the Aare by Vindonissa, as it still does, and a fort in the vicinity to guard the crossing is most probable. It need not have been on the site of the later base; but that is an excellent site, and we have to account for the early sigillata. On these grounds it seems probable that there was a fort at Vindonissa contemporary with those at Basle and Oberwinter-

---

[1] Ettlinger in *Limes-Studien*, p. 46; of earlier discussions, cf. still Oxé, *Germania* xi (1927), pp. 127–32; Simonett, *JGPV* 1945/6, pp. 5–25; Fellmann, *JGPV* 1953/4, pp. 34–8. [Add.]

[2] Kraay, *Die Münzfunde von Vindonissa*, tables, pp. 25, 30.

thur, dating from about 20 B.C., probably on the plateau between the Reuss and the Aare where the base later stood.[1]

3. 3. ZÜRICH AND THE WALENSEE

The Lindenhof at Zürich (Turicum), on which excavation has revealed the remains of an Augustan fort, is in the very heart of the modern city, its summit now forming a flat gravelled area planted with trees and surrounded by a low wall. The tall city buildings which hem it in make it difficult to realize how completely the Lindenhof, before the city grew up, used to dominate what is now the site of the city and particularly the exit from Lake Zürich along the River Limmat. Not nearly so high as the hills which shut in the lake and the river on either side, the Lindenhof nevertheless completely commands the valley in which it stands, together with the natural lines of communication up and down that valley.[2]

The definitive work on the Lindenhof site is by Vogt, based on excavations in 1937–8.[3] The first occupation was undoubtedly military and the garrison was composed of or at least included cavalry.[4] This occupation was also relatively short. The buildings associated with it showed no signs of repair or rebuilding,[5] and the pottery on which the dating hangs, there being no coin evidence,[6] is very homogeneous. Vogt discusses it at some length and establishes that it includes sigillata earlier than any from Haltern or Oberaden, and earlier than was at that time known from any other site in Switzerland, whereas later Augustan sigillata is totally lacking.[7] This early sigillata is paralleled by subsequent finds from Vidy, though in very small quantities, a fact which makes the two very early pieces

---

[1] Cf. Laur-Belart in *Carnuntina*, p. 91, on possibility of 'ein kleineres Kastell als Strassen- und Brückensicherung'; more fully, Wiedemer, *JSGU* liii (1966/7), pp. 67–70.

[2] This relationship can clearly be seen from two relief models built by J. U. Bachofen (1598–1670) now in the Schweizerisches Landesmuseum, Zürich, one showing the city as it was in his day, the other a plan for the fortification of the city, dated 1638.

[3] Vogt, *Der Lindenhof in Zürich*, esp. pp. 28–35, 'Die frührömische Anlage', superseding Stähelin, *Die Schweiz in römischer Zeit*, p. 187.

[4] Ibid., p. 34.   [5] Ibid., pp. 32, 147.

[6] Ibid., p. 34, on the absence of coin finds.

[7] Ibid., pp. 146–70, esp. pp. 147–53.

among the small number of sherds found at Zürich especially significant.

Apart from this very early sigillata, the so-called Service I is not only comparatively well represented, but represented by early forms, which Vogt labels Service I*a*, not found at Haltern and very rare at Oberaden; the later forms of Service I, which Vogt calls I*b* and I*c*, are found at both Haltern and Oberaden, but I*b* is extremely rare at Haltern, a fact which reflects the difference between the dates of foundation of Haltern and Oberaden. Service I*a*, which in Vogt's day was unknown at Basle, has since been found there,[1] though not in as primitive a form as at Zürich.[2] The later Service II is rare here at Zürich.

Vogt thought, largely on general historical grounds, that Zürich was probably founded in 15 B.C. in connection with Tiberius' campaign of that year, or else perhaps rather earlier as a frontier post against the Raetians.[3] The evidence of the sigillata supports the latter alternative, as far as the date is concerned, while the hypothesis that the Zürich fort was designed primarily to block Raetian raids down the Limmat appears to find confirmation not only in its location, but also in the subsequent discovery of remains of watch-towers along the Walensee, above Lake Zürich, which will have given the garrison of the fort advance warning of such raids.

Three such towers are known, strongly built in stone, one at Voremwald, near Filzbach on the south side of the Walensee and 300 m. above it, one at Strahlegg on a low promontory on the north side with a commanding view along the whole length of the lake, and one at Biberlikopf, high above the lake at its western end.[4] Voremwald and Biberlikopf have yielded finds of weapons and of datable pottery. From Voremwald

---

[1] Fellmann, *Basel in römischer Zeit*, p. 89.

[2] Cf. esp. the sherds illustrated by Vogt, op. cit. fig. 30, nos. 14, 15. [These two pieces are now dated by Goudineau, *Bolsena* iv: *La Céramique arétine lisse*, p. 284 (cf. below, Appendix I, p. 253, n. 2) to perhaps slightly after 30 B.C., although certainly not long after.]

[3] Vogt, op. cit., pp. 34–5; on danger of Raetian raids, Strabo iv. 206.

[4] Laur-Belart, *Ur-Schweiz* xxiv (1960), pp. 7–18 (Voremwald), pp. 51–69 (Strahlegg and Biberlikopf); id., *JSGU* xlviii (1960/1), pp. 151–60; id., *JSGU* xlix (1962), p. 83; further reporting on systematic excavations at Biberlikopf, id., *Ur-Schweiz* xxvi (1962), pp. 35–51. Cf. Hübener, *Militärgeschichtliche Mitt.* ii (1968), p. 20.

come two *pilum* heads with barbed tips, of a type found at Numantia, but already obsolescent in Augustan times and unparalleled elsewhere in Switzerland.[1] The pottery includes sherds of Aco-ware resembling sherds from Oberaden and early sigillata sherds (Services I*b* and I*c*) paralleled at Basle and Haltern. Biberlikopf yielded a *pilum* of similar pattern, six arrow-heads, and other small finds, including sherds of Aco-ware and Arretine, one of Service I*c* resembling, though not identical with, Arretine from Zürich.[2] A *denarius* of Antony's *legio VI* was also found here in 1914.

The datable finds, though not numerous, are sufficient to date the towers to the reign of Augustus, and probably, to judge from the old-fashioned *pila* and the absence of Service II sigillata, comparatively early in the reign.[3] Although none of the pottery is as old as the earliest of the Zürich pieces, that need not be significant when the total amount of pottery found here was so small. Watch-towers like this make sense only if linked to a fort from which they can summon help, and the finds in general would be consistent with the hypothesis that these towers are contemporary with the Zürich fort.

When the Voremwald tower was first discovered, Laur-Belart suggested that it was meant to guard the route along the south side of the lake over the Kerenzerberg, linking Augst and Zürich with North Italy via the Upper Rhine and the Septimer Pass. Because the mountains on both sides of the lake fall sheer into its waters, there is no possible way in antiquity or indeed at the present day along the edge of the lake itself (the modern road still climbs the Kerenzerberg). The tower at Strahlegg therefore, on the lake shore below the Kerenzerberg, can only have watched boat traffic on the lake. Voremwald and Strahlegg alike are so placed as to be able to signal to Biberlikopf, which could relay the signal to the west. Other towers may have existed as well, still undiscovered.

Meyer, however, accepting Laur-Belart's view that the towers were meant to watch the Kerenzerberg and the lake, argued rightly that their task was rather to prevent Raetian

[1] Grüninger, *Ur-Schweiz* xxiv (1960), pp. 18–24.
[2] Ibid., pp. 69–72; further, Laur-Belart, *Ur-Schweiz* xxvi (1962), pp. 44–8.
[3] Strahlegg is not dated by finds, but so closely resembles the other forts in construction that we can scarcely doubt that it was built at the same time.

raids from the Upper Rhine and the heart of the Alps down the Walensee and Lake Zürich into North Switzerland.[1] The Zürich fort, as pointed out above, so controls the Limmat valley leading out of Lake Zürich, and that valley alone, that it is perfectly placed to block such raids, especially if supported by advanced look-outs. On the other hand it does not naturally link up with Oberwinterthur and the road going east into the Voralpenland.

The hypothesis that towers and fort go together explains perfectly the function of both; and explains why the fort, and presumably therefore the towers, were soon abandoned. They were founded, as we have seen above, between 25 and 20 B.C., while the absence of later sigillata and the scarcity even of Service II suggest that they were abandoned perhaps before the end of the first century B.C., once the campaign of 15 B.C. and the consolidation of Roman occupation had removed the threat of Raetian raids which the fort and towers were meant to counter.

3. 4. OBERWINTERTHUR

The presence of an Augustan fort lying beneath the Late Roman fort at Oberwinterthur (Vitudurum) has long been conjectured, largely on the strength of early Arretine pottery, among which the commonest stamps are those of Ateius, a fact which might suggest that the site was occupied during roughly the same period as Haltern.[2] The site in question lies on top of a small but steep and prominent hill, where the village church now stands; it is an ideal defensive position.[3] Among the finds from this area are four Arretine sherds with potters' stamps of early Augustan date, namely one of L. TITI THYRSUS, one of LSG (Lucius Saufeius Gausa), and two of L. TETTI SAMIA,

---

[1] Meyer, *MH* xix (1962), p. 147; this is not to deny that the Chur–Walensee–Zürich route was used by the Romans from the early days of the occupation, as were the Vindonissa–Oberwinterthur–Konstanz and Chur–Bregenz routes, see Wiedemer in *Helvetia Antiqua*, pp. 167–72.

[2] Stähelin, *Die Schweiz in römischer Zeit*, p. 186, n. 2, with bibliography; see esp. Bouffard, *Neujahrsblatt der Stadtbibliothek Winterthur* cclxxvi (1943), pp. 5–33.

[3] Wiedemer, *Ur-Schweiz* xxiii (1959), p. 49; cf. also the comprehensive study of the Oberwinterthur site by Wiedemer, *Ur- und Frühgeschichte der Winterthurer Gegend*. I am grateful to Dr. Wiedemer for corresponding with me on the relative dating of the Winterthur and Zürich finds.

one of the latter being radially stamped.[1] The presence of four such early pieces among the comparatively limited quantity of sigillata from the site is particularly noteworthy, and probably on such a site and in the context of the evidence from the other sites mentioned in the preceding chapters betokens the presence of a Roman garrison, even though no buildings or defences are known which can be attributed to this early period.

No piece of pottery from Oberwinterthur is so obviously early as the earliest from Zürich. The four pieces mentioned above are rather to be classed with the earliest pieces from Basle and Vindonissa. General considerations of probability, such as are discussed above, favour the date which the pottery evidence suggests, making the foundation of Oberwinterthur contemporary with that of Basle and shortly after that of Zürich, probably around 20 B.C., as part of the preparations for the campaign of 15.

3. 5. DANGESTTETEN

Dangstetten lies on the north bank of the Rhine, facing the important Rhine-crossing at Zurzach, and commanding the mouth of the Wutach valley, an important line of communication between the Rhine at this point and the Upper Danube.[2]

At Dangstetten in 1967 there came to light the remains of an Augustan legionary base, either for one or for two legions, which is being excavated under the direction of Dr. G. Fingerlin (Freiburg i. Br.). Preliminary reports suggest that it was given up, like Oberaden (Chapter 6. 3) and Rödgen (Chapter 6. 8), soon after 10 B.C., since coin-finds to date are preponderantly of the Nemausus issues; the Lugdunum altar-series is totally absent.[3] The evidence of the pottery finds is consistent with this dating. Other finds include a small bronze plate marked with the name of *legio XIX*. More excavation is however needed

---

[1] Preliminary report on 1949–51 excavations by Bloesch and Isler, *Neujahrsbl. der Hülfsgesellschaft Winterthur* lxxxiii (1952), with note on these four sherds by Ettlinger, pp. 31–2.

[2] Cf. Schönberger, *JRS* lix (1969), p. 154.

[3] Brief references by Hübener, *Militärgeschichtliche Mitt.* ii (1968), p. 16; Schönberger, loc. cit., pp. 145, 149. [ADD.]

before we can determine the exact size of the base and when it was established.

This site may prove to be one of the most significant discoveries of recent years for our understanding of Augustus' campaigns and strategy, and the results of further excavation will be eagerly awaited.

4

THE OCCUPATION OF THE ALPS
AND VORALPENLAND

SOUTH of the Alps, in the valleys which lead up from the Cisalpine plain to the passes of the Central Alps, we can discern,
albeit dimly, the same sort of military preparations going on
as were afoot in Helvetia in the years before 15 B.C. Archaeological evidence is virtually non-existent; we must therefore
do what we can with the literary and epigraphic evidence at
our disposal. Once we cross the Alps with Drusus' army in 15,
archaeological evidence from the Voralpenland becomes more
abundant. We shall consider it in due course.

Any investigation of the actual conquest of the Alpine
regions should begin with Augustus' own monument to his
success, the Tropaeum Alpium at La Turbie in the Alpes-
Maritimes.[1] The list of the 'gentes Alpinae devictae' comprises
the names of forty-five tribes. The names of those who submitted without a struggle are naturally excluded. There is a
persistent view, backed by the immense authority of Mommsen,
that the order of the tribes on the monument is that in which
they were conquered, from which it would follow that the
groups and sequences of names as they appear should reveal
the routes taken by the various Roman forces which conquered
them, whence much fruitless speculation and misplaced
ingenuity.[2] Such an arrangement in order of conquest is

---

[1] Pliny, *NH* iii. 136; *CIL* v. 7817; the monument has now been restored, Formigé, *Le Trophée des Alpes*, with the most accurate text of the inscription; Formigé's
photograph of the restoration is not good, but there is an excellent one in Howald
and Meyer, *Die römische Schweiz*, plate 1.

[2] Cf. Howald and Meyer, p. 357: 'Plinius' Liste . . . zählt die Völker in der
Reihenfolge ihrer Unterwerfung unter Rom auf, wodurch natürlich auch eine
geographische Folge entsteht, die aber nicht in erster Linie beabsichtigt ist.
Andererseits ergibt die Reihenfolge der Liste den Verlauf der betreffenden Feldzüge.' Also Meyer, *MH* xix (1962), pp. 146–7, with bibliography.

however, as one of the scholars who nevertheless believes in it points out, unparalleled.[1] The theory was moreover demolished long ago by Oberziner in a single paragraph, and should be forgotten. The arrangement is geographical, and against the 'order of conquest' theory Oberziner needs to invoke one argument only, namely the position in the list of the Salassi: πόλλ' οἶδ' ἀλώπηξ, ἀλλ' ἐχῖνος ἓν μέγα. They come in twenty-third place, after all the tribes of the Central Alps, the Upper Rhine, and Vindelicia, which is, as Oberziner says, 'absolutely contrary to the order of conquest according to the ancient writers'.[2] We might put it still more strongly: the final conquest of the Salassi in 25 B.C. is, as we saw in Chapter 3, one of the few events in the conquest of the Alps about which our information is relatively full and precise, and a theory which requires us to ignore this evidence, or to postulate an unheard-of Salassian revolt in 15–14 B.C., is perverse indeed.[3]

The order of the names would appear in fact to be basically geographical. Tribes conquered successively are indeed often named successively; the succession is in each case the result of the same geographical contiguity. Naturally there are also oddities and irregularities in the geographical order; untidy agglomerations of tribes dwelling in a tangle of mountain valleys cannot be listed and numbered with the same precision as squares on a snakes-and-ladders board. It would be an odd coincidence if out of half a dozen lists, supposedly in geographical order, of the present-day Swiss cantons or, for that matter, of the London postal districts, any two lists were identical.[4] How this geographical order is arrived at, we shall see below. But almost at the start of the list we are faced with a tribe whose location is uncertain, and whose relationship to other tribes of similar name in other sources has been a matter of dispute. Since the elucidation of these problems may give us the key to Roman strategy on this side of the Alps, let us begin here. Where did the Vennonetes live, who appear in third place on this list, after the Trumpilini of Val Trompia and the Camunni of Val Camonica, and immediately before

---

[1] Christ, *Historia* vi (1957), pp. 418–19.
[2] Oberziner, *Le guerre di Augusto contro i popoli alpini*, p. 11; forcibly restated by Heuberger, *RE* ixA, col. 7.
[3] So postulated by Formigé, op. cit., p. 59.
[4] *Experto crede*: I have tried it with students, not explaining the purpose.

the Venostes of Val Venosta, the upper valley of the Adige, on the Italian side of the Reschenscheideck Pass?[1]

The form 'Vennonetes' does not reappear in other writers, but a number of similar tribal names do: Vennonenses, Vennones or Vennontes, Vennii—how many tribes are we dealing with? Are these all different forms of the same name? There is considerable variation in the ways in which Greek and Latin writers spell the barbarous and unfamiliar tribal names they have to deal with, and in the Alpine regions, with their multiplicity of racial stocks, the problems must have been complicated by local dialects. English writers have faced the same problem in Arabia and on the North-West Frontier.[2] There can be no doubt that the Vennonenses and the Vennonones or Vennontes at least are identical. The former appear in Pliny, only two sentences before his citation of the Tropaeum inscription: 'Raetorum Vennonenses Sarunetesque ortus Rheni amnis accolunt.'[3] The Sarunetes mentioned here are identical with the Suanetes, who appear in fifteenth place on the Tropaeum along with the Rugusci, Calucones, and Brixentes (fourteenth, sixteenth, and seventeenth respectively), and all four of these reappear in Ptolemy, along with the Vennones or Vennontes. The latter appear in a similar Upper Rhine context in Strabo, although there regarded as Vindelici instead of Raeti and linked with the Brigantii, the Tropaeum's Brixentes, to whom belonged Bregenz (Brigantium, see Chapter 4. 2).[4] A second passage where Strabo mentions this tribe will be considered later.

The Vennonenses then, alias Vennones or Vennontes, lived somewhere on the Upper Rhine. Many scholars have assumed that the Tropaeum's Vennonetes are the same people, and the names are close enough to make it plausible.[5] But before we accept this identification, we must first ask whether there is any evidence for a tribe of this or similar name elsewhere in

---

[1] Pliny gives the order 'Venostes, Vennonetes', but the existing fragments of the inscription itself show that the actual order was the reverse, Formigé, op. cit., p. 58.

[2] Cf. Lawrence's comments in *Seven Pillars of Wisdom*, pp. 24–6; similarly, compare Caroe's spelling of names in *The Pathans* with the less scientific and more heavily Anglicized versions used by Kipling and earlier writers.

[3] Pliny, *NH* iii. 135.

[4] Ptol., *Geog.* ii. 12. 2; Strabo iv. 206.

[5] Cf. Heuberger, *Rätien im Altertum und Frühmittelalter*, pp. 58–9, 226–8; also Stähelin, *Die Schweiz in römischer Zeit*, p. 635.

the Alps, and particularly to the south of the main chain. Two passages in the ancient writers must be considered, the first in Strabo, mentioned in the last sentence of the previous paragraph.[1] He is describing the various Alpine tribes: after listing those of the Western and Pennine Alps, and mentioning the sources of the Rhône and the Rhine, he comes to the tribes, 'above' (ὑπέρ) Como. On the one side (τῇ μέν), where the land slopes towards the east, live the Raeti and Vennones, on the other (τῇ δέ) the Lepontii, Tridentini, Stoni, and several smaller tribes. What picture does Strabo have in his mind? I have seen no satisfactory explanation of this passage. Meyer, who at least recognizes that it presents a problem, explains that the Raeti and Vennones lived to the east of Como, the Lepontii to the west, while the Tridentini and Stoni are 'lose angehängt' east of the Raeti and Vennones.[2] Why then the contrast, τῇ μέν and τῇ δέ? Strabo at least claims to arrange his material logically,[3] and his knowledge of this material, as far as the Alps are concerned, has impressed at least one modern authority.[4]

The only geographical unity which the second group of tribes possesses, Lepontii, Tridentini, and Stoni, is in fact that they all lie south of the main chain of the Alps. If Strabo sees the Raeti and Vennones as being 'on the other side' to these three tribes, it is not on the other side of Como, but of the Alps. And this is also what he is trying to indicate when he says that their land 'slopes towards the east'. He pictures the Alps as running in a semicircle, with the St. Bernard at the top of the curve.[5] Above Como he therefore pictures the main chain as already running southwards, rather than eastwards, as in fact it does, and so for him the further slope of the mountains faces east. This passage too then corroborates the others previously cited and discussed: the Vennones are a tribe north of the main chain, and neither this nor any other passage serves as evidence that there were Vennones south of it, for instance in the Valtelline, as some scholars have supposed.[6]

[1] Strabo iv. 204.
[2] Howald and Meyer, op. cit., pp. 48–9.
[3] Strabo iv. 201, cf. v. 210–11.
[4] Chilver, *Cisalpine Gaul*, p. 5.
[5] Strabo v. 211; cf. also iv. 206.
[6] The Valtelline was and is prosperous and fertile, and probably came under

The final passage that requires study, and the one which gives this whole inquiry its importance for our present investigation into Augustan strategy, is in Dio. Under the year 16 B.C. he reports the operations of P. Silius Nerva, independently attested as proconsul of Illyricum,[1] against two Alpine tribes, the Camunni and the Vennii; Silius and his lieutenants are also credited with repelling raids by the Pannonians and Norici on Istria, and reducing both peoples to subjection.[2] The date is the first difficulty. The passage is one where Dio is clearly resuming a series of events, some of which may have happened in preceding years. We should not necessarily assume that Silius' operations were confined exclusively to the year 16. The second difficulty is the identity of the Vennii. Are they too identical with the Vennones–Vennonetes–Vennonenses of the Upper Rhine area, north of the Alps, or a new tribe that we have not previously heard of?

Now the Camunni, with whom Dio links them here, are well known. They appear on the Tropaeum in second place, after the Trumpilini.[3] Trumpilini and Camunni lived above Brescia (Brixia) in the Val Trompia and the Val Camonica respectively. Silius was operating in this area against the Camunni. Was he also responsible for the conquest of the Trumpilini? They were undoubtedly subdued by force, or their name would not be on the Tropaeum, and at a relatively early date: a *cohors Trumplinorum* under the command of Staius, son of Esdragassus, 'princeps Trumplinorum', is found serving under one C. Vibius Pansa, *legatus pro praetore in Vindolicis*, (the inscription itself is discussed further below),[4] and such a cohort cannot have had a long life, for the tribe was soon

Roman rule peacefully, like the neighbouring Val Bregaglia, cf. Oberziner, op. cit., p. 52; Casimir, *Le Trophée d'Auguste à la Turbie*, p. 67; it has yielded few Roman remains, Chilver, op. cit., p. 44.

[1] *CIL* iii. 2973 = *ILS* 899, and surely in this capacity he carried out these operations; on military jurisdiction in Cisalpina, see Syme, *The Roman Revolution*, p. 329, cf. id. on military operations of another proconsul of Illyricum, M. Vinicius, *Historia* xi (1962), p. 148.

[2] Dio liv. 20. 1. 2; on the date, Ritterling, *RE* xii, col. 1226. Orosius also has a Piso, presumably L. Calpurnius Piso (cos. 15 B.C.) operating 'adversus Vindelicos' at this time, but the passage is very puzzling, cf. Syme, *The Roman Revolution*, p. 329 and p. 398, n. 6; Orosius vi. 447.

[3] This is the actual spelling of the Tropaeum inscription; Pliny's MSS. here have 'Triumpilini'; *CIL* v. 4910, discussed in this paragraph, 'Trumplini',

[4] See below, p. 74 n. 4.

attributed to Brescia, and Trumpilini are already found in the legions under Augustus.[1] Perhaps they fought for the Romans in the campaign of 15 B.C., as they had fought against them a year or two before. This would explain Pliny's sneer, 'venalis cum agris suis populus'.[2]

Dio then records operations by Silius extending from Istria in the east to at least as far west as the valleys above Brescia. These valleys however, the Val Trompia and Val Camonica, do not lead directly to any of the major Alpine passes. The valleys east and west of them, which do, had been brought under Roman control somewhat earlier. To the east, the key position of the Dos Trento above Trent, commanding the road along the Adige, which leads up to the Brenner and Reschenscheideck Passes, was fortified by M. Appuleius (cos. 20 B.C.) at Augustus' command in or after 23 B.C.[3] The tribes of this area are not among Augustus' conquests: Tridentini around Trent itself, Benacenses on Lake Garda, Stoeni or Stoni east of it in the Giudicarie, Arusnates in the Val Policella, Feltrini around Feltre, Anauni in the Val di Non.[4] Nor are those around Lake Como, west of Brescia, such as the Ausuciates and Galliantes, nor the Bergalei in the Val Bregaglia above Lake Como on the way up to the Septimer and Maloja Passes.[5] It looks as if Rome had already taken a firm grip on the approaches to the most important passes of the Central Alps; was it merely Silius' job to mop up in those valleys that had been bypassed earlier?

We have already seen that there is no other evidence for the Vennones–Vennonetes–Vennonenses south of the Alps. If then we wish to locate the Vennii here, are we to assume that they are quite distinct from the other Venn- tribe? If so, it is somewhat surprising that they appear neither on the Tropaeum nor anywhere else in all the references we have to Alpine tribes. After all, Dio records their subjection as if they were a tribe of some importance. We have seen what variety there is in spelling

---

[1] Ritterling, *Klio* xxi (1927), p. 85.

[2] Pliny, *NH* iii. 133.

[3] *CIL* v. 5027 (= *ILS* 86). On its significance and dating, see Chilver, op. cit., p. 12; Augustus' titles include *trib. pot.*, but without a number.

[4] Howald and Meyer, p. 358; on the Stoeni, ibid., pp. 48–9, n. 6.

[5] *CIL* v. 5050; Howald and Meyer, pp. 193, 358; Stähelin, *Die Schweiz in römischer Zeit*, p. 106; cf. also Howald and Meyer, pp. 187–9.

the Venn- tribe's name, and it would not be remarkable if Dio had adopted yet another form of it. Most scholars have in fact assumed this identity, probably rightly.[1]

If this is so, however, the natural conclusion is that Silius' operations took him beyond the main chain of the Alps into the valley of the Upper Rhine or one of its tributaries, where alone, as we have seen, is there any ancient evidence for these Vennii–Vennonetes–Vennonenses–Vennones. Let us then return to the question of the order of tribes on the Tropaeum, to see whether from this we can get more geographical and therefore strategic precision. The Trumpilini, who begin the list, are the most southerly of all the tribes in the Central or Eastern Alps who appear, Trumpilini, Camunni, Vennonetes (=Vennii etc.): a row running from south to north, and probably also a group of tribes conquered by Silius in the same campaign or series of campaigns, in which he will have marched and fought from south to north also. Then another south–north row begins, Venostes, Isarchi, Breuni, Genaunes, Focunates, the tribes of the Brenner and Reschenscheideck area.[2] Then we read, 'Vindelicorum gentes quattuor, Cosuanetes, Rucinates, Licates, Catenates', followed by the Ambisontes.[3] Then the tribes of the Upper Rhine, whom we have already met in Pliny and Ptolemy also. Then, moving westwards, we have the Lepontii, the tribes of the Valais, the Salassi, and finally the numerous tribes of the Western Alps.[4] The Vennonetes, then, are listed after Trumpilini and Camunni, rather than with the other Upper Rhine tribes later, because they are the most southerly of these tribes, and because their association with the Trumpilini and Camunni in Silius' campaign made it seem natural to list these three tribes together.

If then the Vennonetes–Vennii lay 'above Como', north of the Val Camonica, beyond the main chain of the Alps, this would indicate the area on the north side of the Splügen,

---

[1] See above, p. 61, n. 5.

[2] Venostes and Isarchi do not appear in Ptolemy, whence Heuberger, op. cit., p. 65, suggests that they were so severely handled in 15 B.C. as to be almost wiped out. Breuni and Genaunes appear categorized as Illyrians in Strabo iv. 206; again linked by Horace, *Od.* IV. xiv. 10–11. Focunates otherwise unknown.

[3] Howald and Meyer, pp. 70–1, are surely right to take the phrase 'Vindelicorum gentes quattuor' as introducing the four tribes which follow.

[4] On Lepontii and Uberi, dwelling round the St. Gotthard massif, see Meyer, *MH* xix (1962), pp. 141–4. On Vallis Poenina tribes, see above, p. 40.

Septimer, or Maloja Passes, the first two of which lead directly, the third via the Julier Pass, into one of the valleys of the Upper Rhine system. All these passes were known to the Romans,[1] the Splügen and Maloja–Julier were paved, though nobody knows when,[2] and an early Roman station, possibly Augustan, has been found beneath the medieval hospice on the Septimer,[3] while Chur (Chapter 4. 1), where the various routes into the Upper Rhine valley converge, was the site of a Roman settlement, military or civilian, under Augustus. This region round the Maloja–Julier and the Splügen is the nodal point of communications in this part of the Alps. If we can suppose that Silius' attack on the Vennii gained him control of this area, the Romans would then be ready the following year to launch their columns down the Julier into the Upper Rhine or down the Inn. And while we cannot reconstruct the details, it seems likely that this is what happened.

Inadequate as the evidence is, therefore, we are none the less left with the suspicion that the campaigns of Silius and his lieutenants were more extensive and important than Dio's brief notice would suggest. Augustus' plans called not merely for the conquest of the Alps, but for the glory accruing from that conquest to fall to members of his own family. It is, as we shall see, especially in Chapter 6, not the only time that others were defrauded of their due by official propaganda or sycophantic chroniclers. When in 15 Drusus and Tiberius took command and the two armies, each divided into several columns, poured through the Alpine valleys,[4] we are better informed about their doings.[5] Deceptively well informed, in fact: detailed modern reconstructions do not always agree on the details.

[1] Stähelin, op. cit., pp. 380–8; Hyde, *Roman Alpine Routes*, pp. 87–113.

[2] No warrant for Augustan date, as assumed by Hyde, p. 103; cf. Syme, *JRS* xxvi (1936), p. 113.

[3] *JSGU* xxix (1937), p. 99, allegedly Augustan, but without details; the finds subsequently published by Wiedemer in *Helvetia Antiqua*, pp. 168–71; they include a sherd of terra sigillata, and sherds of Aco-type beakers and imitation sigillata. They cannot be precisely dated, but are certainly early and together with the Augustan finds from Chur suggest use of the Septimer under Augustus. [ADD.]

[4] Vell. ii. 95. 2; Dio liv. 22. 4; cf. Christ, op. cit., p. 421; was Calpurnius Piso perhaps a column commander, possibly of one of the columns from North Italy? (Oros. vi. 447; Suet., *de rhet.* 6).

[5] Vell. ii. 39. 3, 95. 2, 104. 5, 122. 2; Dio liv. 22; Strabo iv. 26, vii. 292; Suet., *Aug.* 21, *Tib.* 9; Florus ii. 22; Oros. vi. 445–6; Livy, *epit.* 138; Hor., *od*, IV. iv. 17–28, xiv. 6–24; *cons, ad Liviam*, 15–16, 175, 385–6,

Which pass did Drusus take, Brenner or Reschenscheideck?[1] The battle, the scholars' battle, rages. Local pride is involved. 'What porridge had John Keats?' The controversy is nonsense. Drusus' forces will have used both passes, as well as descending from Silius' eyrie. This was what the Roman strategy was. Tiberius started from Gaul, and if his main body followed the Rhine eastwards from Basle to the Bodensee, where, as we saw in Chapter 3, he fought his naval battle against the Vindelici, another column will have invaded the Upper Rhine via the Walensee route (above, Chapter 3. 3), and probably another from the Valais over the Furka Pass.[2] The natives failed to unite when compelled to resist so many thrusts at once and were subdued piecemeal. It was the common failing of barbarians: 'dum singuli pugnant, universi vincuntur'.[3] The reputed savagery, perhaps exaggerated by Roman propaganda beforehand to justify the Roman aggression,[4] was of little avail. One summer's campaign was enough.[5] Once the Romans held the valleys, the natives could submit or take to the high peaks and, when winter came, starve. The country overrun, the young men were deported[6] and the rest settled down peacefully, if not contentedly, to pay tribute. Strabo records 33 years of peace and taxation down to the time at which he was writing.[7] The conquest of the Alpine lands was finally completed the following year, 14, by the subjection of the Ligurian tribes in the Alpes Maritimes.[8]

As a result of the campaign of 15 B.C., not only the Alpine regions passed under Roman control, but the Voralpenland as well, the land lying between the Alps and the Upper Danube. Now the Upper Danube near its source, in the reach between Donaueschingen and Sigmaringen, comes to within some 15

[1] For the Brenner, Heuberger, op. cit., pp. 57–9; id., *Das Burggrafenamt im Altertum*, pp. 24–9; for the Reschenscheideck, Stähelin, op. cit., pp. 107–9, with bibliography, p. 107, n. 3; see further Christ, op. cit., p. 419, n. 17, and Meyer, loc. cit.

[2] For the Furka, Miltner, *Römerzeit in österreichischen Landen*, p. 34.

[3] Tac., *Agricola* 12.

[4] So suggested by Kraft, *JRGZ* iv (1957), pp. 90–1; cf. Heuberger in *Festschr. Wopfner*, pp. 97–104; Augustus boasted that he had made war on none of the Alpine tribes unjustly, *RG* 26; there might be two views on what constituted *iniuria*.

[5] Strabo iv. 206.

[6] Dio liv. 22. 4–5; Raetian cohorts are found in the Roman army, cf. Nuber in *Studien zu den Militärgrenzen Roms* (1967), pp. 90–1.

[7] Strabo, loc. cit.   [8] Dio liv. 24. 3.

miles of the Rhine at Schaffhausen and the northern tip of the Bodensee. But below Sigmaringen it runs north-eastwards for about 150 miles, all the way to Regensburg, steadily diverging from the northern edge of the Bavarian Alps, so that a great expanse of country opens out between, until Regensburg is nearly 100 miles north of the Alps. The Voralpenland is hard to define in terms of administrative boundaries, ancient or modern. Its heartland is Schwaben and Oberbayern, but it is not coterminous with them. In the west it is bounded by the Black Forest region, hilly, thickly forested, sparsely inhabited. In the east, the Lower Inn is a convenient demarcation line, corresponding to the Roman frontier of Raetia and Noricum.[1] Below the confluence of the Danube and the Inn at Passau, the joint stream forms a considerable barrier, without any major crossing until Carnuntum, whereas above Passau the conditions are quite different. There the Danube flows for the most part through a flat plain, often boggy, seldom, as between Weltenburg and Kelheim, confined between high banks. There are stretches of bog also in the valleys of the tributaries which rise in the Alps and flow northwards into the Danube, but the land naturally rises to the foothills of the Alps, and the greater part of the Voralpenland comprises rolling country, green and fertile, still today with its miles of pine forest the idyllic countryside, the 'hell blau und weisses Himmel' of Bavarian sentiment.

The main tributaries are the Iller, the Lech, and the Isar. It is clear from coin and other finds that for nearly a century after their first coming into the land, Roman influence and trade were concentrated principally in the western part of the area, between the Iller and the Lech. The principal towns of the Flavian period were Kempten (Cambodunum) on the Iller and Augsburg (Augusta Vindelicorum) on the Lech, both of which were Tiberian foundations.[2] East of the Lech, there are comparatively few traces of Roman influence in this early period north of the important prehistoric route, whose significance we shall discuss below, running from Salzburg to Augsburg and beyond,[3] and crossing the Danube at Aislingen, the site

---

[1] Nierhaus in *Ur- und Frühgeschichte als historische Wissenschaft*, pp. 177–88.

[2] See Chapters 4. 3 and 4. 7 respectively.

[3] Kraft, *JNG* vii (1956), p. 67; Christ, *Historia* vi (1957), pp. 422–3; on the road

of the earliest known Roman fort on the Upper Danube, founded in the latter part of Tiberius' reign.[1]

The fort at Burghöfe, on the other hand, where the Lech valley opens out into the Danube plain, is to all appearances Claudian, contemporary with those at Risstissen, Unterkirchberg, and probably Hüfingen, built perhaps when the Via Claudia Augusta was put through to the Danube in 47, with a possible extension running westwards along the south bank of the river and through the Black Forest region to link up directly with the Rhine front.[2] East of the Lech, even under Claudius, forts are known only from Oberstimm[3] and perhaps on the Frauenberg, near Weltenburg,[4] in the neighbourhood of the large Celtic *oppida* of Manching and Kelheim respectively, which we shall discuss below, and of important Danube-crossings,[5] which would account for the presence both of the *oppida* and of the Roman forts.

Further east again, Regensburg, Straubing, and Passau, despite their later importance, were not apparently occupied until Flavian times,[6] while below Passau, until Carnuntum is reached, the river was so well defended by nature that it offered little scope for military operations in either direction, and was consequently neglected.[7] The importance of Carnuntum itself is apparent from the Roman strategy against Maroboduus (Chapter 6), but Noricum as a whole was by-passed by the lines of Roman advance, although important as a communications link between the armies of Illyricum and those of Raetia and Germany. It retained its own king, with a Roman *praefectus* as adviser,[8] but its nominally independent status

itself, Eberl, *Das Schwäbische Museum* 1928, pp. 89–97. It is tempting to conjecture a fort of this period in the Salzburg area, though without evidence, cf. Schönberger, *JRS* lix (1969), p. 151.

[1] Ulbert, *Die römischen Donaukastellen Aislingen und Burghöfe*, p. 83.

[2] Filtzinger, *BJ* clvii (1957), pp. 196–8. Roman finds which may indicate a Claudian fort are also recorded at Neuberg a.d. Donau, see Eckstein, *Bay. Vorgbl.* xxx (1965), pp. 135–51, with Ulbert, ibid., pp. 151–3.

[3] Ulbert, *Germania* xxxv (1957), pp. 318–27.

[4] Ibid., pp. 326–7; Reinecke, *BerRGK* xxiv/xxv (1934/5), pp. 166–7.

[5] Cf. Ulbert, op. cit., esp. pp. 324, 327; Krämer, *Germania* xxxv (1957), p. 33.

[6] Ibid., p. 84.

[7] Swoboda, *Carn. Jb.* 1959, pp. 20–1, cf. Cary, *The Geographical Background of Greek and Roman History*, p. 279; also Pascher, *RLÖ* xix (1949), and Noll, *RLÖ* xxi (1958).

[8] Vell. ii. 109. 5, 'regnum Noricum'. On Noricum and its incorporation within

was not found inconsistent either with the setting-up of a legionary base at Carnuntum, or with the presence of a Roman garrison at the town on the Magdalensberg, almost certainly Noreia, where the *conventus Noricorum* met.[1] By the time of Claudius, Noricum can be considered one of the *provinciae togatae*.[2]

Raetia on the other hand was anything but a backwater. It was a base for further Roman penetration of Germany, like the expedition of L. Domitius Ahenobarbus in 2 B.C., discussed below in Chapter 6. If, as we have seen, there is no evidence for Roman forts on this stretch of the Danube before Claudius' reign, except for that at Aislingen, this is not because Roman control did not extend so far, as has been suggested,[3] but because the Upper Danube was not a frontier, in the sense of a fixed, garrisoned frontier, until the time of Claudius, if then. For the Claudian foundations to which we have already referred appear designed to watch river-crossings and guard a lateral river-bank road, and may well do no more than control traffic across the river, rather than acting as frontier-posts of the later, Flavian *limes* type. It is impossible to trace a pre-Claudian *limes* anywhere in the Voralpenland. The pre-Claudian frontier was not a fixed line to be defended. Roman control extended as far as her armies could reach, and Ahenobarbus' expedition showed how far that was, with Raetia as a base. If he could settle the wandering Hermunduri on vacant lands, probably in the Upper Main area, where they remained Rome's faithful clients, there can be no doubt that the Romans had the power to establish forts on the Danube itself, had they wished to do so.

the Empire, see esp. Miltner, *Klio* xxx (1937), pp. 208–11, refuting Swoboda, *Klio* xxviii (1935), pp. 180–6, and cf. Polaschek, *RE* xvii, cols. 987–9.

[1] Vell., loc. cit., explicitly states that Carnuntum was in Noricum; it was later transferred to Pannonia, Pliny, *NH* iv. 80. Apart from the garrison, the Magdalensberg is notable for the number of inscriptions in honour of the imperial family; see reports of the extensive excavations almost annually in *Carinthia I* from vol. cxxxix (1949) onwards; summaries by Vetters, *RE* ixA, cols. 262–5, and *JÖAI* xlvi (1961/3), pp. 219–28. Ertl, *Topographia Norici*, pp. 139–42, argues that the Magdalensberg settlement was called Virunum, just like the Claudian *municipium* in the valley below, but the identification with Noreia seems more probable, cf. Alföldy, *Historia* xv (1966), pp. 239–40.

[2] Sherwin-White, *The Roman Citizenship*, pp. 186–7.

[3] Christ, *Historia* vi (1957), p. 427; better however Filtzinger, *BJ* clvii (1957), pp. 196–8, speaking in terms of 'die römische Einflusszone'.

The earliest traces of Roman occupation so far known to archaeology lie further back in the Lech valley. Forts on the Lorenzberg at Epfach (Chapter 4. 5) and probably at Augsburg-Oberhausen (Chapter 4. 7) guarded important river-crossings, and formed with Gauting (Chapter 4. 6), where no Roman occupation before Tiberius' reign can be proved, although it may be inferred, the points of a triangle which was of the utmost importance to the Roman communications network in the area. A road coming eastwards from Helvetia via Bregenz (Chapter 4. 2), Kempten (Chapter 4. 3), and the Auerberg (Chapter 4. 4), all sites occupied early in Tiberius' reign, if not before, crossed the Lech just above the Lorenzberg and at Gauting met the Salzburg–Oberhausen–Aislingen route mentioned above,[1] while the road from Italy over the Reschenscheideck Pass and down the Lech valley, the later Via Claudia Augusta, in use from the first days of the conquest onwards,[2] intersected the first of these roads at the Lorenzberg and the second at Oberhausen.

The importance of Raetia to the Romans for its position on their lines of communication is sufficiently demonstrated by the administrative organization of the area, the Vallis Poenina, Raetia, and Vindelicia forming one single administrative unit which embraced all the major north–south passes of the Central Alps, Great St. Bernard, Splügen, Maloja, Julier, Reschenscheideck, Brenner, as well as the communications between the Vallis Poenina and the upper Rhine over the Furka Pass, and between the upper Rhine and upper Inn valleys by the Arlberg Pass. We find prefectures in the Western Alps similarly arranged so as to group lines of communication under one command.[3] In this context, the use of forts like those on the Lorenzberg and at Oberhausen to guard important river-crossings is understandable. Strategic points

---

[1] There is no evidence that this road continued beyond Gauting, though the Würm valley offers a suitable route, see Wagner, *Denkmäler und Fundstätte der Vorzeit Münchens und seiner Umgebung*, p. 20–1.

[2] *CIL* v. 8002, 8003: '. . . viam Claudiam Augustam quam Drusus pater Alpibus bello patefactis derexerat'. See further Wells, *Phoenix* xxi (1967), p. 66.

[3] Such was the kingdom and prefecture of Cottius along the Cols du Mont Genèvre and du Mont Cénis (*CIL* 7231, from the arch at Susa), and later the Bricianii, Quariates, and Adunicates are found under one command, which thus embraced the Cols d'Izoard, de Vars, and de la Cayolle (*CIL* xii. 80), cf. Jullian, *Histoire de la Gaule*, vi, p. 509, n. 3.

along the whole road network were probably protected in this way.[1]

The Roman grip on Raetia must have been very firm. We have already referred to Strabo's explicit testimony that, despite the fierceness of their resistance, the Raeti settled down with remarkable docility to Roman rule and taxation. Was it the peace of acquiescence or of harsh repression? Roman methods of pacification could be ruthless: 'ubi solitudinem faciunt, pacem appellant'.[2] But the archaeological evidence, above all from Kempten, suggests that peace was not brought about by depopulation here, even if the repression of the resistance offered to the invading forces was sufficient to deter further recalcitrance, and the view that the excavations in the Celtic *oppidum* at Manching provide evidence to the contrary cannot be sustained, although it merits close examination.

The village of Manching lies south-east of Ingolstadt and almost due north of Munich, on the right bank of the River Paar and about two miles south of the Danube. Here lay a vast Celtic *oppidum*, surrounded by a true *murus Gallicus*, as described by Caesar, over 7 km. in circumference, enclosing an area of about 380 ha.[3] The land is so flat that there is now an airfield within the *oppidum*. The whole Manching area was of considerable importance already in pre-Celtic times,[4] as in later Roman and medieval times, because there is a crossing of the Danube here.

Excavations carried out in the *oppidum* in 1955 and again in 1957–61 have clearly shown that it was occupied until late in the La Tène period.[5] The latest finds here are also the latest anywhere in the Upper Danube lands west of the Isar, except two sites near the mouth of the Isar.[6] In the area so far excavated at least 200 skeletons have been found, overwhelmingly

---

[1] Cf. Ritterling, *BJ* cxiv/cxv (1906), p. 171, lucidly expounding Augustan policy on use of detachments and forts to guard important lines of communication or penetration.

[2] Tac., *Agr.* 30. 7.

[3] Krämer, *Germania* xxxv (1957), p. 33, with maps and history of research into the *oppidum*, pp. 32–44; on *muri Gallici*, see above, p. 15.

[4] Rochna, *Germania* xli (1963), pp. 92–9.

[5] Reports in *Germania* xxxix (1961) and xl (1962); most important, Krämer, *Germania* xl (1962), pp. 293–317.

[6] Krämer, op. cit., pp. 315–16, with map, fig. 4, p. 314; cf. also Maier, *Germania* xxxix (1961), pp. 366–8, discussing the La Tène pottery.[1]

those of adult males, their bones often scattered and gnawed by canine teeth.[1] Though a few scanty objects of Roman provenance, including fragments of black-gloss sigillata, have been found, there is nothing which need be dated after 15 B.C., and Krämer has argued that the *oppidum* was captured by the Roman forces in that year and thereafter ceased to be occupied. The absence of later finds west of the Isar indicates, he suggests, that the Romans uprooted the natives from this area, whereas east of the Isar they controlled them without garrisons by fear and influence from what Krämer takes to be the legionary base at Oberhausen, since this area was militarily and strategically less important.[2]

Against Krämer's theory however is the total absence of any evidence of Roman assault on the *oppidum,* such as Roman missiles or weapons of any sort. Krämer has suggested that this is because the attackers collected up their weapons and took them away with them. This seems in itself unlikely. Did a fatigue party go carefully over the vast area of the *oppidum,* picking its way through the unburied bodies of the inhabitants, gathering in leaden *glandes,* artillery bolts, bent *pila,* and all the debris (Roman) of the fight, such as other sites reveal? Ulbert, vigorously opposing Krämer's views, points out how different a picture we get from Maiden Castle.[3] We might also point out that none of the skeletons from Manching bears evidence of 'the murderous effect of the Roman weapons' so graphically described by Richmond at Maiden Castle.[4] Broken weapons of Celtic type were however found in abundance at Manching. Should we not then with Kunkel see these as testifying, like the skeletons, to the bloody end of the *oppidum* brought about, not by the Roman invaders, but by Celtic rivals?[5]

It is undoubtedly hard to see any explanation of so many scattered skeletons other than hostile action. If there was a

---

[1] Krämer, op. cit., p. 311.   [2] Ibid., pp. 315–16.

[3] Ulbert, *Die römischen Donaukastellen Aislingen und Burghöfe,* pp. 78–9; id., *Der Lorenzberg bei Epfach,* pp. 102–7; cf. id., *Germania* xxxv (1957), p. 324.

[4] Richmond, *Roman Britain,* p. 24.

[5] Kunkel, *Ausgrabungen in der Keltenstadt bei Manching an der Donau,* p. 18; speaking of 'jene innerkeltischen Wirren, . . . mit deren Auswirkungen die Römer ihr Eingreifen nördlich der Alpen rechtfertigten'. Kunkel's theory seems more likely than Krämer's, that the weapons were perhaps deliberately broken, speaking of 'Schatz- und Sammelfunde'.

plague, one would expect the dead to be found all together in their huts, if the survivors had abandoned the place without burying them; and plague would not account for the preponderance of adult male skeletons. Wiedemer, comparing numerous finds of human bones from Swiss sites of the La Tène period, considers and rejects for so large a number of dead the explanation of human sacrifice.[1] The most likely solution remains Kunkel's, that Manching was taken and destroyed by other Celts. Its cultural affinities and trade connections, as Kunkel observed, appear to be with Helvetia and Gaul rather than Noricum,[2] and its *murus Gallicus* is the most easterly example of this type of fortification known, with the exception of one somewhat dubiously reported from Židovar in Jugoslavia.[3] We should perhaps see Manching as an outlier, sacked by tribes from further east. It is only some 20 miles as the crow flies from the other great, but as yet unexcavated, *oppidum* on the Michelsberg at Kelheim, on the north bank of the Danube at the mouth of the Altmühl. If excavations there ever reveal in what relation these two *oppida* stood, we may be closer to solving the problem of the destruction of Manching. That it had anything to do with the Romans is unproven and improbable.

If then the conquest of Raetia was due to the legions, we do not know, in the absence of archaeological evidence, how long after the conquest Raetia retained a legionary garrison. Epigraphic evidence however suggests that the legions were withdrawn from Raetia between 12 B.C. and A.D. 12, and other considerations lead us to narrow this down to the period A.D. 6–12. Our starting-point is the inscription mentioned earlier which attests a certain C. Vibius Pansa, probably the son of the consul of 43 B.C., but not otherwise known, who was *legatus pro praetore in Vindolicis*, possibly the first governor of the newly conquered territory, for the date is within a year or two of the conquest.[4]

---

[1] Wiedemer, *Germania* xli (1963), pp. 277–8, cf. p. 269.
[2] Kunkel, op. cit., p. 16.   [3] See above, p. 15.
[4] *CIL* v. 4910 = *ILS* 847, already referred to above, p. 63, n. 3, and frequently discussed, see refs. in Howald and Meyer, *Die römische Schweiz*, p. 196; the correct reading vindicated by Ritterling, *RE* xii, col. 1226, against Mommsen, *CIL* ad loc.; on the date, Ritterling, *Klio* xxi (1927), p. 85, and id., *Fasti des römischen Deutschland* (1932), p. 108; cf. also Wagner, *Germania* xli (1963), pp. 324–7.

A second inscription refers to a man who may have served under him or his immediate successor: 'Q. Octavius L. f. C. n. L. pron. Ser. | Sagitta, | IIvir quinq(uennalis) III, praef(ectus) fab(rum), prae(fectus) equi(tum), | trib(unus) mil(itum) a populo, procurator Caesaris | Augusti in Vindalicis et Raetis et in valle Poe|nina per annos IIII et in Hispania provincia | per annos X et in Suria biennium.'[1] It has been supposed that this man was actually governor of the Raetian area with the title of procurator, probably in the early years of Tiberius' reign, but wrongly. As Heuberger recognized, he was not governor, but financial procurator, before going on to fill the same post in the more important provinces of Spain and Syria.[2] His military career, if we allow one year for each of the tours as *praefectus* and *tribunus militum*, lasted nineteen years; it may in fact have lasted longer. His civilian career, since he was thrice *quinquennalis*, occupied at least eleven years. He could not hold any municipal office before the age of thirty and could scarcely have become *quinquennalis* at that age without previously holding minor office. If then his civilian career preceded his military career, we should probably allow some fifteen years for it, in which case he would have started off in the army at the age of about 45, which is absurd.[3] The military career therefore came first. He may on retirement have gone at once to the highest magistracy in the town where he settled

---

[1] *ILS* 9007 = Howald and Meyer, op. cit., no. 35; on this and other inscriptions cited here, see also Stähelin, *Die Schweiz in römischer Zeit*, pp. 110–14, with further bibliography.

[2] Heuberger, *Klio* xxxiv (1942), p. 291. So too Pflaum, *Les Carrières procuratoriennes équestres* i, pp. 13–16. Later Raetia, Vindelicia, and the Vallis Poenina became a regular province, with a governor bearing the title of procurator, attested *CIL* v. 3936 = *ILS* 1348 = Howald and Meyer, op cit., no. 36: 'Q. Caicilio | Cisiaco Septicio | Picai Caiciliano, | procur(atori) Augustor(um) et pro leg(ato) provinciai Raitiai et Vindelic(iai) et vallis Poenin(ai), auguri, | flamini divi Aug(usti) et Romai, | C. Ligurius L. f. Vol. Asper | c(enturio) coh(ortis) I c(ivium) R(omanorum) ingenuor(um)', probably under Gaius and Claudius, to judge from the spelling, though a 2nd-century date has also been suggested. The evidence suggests that *praefectus* rather than *procurator* is the title to be expected under Augustus and Tiberius, cf. Sherwin-White, *Roman Society and Roman Law in the New Testament*, pp. 6, 12, with further refs., discussing the Pontius Pilate inscription.

[3] On minimum age for holding office, see the Table of Heraclea, *CIL* i². 593, lines 89 ff.; on *duoviri* who subsequently enter the army in their thirties, Birley, *Roman Britain and the Roman Army*, pp. 139–40. There is theoretically the possibility that Sagitta's two careers overlapped, but I can find no parallel, and it seems intrinsically less likely.

(this was Superaequuum Paelignorum, now Castelvecchio Subequo, where the inscription was found), but even so the military and civil careers together take up a minimum of thirty years. The inscription however appears to have been set up before the death of Augustus, who is not called *divus*. The military career therefore begins not later than 16 B.C., and the Raetian procuratorship ends not later than 10 B.C., nor of course earlier than 12 B.C., since it lasted four years, and Raetia was not conquered until 15.

Another inscription, however, shows that by A.D. 12 Raetia no longer had a legionary garrison: '[S]ex Pedio Sex. f. An. | Lusiano Hirruto, | prim(o) pil(o) leg(ionis) XXI, pra[ef](ecto) | Raetis, Vindolicis, valli[s | P]oeninae et levis armatur(ae), | III vir(o) i(ure) d(icundo), praef(ecto) | Germanic[i] Caesaris quinquennalici | [i]uris ex s(enatus) c(onsulto), quinquen(nali) iterum. | hic amphitheatrum d(e) s(ua) p(ecunia) fecit. M. Dullius M. f. Gallus.'[1] The most likely year for Germanicus' honorary office is 16/17, when he was in Italy as conquering hero, and certainly no later than 18/19, when he went east. Pedius will probably have held the quattuorvirate before the honour of standing in for Germanicus, in which case, if his military career preceded his civilian one, he will have retired from the army not later than A.D. 16, and probably not later than 14, having commanded in the Raetian area, which cannot have had a legionary garrison at the time, since the legionary legate would have outranked Pedius. Kraft's argument that Pedius did not become prefect before 14, on the grounds that his subsequent municipal career proves him to have attracted Germanicus' attention during his active service, probably during the mutiny of A.D. 14, in which *legio XXI* took part,[2] cannot be accepted, first because he could have served under Germanicus in Illyricum in A.D. 9; secondly, we cannot suppose that members of the imperial house accepted honorary office only in those municipalities where they knew someone personally; and thirdly, a *primus pilus* posted out of *legio XXI* immediately after the mutiny, as Kraft supposes Pedius was, would not have left in glory to go to an independent command,

---

[1] *CIL* ix. 5044 = *ILS* 2689 = Howald and Meyer, no. 34.
[2] Kraft in *Aus Bayerns Frühzeit*, pp. 153–6; cf. Schleiermacher, *Germania* xxxi (1953), pp. 200–1.

for the mutiny reflected no credit on the officers of the legion, nor was an experienced *primus pilus* to be spared in the difficult period after its suppression, if he were any good.

It is of course possible, though less likely, that Pedius entered the army after his municipal career. He would then have been at least 37, rather old, but not impossibly so. This would put his Raetian command in the 20s or 30s, and would tell us nothing about Raetia in Augustan times. Under Tiberius, however, *legio XXI* was on the Rhine, moving to Vindonissa early in Claudius' reign.[1] The appointment of its *primus pilus* to the Raetian command is less probable at this period, when the legion had no links with Raetia, than it would have been under Augustus. *Legio XXI* may have been raised specially for the attack on the Alps and the Voralpenland, and probably formed part of the Raetian garrison as long as it had a legionary garrison:[2] what is more likely than that its *primus pilus*, who knew the area, stayed on to govern it and to command its garrison of auxiliaries and militia when the legions were withdrawn? The argument that this took place before the end of Augustus' reign is further strengthened by the passage in Tacitus where he records that in A.D. 14 'veterani . . . in Raetiam mittuntur, specie defendendae provinciae ob imminentis Suebos',[3] a pretext that may have been invented to get the men quietly away from the Rhine army, but which would have lacked somewhat in plausibility, had Raetia already had at that time a legionary garrison.

The epigraphic evidence therefore suggests that the legions were withdrawn from the Raetian area some time between 12 B.C. and A.D. 12. Is it possible to narrow this down still further? Not with any certainty perhaps, but if we examine the role of the Raetian garrison, and try to place our knowledge of Roman dispositions in the Raetian area under Augustus in the context of the Augustan campaigns in Germany, we can hazard a probable solution of the problem. Two facts: first, when L. Domitius Ahenobarbus led an army across the Elbe some time between 6 and 1 B.C., crossing the river unopposed,

---

[1] Ritterling, *RE* xxi, cols. 1782-5.

[2] Ibid., col. 1781, pointing out that many recruits from the newly conquered Alpine tribes, now attributed to North Italian communities, are found in its ranks.

[3] Tac., *Ann.* i. 44. 6.

erecting an altar to Augustus, and receiving the tribes beyond the river into Roman *amicitia*, his starting-point was Raetia;[1] secondly, in A.D. 6 the attack on Bohemia was to have been launched from two directions simultaneously, by Tiberius from a base at Carnuntum with the army of Illyricum, and by Sentius Saturninus from the west.[2] Tacitus makes Maroboduus say that he had twelve legions deployed against him,[3] which may represent the total number of legions stationed in Illyricum, Raetia, and Germany at the time, whether or not they were actively engaged in the projected Bohemian expedition. If so, then this gives us some grounds for thinking that Raetia in A.D. 6 still had a legionary garrison, possibly of two legions,[4] Illyricum and Germany having each five legions. We might suppose, purely as a hypothesis, that the Raetian legions were perhaps withdrawn that year, when reinforcements for Illyricum were urgently assembled from all quarters (below, Chapter 7).

Where then were the Raetian legions stationed? The traditional view, which has a legionary base at Oberhausen as the most advanced of all Augustan military installations in the Voralpenland, is both unparalleled and militarily unsound. We should expect an advanced legionary base to have a screen of forts in front of it.[5] The Romans moreover must have used both the Aislingen crossing and that facing the mouth of the Lech during the campaigns under Augustus. Whatever else may be hypothesis, the operations of Aheno-barbus and Saturninus are fact. Is it possible that the legions lay on the very bank of the Danube, as they lay on the Rhine? There is no lack of suitable sites.[6] We have no evidence, but

---

[1] Dio lv. 10a. 2; Tac., *Ann.* iv. 44. 3; Syme in *CAH* x, p. 366.

[2] Vell. ii. 109. 5.   [3] Tac., *Ann.* ii. 46.

[4] There is some evidence that *XXI* was one of the Raetian legions; Ritterling, *RE* xii, cols. 1226, 1711, supposing that Raetia had two legions, conjectured *XIII* as the other. Syme, *JRS* xxiii (1933), p. 28, suggested *XVI* instead of *XIII*, and this is supported by the recent find of a helmet inscribed with this number at Burlafingen near the confluence of the Iller and Danube, see Radnóti in *Aus Bayerns Frühzeit*, pp. 157–73; id. in *Quint. Cong. Int. Lim. Rom. Stud.*, pp. 177–82. If *XVI* and *XXI* were once part of the Raetian garrison, both legions were on the Rhine by A.D. 14 (Tac., *Ann.* i. 31. 3, 37. 4).

[5] Cf. Frere on the Inchtuthil fortress: 'It is inconceivable that the fortress of Legio XX had no screen of forts beyond it' (*JRS* lvi (1966), p. 270); the same would be true of a base at Oberhausen.

[6] Cf. Ulbert, *Der Lorenzberg bei Epfach*, p. 100: 'Günstige Geländegegebenheiten gibt es dort genügend.'

Carnuntum offers a parallel, for here we know that in preparation for the campaign of A.D. 6 'praeparaverat iam hiberna Caesar [i.e. Tiberius] ad Danubium',[1] and yet no trace of his base has ever been found, for the known legionary base at Carnuntum cannot be shown to date from before the reign of Claudius.[2] On the other hand, the legionary base or bases may have lain further back, at the foot of the Alps. Dangstetten (Chapter 3. 5) would seem to be too remote. It would not be surprising to come upon such a base in the Füssen area. Meanwhile the whole question remains open.

4. I. CHUR

Chur (Curia) occupies an important strategic position commanding the Upper Rhine valley at a point which must be passed by anyone who has crossed the Furka, Splügen, or Maloja and Julier Passes and who wishes to descend the valley; it is a site likely to have attracted the Romans' attention from their first coming into the area.[3] Only recently however has evidence of occupation under Augustus come to light, the result of considerable archaeological activity in the region due to much construction work, gravel-digging, and quarrying, which indeed led to the appointment of a cantonal archaeologist for Graubünden.[4]

The most important finds for the history of the earliest period of Roman occupation were two fragments of an inscription in very fine monumental lettering which fitted together to read L. CA[and in the line below PRINC]; clearly L. CA[ESARI AVGVSTI. F.] PRINC[IPI IVVENTVTIS]. The date must be between 3 B.C. and A.D. 2 or soon after; we are reminded of the similar inscriptions from the Vallis Poenina, which was under the same command as the Upper Rhine at this period.[5] Also in the same area at Chur-Welschdörfli were found some

---

[1] Vell. ii. 110. 1.

[2] Wells, in the proceedings of the Eighth International Congress of Roman Frontier Studies, 1969 (forthcoming).

[3] See above.

[4] Erb in *Helvetia Antiqua*, p. 223; bibliography of reports on excavations in various local newspapers and journals, ibid., p. 231, n. 30.

[5] Meyer in *Helvetia Antiqua*, pp. 228–30; the rather unusual word-divider between L. CA[tends to confirm a Late Republican or Early Empire date, cf. Howald and Meyer, *Die römische Schweiz*, nos. 37–41, and *CIL* xiii. 5796 = 11879.

fragments of Italian sigillata.[1] The finds do not of course prove that there was a military base here, but in view of Chur's strategic position it is not easy to suppose that the area was left to the newly conquered civil population totally without a garrison. A fort on this site or nearby is therefore extremely probable.

4. 2. BREGENZ

Bregenz (Brigantium) lies at the eastern end of the Bodensee. The remains of a Roman military post here on the so-called Ölrain were discovered during building operations and were made the subject of extremely limited excavations between 1920 and 1944.[2] There was a previous Celtic occupation of the site, of unknown extent.[3] The finds, which still await adequate publication, included many objects typical of the Roman army, as well as coins and pottery. The latter included Italian sigillata, although South Gaulish predominated; without full details, we cannot tell how early this Italian sigillata was, but it would appear to be an indication of Augustan or early Tiberian date.

In addition there comes from Bregenz a stone, not found *in situ*, inscribed DRVSO TIB. F. CAESARI.[4] Hild sees this as proving that the fort was built and dedicated in Drusus's presence in A.D. 14 or 17 during his visits to Pannonia and the German front.[5] This is quite arbitrary. In the first place, there is no proof that the stone comes from the fort. The traces of previous Celtic occupation on the Ölrain seem scarcely adequate to be those of the important *oppidum* of Brigantium which Strabo records,[6] and it is probable that this lay elsewhere in the area, while there may well have been (though this is quite conjectural) a new Roman-style civil settlement established in early Tiberian times, as at Kempten (Cambodunum), with which Brigantium is linked by Strabo. If so, the Drusus

---

[1] Wiedemer in *Helvetia Antiqua*, p. 168.

[2] Hild, *JÖAI* xxxvii (1948), *Bbl.*, cols. 123–60; id., *Festschrift Egger* ii (1953), pp. 257–60, = *Carinthia I* cxliii (1953), pp. 711–14.

[3] Hild, opp. citt., col. 123 and p. 257 respectively.

[4] *CIL* iii. 5769 = 11879; photograph in Hild, *Festschrift Egger* ii, p. 260, makes it clear that this is the correct reading, not CESARI, as Hild prints in his text.

[5] Tac., *Ann.* i. 24, ii. 44, 62.   [6] Strabo iv. 206.

inscription might well be connected with the founding of this town.

But even if it did come from the military post on the Ölrain, as Hild assumed, there is the further objection that it might just as well celebrate a rebuilding of the fort, or of some part of it, as the original building.[1] The inscription, like the sigillata, even supposing that it is connected with the fort at all, only tells us that it was in existence early in Tiberius' reign. Only the full publication of the finds and further extensive excavation down to undisturbed subsoil can tell us when it was founded.

4. 3. KEMPTEN

Roman military objects have been found at two separate sites at Kempten (Cambodunum), one on the Lindenberg on the right bank of the River Iller, the site of a civilian settlement which appears to date from the reign of Tiberius, and the other on the Burghalde on the left bank, the site of a fortified town of the period from about 260 onwards. The extensive archaeological activity at Kempten in recent years has concentrated on the civil settlement on the Lindenberg. What evidence we have for military occupation has come almost by accident. We must consider the Lindenberg and the Burghalde separately, noting that neither has revealed any trace of native settlement, and that therefore the original Celtic Cambodunum to which Strabo refers[2] must be sought at yet a third site in the area, still unknown.[3]

The settlement on the Lindenberg is judged by Krämer to date from about the same time as the fort at Bregenz and the legionary base at Vindonissa, that is to say, from the early years of Tiberius' reign.[4] He bases his dating on the finds of coin and pottery from the site, which are the subject of detailed reports by Kellner and Fischer respectively.[5] The military

---

[1] Cf. my discussion of the inscription from Emona (Ljubljana) in the proceedings of the Eighth International Congress of Roman Frontier Studies, 1969 (forthcoming).

[2] Strabo iv. 206.

[3] Krämer, *Cambodunumforschungen 1953–i*, pp. 118–19.

[4] Krämer, op. cit., p. 117; on the insecurity of the dating of both Bregenz and Vindonissa see however the previous chapters 4. 2 and 3. 2 respectively.

[5] Kellner in Krämer, op. cit., pp. 54–9; Fischer in *Cambodunumforschungen 1953* ii, esp. pp. 36–7, with table, p. 34.

finds already mentioned came from within the area of the civil town, being most frequent in the northern part of it, so numerous that Krämer thinks it impossible to doubt that in the first half of the first century there was a military garrison here somewhere in the Lindenberg area.[1] He observes however that these objects, where stratigraphically datable, are found not in the lowest, Tiberian level, but in the next of the period of Gaius and Claudius,[2] and moreover for the most part in gardens and farmland, outside the buildings of that period, where he supposes that they may have been thrown away, outside the actual fort.[3]

There can be no doubt of the military character of the objects concerned. Fellmann rightly notes their similarity to finds from Vindonissa.[4] But what does the evidence amount to? No sign of the buildings or defences of a fort has been found on the Lindenberg. The obvious site for any military post would however be such as to include within its defences the summit of the Lindenberg, which lies outside and to the east of the town, an area which the excavations did not reach.[5] But the military finds from the gardens within the town are not evidence for a fort at this point. And as Krämer points out, there is nothing to link the finds with the pre-Claudian period. His explanation of how they got into the gardens is ingenious, but not ingenious enough. What actually happened? Did the garrison come down into the town to plant its debris among the houses? Why not abandon it with the fort, or throw it on a

---

[1] Krämer, op. cit., pp. 119–20.

[2] It might seem from the phrasing of the account on p. 120 that period 2 is assigned to the period of Gaius and Claudius solely because the earliest coin found in it is a coin of A.D. 41. That is not so, nor is this the earliest coin, as is clear from the table on pp. 29–30.

[3] Krämer, op. cit., p. 120: 'Möglicherweise deutet das fast ausschließliche Vorkommen in dem Hof- und Gartengelände außerhalb des eigentlichen Hauses darauf hin, daß es sich um weggeworfenes Gut aus der Zeit der Auflassung der Garnison in claudischer Zeit handelt, das hier wohl auch außerhalb des eigentlichen Lagers in den Boden kam. Wenn man so in dem Befund unserer Grabung auch keine Anhaltspunkte dafür hat, daß die Garnison in frühtiberische Zeit zurückreicht, so wird man doch aus diesem sehr kleinen und zufälligen Ausschnitt auch nicht des Gegenteil schließen dürfen.'

[4] Fellmann, *JSGU* xlvii (1958/9), p. 264.

[5] Map of Lindenberg and Burghalde in Kleiss, *Die öffentlichen Bauten von Cambodunum*, plate 42; plan of Lindenberg, somewhat schematic, Krämer, op. cit., p. 14; photo., ibid., plate 1a; the lie of the land is most clearly to be seen in a photograph of a diorama of the area in *Jber. Bay. Bodendenkmalpflege* 1962, p. 116.

dump beside the fort? But if the north part of the town where
the finds came from *was* just beside the fort, then why no
trace of the fort itself in this area in the Tiberian layer? The
presence of military finds among the houses of the civilian town
suggests that this was where the users of the objects were also,
yet we cannot think of a military detachment as simply living
in the town rather than separate from it in a regular camp.
And this still would not explain why their equipment was
found in the gardens.

To sum up then: the Lindenberg was the site of a town from
early Tiberian times on. There is no evidence for prior occupation by native settlers or Roman soldiers. Yet somehow in
the Claudian period, and apparently in this period only,
military equipment came to be buried in farmland and gardens,
especially in the northern part of the town. This is not, *pace*
Krämer, evidence for the existence of an early Tiberian fort on
the Lindenberg. I confess myself unable to suggest a satisfactory explanation. Could fill containing the military objects
have been brought from another site? But there appears to be
no evidence for deliberate fill. Could the equipment have been
lost by soldiers called in to suppress a riot? Far-fetched and
implausible? The problem remains.

The Burghalde on the other hand would be an excellent
site for a small fort, as its choice for the later fortified town
shows. It is roughly triangular, some 400 m. in circumference,
an isolated knoll some 200 m. from the river. The presence of an
early fort here is conjectured from finds of military objects,[1]
and I think it probable, but there is no evidence to determine
the date of the first occupation. A fort on the Burghalde however
would naturally be designed to guard the crossing of the
Iller. The Lorenzberg fort also suggests very strongly that a
road from west to east across the Voralpenland was in use
when it was established; such a road must have joined up with
the Basle–Oberwinterthur road; and one naturally then thinks
of the Burghalde fort at Kempten as contemporary with the
Lorenzberg. Excavation is now needed to test this hypothesis.

[1] Reinecke, *Germania* xvi (1932), pp. 133–4; *Germania* xxix (1951), p. 42;
Krämer, suggesting either two forts existing simultaneously, or an original fort on
the Burghalde, later transferred to the Lindenberg, op. cit., pp. 119–20.

4. 4. THE AUERBERG

The Auerberg is a steep, isolated hill which dominates the whole surrounding countryside. Its twin peaks are surrounded by a clearly visible 'Ringwall', forming what most scholars have assumed to be a strong and extensive hilltop *oppidum*, possibly Strabo's Damasia, resembling other known Celtic *oppida* such as Bibracte, though typically Celtic finds are not yet to hand.[1] The exact date and nature of the occupation of the site await elucidation by excavation.[2] Our knowledge of the site at the moment depends upon very limited and inadequate excavations carried out at a number of separate points in 1901–6.[3] The excavators suggested that the period of Roman occupation was 30–50, but Loeschcke, relying on the high percentage of Italian as against South Gaulish sigillata and the comparative closeness of the pottery finds from the Auerberg on this occasion to those from Haltern, dated all the Auerberg material to Tiberius's reign, probably beginning in the 20's and finishing before 40.[4] More recently Ulbert notes that the Auerberg finds are parallel to those from Kempten and Bregenz and sees all three as part of a chain of early Tiberian forts.[5] Loeschcke's dating should be set back a few years, since he was assuming that Haltern was given up in 16 instead of 9, so that Ulbert and Loeschcke are substantially in agreement: the earliest finds yet known from the Auerberg are to be dated around the beginning of Tiberius' reign.

The key words in that sentence, however, are 'yet known'. For the Auerberg, like the Ölrain at Bregenz (above, Chapter 4. 2), has been so little excavated that the finds so far made

---

[1] Strabo iv. 206, cf. Krämer, *Cambodunumforschungen 1953* i, pp. 118–19; Reinecke, *Bay. Vorgbl.* xxii (1957), p. 99; Hübener, *JRGZ* v (1958), p. 210. The identification of Damasia with Augsburg is now quite exploded after Ohlenroth's excavations, *Germania* xxxii (1954), pp. 76–85, cf. also Wagner's criticisms of the theory, *Die Römer in Bayern*, p. 10.

[2] Further excavations were begun in 1966 by Dr. G. Ulbert (Munich), to whom I owe a particular debt for discussing the problems of the Auerberg with me and for taking me over the ground and pointing out the features of the site in abominable weather.

[3] Report by Frank and Jacobs, *Beitr. zur Anthrop. u. Urgesch. Bayerns* xvi (1907), pp. 63–84; see esp. on the site itself and its resemblance to other known *oppida*, pp. 63–5, and on the dating, p. 69.

[4] Loeschcke, *MAKW* v (1909), p. 141, n. 2.

[5] Ulbert, *Die römische Donaukastellen Aislingen und Burghöfe*, p. 82.

should be considered as giving no more than a *terminus ante quem*. Nor is the nature of the Roman occupation yet clear. Barracks are reported, and three fine daggers attest the presence of legionaries.[1] Terraces cut into the steep slope of the higher of the twin peaks, which have not been excavated,[2] closely resemble the building platforms constructed in this way in the Magdalensberg, a native *oppidum* in which Roman merchants and the Roman administration also established themselves. Whether there is in fact any real parallel is a question which, like so many others, awaits further excavation before an answer can be expected.[3]

4. 5. THE LORENZBERG AT EPFACH

The Lorenzberg is an isolated knoll on the left bank of the Lech close by the village of Epfach (Abodiacum). High steep cliffs across the river on the right bank look down on it and cut off any view to the east. If you drive up from the west, from the direction of Kempten and the Auerberg, the Lorenzberg cannot be seen at all, until you come over the brow of the hill at Epfach and look down into the valley. It commands that stretch of the valley in which it stands, but nothing more.[4] A small Augustan fort for a mixed detachment of cavalry and legionaries stood here, and a fort here is inexplicable except to control the river-crossing, since that is all it can control. There can be no doubt at all that during the period when they were occupying the Lorenzberg, the Romans were using the road which crosses the Lech at this point. To the east this road continues to Gauting where it links up with the pre-Roman road leading from Noricum via Salzburg to Augsburg and on to the Danube and beyond. Westwards the road links the Lorenzberg with the Auerberg, Kempten, Bregenz, and the Augustan forts of North Switzerland, Oberwinterthur,

---

[1] Frank and Jacobs, op. cit., pp. 67–8 (barracks), 71–3 (daggers); further, Ulbert in *Aus Bayerns Frühzeit*, pp. 175–85.

[2] Cf. Frank and Jacobs, op. cit., pp. 68–9.

[3] Dr. Ulbert had kindly informed me that his first three years of digging have yielded neither Late La Tène nor Augustan finds. There is however evidence of iron-working on the hill in Roman times, which raises the question whether the Roman occupation was primarily dictated by military or by other considerations. Cf. also now Schönberger, *JRS* lix (1969), p. 188, no. 44.

[4] Ulbert, *Der Lorenzberg bei Epfach*, pp. 1–3, with photographs, plates C, D.

Vindonissa, and Basle.[1] The presence of an Augustan fort on
the Lorenzberg is a strong argument for the conjecture that
the intervening points were also garrisoned from the earlier
part of Augustus' reign on.

There can be no doubt that the fort on the Lorenzberg is
Augustan. The excavations in 1953–7 brought to light not
only quantities of military finds (including a *pilum*-head, a
spearhead, and a spear-butt)[2] but sufficient coins and pottery
to enable us to determine the dates of the Roman occupation.
The coins include 17 bronze coins of the reign of Augustus, 1
of them halved, the most frequent issues being those of the
tresviri IV of 3–2 B.C. (5 in all) and Lugdunum I (4). There
are 7 coins of Tiberius' reign, 1 of Caligula's, and 2 whole
and 2 halved Republican *asses*. After Caligula the series breaks
off.[3] The pottery includes Service I sigillata, though not I*a*.
Service II however predominates, as is natural at a site occupied into post-Augustan times.[4] Other significant finds included both Aco- and Sarius-ware.[5] Late Arretine, Po Valley,
and South Gaulish sigillata completes the picture. The site
appears to have been occupied at the same time as Oberhausen and abandoned in the middle of the 1st century.
Ulbert appears justified in his dating of the occupation to the
period ±10 B.C. to ±A.D. 50. There was also a second, completely separate, late Roman occupation. As Ulbert points
out, the Lorenzberg itself is small, and the area covered by the
early fort appears to have been only about 0·25 ha., enough
for a garrison of not more than eighty men, infantry and
cavalry together.[6]

4. 6. GAUTING

Reinecke, having assembled the evidence to show that Gauting
was the Roman Bratananium, at the point where the road

---

[1] On the importance of the road-system in this area, Wells, *SJ* xxviii (1970),
p. 68 with p. 69, fig. 3.

[2] Ulbert, op. cit., pp. 45–7.

[3] Ibid., pp. 35–41, pointing out that earlier finds stated to be from the Lorenzberg (list, p. 35) are largely not, and that this list should therefore be ignored; cf.
FMRD i. 1, pp. 242–58.

[4] Ulbert, op. cit., pp. 51–64.

[5] Ibid., pp. 64–8; see also below, p. 263.   [6] Ibid., pp. 33–4.

from Bregenz and Kempten joined the Salzburg–Augsburg road,[1] later reports the chance find of a cellar there, containing South Gaulish sigillata, coarse pottery, brooches, and other finds, which Reinecke dates to the period A.D. 20–46.[2] No specifically military finds were made. These finds from the cellar are the earliest yet made at Gauting, but they provide no more than a *terminus ante quem* for the start of Roman occupation. Whether it was civil or military occupation is not known. It is a reasonable conjecture that a fort lay there or in the vicinity from early Tiberian times or earlier, since the Lorenzberg fort would seem to show that the Romans from Augustan times onwards were using the road leading thence to Gauting, but to speak of an early Tiberian fort at Gauting on the basis of Reinecke's two articles is to go beyond the evidence, which shows only that there was Roman occupation of some sort here, probably beginning not later than Tiberius' reign.

4. 7. AUGSBURG–OBERHAUSEN

Oberhausen, once a village outside Augsburg, is now a suburb of it, separated from the town proper by the River Wertach. It is commonly supposed that there existed at this point a base for two legions under Augustus, although the only evidence is the finding before the First World War of a large quantity of Roman artefacts in a gravel-pit dug in an old river-bed beside the Wertach, and no trace of buildings or defences has ever been discovered. I have set out at length elsewhere why I believe this theory to be misconceived, and would refer my readers to that article for a full examination of the evidence and of the conflicting interpretations that are possible.[3]

The gravel-pits from which the finds in question came lay at the confluence of the Wertach and the little Hettenbach, about a mile above the point where the Wertach joins the Lech. The site is now occupied by a factory. The only excavation ever attempted took place in 1913, and brief

---

[1] Reinecke, *Bay. Vorgbl.* xviii/xix (1951/2), pp. 195–220.

[2] Id., *Bay. Vorgbl.* xxii (1957), pp. 96–9.

[3] Wells, *SJ* xxviii (1970), pp 63–72, with full refs. to original reports and publications of finds.

published accounts survive, but the original plans are lost. Apart from the finds themselves, the only structural feature observed was a massive revetment of the old river-bank. The excavators likened it to a landing-stage, in which case we might suppose that it was for the loading and unloading of supplies. It might on the other hand mark the site of a ferry, or else of a bridge.[1] Either would be easily explicable, since the route later to be known as the Via Claudia Augusta, established by Drusus as the main road from Italy over the Reschenscheideck Pass to the Danube, crossed the Wertach here or very close by.[2] The revetment might on the other hand be merely a defence against erosion. In any case it shows that this stretch of the river-bank had some particular importance for the Romans. The opposite bank of the old river-bed was not found, or not recognized, so that we do not know how wide the bed was, nor unfortunately do we have any clear indication of how great was the area of the gravel-pits. The excavators assumed right from the start that the finds represented the remains of a legionary base, eroded by the river. If this were so, however, one would expect some of the remains of the camp to have survived, yet no trace has ever been found, despite the watch that has been kept during the extensive construction work in the Oberhausen area over the last half-century.

One explanation for this may be that there was in fact no legionary base here, but only a small fort, perhaps in the angle between the Wertach and Lech, in the area known as the Pfannenstiel, where military equipment, including horse-gear, and cavalry gravestones have been found. A length of typical V-shaped defensive ditch with rampart postholes is also reported from this area, associated with Claudian finds, beneath the St. Sebastian church. The gravel-pit finds themselves contain much cavalry equipment, and a small fort here, which could watch the crossings over both Wertach and Lech, would fit in well with what was said above about the importance of the Lorenzberg–Gauting–Oberhausen triangle in the Roman system of communications.[3] A legionary base, on the other

[1] Cf. the quay or embankment beside the bridge, almost certainly Roman, crossing a tributary of the Lippe just east of Haltern, below, p. 165.

[2] *CIL* v. 8002: 'viam Claudiam Augustam quam Drusus pater Alpibus bello patefactis derexerat'. See Ulbert, *Der Lorenzberg bei Epfach*, p. 95.

[3] See above, p. 71.

hand, would more naturally have occupied the Augsburg hill itself, the site of the later civil settlement of Augusta Vindelicorum, which excavation has shown to have been first occupied late in Tiberius' reign, although it is just the sort of commanding site beside a river which the Augustan generals often chose for their legionary bases, as for instance at Vetera, Oberaden, Haltern, and Mainz.

Even if there was a Roman fort in the vicinity of the Oberhausen find-spot, however, it does not necessarily follow that the finds came from the erosion of this fort. They might have been spilt in the river as a result of an accident or accidents to boats or wagons. Goods being brought by wagon or pack-animal from Italy or Gaul along what was to become the Via Claudia Augusta, including supplies for Roman forces operating beyond the Danube, will have had to cross the Wertach at this point, or possibly have been loaded into boats for shipment onwards, and wagons may have overturned or boats capsized, dumping their contents into the river, which has a strong current, especially in the spring. The most we can say for certain is that we do not know exactly how the finds got into the river, nor their actual connection with the fort, so that we are not entitled to use the dates for the earliest and latest finds as evidence for the dates at which this fort was established and abandoned. In any case the evidence of coins and of sigillata is conflicting.[1] It might be suggested, purely as a hypothesis, that the fort may have been occupied over roughly the same period as the Lorenzberg was, from soon after the conquest until the reign of Claudius. Dates remain obscure; but at least we can be certain that the supposed legionary base at Oberhausen should disappear from histories, and be replaced by a conjectural fort to guard the river-crossing.

[1] Goudineau, *Bolsena* iv: *La Céramique arétine lisse*, p. 315: 'L'argument des numismates [sc. on the date of Oberhausen] se fonde sur l'aspect plus ancien du "faciès numismatique" de Haltern; mais on peut rétorquer que la confrontation des "faciès céramologiques" conduit à des conclusions opposées.'

PART II

THE PERIOD OF CONFIDENT
EXPANSION

5

THE BASES ON THE RHINE

THE date when legionary bases were first established on the
Rhine itself is obscure, like much else in the history of Gaul
between the departure of Caesar and the start of Drusus'
campaigns in 12 B.C. Caesar left Gaul conquered, but not
wholly acquiescent; troops were needed for internal security,
and the Rhine frontier had to be defended. After the civil wars
which followed Caesar's death and the subsequent agreement
with Antony which we sometimes know as the Peace of Brun-
disium, Octavian significantly judged it necessary to send his
best lieutenant, Agrippa, to stabilize the situation in Gaul.[1]
Agrippa put down disturbances, laid out a strategic road-
system based on Lugdunum (Lyons), and confirmed the Ubii
in possession of the territory which they had occupied around
the site of what was to become Cologne (Oppidum Ubiorum).
The Ubii, good farmers who could be relied upon to defend
their rich new lands, had crossed the river some time between
Caesar's departure and Agrippa's arrival, no doubt when the
Romans were too busy with internal struggles to stop them.[2]

Within the next ten years we hear of fighting against re-
bellious tribes or invaders from across the Rhine by three
Roman commanders, C. Carrinas, Nonius Gallus, and M.
Valerius Messalla Corvinus.[3] Then in 25 M. Vinicius led a
punitive expedition into Germany to avenge murdered Roman
traders, and earned for Augustus an imperatorial salutation.[4]

---

[1] Appian, BC v. 386; Dio xlviii. 49. 3.

[2] Schmitz, Klio xxxiv (1942), pp. 239–63; id., Stadt und Imperium, pp. 38–40;
id., Colonia Claudia Ara Agrippinensium, pp. 22–4; cf. Nierhaus, BJ cliii (1953), pp.
48–9; von Petrikovits, Das römische Rheinland, pp. 16, 85. On the Ubii as farmers,
Pliny, NH xvii. 47. See also above, p. 27.

[3] Carrinas triumphed 30 May, 28 (CIL i², p. 77), cf. Dio li. 21. 6; Nonius Gallus
saluted as imperator (ILS 895), cf. Dio li. 20. 5; Messalla triumphed 25 Sept. 27
(CIL i², pp. 50, 77, cf. Tib. i. vii. 3–12).

[4] Dio liii. 26. 4.

In 20–19 we again hear of unrest and raids; Agrippa in his second governorship rapidly restored order.[1] Throughout this time the old Gallic *oppida* continued to be occupied, even including such notable centres of resistence as Avaricum (Bourges) and Alesia (Alise-Sainte-Reine), while excavation reveals increasing use of Roman goods, including sigillata, most notably perhaps at Bibracte (Mont Beuvray).[2] Trade and wealth were increasing, and the Roman rulers eager to spread the blessings of peace. In 27 Augustus himself was in Gaul to address the tribal nobility and institute a census, the prelude to regular taxation.[3] In 22 Narbonensis, which had especially benefited from the benefactions of Augustus and Agrippa, was handed over to the jurisdiction of the Senate.[4] The remainder of Gaul, together with the army, remained under Augustus' own direct control.

The army throughout this period would appear to have been concentrated in three areas, in Aquitania, and in the territories of the Lingones (Plateau de Langres) and the Remi.[5] The latter two areas were logistically and strategically important, the Plateau de Langres especially so after the opening-up of the Great St. Bernard and the route from Italy through Helvetia to the Rhine in 25.[6] Nothing however permits us to decide when the legions moved their bases from these areas up to the

[1] Dio liv. 11. 1–2.

[2] Archaeologically most important is Bibracte (Mont Beuvray), discussed below, Appendix II; sigillata in Déchelette, *Les Fouilles du Mont Beuvray*, pp. 26, 54–5, 65, pl. 22. Sigillata closely resembling that from Bibracte also found on the Titelberg (Luxemburg), a site which cries out for excavation: Steinhausen, *Arch. Siedlungskunde des Trierer Lands*, pp. 275–6; Koethe, *Germania* xxi (1937), p. 104; von Petrikovits, op. cit., p. 34, n. 40; on sigillata, Oxé, *Germania* xxii (1938), pp. 236–40; further, with photographs of site, *Tetelbierg, site archéologique*. List of *oppida* where there is evidence for continued occupation after Roman conquest by Cotton in Wheeler and Richardson, *Hill Forts of Northern France*, pp. 180–98, with refs. [ADD.]

[3] Dio liii. 22. 5; Livy, *epit.* 134.

[4] Dio liv. 4. 1, cf. Balty, *Revue belge de philologie* xxxviii (1960), pp. 59–73. [ADD.]

[5] Ritterling, *BJ* cxiv/cxv (1906), pp. 159–88, an article justly described as 'grundlegend'; our knowledge of where the legions were in Gaul between Caesar's departure and their move to the Rhine has unfortunately advanced hardly at all since Ritterling wrote. Augustan forts, perhaps to guard a road network, are however known or suspected on the basis of early Italian sigillata at various sites, especially in Gallia Belgica, e.g. Heerlen (near Aachen), Liberchies, Bavai, Tongres, Trier, Rheims, Soissons, Arlaines, La Hérie (Aisne), Troyes, etc.; cf. Schönberger, *JRS* lix (1969), pp. 146–7. On Italian sigillata from Langres, see briefly Drioux, *Pro Alesia* xii/xiv (1926/8), pp. 132–4. [ADD.]

[6] Stevens, *JRS* xxvi (1936), p. 126.

Rhine bank itself. It must have been before the start of Drusus' campaigns.

These campaigns were not improvised at short notice: as we have seen in Chapters 3 and 4, plans and preparations for the conquest of Germany go back to the twenties, before even the war in Spain was over, and certainly to before 17, when M. Lollius, then legate in Gaul, suffered a reverse in a German raid, a reverse which the malice of his enemies dignified with the appellation of *clades Lolliana*.[1] Such a raid was, as we have seen, nothing unusual, and when Augustus himself came to Gaul the following year, everything was quiet.[2] He spent three years there, supervising in person the final preparations for the campaigns of 12 and the following years.[3] Perhaps on his arrival the Rhine bases were established, perhaps earlier, in 18 or 17, when the long-awaited end of the war in Spain released troops for service in Gaul.[4] The archaeological evidence which might help to decide is not forthcoming.[5] Although we now know where the Rhine bases were, in no case can we securely and accurately date the first occupation of the site by a legionary garrison.

Six legionary bases of the Augustan period are known on the Lower and Middle Rhine, all of which are discussed in detail in Chapter 5. 1–5. 5 and 5. 8. Of these Vechten (Fectio), Vetera (near Xanten), Neuss (Novaesium), and Mainz (Mogontiacum) belong to the period of Drusus' campaigns; Nijmegen (Noviomagus) appears to be late Augustan; and from Cologne (Oppidum Ubiorum) the evidence suggests that the site was occupied before A.D. 9, although we cannot tell how long before. The

---

[1] Dio liv. 20. 4–6; Suet., *Aug.* 23. 1; Vell. ii. 97; Tac., *Ann.* i. 10. 3; Julius Obsequens 71, to whom we owe the date, cf. Syme, *JRS* xxiii (1933), p. 17, n. 23, and Ritterling, *RE* xii, col. 1571; one legion, probably *V Alaudae*, lost its eagle, but apparently it was soon recovered, see Syme, op. cit., pp. 17–19. On the true importance of the incident, Syme, *The Roman Revolution*, p. 429; yet even Ritterling holds it responsible for Augustus' decision to invade Germany, op. cit., col. 1225.

[2] Dio liv. 19. 1, 20. 6.

[3] Dio liv. 25. 1.

[4] Cf. Syme, *JRS* xxiii (1933), pp. 22–3.

[5] The places to look for it might be the areas indicated above as those where the legions were based before the move to the Rhine. A survey of early sigillata and coin finds, backed by thorough field-work might lead to the identification of one or more legionary sites, the excavation of which would elucidate not only this problem, but that referred to below, the development of Caesar's temporary *hiberna* into the more permanent Augustan bases found on the Rhine.

first occupation of Strasbourg (Chapter 5. 9) by a legion appears to be early in Tiberius' reign.

The purpose of the bases at Vechten, Vetera, and Mainz is clear: they stand at the head of the three main invasion routes which our sources record not only Drusus, but later Germanicus also, as using. Vechten was apparently under Drusus, as later, a naval base and stores depot. Closely associated with it was the canal built by Drusus, the *fossa Drusiana*, which made the River Vecht into a navigable water-way and so enabled the Roman fleet to sail from the Rhine into the IJesselmeer (Zuider Zee) and thence along the Frisian coast to the mouths of the Rivers Ems, Weser, and Elbe. Both Drusus and Germanicus mounted amphibious operations along this route.

Vetera, near Xanten, faces the mouth of the River Lippe. The Lippe valley was a great invasion highway into the heart of North Germany; the various Roman military sites which have been discovered along the river are discussed below in Chapters 6. 1–6. 4. Both at Vetera and at Neuss, some 50 km. further south, the remains of six successive legionary installations of different sizes and layouts, all of the Augustan or Tiberian periods, were found, quite distinct from the stone-built Claudian fortresses erected on the same site (at Vetera) or on one nearby (at Neuss).

At Neuss the legionary base was preceded by a much smaller fort, dating from some time in the third decade B.C., and superseded by a legionary base for two legions, probably during the next decade. This was replaced by a four-legion base, but later ones were for a single legion. From Vetera also a two-legion base is known, but the fact that here the Claudian fortress was built over the Augustan–Tiberian remains, and the relatively early date of the excavations on the site, combine to make our information far less complete than it is at Neuss.

The third invasion-route (for there is no invasion-route directly facing Neuss) is that leading via the Lower Main either northwards through the Wetterau to link up with the Lippe route on the Upper Weser or in the Teutoburger Wald area, or east and south-eastwards along the Main itself and its other tributaries. Directly opposite the mouth of the Main stood the legionary base at Mainz, presumably founded some time before 12 B.C., and continuing in existence on the same site throughout the Roman period. There were other military installations nearby, and the Rhine-crossing below the base was in use, whether or not a bridgehead fort on the right bank was already established at this time, as it certainly was later.

Of the two remaining Rhine bases previously mentioned, Nijmegen lay in an area inhabited by Rome's Batavian allies. Evidence to date suggests that the base was occupied only briefly in the latter part of Augustus' reign, and that the site was then abandoned until Flavian times. Apart from native settlements nearby, there was also a fort, occupied probably by native auxiliaries and dating from the time of Drusus' campaigns. At Cologne both a base for two legions and a summer camp for four in the vicinity are mentioned by Tacitus; archaeologists have identified the site of the base, without however adding to our knowledge of its history.

A number of forts are also known, although over half a century of intensive search has failed to produce evidence to support Florus' statement that Drusus established over fifty such forts on the Rhine bank alone.[1] There were forts at Nijmegen and, preceding the legionary bases, at Neuss and Strasbourg. To these should be added Asberg (Asciburgium), where excavation has revealed three successive forts of the late Augustan, Tiberian, and Claudian periods, with pottery that includes a considerable quantity of Italian sigillata;[2] Bonn and Koblenz, discussed below in Chapter 5. 6 and 5. 7; probably Andernach, and Urmitz;[3] Bingen, where an Augustan or early Tiberian fort guarded the crossing of the River Nahe; and now Speyer.[4] No other site can be shown to have been

---

[1] Florus ii. 30. 26; unnecessarily emended to Ems–Lippe–Weser, cf. von Petrikovits, *Das römische Rheinland*, p. 34, n. 38. Ritterling's conjectural list, *BJ* cxiv/cxv (1906), p. 177, has been very influential and lies behind many of the later lists, often unacknowledged, cf. Schumacher, *Siedlungs- und Kulturgeschichte der Rheinland* ii, pp. 20–30; Stähelin, *Die Schweiz in römischer Zeit*, pp. 118–19; rejected by Schleiermacher in *Analecta Archaeologica*, pp. 231–3; cf. also von Petrikovits, op. cit., pp. 33–4. Rüger, *Germania Inferior*, pp. 18–19, rightly points out that it is anachronistic to expect 50 forts strung along the river bank, 'im Sinne einer späteren Defensiv-Konzeption'.

[2] Tischler, *Duisburger Forschungen* ii (1959), pp. 162–88; von Petrikovits, op. cit., pp. 13, 51. [ADD.]

[3] Filtzinger, *BJ* clx (1960), pp. 168–9; Nesselhauf, *JRGZ* vii (1960), p. 157; von Petrikovits, *Das römische Rheinland*, p. 15, n. 12. [ADD.]

[4] On Bingen, see below, Appendix II, p. 283. The finds from Speyer do not

occupied before Tiberian times; it must remain an open question whether more forts were established under Tiberius to guard the vital Rhine-bank road when the territory east of the Rhine was given up, or whether further Augustan forts still remain to be found.[1]

At Neuss, in addition to the Augustan–Tiberian legionary installations, the extensive remains of the *canabae* belonging to them were also found on the so-called Selssche Zeigelei site. Similar remains outside the defences have also been found at Mainz, Haltern, Wiesbaden, Höchst-am-Main and Basle. Such *canabae* are not to be confused with the quite different civil settlements which commonly grew up a mile or two away from the legionary base, often clearly separated from it by the graves lining the road between the two. Such a civil settlement, later to develop into the Colonia Ulpia Traiana, already existed in Augustan times at Vetera, north-west of the legionary base,[2] whereas the civil settlement at Neuss, on the other hand, cannot be traced back before the middle of the first century.[3] There are other examples of settlements developing under the protection of, but at some distance from, a legionary base, as at Nijmegen, Cologne, Strasbourg, Carnuntum, and Burnum (Šuplja Crkva, in Dalmatia).[4]

I have deliberately retained the word *canabae* for these agglomerations outside the defences. In the Augustan period the ovens and workshops of the legion were still located inside the fortress, as we clearly see at Vetera, Haltern, Oberaden, Mainz. Later, perhaps because of the danger of fire, they were moved outside. Once this happened, we find the *canabae* starting to be laid out in regular military style, until by the beginning of the second century they and their inhabitants were strictly administered in para-military fashion. But they

suggest a date as early as the time of Drusus, cf. Schönberger, *JRS* lix (1969), p. 145; they are however not yet published in any detail, and I am grateful to Dr. O. Roller for discussing them with me.

[1] The evidence for Roman sites from A.D. 16 to A.D. 69 is now conveniently summarized by Schönberger, op. cit., pp. 151–5.

[2] Von Petrikovits, op. cit., p. 103.

[3] Ibid., p. 106.

[4] On Burnum, see Patsch, *RE* iii, col. 1070; Wilkes, 'Studies in the Roman Province of Dalmatia', p. 279; the civil settlement was at Ivoševci, some two miles from the base. On the distinction between such civil settlements and *canabae*, see Mócsy, *AArchHung.* iii (1953), pp. 184–6. [ADD.]

began as an irregular huddle to accommodate the petty traders and the like, the unofficial camp-followers who ministered to the army's wants. The process has been excellently described by Mócsy, while Baatz, with adequate support from literary sources, has well emphasized the difference between the regular baggage-train of the army, which marched with it and camped with it inside the *vallum*, and the unofficial camp-followers.[1] Von Petrikovits has emphasized that *canabae* in the strict sense, which means *canabae* laid out in military style and accommodating the legionary workshops, do not exist before the Claudian period, whence the somewhat greater extent of the pre-Claudian bases.[2] This is true, but I do not think we need scruple to use the term *canabae* of the pre-Claudian settlements of traders outside the *vallum*, which archaeology has clearly shown to exist. To suppose, on the strength of von Petrikovits's argument, that in the Augustan–Tiberian period there cannot be any remains outside the fortifications, is quite wrong.[3]

These legionary bases of the Augustan period appear to have been permanent or semi-permanent bases, from which the army operated and was supplied, unlike the camps of Caesar's day in Gaul, which were *hiberna* in the literal sense, abandoned each summer and rebuilt each winter. This was denied by Lehner, arguing that the six successive camps or bases of the Augustan–Tiberian period at Vetera showed them still to be, literally, *hiberna* only.[4] But as von Petrikovits pointed out, on Lehner's theory, one would expect, not six, but twenty-five or more.[5] Citing the parallel of Neuss and observing that more permanent wooden buildings might have been found at Vetera with modern techniques of excavation, he argues that Vetera and Neuss were permanent bases, and that the successive re-buildings are due to the fact that wooden buildings have only a comparatively short life-span. Wood was used because there was a plentiful supply of it to hand and because, no

[1] Mócsy, op. cit., p. 179; on later organization of *canabae*, pp. 180, 182–4; also Baatz, *Germania* xlii (1964), pp. 260–5.

[2] Von Petrikovits, op. cit., pp. 55–72; cf. id., *Neue Ausgrabungen in Deutschland* p. 289; id., *BJ* clxi (1961), pp. 459, 478–9.

[3] Cf. below, on Wiesbaden (Chapter 6. 5).

[4] Lehner, *Vetera* (1930), pp. 8, 12.

[5] Von Petrikovits, *RE* viiiA, cols. 1815–16.

doubt, the army was not building for permanence.[1] Stone came in on the Rhine and Danube with Claudius. By that time there was no longer any thought of conquering Germany.

The short life-span of wooden buildings does not however of itself account for the complete replanning and rebuilding of the bases at Vetera and Neuss. That at Mainz was built of wood too, and whatever repairs were needed here were carried out without razing the existing installations and starting afresh. Indeed, even if the buildings had to be rebuilt, why scrap the defences? It is always easier to recut or reopen old ditches than to build new ones. Curle once wrote to Haverfield: 'If Lollius Urbicus returned tomorrow to establish a fort at Makendon, it would be twenty times easier to clear out the old ditches than to begin afresh, and that is after 1,700 years of weather in the Cheviots.'[2] If the base had to be replanned for a garrison of a different size, a fresh start is explicable, but at Neuss bases D, E, and F all appear to be the same size. Was it perhaps thought to be good training for the men to build a new camp, perhaps on reoccupying a site after a year or two's absence? For it seems that we should allow for such absences. From about 10 B.C. to A.D. 9 one legion at least, if not more, was permanently stationed in Germany, as the evidence from Oberaden and Haltern shows (Chapter 6. 3 and 6. 2).[3] Were the left-bank bases kept up as well? In A.D. 4, according to Velleius, the whole army wintered in Germany, so that the bases on the Rhine cannot have had more than a holding garrison at the most.[4] The upper army appears to have had one regular base only, Mainz, just as it had only one gateway into Germany, namely the Lower Main, whereas the lower army, responsible for the Lippe, for amphibious operations along the coast from Vechten, for watching (from 8 B.C. onwards) the transplanted Sugambri and Suebi, needed more than one. The bases were permanent or semi-permanent, built for more than one winter's occupation, but legions might be transferred from one to another as the situation demanded. In A.D. 14, for instance, when for once we have definite

[1] Cf. Oelmann, *Germania* iv (1920), p. 7, n. 1.

[2] Letter from Curle to Haverfield, dated 2 March 1913, bound into a copy of Curle, *A Roman Frontier Post and its People*, in the Haverfield Library, Oxford.

[3] On strength of Haltern garrison see Syme, *Germania* xvi (1932), pp. 109–11.

[4] Vell. ii. 105. 3.

information, we learn that the four legions of the lower army were divided between Vetera and Cologne, which means that the other bases, Vechten, Nijmegen, and Neuss, had no regular garrison at this time.[1]

5. I. VECHTEN AND THE *FOSSA DRUSINA*

Ritterling in 1906 recognized Vechten (Fectio) and Nijmegen as the only Roman sites of indisputably Augustan date in what is now Holland;[2] this is still so. Vechten, he points out, had even then yielded an exceptional quantity of what he called Arretine, that is to say, Italian sigillata. Indeed in the middle of the last century it was possible to pick up in a few minutes on the mound known as 'de Burg' at Vechten after ploughing a mass of Roman sherds, sigillata in particular, and a great quantity of Roman material had come into local collections without any sort of organized excavation, quite apart from the finds that must have been taken away and dispersed before scientific interest was aroused.[3]

In 1870 the Dutch authorities built a fort, part of which now overlies the old Roman site, and in the course of the building the Roman layers were destroyed over a large area (fig. 3). This construction work, however, and a small archaeological excavation in 1892–4 sensibly increased the amount of Roman pottery from the site. Holwerda followed Ritterling in restricting proved Augustan date to Vechten and Nijmegen alone in Holland, regretting that no properly organized scientific excavation had taken place and deploring the excavations by incompetents, which had caused great damage.[4] It was given to Holwerda himself to conduct the first skilled investigation of the site and his excavation in 1914 revealed the first trace

---

[1] Tac., *Ann.* i. 31. 3. Cf. also Schönberger, op. cit., p. 145, coming independently to the same conclusion.

[2] Ritterling, *BJ* cxiv/cxv (1906), pp. 179–80; cf. Kropatschek, *RGKbl.* ii (1909), p. 7, commenting on the early LSG and Tettius sigillata stamps, on which cf. Oxé–Comfort, *Corpus vasorum arretinorum*: LSG is relatively common at Mainz, Xanten, and Oberaden, and is found at Bibracte, Oberwinterthur and Nijmegen (Kopse Hof).

[3] Janssen, *Jb. Altfr. Rh.* ix (1846), pp. 20–35.

[4] Holwerda, *BerRGK* iv (1908), pp. 86–8; on two pieces of leather from the excavations of 1892–4 see also van Hoorn, *Berichten van de Rijksdienst voor het Oudheidkundig Bodemonderzoek in Nederland* iv (1953), pp. 13–14.

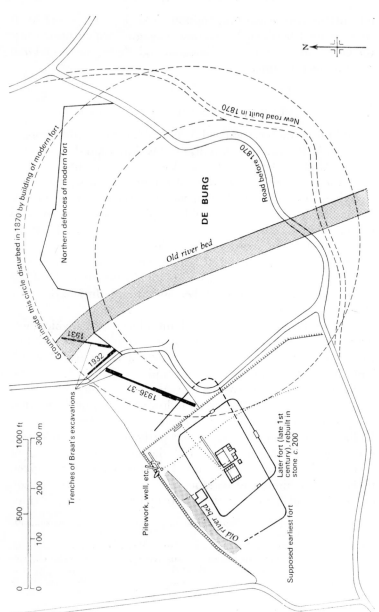

FIG. 3. Vechten: plan of site

of Roman fortifications.[1] The ditches which he found yielded
a little pottery, mostly of the middle of the first century, but
including two pieces which Holwerda judged to be Augustan
or Tiberian. The upper levels of the site yielded more Augustan
pieces, a late Augustan cup of Italian sigillata, and finds rang-
ing down to Domitianic times. Nowhere did he find any post-
Flavian remains or artefacts, and he suggested that this was a
fort occupied for most of the first century and destroyed or
abandoned under Domitian.

Between the wars further excavations took place, under
Holwerda in 1920–1, Remouchamps in 1922–6, and Braat
in 1931–2 and 1936–7.[2] Holwerda's and Remouchamp's
excavations revealed three forts, the first of wood, dated to the
beginning of the first century, the second also of wood, and the
third of stone. Of the earliest fort, the defences on the south and
west were known; on the north it was thought to have had
neither ditch nor rampart, but to have relied for protection
on the Rhine, which came right up to the fort on this side in
Roman times. This however is unlikely. On this low-lying
site the river-bank offered no obstacle to attackers, and the
river itself was no defence against men who could swim
or had boats. It is better to say that the defences of the fort on
the riverside have not been found. Along the old river-bank,
however, were found wooden piles, of undetermined significance. In the second half of the first century the site had been
artificially raised some 2 m. and a new, rather smaller, wooden
fort built, to be rebuilt in stone about 200; the whole circuit
of its fortifications was traced.

Braat's own excavations lay mostly to the east of the area
previously excavated. Here he found what he took for the
remains of a sort of quay or landing-stage, which we shall
consider in a moment. He also discovered the east side of
Holwerda's and Remouchamps's Augustan fort, traced it
northwards to the old river-bank, found the east gate, and

---

[1] Holwerda, *Germania* i (1917), pp. 57–60.

[2] Holwerda, *Germania* v (1921), pp. 22–5; Remouchamps, *Opgravingen te Vechten*;
Braat, *OMRL* xx (1939), pp. 47–63, with English résumé, pp. 64–5, summarizing
Holwerda's and Remouchamps's findings and reporting on his own; see also briefly
Remouchamps, *Jaarverslag van het Provinciaal Utrechtsch Genootschap* 1928; a brief
account of the history of excavations at Vechten by van Giffen appeared in *Quint.
Cong. Int. Lim. Rom. Stud.*, pp. 142–3.

noted the traces of posts and post-holes along the outer face
and in parts along the inner face also of the rampart on this
side. A trial trench extending from the rampart westwards some
25 m. into the interior of the fort yielded no trace of occupation,
save for one well. All higher levels had been destroyed in
1870.

Braat's east side was again excavated over part of its length
when excavation resumed after the Second World War under
the direction of van Giffen.[1] There were the posts again, the
V-shaped ditch 5·4 m. wide and at least 1·4 m. deep, and in
addition van Giffen found a tower 4 m. square. A few posts
were duplicated, indicating repairs. Van Giffen confirmed the
dating arrived at by his predecessors; the remains belonged
to 'the first decennia A.D.'. The whole site however was revealed
by van Giffen's investigation to be far more complicated than
previously suspected. The mound on which the remains lay
was a purely artificial construction, all Roman, apart from the
works of 1870 and typical of the low mounds known as 'terpen'
raised above the flat Dutch plain by the debris of successive
occupations. Another such mound is the site of Valkenburg,
occupied by the Romans first in Claudian times, extensively
and brilliantly excavated by van Giffen, the acknowledged
master of the technique of excavating in these most difficult
conditions. At Vechten the mound was 'raised in several stages
on and over the former Rhine-bed', and stratification revealed
at least five different layers of different periods at heights of
from 2·5 to 4·3 m. above sea-level, the bottom four strata being
marked by burnt layers.

Van Giffen distinguished not only the three periods of
building which his predecessors had identified, but more beside, so-called 'outworks'' lying in part beneath the two later
Holwerda–Remouchamps forts, and 'a number of variously
orientated buildings', including three *horrea* and a very large
oblong building around a square courtyard. From the evidence
of these 'habitation layers, ramparts and ditches', van Giffen
concluded that there was 'a total of at least eight different
periods of Roman building'. And he observed: 'The finds
outside the ditch of the stone fortress were nearly all

---

[1] Van Giffen, *Jaarverslag van de Vereeniging voor Terpenonderzoek* xxix/xxxii (1944/
8), pp. 50–6, with somewhat abridged English version, pp. 56–8.

pre-Claudian.' It is clear that, while the earlier excavations were correct as far as they went, they had failed to find a great deal which van Giffen's experience in the conditions of such sites enabled him to observe and interpret correctly.

In the course of his excavations, van Giffen succeeded in tracing an old river-bed underlying the Roman fort over a stretch of 110 m. Some 36 m. wide and 11 m. deep, it ran roughly from north-east to south-west. Another river-bed, 60 m. wide and 6 m. deep, running more or less at right angles to this one, was discovered in 1870 under the modern fort then being built, and Braat speaks of yet a third, an arm of the river already silted up in Roman times, apparently west of and parallel to that discovered in 1870.[1] There was, however, no trace of flooding during Roman times. This is consistent with the evidence from excavations by van Giffen at two other Roman sites, Valkenburg and Utrecht: 'No trace whatever was found of flooding in Roman times and there is no evidence for the construction of dikes or embankments to keep out the water, not even where they might reasonably be expected.'[2] Valkenburg was first flooded some time between the third century A.D. and the Carolingian period,[3] and evidence from North Holland suggests that a rise in the sea level occurred perhaps about 400, affecting the coastline and causing for the first time flooding on sites which previously were free from it.[4]

So far our account has dealt with the area known to have been occupied by the successive Roman forts. The greater part of Braat's excavations, however, lay outside this area, in the area east and north-east of this fort, where Remouchamps had found traces of pilework of undetermined significance along the bank of the old river-bed which delineated the north side of the fort. Braat set out in 1931 and 1932 to see what the pilework might be. His trenches extended for nearly 300 m. to the north-east of the fort itself (though the position of the east side of the fort was not yet known) and revealed further

---

[1] Braat, op. cit., p. 58.

[2] Van Giffen in *Congress of Roman Frontier Studies, 1949*, p. 38; Braat however had, wrongly as it appears, supposed the site to have been artificially raised against flooding in the second half of the first century A.D., op. cit., p. 48, with p. 49, plan 36.

[3] Ibid., p. 39.

[4] Id., *Jaarvers. Ver. v. Terpenonderzoek* xxix/xxxii (1944/8), p. 58.

pilework and other remains of timber constructions. Braat interpreted these remains as those of 'a sort of embankment, built of clay and treetrunks, lying horizontally and kept together by piles, rammed in the earth. This embankment was necessary in order to reach the deeper navigable passage in the middle of the river, for ships could not come up to the bank.'[1] The term which Braat uses most frequently in the Dutch text to describe this construction is however 'aanleg-steiger', of which 'landing-stage' would seem a better translation than 'embankment', and indeed 'landing-stage' better describes what he thought he had found.

The remains of this construction were again found in the trenches dug in 1936–7, giving the 'embankment' a known length of at least 550 m., with its full extent still unrevealed. In the low-lying ground between the so-called embankment and the then still-undiscovered east side of the fort Braat in 1936 discovered another, similar construction, consisting of 'long rows of posts and postholes', which at first he took for remains of barracks, but, he explains, 'at a further examination the groundplan proved to have nothing in common with that of any known barracks and moreover these remains were only found in the lowest part of the meadow, probably a moor [sic! better, morass] or silted-up river-arm in Roman times'.[2] The reason why Braat at first interpreted these remains as those of barracks is interesting: 'We had always thought that the oldest fort had stretched along the whole length of the embankment and reckoned with the possibility to find remains of its inner building on the . . . meadow' (the meadow, that is, lying immediately north-east of the forts). But with the finding the following year of the east side of the earliest of the three forts, Braat apparently concluded that the remains lying east and north-east of this could not belong to a fort, though he refers later on to 'those of Germanicus' troops that could not find room in this rather small fort'.

Now Braat formed the hypothesis that he was dealing with some sort of landing-stage ('een aanlegsteiger of -kade') in his very first season of digging at Vechten. The next year, 1932, he was consciously seeking evidence to prove his hypothesis, and

---

[1] Braat, op. cit., English summary, p. 64.
[2] Cf. further, ibid., p. 58.

thought he had found it. Yet if we examine closely the plan and section of the 1931 trench and the description of it in Braat's Dutch text,[1] it is not easy to see whence this hypothesis sprang. Braat was clearly himself at a loss to interpret the mass of building remains which he found, remains of at least two periods, for at one point, down at the level of the water table, he found not only a mass of pilework with one or two timbers lying amongst it, but also two wells, one of which was overlaid by a length of timber and was therefore, as Braat notes, of an earlier period. Nor need we wonder at his bewilderment, when we note that his trench, though nearly 110 m. long, was only 3 m. wide at one end and narrowed in two stages to less than half that width at the other.

The other major difficulty with which Braat had to contend, and which made it impossible for him to excavate down to undisturbed subsoil, was the level of the water table, now higher than in Roman times. For instance, the 20-metre-wide old river-bed which the 1931 trench crosses is clearly visible in the section. Over the greater part of this old watercourse the lowest layer reached was one or other of the layers which Braat himself assigns to the end of the first century. Again, in the 1932 excavations, at the south end of the trench, Braat got down to a layer of sand, but after about 8 m. it sinks below the lowest level excavated, and thereafter the lowest layer shown is either that assigned to the beginning of the first century, or 'veenachtige grond', or wooden posts or baulks resting on the bottom of Braat's trench, beneath which he did not dig. The earliest remains on the site were therefore never reached.

But if Braat did not find all that he might have done, what of the construction work that he did find, and took to be the remains of a landing-stage? A striking feature of both the 1932 and the 1936 and 1937 excavations was the great rafts of timber, held together by a frame of planking around the edges, which can clearly be seen in plan and sections alike; the purpose of these rafts, according to Braat, was to stretch out across the low-lying ground until the main channel of the river

---

[1] There are certain discrepancies between the plans and the sections of both 1931 and 1932 excavations, which however are not set out in detail in this present chapter. A fuller study will be found in my Oxford D.Phil. thesis, 'The Frontiers of the Roman Empire under Augustus', pp. 98–108.

was reached. Thus a landing-stage was created.[1] The main channel, he suggests, was flanked by a wide stretch of marshy land into which the river overflowed in winter, whence the need for an elaborate structure like this.

Braat compares this landing-stage with others known from Vetera and Haltern. The one at Vetera is quite unlike what we have here at Vechten, as Braat rightly points out, but rather surprisingly he suggests that the Haltern and Vechten examples are of similar construction. They are not, nor is the work at Haltern a landing-stage at all, but merely weiring to protect the river-bank against erosion, and not even Roman.[2] We are left with the Vetera example of what a Roman landing-stage did look like, and fortunately there are excellent photographs which show us great upright timbers, firmly planted, joined together by horizontal beams to form a solid, continuous wall—we may compare any modern landing-stage of similar type.[3] As Braat rightly says, it is quite different from the Vechten structure.

Is then the Vechten structure a landing-stage at all? The great rafts of logs, which Braat sees as forming the main body of the work, appear from plan and from photographs to resemble very closely the timber platforms for buildings found at, for instance, Valkenburg and Oberaden, both sites where, as probably was the case at Vechten also, mud was a problem.[4]

---

[1] Braat, op. cit., pp. 56–7, describes the rafts in the following terms: 'Wij zien een schoeiing van planken, door paaltjes op hun plaats gehouden, loopen in de lengterichting van de sleuf. Achter deze schoeiing boomstammen, dwars op de righting van de sleuf. Deze boomstammen lagen op een laag rijshout, grootendeels tot veen vergaan. Aaan het profiel kan men zien, dat er oorspronkelijk meer lagen boomstammen geweest moeten zijn, want een drietal is in het midden nog op hooger niveau blijven hangen.' The method of construction of the whole embankment is summed up thus: 'Dit geweldige damwerk is dus in perceelen gemaakt. Eerst heeft men langs den oever een strook gemaakt, toen weer een, toen nog een; vervolgens is men in perceelen, het eene tegen het andere aansluitend, verder de rivier in gaan uitbouwen, tottenslotte het diepere stroombed berikt werd . . . Het doel ervan is duidelijk; het is een aanlegplaats.'

[2] See below, pp. 207–11.

[3] Von Petrikovits, *Das römische Rheinland*, pl. 6, cf. p. 99; id., *BJ* clii (1952), pp. 138–55, with plates 21–4, cf. bibliography, p. 145, n. 80; Scheller, *BJ* clvii (1957), pp. 288–9, shows how closely a quay built at Lobito (Angola) in 1957 follows the Roman technique.

[4] Cf. esp. *OMRL* xx (1939), p. 52, fig. 41, and p. 54, fig. 43, with *Jaarvers. Ver. v. Terpenonderzoek* xxix/xxxii (1944/8), p. 9.

What on Braat's hypothesis lay between the rafts? How were they linked up? Why do we not find them in the 1931 trench? And suppose Braat to be correct, what are the buildings, of which we see traces in the 1931 trench, doing so far out into the embankment?

Then again there is the problem of the wells. We have mentioned the wells found in 1931; more wells were found in 1932 and 1936–7 and, as Braat himself states, not only on the river-bank, as he takes it, but also in the middle of the pilework of the landing-stage and covered by it,[1] where they must have been dug by troops before the landing-stage began to be built— and dug in the low-lying, marshy ground, subject to flooding, which later the landing-stage had to cover. Again, the scattered baulks and timbers at the north end of both 1931 and 1932 trenches are hard to fit into the plan of a landing-stage.

The construction in the low-lying ground immediately east of the east ditch of the fort has already been referred to. Braat decided it was not the remains of barracks, but a similar work to the main landing-stage, an embankment or bridge-work built up over marshy ground. It exhibits no trace of the most conspicuous feature of the main work, the rafts of timber. It again has wells underlying the later remains, and we note a further well underlying the front bedding-trench of the rampart of the east side of the fort. This seems conclusive evidence that the wells, or some of them, antedate not only the supposed embankment, but also the fortification of what is supposed to be the earliest fort on the site. Can the 'earliest fort' really be the earliest? And granted that these remains do not look like barracks, what resemblance is there between them and the remains exhibited in the 1931 and 1932 trenches? Unfortunately Braat does not publish a section of this part of the excavations. It seems unlikely, however, that he got down to undisturbed subsoil here, any more than he did else-where.

This failure to reach the lowest levels must also cast con-siderable doubt upon Braat's conclusions regarding the date of these remains. He thought that, in the words of his English summary, 'the pottery, found at the bottom [sc. of the embank-ment or landing-stage], between the woodwork, proved that

[1] Braat, op. cit., p. 60.

this embankment was built in the time of Tiberius, evidently
for the naval expedition of Germanicus in A.D. 16 to the mouth
of the river Eems'. The connection with the expedition of A.D.
16 is however not clearly supported by the evidence, for the
Tiberian sherds were in fact mixed with material dated as late
as A.D. 70,[1] which might equally well lead us to suppose that
the whole construction is Flavian, not Tiberian. It is of course
possible that the pilework was of sufficiently open construction
for the sherds to fall through after it was built. In this case
however it might date from the pre-Tiberian period, Drusus
rather than Germanicus.

Germanicus' forces, however, as Braat himself notes, were
too large for the rather small fort, and Braat suggests that
the *auxilia* must have camped outside, and that they dug the
wells. But who then built the landing-stage over the wells,
and where did the *auxilia* camp thereafter? If Vechten really
was Germanicus' base, as Braat assumes, it must have been a
supply base. Granaries will have been needed.[2] Where did
they lie? Not in the little 'Augustan' fort, which is in any case
later than the wells which Braat attributes to Germanicus'
auxiliaries. What Braat found is not a landing-stage, but the
remains of a large camp, complete with barracks, granaries,
and roadways, the limits and fortifications of which are not yet
known. This will have accommodated a large force, legionaries
or auxiliaries or both; we cannot say how long it was occupied.
If it were Germanicus' base, this would account for the preponderance of Tiberian pottery, and the later Flavian construction would lie on top of that belonging to the Tiberian
period. Vechten is epigraphically attested as a naval base at
least into the third century.[3] The upper layer may belong to
this period. The actual known fort, dated by van Giffen to 'the
first decennia A.D.' may belong to the period between Drusus
and Germanicus, when no large-scale naval operations were
undertaken, and a large base-camp did not need to be kept up.

[1] Braat, op. cit., p. 62: Tiberian sherds, which are not illustrated or described,
were found 'in de diepte tusschen de palen'; and again, 'onderin, tusschen het paal-
werk en het rijshout, had materiaal uit den tijd van Tiberius (tusschen Haltern en
Hofheim in) de overhand en verder reikte de chronologie tot omstreeks 70'.

[2] Cf. Tac., *Ann.* ii. 8. 1, 'praemisso commeatu'.

[3] Byvanck, *Excerpta Romana* ii, nos. 290, 291, 297, 302 (= *CIL* xiii. 8811, 8810,
8815, 12086a).

The sigillata finds from the area noted by Ritterling and others include early pieces from the time of Drusus. The absence of such finds in Braat's excavations may be due to his not having dug deep enough. Once we accept the Tiberian pottery as coming from an occupation under Germanicus, however, let us remember how Germanicus in A.D. 16, before setting sail, prayed to his father 'ut se eadem ausus . . . exemplo ac memoria consiliorum atque operum iuvaret'.[1] If Vechten was Germanicus' base, it was also Drusus'.

Why then was Vechten so important, maintaining, as we have seen, its importance into the third century? The answer lies almost certainly in the *fossa Drusiana*, referred to in ancient sources, identical with the River Vecht, which runs from the Old Rhine (Oude Rijn) near Vechten into the Ijsselmeer (formerly the Zuider Zee).[2] This identification was strongly urged by Ritterling,[3] arguing that this was a ship-canal, and challenging the old view that identified it with the Nieuwe Ijssel, which links the Rhine at Westervoort, above Arnhem, to the Ijssel.[4] The importance which the Romans attached to the Old Rhine branch of the river as a waterway is brought out by Tacitus in a passage where he refers to another of Drusus' engineering projects, the construction of what he calls a *moles*,[5] and the line of later Roman forts along the Old Rhine[6] corroborates what Tacitus says about its importance. We hear also of an *agger*,[7] and the controversy over the identity and the location of both *moles* and *agger* has greatly complicated that over the *fossa Drusiana* itself. Ritterling's identification of the latter with the Vecht was for instance immediately accepted by Holwerda, who put forward, not for the first time, the not unreasonable theory that the *moles* was some sort of complementary structure designed to make navigation easier on the

---

[1] Tac., *Ann.*, loc. cit.

[2] 'Fossa Drusiana' in Tac., *Ann.* ii. 8. 1; 'fossae Drusinae', Suet., *Claud.* 1; 'Drusianus' would appear the more normal form, on the analogy of 'theatrum Marcellianum' (Suet., *Vesp.* 19), 'clades Variana' (Suet., *Aug.* 23, 49, *et al.*), etc.; on *fossa* or *fossae*, see below, pp. 115/6.

[3] Ritterling, *BJ* cxiv/cxv (1906), pp. 179–80.

[4] So, e.g., Blink, *Forsch. zur deutschen Landes- und Volkskunde* iv. 2 (1889), pp. 93–5, and accepted without question by Furneaux ad Tac., *Ann.* ii. 8.

[5] Tac., *Hist.* v. 19.

[6] A more up-to-date list of these forts than Ritterling's is given by Braat, *OMRL* xx (1939), p. 63.   [7] Tac., *Ann.* xiii. 53.

Old Rhine by diverting into it water from the Waal.[1] Unfortunately he also identified the *moles* with the *agger*, a confusion
which we shall consider below. The case for supposing the
Nieuwe Ijssel to have been the ship-canal was subsequently
restated by Hennig, Ramaer, and Vollgraff,[2] while Hettema
has urged that there were two canals, a ship-canal, which is the
Vecht, and a drainage-cut, which is the Nieuwe Ijssel.[3]
Since for most of these writers the identification of the canal
is closely linked with the identification of the other works, we
must first consider these.

Now Sebus, who set out to consider the works from an engineering point of view, rightly pointed out that by normal usage
an *agger* is something built on dry land, while a *moles* is commonly a structure set out into the water.[4] There is no reason
to suppose that we are concerned with only one structure. What
the *agger* was we shall consider below. But the *moles* at least
must have been what Holwerda originally suggested it was,
namely a structure which stood at the bifurcation of the
Rhine and the Waal, intended to divert water from the one
into the other. This is confirmed by what happened when
Civilis destroyed it: 'abacto amne tenuis alveus insulam inter
Germanosque continentium terrarum speciem fecerat.'[5] The

---

[1] Holwerda, *BerRGK* iv (1908), pp. 86–7; his theory that Flevum (Tac., *Ann.*
iv. 12) was Vechten, has nothing to recommend it; Holwerda later decided that
the *agger* was after all a different structure, namely a dyke, still visible today, along
the River Linge, which flows between and parallel to the Waal and the Neder
Rijn, *OMRL* ii. 1 (1921), pp. 41–53, esp. 47–8; and later still that *agger* and *moles*
were the same, and that both were this Linge dyke, 'der sogennante Zwischen-
damm', *Germania* xxiii (1939), pp. 31–3. Cf. also Vollgraff, *REA* xliii (1940), pp.
692–5, citing instances from the late 17th century to show how feeble the flow into
the Neder Rijn was then, leading to the construction of works early in the 18th
century to distribute the waters more evenly.

[2] Hennig, *BJ* cxxix (1924), pp. 176–91; Ramaer, *Tijdschrift van het Koninklijk
Nederlandsch Aardrijkskundig Genootschap*, Amsterdam, 2nd series, (hereinafter referred to as *TKNAG*) xlv (1928), pp. 207–18; Vollgraff, op. cit., pp. 695–8.

[3] Hettema, *De Nederlandse wateren en plaatsen in de Romeinse tijd*, pp. 133–56, esp.
155–6, 170–82, 271–8. This work, which discusses comprehensively previous
writers' contributions to the subject of Dutch topography in Roman times, first
appeared in 1938. The second edition is expanded (328 pp. instead of 206) and
extensively revised (even the preface to the first edition, reprinted under that title
in the second, has been altered). Hettema in this edition abandons the view, which
he put forward in the first edition, that Drusus' canal was the Linge.

[4] Sebus, *TKNAG* xxxvi (1919), pp. 686–96, esp. p. 691, on difference between
moles and *agger*. The identity of the two is assumed by others apart from Holwerda,
e.g. Furneaux ad Tac., *Ann.* xiii. 53.   [5] Tac., *Hist.* v. 19.

water must have rushed back into the Waal, leaving the bed of the Neder Rijn and Oude Rijn almost dry. The only question is what form the structure took. Vollgraff and Hettema favour a cutwater or groyn, 'een imposante stroomleidende krib',[1] against which Schönfeld argued that the destruction of such a work would not be enough to cause the immediate and copious flood of water into the old Waal channel which Tacitus described: 'diruit molem . . . Rhenumque prono alveo in Galliam ruentem disiectis quae morabantur effudit.'[2] This certainly suggests the bursting of a dam which had been holding back a considerable force of water. The *moles* then was probably a dam or weir of some sort which permitted only a small flow into the Waal.

The location of this dam at the bifurcation of the two streams finds further confirmation, if confirmation were needed, in the discovery of two inscriptions just before the Second World War during gravel-dredging operations at Herwen, just east of the present bifurcation. One is a dedication by the prefect of *coh. I civium Romanorum equitata*, the other commemorates M. Mallius, soldier of *legio I*, 'Carvio ad molem sepultus est; ex test(amento) heredes duo f(aciendum) c(uraverunt).'[3] Holwerda sees the phrase 'Carvio ad molem sepultus est' as implying that the stone was *not* set up at Carvium, and that therefore Carvium and the *moles* are *not* near Herwen. Carvium he identifies with the Carvo of the Peutinger Table, whose exact site is not known—Holwerda thinks it lay in the Betuwe. Nesselhauf rejects the Carvium = Carvo equation, but accepts the implication that Carvium is not here, and that the stone does not mark the grave. What then is the stone doing at Herwen? A stone normally marked the soldier's grave; if his body was not available, it stood as a memorial to him in the legionary cemetery.[4] If Mallius' stone neither marks his grave

[1] Hettema, op. cit., pp. 158–9, 162, with a sketch copied from Sebus, op. cit., p. 692; Vollgraff, op. cit., pp. 695–8.

[2] Schönfeld, *TKNAG* lvii (1940), p. 555, n. 1.

[3] First published by Vollgraff, *Meded. Kon. Ned. Akad.* 1938, pp. 555–76 (= *AE* 1939, nos. 129, 130); further id., *REA* xlii (1940), pp. 686–98; Holwerda, *Germania* xxiii (1939), pp. 31–3 (with photographs and improved reading); Schönfeld, *TKNAG* lvii (1940), pp. 549–70, with photographs; Byvanck, *Excerpta Romana* iii, pp. 231–2, no. 379B; Nesselhauf, *BerRGK* xl (1959), p. 213, no. 258.

[4] E.g., *inter alia*, gravestone of M. Caelius, *CIL* xiii. 8648 (*Vetera*); EE ix. 1064 (Chester) = Collingwood and Wright, *Roman Inscriptions of Britain* i, no. 544.

nor stands in the cemetery outside the legionary base, why is it
here? Since 1939, moreover, the gravel-pits have yielded numerous other finds, including weapons and building material.[1]

Right from the start Vollgraff had assumed that the place
where the stone inscribed 'Carvio ad molem' was found was
Carvium (it never seems to have occurred to him to suppose
otherwise), and he quotes a letter from the philologist, von
Hamel, to the effect that Carvium and the modern Herwen
are probably the same, being derived from a Germanic root,
whereas the Carvo of the *Tabula Peutingeriana* is a different
place and the name Celtic.[2] Moreover, since the gravel denotes
a former river-bed, and since the dredging found the stones in
question some 10–12 metres down on the edge of 'un vaste
amoncellement de moellons de tuf' 200 × 70 metres in extent,
Vollgraff deduces triumphantly that this is in fact the remains
of the *moles* itself.[3]

What then of the *agger*? 'Ne tamen segnem militem attinerent,
ille [*sc.* Pompeius Paulinus] inchoatum ante tres et sexaginta
annos a Druso aggerem coercendo Rheno absolvit.'[4] The troops
were set to finishing the *agger*—finishing, not repairing—and
not as a matter of urgency, but to keep them occupied: 'quietae
ad id tempus res in Germania fuerant.'[4] Is then this *agger*, as
Vollgraff, Hettema, and others suppose, an essential part of
Drusus' great scheme of hydrological engineering? Vollgraff,
for instance, arguing that the *agger* was an embankment along
the left bank of the Neder Rijn from the *moles* to the new canal
at, as he thinks, Westervoort (i.e. the Nieuwe Ijssel) to keep in
the now greatly increased volume of water, speaks of Pompeius
Paulinus' troops as strengthening or lengthening the *agger*,
'devenu plus ou moins caduque au bout de soixante ans'[5]—a

---

[1] Vollgraff and Roes, *REA* lvii (1955), p. 291; 'd'autres inscriptions, des armes
romaines, de la vaisselle de bronze, des fragments de sculpture et d'architecture
(signalons, notamment, un chapiteau, un fragment d'une grande corniche, un grand
fragment du revêtement d'un mur orné de peintures) et de vastes arras de tuiles,
de carreaux, de briques, de moellons de tuf, le tout provenant, à n'en pas douter,
du camp des soldats romains chargés de la garde de la moles Drusiana, et de la
super-structure de la moles même . . . Les objets trouvés s'échelonnent entre la
première moitié du Ier siècle et le début du IIIe.'

[2] Vollgraff, *REA* xlii (1940), loc. cit. Further argument in support of Vollgraff's
position by Jongkees in *Romana Neerlandica*, pp. 16–18.

[3] Vollgraff, ibid., pp. 692–5.

[4] Tac., *Ann*, xiii. 53.   [5] Vollgraff, op. cit., pp. 695–8.

very strange interpretation of 'inchoatum aggerem absolvit'. Hettema follows him.[1] Yet it seems clear that, if an embankment was necessary to keep in the water diverted by the new dam into the Rhine channel from the Waal, it must have been built and completed by Drusus at the time, and assiduously kept in repair since. This embankment or dyke is probably something different. Nothing connects it with the other works. 'Coercendo Rheno'—this may indeed be flood prevention, a task, as we saw in the previous section, of far less urgency in Holland then than now. It seems best to conclude that we do not know what or where the *agger* was.

Vollgraff however makes his theory of the *agger* one of his arguments in support of the Nieuwe Ijssel as Drusus' canal, on the grounds that the Vecht is too far below the dam for the troops to have built an *agger* all the way from Herwen to Vechten. He argues further that the Vecht was too far from the Roman bases in the Rhineland, forgetful that Vechten was itself probably a large base. This argument, both in itself and in the details of the language in which it is expressed, reveals a failure to grasp the essentially offensive nature of Drusus' operations and the great mobility of his troops.[2] The same argument is also used by Ramaer, who suggests further that a well and some Roman coins found near the Nieuwe Ijssel prove that it was used by the Romans,[3] although not only is there no reason to think the well Roman, but if chance Roman finds along a route are to be accepted as evidence of Roman use, it is possible to prove that the Romans used all the main railway lines out of London.

Hettema tries to combine the views of both sides of the controversy,[4] resting his case heavily on Suetonius' use of the plural, *fossae Drusianae*, as indicating the existence of two canals. This argument at least can be swiftly disposed of. Marius built a canal on the Rhine, of which Mela writes: 'Fossa Mariana partem eius amnis navigabili alveo effundit'; Strabo

---

[1] Hettema, op. cit., pp. 156–70.

[2] Vollgraff, op. cit., p. 697, with such phrases as, 'le gros des troupes romaines chargées de défendre les deux Germanies est toujours resté concentré dans les camps de Rhénanie', and 'étant donnée la possibilité d'incursions subites de Germains venant du Nord'.

[3] Ramaer, *TKNAG* 1928, pp. 207–18, esp. pp. 213 (well), 217 (coins).

[4] Hettema, op. cit., pp. 133–56 (esp. 155–6), 170–82, 271–81.

and Plutarch also refer to it in the singular, whereas Pliny has 'fossae ex Rhodano C. Mari opere et nomine insignes', and the plural appears again in Ptolemy and the itineraries.[1] So Cicero uses 'pontem' and 'pontes' of one and the same bridge.[2] Hettema argues that only his theory that the Nieuwe Ijssel is a drainage-cut can explain the building of a dam to divert water from Waal to Rhine, since the ship-canal on the Vecht is too far away to be affected.[3] Granted this, granted that water channelled into the Rhine at Herwen would have every chance to dissipate itself before reaching the Vecht, yet Drusus had every reason to improve the flow of water in the Rhine at the expense of the Waal. For the Roman use of the Vecht and their establishment of a base at Vechten presuppose the navigability at all times, and especially in the time of low water, the summer, the campaigning season, not only of the Vecht itself, but of the whole length of the Rhine from Vechten back to the Rhineland. Water flowing into the Waal was wasted; hence the dam, to divert it, or some of it, into the Neder Rijn below Herwen. Thus is the whole series of Drusus' works explained. There is no reason to suppose that the Nieuwe Ijssel was dug by the Romans, or that Drusus was responsible for any canal other than the Vecht, where he may either have improved an existing channel to make it navigable or cut a new channel to provide the Rhine with an outlet to the Ijsselmeer. With this channel and their base at Vechten, the Romans were admirably placed to launch those amphibious operations along the North Sea coast which were, as we have seen, a feature both of Drusus' and of Germanicus' campaigns.

5. 2. NIJMEGEN

The area of Nijmegen (Noviomagus) has a wealth of Roman and native Batavian sites. The most important of these for our present purposes is the Roman legionary base (fig. 4) some 2 km. east of the modern city-centre on the edge of a high steep escarpment overlooking the Betuwe, the flat plain between the

[1] Mela ii. 79; Strabo iv. 183; Plut., *Marius* 15; Pliny, *NH* iii. 34; Ptol., *Geog.* ii 10. 2; for the itineraries, cf. Ihm, *RE* vii, col. 75–6.

[2] Cic., *ad fam.* x. 18. 4, 23. 3.

[3] Hettema, op. cit., p. 142, n. 4.

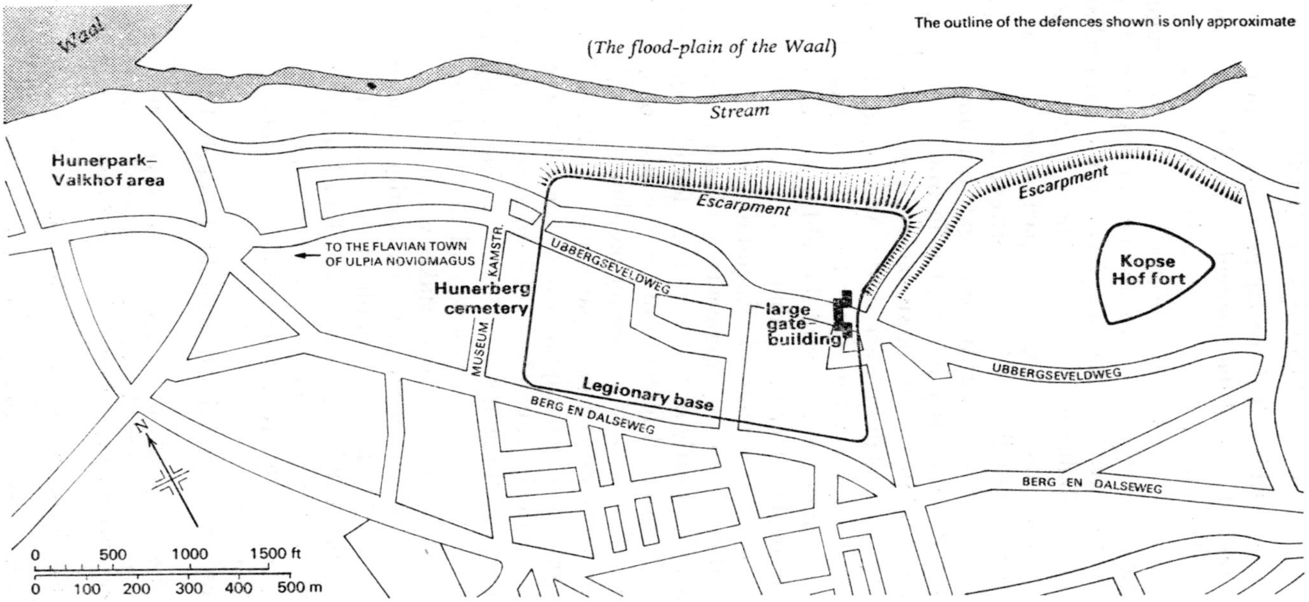

The outline of the defences shown is only approximate

(The flood-plain of the Waal)

Stream

Waal

Kopse Hof fort

Escarpment

Escarpment

UBBERGSEVELDWEG

BERG EN DALSEWEG

large gate-building

UBBERGSEVELDWEG

Legionary base

BERG EN DALSEWEG

MUSEUM

TAMSTR.

Hunerberg cemetery

TO THE FLAVIAN TOWN OF ULPIA NOVIOMAGUS

Hunerpark–Valkhof area

N

0   500   1000   1500 ft

0   100   200   300   400   500 m

Fig. 4. Nijmegen: the Roman military sites

Waal and the Rhine. This escarpment seen from the Betuwe strongly reminds one of the Fürstenberg at Xanten, on which stood the Augustan base of Vetera. The Flavian fortress on this site at Nijmegen has long been known, but the Augustan base lying underneath the Flavian one did not come to light until 1960.[1] Excavations that year revealed the extraordinarily large east gate-building of the early base right alongside the smaller Flavian gate-building and in part underneath the stone gate of the stone-built post-Flavian fortress, dating from about 100.[2] Connected with the Augustan gate-building was a pair of ditches, the outer one interrupted in front of the gate, the inner one continuous and presumably therefore once crossed by a bridge, although no trace of this was found. The ditches had been allowed to silt up naturally and were securely dated by the finding of two graves of the mid first century dug into the filling of the inner ditch about 40 m. north of the gate.[3] The outer ditch contained Augustan pottery. The gate-building itself is dated by fragments of a jug-handle, said to be unmistakably of early-first-century type, found in the hard top layer of the rammed filling of one of the post-holes, and by a sherd of Italian sigillata in another post-hole. The filling of the post-holes was observed to be particularly clean, as if the area was not yet soiled by occupation when the holes were dug.

The outer ditch came to an end somewhere between 20 and 45 m. north of the gateway, where a ravine dropping down the face of the cliff renders a second ditch neither necessary nor possible. Instead a row of stakes was driven in along the outer edge of the inner ditch, which continues along the edge of the ravine. About in the middle of the stretch within which the outer ditch finishes, a tower was found of the same construction as the gate-building, and a rampart was traced running between the two. A second tower was observed further along the rampart.

The only other remains that could definitely be assigned to

[1] Brunsting, *Numaga* viii (1961), pp. 49–67; summary of results in id., *400 Jaar Romeinse Bezetting: Noviomagus Batavorum*, pp. 7–9; there is an account of earlier research and excavations up to the end of 1959 by Brunsting, *Numaga* vii (1960), pp. 6–27.

[2] Brunsting, *Numaga*, viii (1961), pp. 55–6, cf. plan, p. 52; on the date of the stone fortress see id., *Numaga* vii (1960), p. 24.

[3] Brunsting, *Numaga* viii (1961), p. 61, cf. photographs, pp. 63–4.

the Augustan period were a number of rubbish pits from inside
the base, which yielded sigillata and other pottery of the early
first century.[1] Until the big Augustan gate-building was found,
the excavators did not associate these pits with military
occupation of the site at all, but thought of ribbon-development
between the Kopse Hof and Hunerpark–Valkhof settlements,
to be discussed below. Although the quantity of Augustan
finds has been increased by subsequent years' excavations,[2]
it remains slight. Brunsting tried to explain this by suggesting
that the defences were erected by a small advance-party only
and that the base was never occupied, the legion for which it
was built having perhaps been one of those lost with Varus.
'Never occupied' probably goes too far, but the period of occupation must have been short, and the finds point to the late
Augustan period, whether before or after A.D. 9. A study of the
sigillata finds from the base and the cemeteries to the south and
south-east which belong to it is said to be in preparation, and
may help us to establish just how much evidence of Augustan
occupation there is, and what the limits of this occupation
were. A recent account of the coarse ware by Stuart speaks of
an early period extending from 15/12 B.C. to A.D. 37, but precise
dating of such ware is of course extremely difficult.[3]

Stuart has put together all the evidence that can help us
to trace the circuit of the defences in the different periods of
occupation.[4] Unfortunately our knowledge comes from different
excavations by different people at different times, or from
chance observations in the course of building operations, all
of which have revealed along the west and south sides only a
number of disconnected sections of ditch, and the evaluation of
these is complicated by the absence of adequate large-scale

[1] Brunsting, op. cit., p. 65.
[2] Bogaers, *Numaga* xii (1965), pp. 12–13; Brunsting, *Nieuws-bulletin van de
Koninklijke Nederlandse Oudheidkundige Bond*, 6th series, xvii (1964), pp. 131–2; xviii
(1965), pp. 62–4, 125–8; xix (1966), pp. 84–7; xx (1967), pp. 7–8.
[3] Stuart, *Gewoon aardewerk uit de Romeinse legerplaats en de bijbehorende grafvelden te
Nijmegen*; this work contains the most up-to-date bibliography and by far the
clearest map of the Nijmegen sites (plate 29); on dating, see p. 112, where 35
pieces are listed as 'pre-A.D. 37'; but if we trace these back, with the help of the
tables on pp. 113–17, to Stuart's more detailed discussion in the text, we find
that not one need be dated to the period between A.D. 9 and A.D. 70. Cf. also
Ettlinger's review in *Helinium* iv (1964), pp. 273–4.
[4] Stuart, op. cit., pp. 1–4.

plans in the published reports. It is certain that on the west
side and at least part of the south side there existed at least two
ditches, while sections of stone wall, probably that of the stone-
built fortress, were found on both sides,[1] but it is not certain
whether the two ditches are parallel and contemporary, or on
slightly different alignments and to be assigned to different
periods. The case for the latter interpretation was put by
Breuer, and subsequent discoveries do not affect his case.[2]
Stuart indeed speaks of a double ditch found in 1956 on the
south side of the fortress south of the line of the south front
indicated by previous sections, but it is not clear whether this
is something completely different from the earlier sections or
not.[3] Brunsting has tentatively suggested that there may possibly
have been an annexe on this side.[4]

On the available evidence, it seems we should conclude
that the Augustan base was of approximately the same extent
as the Flavian, though the ditches do not coincide, and that
parts of the ditches of both periods have been turned up by
excavators. This theory, if plausible, can only be tested by
further excavation. Unfortunately, although Holwerda found
and excavated the west gate, he did not carry his trenches
sufficiently far forward of the gate-building to see whether
or not there was a second ditch associated with it.[5] As Brunsting
points out, it is certain that in the Flavian period there was a
single ditch on the east side, and there is no obvious reason
why there should have been stronger defences on the west and
south.[6] For the Augustan period of course we might expect the
double ditch on the east to be an argument for the same on the
south and west. But the east side is the weakest, being on a
reverse slope and more vulnerable to attack from the crest of

---

[1] Vermeulen, *Een Romeinsch grafveld op den Hunnerberg te Nijmegen*, pp. 9–10, reporting the presence of walls on the west side, but doubting whether they are
Roman; Roman however according to Breuer, *L'Antiquité classique* iii (1934), p. 391;
on the accuracy of Vermeulen's excavations, cf. Holwerda, *OMRL* xvii (1936),
pp. 17–18; stone walls south of the fortress again reported by Brunsting, *Nieuws-
bulletin van de Koninklijke Nederlandse Oudheidkundige Bond*, 6th series, xiv (1961),
p. 220.

[2] Breuer, op. cit., pp. 385–92; *contra*, Vermeulen, *OMRL* xii (1931), pp. 123–
32.

[3] Stuart, op. cit., p. 3.

[4] Brunsting, *Numaga* vii (1960), p. 11.

[5] Holwerda, *OMRL* i (1920), plate 7, fig. 19, cf. p. 26.

[6] Brunsting, *Numaga* viii (1961), p. 56.

the hill above, so that a double ditch on this one side only in Augustan times is possible. No precise dates for the period of Augustan occupation can be determined, but it seems to have lasted a comparatively short time, to judge from the scantiness of finds. As Brunsting indicates, a date in the latter part of Augustus' reign, around A.D. 9, seems likely, but we await the forthcoming publication of the sigillata.

The legionary base lies between two native sites, one to the east, on the same escarpment as the base and considerably above it, on the site known as the Kopse Hof,[1] the other to the west in the Hunerpark–Valkhof area. Further west still, on the west of the modern town and over 2 km. from the base, a new civil settlement grew up in Flavian times and flourished throughout the second century.[2] The Hunerpark–Valkhof settlement has never been scientifically excavated, but finds there during road-building operations in the 1930s show that it was abandoned in the late first century and re-established in the third.[3] There was no evidence of military occupation. The finds included sigillata parallel to that at Haltern and Oberaden.[4] Graves associated with this settlement were found on the Hunerberg, which is the lower part of the escarpment below the base.[5] The graveyard extends from the limits of the settlement area, where the earliest graves, dated to the latter part of Augustus' reign, were found, right up to the west ditch of the base. Here, near the ditch, the latest graves were of the 60s, with a few later finds of the latter part of the first century, apparently

[1] Sometimes also Kopse Veld, sometimes too described simply as Ubbergen (so, e.g., Breuer, OMRL xii (1931), pp. 27–121, 'Les objets antiques découverts à Ubbergen près Nimègue').

[2] De Waele, Noviomagus Batavorum (Romeinsch Nijmegen), pp. 38–51, esp. p. 49 (cf. English summary, p. 104); id., RE xviii, cols. 1210–12; Brunsting, Het grafveld onder Hees bij Nijmegen, with bibliography; id., 400 Jaar Romeinse Bezetting, p. 14; Bogaers, Ber. van de Rijksdienst voor het Oudheidkundig Bodemonderzoek x/xi (1960/1), pp. 263–317.

[3] De Waele, op. cit., pp. 16–19; Holwerda, OMRL xxvii (1946), pp. 5–26, with plan, p. 6; the coin finds by Daniëls, OMRL xxxi (1950), pp. 1–32; id., Noviomagus: Romeins Nijmegen, pp. 47–100; earlier account, id., OMRL ii (1921), pp. 6–32.

[4] Holwerda, op. cit. Augustan sigillata from Nijmegen was noticed by Ritterling, BJ cxiv/cxv (1906), p. 180, who links Nijmegen with Vechten as the only undoubted Augustan sites in Holland.

[5] Vermeulen, op. cit.; earlier excavations in this cemetery by G. M. Kam (Vermeulen, op. cit., plates 1, 2: Kam's excavations labelled O, E, and S) are still not published, cf. Stuart, op. cit., p. 1, n. 10.

associated with the base, not with the cemetery.[1] The fact that the graves stop at the ditch creates a presumption that the ditch of the Augustan base was still open throughout Claudian–Neronian times so as to discourage encroachment on the base area, even though this was now unoccupied.[2] Vermeulen, knowing nothing of an Augustan occupation, suggested that the Flavian fortress was scrupulously planned to avoid disturbing the graves. Lehner rightly pointed out that Roman piety did not stop them doing this elsewhere, at Neuss, for instance.[3]

The Kopse Hof site presents more of a problem. The area produced sigillata earlier than any at Haltern, notably pieces with the stamps LSG and TETTI SAMIA, while the latest sigillata is said to support an end-date of around 70.[4] There is also much native pottery, which cannot however be dated accurately enough to establish how long the site was occupied before the start of Roman influence.[5] Holwerda, who excavated here, reported a rampart without a ditch surrounding the site and suggested that this was a place of refuge. The internal area of the fort was about 8 ha., mostly without trace of habitations, but with a single track across it, lined with huts.[6] Holwerda identified it with the 'oppidum Batavorum' burnt by Civilis.[7] De Waele on the other hand suggested that it was a fort built by Batavians in Roman service, and pointed out that a tribe the size of the Batavians must have had many *oppida*.[8] This suggestion has now been taken up again by Kam, who points out that in the Kopse Hof fort alone the numerous loom weights which the women would use, found in all other known Batavian

[1] On dating see esp. Vermeulen, op. cit., pp. 217, 221; on the late-first-century finds, p. 5 (= German résumé, p. 251, where however a vital misprint totally changes the sense, stating that apart from potsherds and fragments of glass there were 'kleine Urne' containing bones: comparison with the Dutch text shows that this should read 'keine Urne').

[2] An isolated grave beneath the *principia* of the Flavian fortress probably goes back to the pre-Roman period, Vermeulen, op. cit., p. 220; other prehistoric finds beneath fortress reported by Brunsting, *Numaga* vii (1960), p. 23, and viii (1961), pp. 66–7.

[3] Lehner, *Germania* xvii (1933), p. 155, reviewing Vermeulen, op. cit.

[4] The pottery from the Kopse Hof is published by Breuer, *OMRL* xii (1931), pp. 27–121; further, on sigillata, W. H. Kam, *Numaga* ix (1962), pp. 149–52; also id., *De Versterking op het Kopseplateau te Nijmegen*.

[5] Breuer, loc. cit., p. 29.

[6] Holwerda, *OMRL* ii (1921), pp. 57–78.

[7] Tac., *Hist.* v. 19.

[8] De Waele, op. cit., pp. 11–16; id., *RE* xvii, col. 1207.

sites, are missing, whence he concludes that the fort was
occupied by men alone.[1] Occupation remains extend beyond
the fort on the south and east.[2] At one point about 100 m.
south of the fort a considerable amount of sigillata contemporary with the Oberaden and the earliest Haltern finds was
discovered, but none later, whence Holwerda suggested that
the fort was superimposed on an earlier settlement, which was
given up when the fort was built.[3] If so, then the fort itself
appears to be dated to the earlier part of Augustus' reign.
The absence of a ditch is un-Roman; so is the layout of the
interior, unless, as Kam suggests, Holwerda did not get down
to the lowest occupation layers and therefore failed to recover
the true plan.

It seems then that for the pre-Roman period and the early
part of Augustus' reign we have at Nijmegen two separate
native settlements, one on the Kopse Hof, one on the Hunerpark–Valkhof site, the inhabitants of which rapidly became
Romanized, if one is to judge from the Augustan sigillata on
both sites. In the early Augustan period, perhaps at the time
of Drusus, the Kopse Hof settlers were displaced to make
room for a fort, possibly, as Kam suggests, built and occupied
by Batavian auxiliaries. And later in Augustus' reign a Roman
legionary base was established on the escarpment about 400 m.
below the Kopse Hof, but was soon given up, although the
strength of the defences suggests that this was not the original
intention.

5. 3. VETERA (NEAR XANTEN)

The earliest Roman base to bear the name of Vetera[4] stood on
the Fürstenberg between Xanten and Birten; here, as Tacitus
tells us, two legions were garrisoned in A.D. 14.[5] It was rebuilt
on a different site under Vespasian. Both Vetera I and Vetera
II lay opposite the point where the Lippe probably entered

---

[1] Kam, *Numaga* x (1963), pp. 153–9.
[2] Holwerda, op. cit.; id., *OMRL* xxiv (1943), pp. 35–58, with plans, pp. 36–7;
Brunsting, *Nieuws-bulletin van de Koninklijke Nederlandse Oudheidkundige Bond*, 6th series
(1957), p. 129.
[3] Holwerda, *OMRL* xxiv (1943), pp. 57–8.
[4] The name is pre-Roman, see von Petrikovits, *RE* viiiA, cols. 1804–5.
[5] Tac., *Ann.* i. 45.

the Rhine in Roman times, though now the confluence is further south.[1] The Fürstenberg itself rises about 150 ft. above the flood-plain, sloping gently on all sides but the east, which has been eroded since Roman times and which now drops steeply to an old, marshy, half-dried-up arm of the Rhine.[2] This erosion has destroyed part of the Roman site. Only the amphitheatre remains above ground, but excavation has revealed two Claudian–Neronian fortresses with stone buildings, and traces of several Augustan and Tiberian bases beneath them. From the cemetery south of the hill have come military grave-stones, notably that of M. Caelius, centurion of *leg. XVIII*, 'cecidit bello Variano'.[3]

The pre-Claudian remains described by Lehner, as supple-mented by von Petrikovits, are as follows (fig. 5):[4]

(i) A: the most northerly of the Roman remains on the Fürstenberg, it comprises a single ditch running roughly east to west, with a wood-and-earth rampart on its south side, revealed by the parallel bedding-trenches of the revetment. Two distinct periods of both ditch and rampart were observed. The ditch was traced for over 510 m., beyond which it could not be excavated further, but excavations south of the line of the ditch showed Augustan pits extending at least 70 m. further west. They cannot belong to any of the known stretches of fortification except A or C. The east end of the ditch had been destroyed by erosion.[5]

(ii) C: 420 m. long, running first south-westwards and then westwards from the edge of the hill, its eastern end again having been destroyed, it comprised, like A, a single ditch with a rampart, this time on the north of the ditch, again showing two periods. In the south side was a gate, rebuilt in the later period slightly farther west; in front of the earlier gate a paved road was observed, running south, while in

---

[1] Von Petrikovits, loc. cit., with map, cols. 1813–14.

[2] Lehner, *Vetera* (1930), pp. 8–9 (photo. p. 7); von Petrikovits, loc. cit., col. 1803, cf. Scheller, *BJ* clvii (1957), pp. 272–93; air photograph in Scollar, *Archäologie aus der Luft*, pl. 15.

[3] *CIL* xiii. 8648.

[4] Lehner, op. cit., pp. 12–20, with plan, plate 2; cf. von Petrikovits, loc. cit., cols. 1815–17; Lehner's earlier reports in *BJ*, to which he refers in his book, give fuller details.

[5] Lehner, op. cit., pp. 12–14.

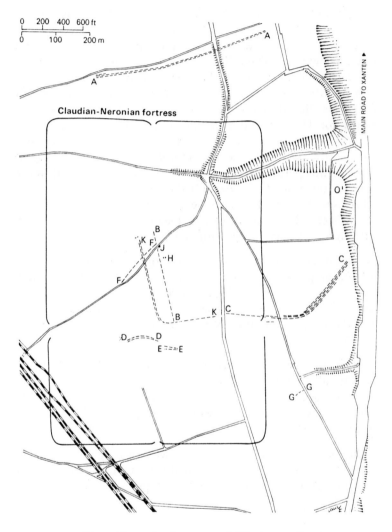

Fig. 5. Vetra: the Augustan and Tiberian remains

front of the later one was a *tutulus*.[1] Von Petrikovits plausibly suggests that A and C are both part of the same base for two legions.[2]

(iii) B: a single ditch 265 m. long running north and south, it cannot from its position have joined either A or C. No trace of a rampart was found, though one made of turf may have existed. The cellar J, which contained pottery of the last decade B.C., seemed to Lehner from its orientation to go with B,[3] while pottery ovens, H, whose contents date them also to the last decade B.C. and mark them down as a source of supply for Haltern and Oberaden,[4] though they may belong to A–C, more probably, I would suggest, go with B, since they lie just behind it, and the *intervallum* is a likely place for ovens in this period, before they were expelled from within the fortifications into the *canabae*.[5] If the cellar J referred to above belongs to B also, the evidence for B's early Augustan date is consistent. But neither H nor J can be ascribed to B with certainty. Either could go with A–C.

(iv) K: this forms two sides of a right angle, the west side 260 m. long, the south side 165 m.; on the west a double ditch was found, on the south, a single. Since K at one point overlies a burnt layer with early Tiberian sherds, and since it lies beneath the Claudian–Neronian remains, its date is beyond question.[6]

(v) Other short, disconnected stretches of ditch, D, E, F, G, O: all but G and O underlie the Claudian–Neronian fortresses and are therefore pre-Claudian, while D and G contained Augustan finds, which however provided only a *terminus post quem*.[7]

The only stretch of defences that we can date with absolute certainty is K, which belongs to the middle or late years of Tiberius. A–C and B are probably parts of two separate

[1] Lehner, op. cit., pp. 15–17.
[2] Von Petrikovits, loc. cit., col. 1815.
[3] Lehner, op. cit., pp. 14–15.   [4] Ibid., p. 20.
[5] Cf. von Petrikovits, loc. cit., col. 1816; ovens in the *intervallum* also at Mainz.
[6] Lehner, op. cit., pp. 20–1.
[7] Ibid., pp. 17–19; for O, see Wieland, *BJ* cl (1950), p. 156; the finds from D and G in *BJ* xix (1910), pp. 253–4.

Augustan bases. Von Petrikovits sees D also as Augustan. E, G, and O are in all probability Tiberian, while F, he suggests, need not be a defensive ditch at all. O might well go with one of the other stretches of ditch, but it seems clear that we have the remains, fragmentary though they are, of at least six pre-Claudian bases, one of which (A–C) shows clear evidence of two distinct periods. It is particularly unfortunate that no modern excavations have been done at so important a site, but unfortunately attention since the Second World War has been concentrated on other sites in the Xanten area where need is more urgent, to the exclusion of the Fürstenberg.[1]

5. 4. NEUSS

Neuss (Novaesium) on the left bank of the Rhine opposite Düsseldorf has long been known as the site of a Claudian fortress, extensively excavated by Koenen before the First World War.[2] At about the same time a second Roman site was also investigated within the area of a brickyard owned by a certain Herr Sels (the so-called Selssche Ziegelei site), about half way between the Claudian fortress and the town wall of the civil settlement of Novaesium. It could not be properly excavated because of the modern buildings on the site, but a vast quantity of finds was recovered.[3] Yet a third site came to light in the 1950s, just east of the Selssche Ziegelei, between it and the Claudian fortress, in an area at that time almost totally unbuilt on, but destined for a new autobahn and housing estate. This site proved to have been occupied by seven

[1] Cf. von Petrikovits, *Das römische Rheinland*, p. 38. Dr. C. B. Rüger however informs me that the Fürstenberg is earmarked for building in the 1970s, so that rescue digs may be expected.

[2] Koenen and others, *BJ* cxi/cxii (1904); structures of the same period outside the fortress, Lehner and Oelmann, *BJ* cxxxi (1926), pp. 369–70, and cxxxii (1927), pp. 271–2. This fortress is sometimes referred to as being at Grimlinghausen, and is also known as the 'Koenenlager', cf. von Petrikovits, *BJ* clxi (1961), pp. 471–5.

[3] The site and the story of its discovery set out by Koenen, *BJ* ci (1897), pp. 1–9; on the coins, van Vleuten, ibid., pp. 9–12; on sigillata stamps, Oxé and Siebourg, ibid., pp. 12–21; fuller account of coins by Strack, *BJ* cxi/cxii (1904), pp. 419–53. Minor excavations in the Ziegelei area in 1926 reported by Lehner, *BJ* cxxxii (1927), p. 271. The Ziegelei site is marked as a 'Siedlungsstelle' on the map in von Petrikovits, *BJ* clxi (1961), *Beilage* 1.

successive forts or legionary bases of the Augustan–Tiberian period (fig. 6).[1]

The site of these bases is delimited by an old Rhine channel on the north and by the Ziegelei and other buildings on the west, which prevented any search for the west side of the defences. In most cases only the south and east sides have been traced. The seven fortifications are arranged by von Petrikovits in the following order of date:[2]

A. An irregular fort, whose west side was not found; the other three sides were excavated and enclose an area of over 6·5 ha., the size of an auxiliary (or *vexillatio*) fort. It had two ditches, with no trace of rampart or of inner buildings; native sherds and a few Roman ones probably date the fort to the third decade B.C.[3]

B. Much larger than A, polygonal, with probably at least five sides, three of which have so far been found in whole or part, embracing at least 27 ha. The probable area of the whole is about 40 ha., large enough for two legions. The front bedding-trench of the rampart has been discovered, with in front of it a ditch 8–10 m. wide and 2 m. deep, in some places showing the usual V-shaped section, in others flat-bottomed, while 6 m. in front of this ditch is a smaller V-shaped ditch, which von Petrikovits describes as an 'Annäherungshindernis'. No trace of the gates has yet been found, nor of the inner buildings, though traces of roads may belong to this period.

C. This is apparently the largest of all, 50 ha. for certain and perhaps in all 75 ha. The south-east corner and perhaps part of the west side have been uncovered; the rampart appears to have had a revetment on the front only. The ditch is over 5 m. wide, and 2 m. deep. The east gate was found near the south-east corner, with what appears to be a *tutulus* in front,

---

[1] Report covering excavations to the end of 1961 by von Petrikovits, *BJ* clxi (1961), pp. 449–85; earlier reports and discussions, idem, in *Neue Ausgrabungen in Deutschland*, pp. 286–302, and *Das römische Rheinland*, pp. 19–26, 31–3; cf. also idem, *Novaesium: Das römische Neuss*. Final reports to be published in *Limesforschungen*, cf. Mary, *Novaesium* i, and Schönberger, Simon, and Vegas, *Novaesium* ii. [ADD.]

[2] Von Petrikovits, *BJ* clxi (1961), pp. 455–71, superseding idem, *Das römische Rheinland*, pp. 17–26; for the plan of the fortifications, *BJ* clxi (1961), Beilage 2, cf. smaller plan, p. 456.

[3] See above, pp. 41–2.

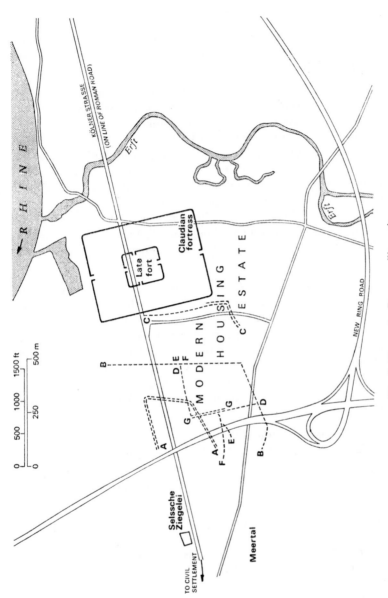

Fig. 6. Neuss: the Roman military sites

as at Vetera C. Within C, but outside all the other fortifications, buildings were found, from one of which comes a *tabula ansata* inscribed '*leg. V*'.

D. Like its successors E and F, D has a big re-entrant right angle facing south-east. In the angle of the re-entrant traces of what may have been a tower were observed, although it is uncertain whether they belong to D, E, or F. It too, like C, had a rampart apparently revetted on the front only, while its ditch was only 2 m. wide. Only the two sides forming the right angle are known, without gates. Buildings were found within D–E–F, but they cannot be ascribed with any certainty to any one of these periods, although traces of roads probably belonging to D are known. The area of D so far ascertained is about 17·5 ha., and the total area is conjectured to be at least 25 ha.

E. This takes over D's big re-entrant, but does not extend so far to the south. There is a wood-and-earth rampart with two bedding trenches, front and rear, and a ditch 4·5 m. wide with a row of pointed stakes or a fence 10 m. in front of it. The area ascertained so far is about 16 ha., the total area estimated to be about 22–3 ha. Both faces of the rampart were buttressed with timber supports let into horizontal baulks, such as are also found in the post-Augustan forts at Köln-Alteburg and Remagen.[1]

F. F has fortifications of the same type as E's, but without timber supports. They follow the same line as E's, except on the south side; but the 'Annäherungshindernis' lies only 4·5 m. in front of the ditch. F and E have the same area.

G. G so far comprises only a single straight length of ditch, traced for 260 m., 3–3·5 m. deep, whose floor was so irregular that it appears sometimes only as pits. No rampart has been found on either side. The ditch is conjecturally ascribed to a fortification, but no one has any idea which side of the ditch the fort (if it was one) lay on, nor what shape or size it had. No buildings are known belonging to it.

The relative dating of these structures offers few difficulties. D–E–F–G are undoubtedly to be dated in that order since they

---

[1] Van Petrikovits *Das römische Rheinland*, p. 22, n. 19.

lie wholly or partially on top of one another. A and B do not intersect, but both in their different places lie beneath D–E–F–G. C intersects no other of the fortifications. The only question then is the order of A–B–C. Now to C von Petrikovits ascribes all the remains of buildings outside the other fortifications, judging them too scattered to be *canabae*. These buildings at two points cut the fortifications of B. If then they do belong to C, C is later than B. But the oldest buildings at another point lie beneath D–E–F and on top of ditches belonging to roads; and these roads have no remains of buildings in alignment with them. Hence it looks as if the roads belong to B and the buildings to C; and von Petrikovits points out that D–E–F for part of their circuit so closely coincide that we expect them to be successive. There appears to be no decisive stratigraphic proof that A is the oldest of all the structures and von Petrikovits still says only that it is probable that A is the oldest. But if A is only an auxiliary fort, and the only auxiliary fort, and if it has produced sherds of the third decade B.C., it is very likely to be the first fortification on the site, as at Strasbourg, where a fort is also succeeded by a legionary base, though after a much greater lapse of time.

The preparation of the definitive publication of the Italian sigillata from the excavations at Neuss, amounting to some 10,000 sherds, is in the hands of Dr. Ettlinger, whose first report states that the earliest pieces from here are earlier than the earliest from Basel or Oberaden, and find their parallels at Zürich, Vidy, Rome, and on the Magdalensberg.[1] They are probably to be dated to 20 B.C. or a little before, as I have argued more fully above, in connection with the Swiss sites. This probably marks the date at which the fort A was established. There is no evidence available, yet, at least, to enable us to date the later fortifications. Ettlinger's preliminary figures show however that there are significant quantities of relatively early pieces, and enough of these come from outside A to establish that B at least is also comparatively early. How long B was occupied, we do not know, but C, which is built for four legions, is most naturally to be dated after A.D. 9, when we know that the army of Lower Germany was increased

---

[1] Ettlinger in *Studien zu den Militärgrenzen Roms*, pp. 77–85. I am grateful to Dr. Ettlinger for further correspondence on this subject.

to this size.[1] It has been conjectured by von Petrikovits that D may have been built by *leg.* XX on its transfer from Cologne, but there is no clear evidence for the date of any of the bases. The polygonal shape and re-entrant angles of these bases are, as von Petrikovits notes, characteristic of the Augustan–Tiberian period.[2] The solidity of the buildings and the evidence of repairs to them argue that they were built for permanent occupation, not for one winter only.[3] The sheer quantity of the finds (over a million and a half potsherds, for instance) also shows that the occupation must have been extensive and well-nigh continuous. The Neuss site cannot have been occupied for as long as Vindonissa was (some 90 years), but the quantity of Roman artefacts recovered must compare with Vindonissa.

The vast quantity of finds from the adjacent Selssche Ziegelei area leads to the conclusion that it too must have been continuously occupied for a considerable period; and if, as I would suggest, this is the area of the Augustan–Tiberian *canabae*, this too is an argument for the continuous occupation of the base also. No plans of buildings were recovered from this area, though Koenen reported that it was covered with holes, some forming irregular rows; numerous fragments of roof tiles were observed and a few traces of stone foundations.[4] Among the finds there were over 3,000 coins, predominantly Augustan, with those of Nemausus especially frequent, followed by those of Lugdunum.[5] Strack originally suggested that there were only three coins dated between 17 and 37, but Kraft has now shown that there are at least 26 of this period; he also notes that there are 25 coins of the Augustan *tresviri* IV issues to 12 of *tresviri* I/II, a proportion typical of a post-Augustan site.[6] Strack was clearly wrong to suppose that there was a break in occupation under Tiberius. Of later issues, Strack gives Claudius

---

[1] Cf. von Petrikovits, *BJ* clxi (1961), p. 468–9. C has been widely hailed as Tacitus' four-legion *aestiva* of A.D. 14.

[2] Idem, *Das römische Rheinland*, pp. 24–6; cf. idem, *BJ* clxi (1961), pp. 470–1.

[3] Idem, *Das römische Rheinland*, p. 31.

[4] Koenen, *BJ* ci (1897), p. 3; the roof tiles were unstamped, except for two with stamps of *legio XVI*.

[5] Strack, loc. cit.

[6] Kraft, *JNG* vii (1956), pp. 26–7; the whole Sels collection, so far as it survives, is being re-examined in connection with the new material from the adjacent fortress site, cf. *BJ* clxi (1961), p. 485.

18, Nero 9, Domitian 5, with scattered second-century coins. There was also much Augustan pottery; Koenen notes the predominance of Italian sigillata over Gaulish, and refers to the discovery of what appears to be genuine, early black-gloss sigillata, as found, for instance, on the Lorenzberg.[1] Other finds include a few lance-heads, which are the only specifically military objects from the site.[2]

The list of sigillata stamps gives 156 pieces with decipherable stamps.[3] Apart from a large quantity of Augustan pieces there is also much Gaulish sigillata, extending down to Claudian–Neronian times or later. The Italian stamps include 33 stamps of the Ateius-group, while of earlier potters' stamps we have 2 of L. Tetti Samia, 9 of C. Sentius, and 5 of L. Titius. The picture which the finds give is of a site first settled early in Augustan times, intensively occupied in the early first century A.D., and not abandoned until some time in the second half of the first century at the earliest, although probably it was significantly less used after the middle of the century. Little weight need be attached to scattered later coin finds, since the whole area continued to be in use throughout the Roman period. The very small number and the nature of the specifically military finds do nothing to support the assumption that the site lay within the area of the Augustan–Tiberian fortifications, though it was assumed both by the excavators and by later scholars that this was the site of the Augustan base;[4] the fact that the coins shows that the site was occupied up to A.D. 70, if not longer, that is to say, that it was still occupied after the building of the new stone fortress further east, tells against the assumption. Now the discovery of the Augustan–Tiberian bases makes it virtually certain that the Ziegelei area was not included within the fortifications. It seems likely then that it was the area occupied by the *canabae*, suffering a decrease in activity but not completely abandoned in Claudian times, when the new fortress was built further east.

The Roman road along the bank of the Rhine, which will have given the garrison at Neuss swift communications northwards

---

[1] Koenen, op. cit., pp. 4–5.
[2] Ibid., pp. 2–3.
[3] Oxé and Siebourg, loc. cit.
[4] Koenen, op. cit., p. 8; Ritterling, *BJ* cxiv/cxv (1906), p. 170; Oxé in Albrecht, *Das Römerlager in Oberaden* i, p. 55; *contra*, Nissen, *BJ* cxi/cxii (1904), p. 7.

and southwards, ran where the modern road now runs.[1] It was possibly carried on a bridge or an embankment over the low-lying, marshy 'Meertal' west of the Augustan–Tiberian site, where iron-shod piles have been found, like those at Oberhausen and on the Annaberg at Haltern.[2] The road was lined with graves, and gravestones of the Augustan–Tiberian period, including one mentioning *leg. XX*, have been found alongside the road and built into the walls and foundations of the Claudian fortress.[3] This may indicate that the road itself is quite early, as is probable, since Neuss does not face an obvious invasion-route into Germany, as do Vetera and Mainz. Its garrison must have depended greatly on this road for its lateral communications and its ability to march north or south, wherever it might be needed.

5. 5. COLOGNE

Tacitus attests the presence of four legions all together in summer quarters 'in finibus Ubiorum' in A.D. 14,[4] two of which had their *hiberna* at Vetera,[5] the other two, *legg. I* and *XX*, at Cologne, 'apud aram Ubiorum',[6] whither Caecina led them back, 'in civitatem Ubiorum reduxit'.[7] It is clear that they shared a single base, and that they had already occupied it for at least the previous winter of 13/14, and were destined to re-occupy it for 14/15.

Filtzinger has now stated the case for believing that the site of this base for two legions was that later occupied by the Colonia Claudia Ara Agrippinensium.[8] Beneath the stone-built north wall of the colony traces of a previous wood-and-earth rampart were found along a short stretch just west of the Cathedral, and this may well belong to the base. Several early pottery ovens are known, producing the same type of pottery as is typical of potteries found in other military sites in the

---

[1] Hagen, *Römerstrassen der Rheinprovinz*, pp. 67–70.
[2] Koenen, *BJ* cxi/cxii (1904), p. 105.
[3] Lehner, ibid., pp. 311–13, 320–2; cf. *CIL* xiii. 8553.
[4] Tac., *Ann.* i. 31. 3.   [5] Ibid. i. 45. 1.   [6] Ibid. i. 39. 1–2.
[7] Ibid. i. 37. 3, on which von Petrikovits, *Das römische Rheinland*, p. 33.
[8] Filtzinger, *Kölner Jb. für Vor- und Frühgesch.* vi (1962/3), pp. 23–57, with further refs.; sigillata stamps generally contemporary with those from Haltern, p. 56, n. 26, citing letter from Ettlinger.

Rhineland in the Augustan–Tiberian period, while stamps found on Italian sigillata within and immediately outside the area of the colony also closely resemble those from other military sites in Germany and Switzerland. A stretch of ditch which may belong to the defences of the military base on the west side has also been reported.[1]

On Filtzinger's hypothesis, however, the base was actually set within the fortifications of the *oppidum Ubiorum*, and further pottery ovens lying outside the area of the later colony were ascribed to this *oppidum*, rather than to the base.[2] It is however somewhat difficult to picture the base totally surrounded by a native civilian settlement, and such an arrangement would be altogether unparalleled. The evidence from Vetera and Neuss shows that at those two sites several successive Augustan–Tiberian military installations on different orientations succeeded one another. It is more likely that this also happened here, and that all the pottery ovens belong to the base in its different phases.

Filtzinger argued that the base could not have been established before A.D. 9, since only in that year did *legg. I* and *XX* come to Germany; we now have, however, clear proof that the site was occupied earlier, in the shape of a sherd of sigillata with the graffito PRIN. LEG. XIX.[3] *Legio XIX* perished with Varus, and was earlier at Dangstetten (above, Chapter 3. 5). The base went through different periods, since earlier buildings are reported on a different alignment from that of the later street-plan which continued to be used for the subsequent colony,[4] and which may have been that of the base in its last phase, the colony being established on precisely the same site and orientation, as happened elsewhere, for instance at Emona and Aosta in Augustan times, or at Gloucester and Lincoln later.

Where and what was the *oppidum Ubiorum* in the Augustan and early Tiberian period? Tacitus speaks of Agrippina,

---

[1] La Baume, *Köln. Jb.* vii (1964), p. 13; the ditch is however described as a *Sohlgraben*, rather than the usual *Spitzgraben*.

[2] La Baume, op. cit., pp. 7–13; cf. also Doppelfeld in Zimmermann, *Kölner Untersuchungen*, pp. 13–28. [ADD.]

[3] Filtzinger, op. cit., pp. 27–8. Sherd with graffito still unpublished (information kindly communicated by Dr. C. B. Rüger). [ADD.]

[4] Ibid., p. 28, with p. 56, n. 30.

Germanicus' daughter, as having been born in the *oppidum
Ubiorum* (6 November A.D. 15), and elsewhere confirms that
Germanicus' residence was outside the base.[1] But it will
scarcely have been inside a native settlement, even though
the word *oppidum* is in fact regularly used by Roman writers,
as we have seen in Chapter 2 for instance, to mean a settlement
of this sort. Apart from the commander-in-chief's house, there
will also have been the cult-centre of the *ara Ubiorum* here. We
should perhaps envisage an official Roman settlement on
Ubian territory, *oppidum Ubiorum* designating the area, rather
than a fixed settlement. Schmitz has commented on the fact
that no native name for the site has come down to us.[2] This
would allow us to reconcile what has been said above about
the colony replacing the base on the same site with Tacitus'
remark that Agrippina 'in oppidum Ubiorum, in quo genita
erat, veteranos coloniamque deduci impetrat', meaning only
that the colony was on Ubian territory, not within the walls
of an existing settlement.

5. 6. BONN

In recent years excavations in the Minoritenplatz and under
the Rathaus at Bonn (Bonna) have revealed an auxiliary fort,[3]
lying about half a mile south of the known Claudian fortress.[4]
Von Petrikovits speaks of defences comprising a single ditch
and a rampart revetted with timber on the front only; three
periods are known, two of wood and one of stone, but no further
details have yet been published. The dating of the fort depends
upon seven sherds of Italian sigillata, two of which are dated by
Ettlinger to the second decade B.C., one to the first decade B.C.,
and four to the late Augustan or early Tiberian period.[5] The
fort would therefore appear to go back to the time of Drusus or
before. Further publication of the finds is awaited, and further
excavations are planned.

It has also been argued that Bonn was a naval base under

---

[1] Tac., *Ann.* xii. 27, cf. ibid., i. 39; see Filtzinger, op. cit., p. 28 and p. 56, n.
27.

[2] Schmitz, *Colonia Claudia Ara Agrippinensium*, pp. 46–7.

[3] Von Petrikovits, *Das römische Rheinland*, pp. 34–5.

[4] Ibid., p. 47; for position of both sites, see map, p. 60; cf. pp. 106–7.

[5] Ibid., p. 35, n. 41.

Drusus, not on the basis of archaeological evidence, of which
there is none to support such a theory, but relying on a doubtful
reference in Florus, 'Bonnam et Gesoriacum pontibus iunxit
classibusque firmavit', where other manuscripts read however
'Bormam'.[1] Gesoriacum is commonly taken to be Boulogne,
although the context would more naturally lead one to suppose
that the two places in question were on the Rhine, in which
case Gesoriacum defies identification. Heurgon, accepting the
identification of Gesoriacum with Boulogne and reading
'Bonnam', which he applied to Bonn, argued that 'pontibus
iunxit' does not mean 'joined to each other', but rather,
referring separately to each place, 'joined to the opposite bank'.[2]
His interpretation of the phrase in question is accepted by von
Petrikovits who, however, declines to identify either Borma
(which is indeed the generally accepted reading) or Gesoriacum
with any particular site.[3] Certainly if Bonn and Boulogne are
intended, the relevance of Boulogne in this context is not clear,
even by Florus' not very exacting standards. It may be that
Florus has so misunderstood his source as to deprive his notice
of all value. The real meaning of the passage must perhaps
still be left open. We are certainly not justified in postulating
either a Rhine bridge or a fleet for Bonn on the basis of this
passage alone, unless archaeological evidence comes to its
support.

5. 7. KOBLENZ

The Altstadt at Koblenz (Confluentes) is an ideal site for a
Roman fort, on high ground commanding the mouth of the
Moselle. It is too intensively built-up to have been excavated,
but in the course of new building in 1952 a length of Roman
ditch was found, containing six pieces of pottery of the mid
first century and belonging almost certainly to a fort; the ditch
will have been filled in probably about A.D. 70 or earlier.[4]
We have no knowledge of a bridge across the mouth of the
Moselle in the first century, though Tacitus refers to a bridge

---

[1] Florus ii. 30. 26.
[2] Heurgon, *REA* li (1949), pp. 324–6.
[3] Von Petrikovits, op. cit., p. 33.
[4] Filtzinger, *BJ* clx (1960), p. 171.

over the Nahe, and indeed we can hardly doubt that the road
along the left bank of the Rhine was carried on bridges across
all the tributaries.[1] Bingen at the mouth of the Nahe shows
signs of early, possibly Augustan, occupation,[2] and if Bingen
was occupied, so probably was Koblenz.

The earlier finds from the Altstadt area were assembled by
Günther, who also refers to what may be another length of
ditch, found in 1903, though he is over-enthusiastic in asserting
that it is the ditch of a 'Drususkastell'.[3] The finds, scanty
enough, comprise 7 coins of the first century, including one of
Nemausus, two fragments of sigillata with the stamp of Ateius,
and a brooch, said to be Tiberian. They increase the presumption that Koblenz was the site of an early fort, but do not help
us to fix the date of its foundation.

5. 8. MAINZ

The most important site of the Augustan period in the Mainz
area is the legionary base at Mainz itself (Mogontiacum), on
the high ground to the west of the present city centre. Its site
was unoccupied in the Middle Ages, but greatly disturbed by the
construction of forts in the eighteenth century. In the 1930s it
was levelled to make a playing field; today it is almost entirely
built up and will soon be entirely so. For our knowledge of the
site we are largely indebted to Baatz for excavations in 1957-8
and for the book in which he published the results of these excavations and collated earlier reports bearing upon the military
antiquities of the Mainz area (fig. 7). The immense value of his
work can at once be recognized by anyone who cares to compare the plan of the base that Baatz has now established with
the conjectural plan given by Behrens a year or two before
Baatz's excavations began.[4]

The site lies about 40 m. above the Rhine, and is notably well-
drained and dry even after heavy rain.[5] Baatz's excavations
centred on the south-east front, through which trial trenches were
dug.[6] The posts of two wood-and-earth ramparts were discovered

---

[1] Tac., *Hist.* iv. 70; cf. Filtzinger, op. cit., pp. 173-4.
[2] On Bingen, see below, p. 283.   [3] Günther, *BJ* cxlii (1937), pp. 48-50.
[4] Behrens, *MZ* xlviii/xlix (1953/4), p. 73, cf. pp. 70-1.
[5] Baatz, *Mogontiacum*, p. 13.   [6] Ibid., *Beilage* 3.

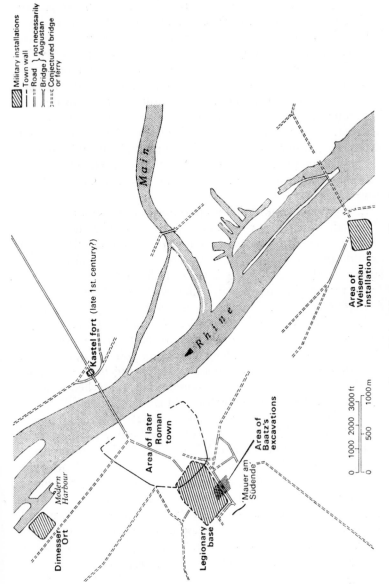

Military installations
Town wall
Road } not necessarily
Bridge } Augustan
Conjectured bridge
or ferry

Main

Kastel fort (late 1st. century?)

Rhine

Area of
Weisenau
installations

Modern
Harbour

Dimesser
Ort

Area of later
Roman town

Legionary
base

Mauer am
Südende

Area of
Baatz's
excavations

0   1000 2000 3000 ft

0   500   1000 m

Fig. 7. Mainz: the Augustan military sites

along with traces of a third period, probably of repairs: the earliest period had posts set in a bedding-trench, the second in individual post-holes slightly in advance of the original line.[1] The position of the south-east front never altered from the first occupation of the site down to the third century or probably the fourth.[2] The foundations of a stone wall found on top of the remains of the wooden period date from the third century or perhaps the second half of the second century, and it was not the first stone wall in this position. Repeated reconstruction and the destruction of the higher Roman levels by the eighteenth- and twentieth-century building and levelling make it impossible to say how many phases of the fortification intervened between the remains of the earth rampart and those which survive of the stone wall.

In front of the line of the rampart and wall seven ditches were observed, which Baatz numbers from 1–7 in what he takes to be the sequence of their construction, warning that this does not exclude the possibility that still more once existed and can no longer be observed.[3] No. 4 is separate from the other ditches, 15 m. further out than no. 2, which is otherwise the outermost ditch;[4] no. 4 is undoubtedly to be dated to the reign of Claudius or Nero;[5] no. 5 is the innermost ditch of all and cuts into the foundations of the wood-and-earth rampart;[6] nos. 6 and 7 are clearly later than no. 5.[7] Hence, as Baatz points out, only nos. 1–3 come into question as possibly belonging to the rampart which he found, and they are moreover distinguished from all the other ditches observed by the light colour of their filling, not yet darkened by continued use and occupation of the terrain.[8]

Of these three ditches, no. 3 cuts into the inner side of no. 2 and is therefore later; no. 1, lying nearer to the rampart than either 2 or 3, neither cuts nor is cut by no. 3. No. 2 alone of the fortification ditches observed is not truly V-shaped, but has a flat bottom,[9] and is too far from the rampart to be the single ditch of the earliest period of it. Baatz therefore suggests that no. 1 belongs to the earliest period of the rampart, no. 2 may go with it to form a double ditch, but is more likely later, while

---

[1] Baatz, plate 21, cf. pp. 17–18.
[2] Ibid., pp. 28, 30, cf. p. 77.
[3] Ibid., pp. 23–4.
[4] Ibid., *Beilage* 4, section A.
[5] Ibid., pp. 23–4.
[6] Ibid., p. 23.
[7] Ibid., p. 26; *Beilage* 4, section B.
[8] Ibid., p. 19.
[9] Ibid., *Beilage* 4, section A.

no. 3, known to be later than no. 2, is probably later than both 2 and 1, and was dug after they had been filled. The finds from all three ditches are scanty and cannot be firmly dated, but are compatible with a dating any time up to the late Tiberian period.[1]

The flat bottom of ditch no. 2 was silted up and the layers of silt had a greenish tinge which led Baatz to conclude that the ditch had once carried drainage water.[2] Ditch no. 3 was also silted, at least in its lower portion; and from section A it appears that ditches nos. 1, 2, and 3 were all preserved for only about 1 m. up from the bottom. The filling of no. 3 contained two un-stamped tiles, whereas elsewhere tiles are not found in Augustan–Tiberian levels, and although it contained no specifically Claudian pottery, what pottery it did contain was not precisely datable.[3] Hence Baatz concluded that no. 3 was filled in late Tiberian or Claudian times, and the evidence of the tiles, while not conclusive, best supports a Claudian date. Although Baatz assumes no. 3 to be later than nos. 1 and 2, there is no evidence to show it later than no. 1 which contained no finds datable more closely than merely to Augustan–Tiberian times.[4] No. 1 stayed open for some time, since a photograph shows it to have been recut and then deliberately filled in at an unknown date.[5]

Baatz observed three periods in the remains of the rampart posts; the plan[6] shows that this means two separate periods of construction, followed by local repairs. The posts of the second period are set in individual post-holes up against the posts in the original bedding-trench of the front revetment, as if planted while the originals still stood, but the rear row cannot have been erected without the complete removal of the original rear revet-ment and the cutting back of the earth core, since it stands in front of the original row. But essentially the rampart remains throughout these three periods in the same place. If ditch no. 1 belonged to it originally, why was no. 1 filled in and replaced by no. 3, which lies 6 m. further out? If Baatz thinks no. 2 is too far out to belong to this rampart in the capacity of its only protec-tive ditch, equally so is no. 3, whose point lies just 1 m. closer to the rampart than the foot of no. 2's inner side, and 10 m.

---

[1] Baatz, p. 19.   [2] Ibid., p. 19, cf. *Beilage* 4, section A.
[3] Ibid., p. 23, cf. pp. 16–19.
[4] Ibid., p. 19.   [5] Ibid., plate 23. 2.   [6] Ibid., plate 21.

away from the foot of the front face of the rampart.[1] If no. 3 does in fact follow the obliteration of no. 1, then either the rampart also was moved forward, and the foundations of the new rampart will have been destroyed by the later ditches, nos. 5 6, and 7, or else no. 3 is the outer ditch of a pair of ditches, and the corresponding inner ditch must have lain somewhere in the area of ditches nos. 1 and 5. But it is here that the profiles of the ditches are clearly distinguishable, and it is hard to believe that no. 3's putative twin either escaped the excavator's notice, or was utterly destroyed without trace by no. 1 (which Baatz of course sets earlier than no. 3 anyway) or by the very narrow, pointed no. 5. There is however no argument at all against supposing that no. 1 is in fact itself the inner ditch and no. 3 the outer, so that the rampart in its second period (i.e. that of the rows of separate post-holes) was defined by a double ditch.

In this case then no. 2 belongs to the earliest period (i.e. that of the bedding-trenches) of the rampart. Despite the greenish tinge of the layers of silt in its bottom, it is clearly not a drainage-ditch, as we can see by comparing it with the other fortification ditches and the other drains, as seen in sections A and B. Indeed the greenish tinge better suits stagnant than running water, and clearly water used to collect here, whether because the bottom of the ditch at this point was rather deeper than elsewhere, or because the causeway of a gate impeded drainage, or for some other reason. Each time that the ditch thus flooded, a fresh layer of silt was deposited, and this accounts for the nature of the filling observed by Baatz.

I would suggest that ditch no. 2, the earliest ditch that was discovered in the excavations, was the outer ditch of the system belonging to the earliest period. It is not the usual V-shaped *fossa fastigata* to which we are accustomed in the early Roman fortifications in the Rhineland, but, as appears from section A–B, a *fossa Punica*. The steep, almost vertical, outer side is unlike that of the other ditches, and the inner side can be clearly seen to turn and slope gently towards the rampart. A Punic ditch cannot stand alone, since an enemy trapped within it becomes desperate and must be faced by a really tough final obstacle,[2]

---

[1] Baatz, *Beilage* 4, section B.

[2] Cf. Richmond on the Punic ditch at Cawthorn, *Arch. Journ.* lxxxix (1932), p. 74, and his drawing of the ditch system at Hod Hill, *PBA* xli (1955), p. 307. I know

but the inner ditch must have lain somewhere in the line of nos. 1 and 5, which have totally obliterated it.

In the interior of the base at least two periods of wooden building could be observed before the earliest stone foundations of about the middle of the first century. Tiles are first found in the Claudian–Neronian levels, together with mortar and window-glass, but lime-plaster as a facing for the walls appears to have been used in the earliest period.[1] Baatz suggests that there may have been stone buildings, as yet undiscovered, in Augustan–Tiberian times; but there is absolutely no reason to suppose that there were, and the analogy of other Rhineland sites is against it.[2] The most notable remains of the earliest period of occupation within the fortifications were however in the *intervallum*, and comprised a road, numerous rubbish pits so collapsed by the decay of organic matter that neither individual pits nor layers could be distinguished, slight traces of buildings, several hearths, and one or perhaps two ovens. The road was about 12 m. from the rampart and originally about 3 m. wide, although it was made 6·5 m. wide in late Tiberian times. It was metalled and had been repeatedly mended until it was 1·4 m. thick and so tough that the mechanical excavator had difficulty in shifting it.[3] In the lowest layer of metalling and the earliest gutter of the road was found sigillata of Service I, while in the next layer and its new gutter there was Service II.

The space in the *intervallum* between the road and the rampart yielded pottery contemporary with that from Oberaden, and the latest pottery was late Augustan or early Tiberian; there was no Gaulish sigillata.[4] During this time the ground had been raised about 1 m. and periodically levelled off. There was no pottery of the middle and later periods of Tiberius' reign, whence Baatz suggested that the wood-and-earth rampart of the usual Rhineland type was at this time replaced by a new rampart revetted on the front only, with a sloping bank to the rear extending right back to the *intervallum* road, the front revetment being later replaced by stone. The only structure or finds

of no other Punic ditch from an Augustan site. Baatz mentions also a so-called 'Wolfsgrube', in front of ditches nos. 2 and 3; if correctly identified, it has no parallel except on the Annaberg at Haltern. [ADD.]

[1] Baatz, op. cit., pp. 14–16, 21.
[2] Cf. Ettlinger, *BJ* clxii (1962), p. 604, expressing surprise at Baatz's suggestion.
[3] Baatz, op. cit., p. 15.   [4] Ibid., pp. 16–17.

from the *intervallum* to be dated after the early Tiberian period was a water-tank, partially stone-built, containing pottery of the middle or second half of the first century, which on this hypothesis had been let into the rear slope of the rampart.[1] There is, however, no apparent reason for this reversion to a single wooden palisade, and 11 m. would be an inordinate and unprecedented width for the earth bank.[2] It might therefore be better to suppose that earth was tipped in the *intervallum* not in order to construct a bank for a new rampart, but rather to raise and resurface this part of the available land within the base. The use of the *intervallum* for garbage disposal had left the ground unstable, and perhaps unsavoury. When under Tiberius it was decided to build here, the whole area was first filled with fresh earth to provide a clean, level, firm surface, and the occupation layers above this have not been preserved, except for the sunken water-tank.

The fill used here may have come from outside the base, where rough pits, perhaps simply one large pit, 14–15 m. wide and 4 m. deep, were cut by four of Baatz's trial trenches, extended over some 125 m.[3] All four pits were very alike in their form and filling. Baatz judged the material dug out to have been used for daubing the walls of the wooden huts and for streetmaking, but it seems somewhat doubtful if this would take as much clay and gravel as was apparently excavated here. In the bottom of one of the pits was a tile of the *legio IV Macedonia*; all the pits had been filled with organic rubbish and charcoal, among which were sherds resembling those of the early period at Hofheim. The pits may also have provided earth to raise a bank (which will not have covered the whole *intervallum*) up to the bank of the new Claudian stone wall. They were then used for tipping the rubbish which had previously been buried in the *intervallum*, and later a road was made along the edge of the pits to facilitate tipping until the filling was completed.

Although Baatz's excavations were limited to this part of the south-east front, he also summarizes early excavations and

---

[1] Baatz, op. cit., pp. 22, 24. Apart from this one tank, no trace of a water supply was found; perhaps we might conjecture a timber aqueduct, rebuilt in stone between 71 and 86 (p. 77).

[2] Cf. the later wall at York, Richmond, *PBA* xli (1955), p. 311, with drawing, p. 312.

[3] Baatz, op. cit., p. 25.

observations bearing on the other sides. A length of fortification excavated in 1910 is the south-west side of the defences;[1] it was traced for about 260 m. and probably extended for about 440 m. Sections of Roman wall observed on the north-west in 1913 and 1919 may perhaps belong to a late period of the north-west front.[2] The north-east front and the north and east corners are not, however, known from any excavation or observation; Baatz shows clearly that this side lay to the north of the later town wall, and estimates its line from the present contours of the ground, but a comparison of the plan with the map shows that the line, especially at the north and east corners, is highly speculative.[3] Thompson, reviewing Baatz, writes: 'One wonders how far he is justified in arguing that the modern crests of the steep slopes on these two sides define the line of defences in a fast eroding subsoil like loess.'[4] The area of 35–6 ha. which Baatz ascribes to the base should be taken as a minimum, though it cannot be far short. Baatz himself comments on its smallness compared with Vetera's 56 ha., and suggests that at Mainz the auxiliaries lay outside the base in their own forts.[5]

The first occupation of the site is not easy to date. The number of early finds is few, and there is no piece of sigillata as early as the earliest finds from Basle, not to mention those from Neuss, Zürich, Augst, and Vidy. This need not be significant, however, when so very little of the base was excavated.[6] The early pottery as a whole resembles that from Oberaden.[7] A date earlier than this, probable on general historical grounds, is not excluded by the absence of earlier finds, though it cannot be proved. Baatz points out that since the interior of the base was not excavated, an earlier and smaller fort on the site, as at Neuss, remains a possibility, though again there is no evidence.[8]

[1] Ibid., pp. 68–71; this is the so-called 'Mauer am Mitteldamm'. The 'Mauer am Südende' discovered in the same excavation is proved by Baatz to have had no connection with the base.

[2] Ibid., pp. 71–2.

[3] Ibid., p. 72, cf. Beilage 1, 2.

[4] Thompson, JRS liii (1963), p. 237.

[5] Cf. table, Baatz, op. cit., p. 80; Baatz sees 18 ha. as the minimum size for one legion; Thompson objects that Lincoln was only 16·8 ha., but this was in Claudian and post-Claudian times, when the bases were generally smaller. Cf. above, p. 98 on canabae.

[6] Cf. Ettlinger, op. cit., p. 605. See above, p. 41.

[7] See table of early sigillata stamps, Baatz, op. cit., pp. 53–7.

[8] Ibid., p. 77, cf. p. 19.

The *canabae* were observed outside the south-east front, where an occupation layer beginning some 35 m. from the outer edge of ditch no. 2 yielded Service II sigillata.[1] There was no sign of substantial buildings. A road of Augustan date leading down to the Rhine shows that the crossing from Mainz to Kastel was already in use at this period,[2] although there is no evidence for a fortified bridgehead at Kastel before the end of the first century.[3] This road was also lined with early occupation remains, as if the *canabae* had extended along here too. A further hoard of sigillata, perhaps a merchant's stock, was found outside the Peterskirche in Mainz; it is probably late Augustan, parallel to the later types from Haltern.[4]

There are two other known Augustan sites in the Mainz area. Firstly, on the left bank of the Rhine about 2 km. downstream, at the Dimesser Ort, lay the Augustan and later Rhine-harbour, where vast quantities of amphorae, whole or broken, have been found, with considerable amounts of sigillata.[5] Secondly, on an escarpment overlooking the river some 3·5 km. south of the Mainz base, at Weisenau, there was probably also some form of military occupation in Augustan or Tiberian times.[6] This was also the site of a pre-Roman settlement and a short-lived legionary base under Caligula, but the whole area has been cut about and the remains largely destroyed by a large quarry and a cement works.[7] Since we do not know where the other two legions were encamped after A.D. 9, when the army of Upper Germany was increased to four legions, it is possible that Weisenau was the site of their base.

[1] Baatz, op. cit., pp. 19–20.

[2] Ibid., p. 82; the piles of the bridge, generally assumed to be Vespasianic, were found in the river-bed and on the bank, see Behrens, *MZ* xlviii/xlix (1953/4), pp. 79–80, with further refs.

[3] Schmidt, *ORL* ii B.30, *Kastel bei Mainz*; Augustan fort conjectured, pp. 19–20; more recently, Schönberger, *SJ* (1961), p. 37, n. 8; id., *Neuere Grabungen am obergerm. und rät. Limes*, p. 72; an Augustan fort is not of course excluded in the Kastel area, which has yielded scattered Augustan and Tiberian finds, cf. Schmidt, op. cit., p. 17; *FMRD* iv. 1, no. 1183. 4–9, with n., p. 136.

[4] Von Pfeffer, *MZ* lvi/lvii (1961/2), pp. 209–12.

[5] First reported in *Westd. Ztschr.* xx (1901), cols. 341–5; see Behrens, op. cit., p. 79; Baatz, op. cit., pp. 82–3.

[6] Baatz, op. cit., p. 81; von Petrikovits, *MZ* lviii (1963), p. 28, suggests Weisenau as the site where the auxiliaries were encamped.

[7] Baatz, loc. cit.; Schumacher, *MZ* iii (1908), pp. 37–8; Klumbach, *Germania* xxix (1951), pp. 165–6; see also below, p. 283.

5. 9. STRASBOURG

The earliest Roman fortification on the site of Strasbourg (Argentorate) was an auxiliary fort measuring about 180 × 350 m., with an area of about 6·3 ha., the same size as the early fort at Neuss and rather smaller than the fort on the Annaberg at Haltern, which has an area of about 7·25 ha.[1] It was succeeded by a legionary base, the east side of the defences of the fort being levelled to form the *via principalis* of the new base (today the Rue du Dôme).[2] The first garrison of the base was apparently *legio II*. Fort and base lie on an island, where now the old quarter of the city stands, with the cathedral and the Château des Rohan. The earliest cemetery was also on the island, yielding Augustan coins and sigillata, military finds, especially those typical of cavalry troops, and a dedication to Mars Loucetius set up by one Fittio of the *ala Petriana Treverorum*, which is hence assumed to have garrisoned the fort.[3] It appears that this was the cemetery belonging to the early fort, while the later cemeteries are not on the island but on the mainland, extending along the road in the usual way; these cemeteries have yielded gravestones of *legio II*.[4] Forrer comments on the absence of weapons and the like in the graves here, in contrast to those on the island, further evidence that the mainland graves are those of legionaries, not native auxiliaries.

The relative order of the various occupations of the site is quite clear. Hatt describes the discovery in the Ruelle Saint-Médard of 'une stratigraphie romaine absolument complète'.[5] The absolute dating of the early period is less satisfactory. Forrer saw Strasbourg as a 'Drususkastelle', dating from 12 B.C. or just after.[6] Hatt would date the first occupation of the site either 'vers 15 av. J.-C.', or else around 12.[7] What is needed is a thorough re-examination of all pottery and coins from within the area of the earliest fort and the area of its cemetery. The publication of coin finds is particularly unsatisfactory. Forrer

---

[1] Forrer, *Strasbourg-Argentorate* i, pp. 220–1, 261–5.

[2] Ibid., p. 222; Hatt, *Cahiers d'arch. et d'hist. d'Alsace* cxxxiii (1953), p. 76, with section, p. 77.

[3] Forrer, op. cit., pp. 221, 268–70.

[4] Ibid. pp. 273–82.

[5] Hatt, *Gallia* ix (1953), pp. 225–8.

[6] Forrer, op. cit., p. 221.

[7] Hatt, *Historia* ii (1953/4), p. 236, and id. in *Limes-Studien*, p. 51, respectively.

in 1927 published all coins found up to 1921 only.[1] Many subsequent finds remain unpublished, and many coins were
apparently lost after the museum had been bombed in the war.
The amount of sigillata in use among the *ala Petriana Treverorum*
is in any case likely to be small compared with that at a site
occupied by a legionary detachment, such as Zürich or Basle.
The suggested dates of *c.* 12 or *c.* 15 B.C. for the establishment
of a fort at Strasbourg are based on general historical considerations, rather than on precise archaeological evidence. Yet there
seems no reason why a fort here should not on historical grounds
go back well before 15 B.C. Auxiliary forts must antedate legionary bases along the Rhine. The first garrison, recruited from
the neighbouring Treveri, may well have had a defensive role
against possible German invaders before the Romans started to
invade Germany in their turn. All is conjecture, and will remain
conjecture, until modern knowledge of coins and pottery can be
applied to the whole mass of Strasbourg finds.

    In the same way, Hatt dates the start of the base that re-
placed it either 'sous Tibère, vers 20 ap. J.-C.', or else to the
year 14.[2] Forrer set the date of foundation rather earlier, in A.D.
9–10 or A.D. 12, apparently because he assumed that the *legio
II* must have come straight to Strasbourg on its arrival on the
Rhine from Spain after the Varian Disaster.[3] A legion at Strasbourg had a purely defensive role to play, at least in pre-Flavian
times. Syme describes the Strasbourg base admirably: 'It is not
a spear-point directed at the inhospitable hills of the Black
Forest or the thin and innocuous population of southern Germany, nor had it been used as a base for the great invasions of
Augustan days. No, the legion at Strasbourg is ready to leap
upon Metz or Belfort, and penetrate into the interior of Gaul
through the gaps north and south of the chain of the Vosges.'[4]
The establishment of a base at Strasbourg is most likely to have
been part of the same defensive plan that placed a legion at
Vindonissa.

    [1] Forrer, op. cit. ii, pp. 578–85.
    [2] Hatt, *Historia* ii (1953/4), p. 236, and id., *Limes-Studien*, p. 51.
    [3] Forrer, *L'Alsace romaine*, p. 32. Forrer, *Strasbourg-Argentorate* i, p. 82, reports a
tile with the stamp of this legion reputedly found in 1908 in the foundation of the
via principalis during the laying of sewers.
    [4] Syme, *JRS* xxvi (1936), p. 125. [ADD.]

6

THE ADVANCE TO THE ELBE

THERE are, as outlined above in Chapter 5, three main invasion routes into Germany from the Rhine, one for amphibious operations from Vechten along the North Sea coast and up the rivers Weser and Elbe, another from Vetera along the Lippe valley, and a third from Mainz up the Wetterau and through the Hessian Gap. Of the first, already discussed in Chapter 5. 1, nothing more remains to be said in this chapter, the first part of which will be primarily devoted to the other two routes. All three routes converge upon the Weser in the Minden–Kassel area and upon the Elbe in the region of Magdeburg. Although not so much as a Roman marching-camp is known from either of these areas, we cannot doubt that they remain to be found. The part played by the three cities named in the military history of Germany at all periods is sufficient indication of their natural strategic importance. A fourth invasion route also exists, not from the Rhine, but leading northwards from Raetia. This was mentioned in Chapter 4, and will also be discussed below.

The river Lippe rises north-east of Bad Lippspringe in the hills now known as the Teutoburger Wald. It flows south-west to Lippstadt and thereafter almost due west, with gentle deviations either side of the straight line, to join the Rhine at Wesel, almost opposite the site of Vetera. It is the most northerly of the westward-flowing tributaries of the Rhine. In Roman times and right into the Middle Ages it was navigable from the Rhine as far up as Lippstadt,[1] while its banks offer an excellent land route into the heart of Germany. It flows for almost all its course through fairly flat or gently rolling country. There are indeed hills at points along its course, but nowhere is it closely hemmed in: most nearly so at Haltern, where the Hohe Mark to the

---

[1] Cf. *MAKW* ii (1901), pp. 24–5, with documents, pp. 31–5; cf. also *MAKW* i (1899), p. 62, and Albrecht, *Das Römerlager in Oberaden* i, p. 23.

north and the Haard to the south approach each other. The Lippe contrasts strongly in this respect with the Ruhr, the next Rhine-tributary to the south, which is serpentine in its lower course, and for much of its length tightly enclosed between hills on either side, while immediately south of the Ruhr begins very hilly and difficult country, intersected by steep valleys and still today heavily wooded, through which the Sieg and the Lahn flow to join the Rhine opposite Bonn and Koblenz respectively. This area was not one to attract the legions. None of these rivers except the Lippe is a suitable route for an invader.[1] Only as you approach the head of the Lippe do the hills start to close in all around. Near Paderborn the river seems to be flowing through a gigantic amphitheatre. The Teutoburger Wald, the Egge-birge, and the Briloner Höhen stand about it in a semi-circle, and an army which marches up the Lippe to Bad Lippspringe must break through the hills in order to go any further east-wards.

Along the Lippe several Roman stations are known. At Holsterhausen (Chapter 6. 1), roughly 36 km. east of Vetera, a marching-camp for two legions plus auxiliaries is known and a permanent fort may remain to be found. At Haltern (Chapter 6. 2), 18 km. further east, there was a legionary base overlying an earlier marching-camp and occupied from perhaps as early as about 8 B.C. until it was destroyed in the Varian Disaster; there were also remains in the area known as the Wiegel, which may be those of a stores-compound or annexe attached to the base; there were also two separate forts over a mile apart, the one on the Annaberg being very early and comparatively short-lived, the other on the Hofestatt showing four distinct periods of occupation, one of which may possibly be post-Varian. At Oberaden (Chapter 6. 3), 36 km. east of Haltern, a base for two legions is known, occupied from c. 11–10 B.C. to about 8 or 7 B.C., and nearby at Beckinghausen (Chapter 6. 4), a small fort which may have gone on being occupied even after Oberaden was given up. The remains of another base were also discovered in the autumn of 1968 at Anreppen, on the south bank of the Lippe some 10 km. north-west of Paderborn (Chapter 6. 5). The

---

[1] It is clear that the valley was not provided with paved roads, see Hagen, *Römerstrassen der Rheinprovinz*, p. 484, just as the Romans did not set about build-ing roads in Gaul until twenty years after Caesar's first arrival.

evidence suggests that there may have been a chain of bases or forts at 18-km. intervals, in which case it is possible that another may yet remain to be found halfway between Oberaden and Haltern in the Datteln–Olfen–Vinnum region, at which point the north bank, being hilly, offers more likely sites than the south, and possibly three more between Oberaden and Anreppen.

A fort has also been conjectured, but on inadequate grounds, near the village of Reckelsum on the north bank of the Stever, a tributary of the Lippe at Haltern, about 10 km. east of Haltern. Here extensive finds of Roman silver coins and of a number of other Roman objects were made, though no trace of buildings or ditches has been found.[1] There were 85 coins, of which 28 are now lost and the other 57 range in date from 180 B.C. to the reign of Augustus, found at three separate places within about 750 m. of one another. A fourth find-spot lay over 2·5 km. away, while two further *denarii* were found some 5 km. away to the north on the Borkenberge. In comparison with the coins the other finds were negligible: fragments of three Roman pots, three brooches, three other articles of bronze, and two of bone, all of them, apart from one third-century brooch, apparently to be dated around the time of Christ's birth. This evidence does not add up to a fort; indeed the presence of many silver coins without any bronze ones rather suggests loot.

Other Augustan forts have been claimed in the Lippe valley or on the heights encircling the upper reaches, but with even less evidence. Kneblinghausen is marked as an Augustan fort in more than one museum, but there is no archaeological evidence whatsoever to support this, although strategically it is not improbable.[2] Similarly a supposed fort at Elsen near Paderborn has had a long run, thanks to the authority of Mommsen, who

---

[1] Albrecht, *Frühgeschichtliche Funde aus Westfalen*, pp. 36–9.

[2] Reports of excavations by Hartmann, *MAKW* iii (1903), pp. 99–126; ibid. iv (1905), pp. 131 ff.; Stieren, *Germania* xi (1927), pp. 70–1; ibid. xv (1931), pp. 157–63; id., *Bod. Westf.* i (1929), pp. 50–3; Samesreuther and Henneböle, *Germania* xxiii (1939), pp. 94–103; cf. id., *Bod. Westf.* vii (1950), pp. 121–2. Henneböle has also restated his own views in a brief pamphlet, *Das Römerlager Kneblinghausen* (1960). The site holds two superimposed camps, both with *claviculae*, hence probably Flavian or Claudian at the earliest, (Kahrstedt, *BJ* cxxxviii (1953), pp. 144–52); the only possible sign of earlier date is a reported fragment of Italian sigillata, with four fragments of La Graufesenque, two of them late first century or later (*Germania* xxiii (1939), p. 97, n. 1).

located Aliso here, on etymological grounds. Strategically this identification was always improbable and is now quite ruled out by archaeological exploration of the area around the village church at Elsen, which has revealed no Roman remains, but only those of a German settlement, apparently of the early first century.[1]

The identity of Aliso is a notorious problem. Dio names it as the place where Drusus established a post in 11 B.C. at the confluence of the Lippe and the Eliso.[2] The Germans attacked and apparently captured it in A.D. 9,[3] but it was again in Roman occupation in 16, when it was linked to the Rhine bases 'novis limitibus aggeribusque', and is probably also referred to as 'castellum Lupiae flumini adpositum' four sentences earlier.[4] Of the known Roman sites on the Lippe, Oberaden is excluded by its short period of occupation, while Haltern is a possible candidate only if we adopt the hypothesis that the Hofestatt fort was rebuilt under Germanicus. In that case, the Annaberg fort would serve for Drusus' original post of 11 B.C., the legionary base was the scene of L. Caedicius' heroic resistance in A.D. 9, and the Hofestatt fort will have been reoccupied, in what we know as the 'blue' period, under Germanicus.[5]

The case for identifying Aliso with Haltern was set out long ago by Schuchhardt, who points out, rightly, that all the references to Aliso imply that the place was not very far from the Rhine.[6] There is no reason whatsoever to identify it with Tiberius' camp 'ad caput Lupiae' of the year A.D. 4, as did Mommsen.[7] Rice Holmes's argument for a site near Hamm, on the grounds that only here could a fort protect the Rhine frontier from raids through the passes of the Teutoburger Wald, is not only strategically incomprehensible (it smacks of the study, and bears no relation to the actual geography of the Lippe area), but also betrays a ludicrous misunderstanding of Drusus' aims, which in 11 B.C. were not to defend a Rhine frontier.[8] No other

---

[1] Cf. *Bod. Westf.* vii (1950), p. 88; further unpublished information from Dr. Aschemeyer.

[2] Dio liv. 33. 4.   [3] Vell. ii. 120. 4, cf. Dio lvi. 22.

[4] Tac., *Ann.* ii. 7.   [5] See below, pp. 198–206.

[6] Schuchhardt, *Sitzber. Kön. Preuss. Akad.* 1900, pp. 303–16; cf. id., *Sitzber. Preuss. Akad.* 1931, pp. 615–26.

[7] Vell. ii. 105. 3, accepting the conjecture 'Lupiae' for 'Iuliae', on which see Furneaux ad Tac., *Ann.* i. 60. See also below, p. 159.

[8] Holmes, *The Architect of the Roman Empire* ii, pp. 164–5.

suggestion deserves serious consideration.[1] The case for Haltern as Aliso cannot of course be proved; but we can say that if Haltern is *not* Aliso, then we have no idea where Aliso was. If on the other hand Haltern and Aliso are the same, the purpose of the different sites there is explained and the other indications fall into place: the short occupation of the Annaberg, the barricades in the fortress gates, the apparent extension of the Hofestatt fort in its last period. Pure hypothesis! But we can hope for nothing better, except in the unlikely event of the discovery of an inscription at Haltern or elsewhere actually naming Aliso.

The other great invasion route was that along the lower valley of the Main, up the valley of its tributary the Nidda, and northward through the Wetterau; it admirably complemented the more northerly Lippe valley route. Directly opposite the mouth of the Main, as we have seen, stood the legionary base at Mainz. East of the Rhine, along the Main–Wetterau route, we know of a supply-depot from the period of Drusus' campaigns at Rödgen (Chapter 6. 8), just north of Friedberg, about 56 km. from Mainz, as the crow flies, close by a large and apparently friendly native settlement at Bad Nauheim (Chapter 6. 9), which probably became the site of a Roman marching-camp in the time of Germanicus. Wiesbaden (Chapter 6. 5), Höchst-am-Main (Chapter 6. 6), and Friedberg itself (Chapter 6. 7) are all the sites of Roman forts. At the first and last of these sites, *canabae* have been identified. Wiesbaden is probably, Friedberg certainly to be assigned to the period of Germanicus' campaigns; Höchst was almost certainly occupied under Germanicus, but may have been established earlier.

Augustan forts have also been conjectured at Praunheim and Heddernheim, just outside Frankfurt, and at Hofheim. Neither at Praunheim, nor at Heddernheim, nor at Frankfurt itself is there evidence for Roman occupation before Flavian times.[2]

---

[1] One of the least plausible identifications is with Wetzlar on the Lahn, on which see Koepp, *Germania* iv (1920), pp. 1–7, and Kahrstedt, *Gnomon* xii (1936), pp. 285–6. Byvanck, *Nederland in den Romeinschen tijd*, p. 95, actually suggests that the name belonged originally to Oberaden, and was transferred to Haltern when the Oberaden base was abandoned. See further bibliography in Koepp, *Varusschlacht und Aliso*.

[2] Schönberger, *Neuere Ausgrabungen am obergerm. und rät. Limes*, pp. 70–3, reviewing the evidence for Augustan occupation in the Main–Wetterau area, esp. p. 72, with map p. 71; cf. id., *SJ* xi (1952), p. 66; on Heddernheim, cf. Wolff, *ORL* ii B.27, *Kastell und die Erdlager von Heddernheim* (1915); on Frankfurt, Wolff, *ORL* ii

Hofheim is the site of the well-known fort dating from about 39–40, excavated by Ritterling, whose report is one of the classics of Roman archaeology in the Rhineland.[1] A grave recently found in the vicinity was at first dated to the time of Germanicus and taken to mean that there was a fort of that period somewhere nearby.[2] Baatz, however, has shown that the grave can scarcely be so early, since it was lined with tiles, which do not begin to appear in the area until Claudian times.[3]

Such then is the archaeological evidence available for the Augustan period from east of the Rhine. It now has to be put together with the literary evidence. We have seen how Augustus was himself in Gaul from 16 to 13 B.C., in charge of preparations. In 12, the great advance began, and Drusus took the field each year from 12 to 9.[4] The first year, having provided for the loyalty of Gaul in his absence,[5] he invaded the lands of the Usipetes and Sugambri, the latter of whom had invited reprisal by raiding into Gaul.[6] He also made a naval expedition from Vechten along the canal which he had dug, the *fossa Drusiana*, and with the help of the Frisii he attacked the Chauci on the Lower Ems and perhaps occupied the island of Borkum (Burchanis) off the mouth of that river, and defeated the Bructeri in a naval battle higher upstream.[7] Although we do not hear of Drusus himself embarking on naval ventures in the following years, it is very probable that his lieutenants did so.

In 11 he again attacked the Usipetes, bridged the river Lippe, and invaded Sugambrian territory, but the Sugambri were not at home. They had gone with their whole tribe to attack their southern neighbours, the Chatti. Drusus therefore went straight through their lands and those of the Cherusci to the east and reached the Weser, where shortage of supplies, the

B.27a, *Kastell Frankfurt a. M.* (1915); cf. Hundt and Fischer in *Neue Ausgrabungen in Deutschland* (1958), p. 402.

[1] Ritterling, *Nass. Ann.* xiv (1912), pp. 1–416; see below, p. 259.

[2] Schoppa, *Nassau. Heimatbl.* xlvii (1957), p. 28; *Germania* xxxvi (1958), pp. 154–6; cf. Schönberger, op. cit., p. 72.

[3] Baatz in Schönberger, op. cit., p. 72, n. 26.

[4] The chief sources for Drusus' campaigns are Dio liv. 32–3, 36, lv. 6; Florus ii. 30. 21–8; Livy, *epit.* 137–40; Orosius vi. 21. 15. On the lost sources, cf. esp. Marx, *Klio* xxvi (1933), pp. 323–9; ibid. xxix (1936), pp. 94–101, 202–18.

[5] Dio liv. 32. 1.

[6] Dio, loc. cit.; Livy, *epit.* 137.

[7] Strabo vii. 290–1, without a date, cf. Holmes, op. cit., pp. 158–60; also Tac., *Germ.* 32–4.

approach of winter, and a bad omen combined to make him turn back. Since we hear nothing of a battle, it is likely that the Cherusci west of the Weser had retired beyond it on Drusus' approach.[1] After severe fighting on the way back, Drusus planted two forts, one at the confluence of the Lippe and the Eliso, which, as we have seen, may be the fort on the Annaberg at Haltern, and one among the Chatti, near the Rhine, the location of which is unknown.[2] Drusus himself with the main body of his army wintered behind the Rhine.

Mention of a fort among the Chatti is interesting. We do not otherwise hear of operations against them in 12 or 11, yet there must have been an invasion of their territory, perhaps by one of Drusus' legates, whose exploits have been overshadowed by his chief's. The Rödgen supply base shows that Drusus' forces were using the Mainz–Wetterau route, which must have brought them into conflict with the Chatti, living at this time north of the Wetterau. Only later, perhaps in A.D. 9, did they move farther south, probably dispossessing the Mattiaci of the Rödgen–Bad Nauheim area and compelling the establishment by Germanicus of a fort on the excellent defensive site of Friedberg, which Drusus had not thought it necessary to occupy. We do not know whether it was before 12 B.C. or after A.D. 9 that they appropriated Mattium, capital of the Mattiaci.[3] Whatever was done to the Chatti in 11, however, it drove them to make common cause with their erstwhile enemies, the Sugambri, for at the start of the campaigning season of 10, when the Chatti were the special object of Drusus' attentions, they are found to have migrated and joined the Sugambri, perhaps forming an alliance for mutual defence centred on the broken, wooded country of the Rothaar Gebirge.

In the meantime, during the winter of 11/10, Drusus returned to Rome to celebrate the first two years' victories, along with his brother Tiberius, who had himself just finished two years' campaigning in Illyricum, completing the conquest of the Sava valley and Bosnia begun by M. Vinicius (14) and Agrippa (13).[4] The brothers received the *ornamenta triumphalia* and other

[1] Klose, *Roms Klientel-Randstaaten*, p. 47.

[2] Dio liv. 33. 4; on the fort among the Chatti, see below, pp. 229–30.

[3] See above, pp. 20–1.

[4] Dio liv. 24. 3, 28. 1–2, 31, 34; Vell. ii. 39. 3, 96 (on which see Hanslik, *RE* ixA, col. 115); Florus ii. 24; Suet., *Tib.* 9; Livy, *epit.* 139; *RG* 30.

honours, while it was voted that the Temple of Janus should be closed, all wars having ceased, at any rate until the next year's campaigning season.[1] Unexpected trouble in Illyricum however thwarted the closure and compelled the hasty return to his province of Tiberius, who had gone with Augustus and Drusus to Gaul, perhaps to attend the dedication of the Lugdunum altar.[2] Augustus at this period was much at Lugdunum, while the conquest of Germany was afoot.[3]

In 9 B.C. the Chatti were attacked again; then the Suebic Marcomanni on the Upper Main, then the Cherusci were defeated. Drusus reached and unsuccessfully tried to cross the Elbe.[4] Augustus' directive to his generals to leave the tribes beyond the river alone, so as not to compel them to make common cause with those on the near side, was clearly not yet in operation.[5] Drusus set up a trophy and withdrew. Somewhere between the Saale and the Rhine he broke his leg in a riding accident and died a month later,[6] 'magna ex parte domitorem Germaniae'.[7] Tiberius, hastening to the death-bed, drove 200 Roman miles through Germany in 24 hours, clear proof that at least a rudimentary Roman administration was already operating in the conquered territory.[8]

Succeeding to the command, Tiberius, fresh from the successful completion and consolidation of the conquests in Illyricum, made a demonstration of Roman arms throughout Germany the following year without meeting serious opposition. All the tribes were ready to submit, except the Sugambri, whose envoys were however arrested and deported, while 40,000 Sugambri and Suebi were forcibly resettled on the left bank of the Rhine.[9] Germany was organized as a province, except that regular taxation was apparently not yet imposed;[10] that was left

---

[1] Dio liv. 33. 5, 34. 3, 36. 2.

[2] Dio liv. 36. 2–3. See also below, p. 267. [3] Dio liv. 36. 4.

[4] Dio lv. 1. 3 is quite clear that he tried, *pace* Holmes, *The Architect of the Roman Empire* ii, p. 79.

[5] Strabo vii. 291. [Add.]

[6] Strabo, loc. cit.; Dio lv. 1. 4; Livy, *epit.* 140; there is no reason to doubt the identification of Strabo's Salas with the Saale.

[7] Vell. ii. 97. 3.

[8] Val. Max. v. 5. 3 ('per modo devictam barbariam'); Pliny, *NH* vii. 84; on the posting service set up by Augustus, Suet., *Aug.* 49. See the excellent note in Holmes, op. cit., ii, p. 80, n. 4. Also Collingwood and Richmond, *The Archaeology of Roman Britain*, p. 4. [9] Suet., *Aug.* 21, *Tib.* 9.

[10] Dio lv. 6. 2–3; Vell. ii. 97. 4: 'peragratus victor omnis partis Germaniae sine

for Varus. At some time between now and A.D. 9 an altar and a cult of Augustus were established at Cologne to be a focus for German unity and loyalty, as was the Lugdunum altar for Gaul.[1] Germany was being incorporated into the Empire more swiftly even than Gaul had been.

The boundary of the province was now presumably the Elbe.[2] From 10 B.C. onwards part at least of the Roman army had been stationed the year round in Germany, as the excavations at Oberaden have shown. Perhaps Tiberius in 8 laid out the permanent bases for the army of occupation, such as that at Haltern, with its attendant stores depot, auxiliary fort, and *canabae*. Very few of the remains that must exist have, however, been found. Apart from the hundreds of marching-camps which must have been built in North Germany, Saxony, Thuringia, and Franconia, we hear from Florus that Drusus planted 'praesidia atque custodias' in many places on the Maas, Weser, and Elbe, the new territory apparently being garrisoned in strength, with forts at strategic points and important centres of communication.[3] Unfortunately the German terrain is not so well adapted to the use of air photography for archaeological purposes as Britain, and on the ground little search has been made for possible Roman sites in these areas, a fact which goes a long way towards explaining why so few have ever been found.[4]

ullo detrimento commissi exercitus . . . sic perdomuit eam, ut in formam paene stipendiariae redigeret provinciae.' On the imposition of tribute by Varus, Dio lvi. 18. 4, and see below, p. 239. Drusus' death in fact made little difference to Roman policy; there is no warrant for taking it as a turning-point, as in, e.g., Gardthausen, *Augustus und seine Zeit* i. 3, p. 1089: 'Grade zur rechten Zeit für die Freiheit Germaniens war Drusus gestorben . . . die ganze Lebensarbeit war vergebens gewesen.'

[1] Tac., *Ann.* i. 39. 1, 57. 2, where the priest is a Cheruscan; cf. Rüger, *Germania Inferior*, p. 20.

[2] Suet., *Aug.* 21, 'Germanos ultra Albim flumen summovit', cf. Tac., *Germ.* 41, 'flumen inclitum et notum olim, nunc tantum auditur'; *RG* 26; Tac., *Ann.* i. 59; Germanicus confined himself to the regions between Rhine and Elbe, Tac., *Ann.* ii. 14, 22.

[3] Florus ii. 30. 26, excellently discussed by von Petrikovits, *Das römische Rheinland*, pp. 33–4; there is no reason to amend Maas–Weser–Elbe to Ems–Lippe–Weser, ibid., n. 38; see also Nesselhauf, *JRGZ* vii (1960), pp. 152–4. Florus' next sentence refers to the fifty supposed 'Drususkastellen' along the Rhine, of which, as we have seen, archaeology knows little, above p. 97. Even if the text is sound, one wonders whether Florus can have misunderstood his source, so that the real meaning would be fifty forts in the whole area from Rhine to Elbe, Rhine bank included.

[4] Cf. comments of Scollar, *Archäologie aus der Luft*, pp. 17–45, esp. pp. 31–5; further, idem, *BJ* clxiii (1963), p. 305.

The story of the next twelve years in Germany is soon told. There was a small disturbance in Germany in 7, easily repressed, nothing worth mentioning.[1] Then in 6 Tiberius retired to Rhodes. Dio's account breaks off, and for the period 6 B.C.–A.D. 4 we are reduced to his epitomists and to inferior sources. Velleius does not care to treat this period in full: 'sensit terrarum orbis digressum a custodia Neronem urbis.'[2] And yet this period saw great activity both in the Balkans and in Germany. In the Balkans Cn. Lentulus and M. Vinicius were operating beyond the Danube, while 50,000 Getae were transplanted to the south bank and the Dacians after a heavy defeat compelled 'imperia populi Romani perferre'.[3] In Germany too it saw the march of L. Domitius Ahenobarbus to the Elbe, which he crossed unopposed, erecting an altar to Augustus and concluding a pact of friendship with the natives beyond the river.[4] It is specifically stated that this happened while he was still ruling 'the parts along the Danube', and Syme rightly points out that, although the shortest way from the Danube to the Elbe is from Carnuntum across Bohemia, nevertheless Ahenobarbus must have crossed the Danube from Raetia, west of Bohemia, for on the way to the Elbe, he fell in with a migrating tribe of Hermunduri and resettled them on lands on the Upper Main formerly belonging to the Marcomanni, who had migrated after their severe handling by Drusus.[5] The Hermunduri were still here in Tacitus' time, faithful allies of Rome.[6] Not only would the route from Carnuntum to the Elbe have brought Ahenobarbus into conflict with the Marcomanni in their new home in Bohemia,

---

[1] Dio lv. 8. 3, 9. 1.   [2] Vell. ii 100. 1.

[3] Evidence cited and date established by Syme, *CQ* xxvii (1933), pp. 144–6; id., *JRS* xxiv (1934), pp. 120–2; id. in *CAH* x, pp. 364–8; the name M. Vinicius depends upon the restoration of an inscription from Frascati, *ILS* 8965, now apparently lost (Miltner, *Klio* xxx (1937), p. 216, n. 1); the restorations proposed by A. von Premerstein, *JÖAI* xxviii (1933), pp. 140–63, and xxix (1934), pp. 60–81, are basically sound, though can be improved in detail, cf., e.g., Miltner, loc. cit., pp. 215–16; see further Mócsy, *RE* Supp. ix, col. 543, against, e.g., Groag, *RE* ivA, cols. 827–8, or von Lunzer, *RE* viiiA, col. 161. On the effect of the Augustan campaigns against the Dacians, see the very interesting article of Vulpe, *Dacia*, N.S. v (1961), pp. 315–19.

[4] Dio lv. 10a; Tac., *Ann.* iv. 44. 3.

[5] Dio lv. 1. 2; Vell. ii. 108. 1; Strabo vii. 290; Florus ii. 30; Orosius vi. 21. 5; see Syme in *CAH* x, p. 366, on Ahenobarbus' route; on the location of their new territories, see Ulbert, *Die römische Donaukastellen Aislingen und Burghöfe*, pp. 85–6, with further refs. [ADD.]

[6] Tac., *Germ.* 41.

but it would not have led him to the Main. Syme thinks that he conducted this expedition as legate of Illyricum. He may have done so, but it is not impossible that he was given command of a force from Raetia, whether or not he was legate *in* Raetia, specifically for an exploratory expedition to the upper reaches of the Elbe. The date is between 6 and 1 B.C.

Moving to the Rhine command, Ahenobarbus was less successful and a diplomatic reverse in negotiations with the Cherusci endangered Roman prestige. War broke out, which M. Vinicius, succeeding Ahenobarbus, conducted for three years successfully enough to earn himself the *ornamenta triumphalia*. The coolness of Velleius' praise for Vinicius contrasts with the superlatives heaped upon Tiberius, who returned to public life and to the German command in A.D. 4, and Velleius appears to exaggerate the seriousness of the situation facing him on his arrival in order to magnify his glory. Tiberius is even credited with being the first to reach the Elbe, 'quod numquam antea spe conceptum, nedum opere tentatum erat',[1] although Drusus had done so, and Ahenobarbus had actually crossed it some years earlier.

The proof that Germany seemed secure is the decision to proceed in A.D. 6 to the next step in Augustus' grand design, the conquest of Bohemia. This was to be accomplished by a pincer movement reminiscent of the campaign of 15 B.C. Tiberius moved from Germany to the Danube, establishing a base at Carnuntum (near Petronell), in prehistoric and Roman times the most important crossing of the Middle Danube: 'praeparaverat iam hiberna Caesar ad Danubium.'[2] Although no trace of

---

[1] Vell. ii. 104–6. Like others, I once took 'in cuius' [*sc.* Germaniae] mediis finibus ad caput Iuliae [so MSS.; Lipsius conj. *Lupiae*] fluminis hiberna digrediens princeps locaverat' (105. 3) as meaning that he was the first to winter his army in Germany, (Wells in *Roman Frontier Studies, 1967*, p. 3). If Velleius does mean this, he is wrong, cf. the Oberaden evidence, Chapter 6. 3, but it is more natural to take *princeps* here in the sense of 'the general'. See also above, p. 152.

[2] Vell. ii. 109–10; Carnuntum was at this time in Noricum; later transferred to Pannonia (Pliny *NH* iv. 80). The strategic importance of Carnuntum well described by Swoboda, *Carnuntum*, pp. 32–3: 'Carnuntums Bedeutung ist eine Folge seiner geographischen Lage. War die Donau die natürliche Leitlinie der Verkehrsbeziehungen zwischen Ost und West, so führte das Marchtal ins Bernsteinland und an die Ostsee, während sich südlich des Stromes der Verkehr durch die Brucker Pforte und östlich des Seithagebirges über Steinamanger (Savaria), Pettau (Poetovio), Cilli (Celeia), Laibach (Emona), Aquileia an die Adria und nach Italien fortsetzte, ohne auf diesem Wege sonderlichen Schwierigkeiten zu begegnen.'

it has yet been found,[1] it will have been a full-scale legionary headquarters, like those we know from the Rhineland, and no mere marching-camp, as is apparently sometimes assumed. For operations across the Rhine, bases were established on the river bank: Vechten, Vetera, Neuss, Mainz. For the conquest of Bohemia, was Tiberius to depend on a base at Poetovio (Ptuj), well over a hundred miles behind the river-crossing? Although no site between Poetovio and Carnuntum can be shown to have been occupied before the reign of Tiberius, this indicates absence of sufficient archaeological exploration rather than inadequate Roman planning.[2]

While Tiberius attacked from Carnuntum, Sentius Saturninus was to bring up an army from the west, 'per Cattos, excisis continentibus Hercyniae silvis', perhaps following the route which the Marcomanni themselves had taken in their successful invasion of Bohemia.[3] The natural invasion route is the Eger valley, in Roman as in later times,[4] unless we might suppose that Saturninus or any part of his forces planned to attack up the Elbe. Where then was Saturninus' base? Surely not at Mainz. Just as Tiberius had moved up from Poetovio, over a hundred miles behind the Danube, to a new base at the limit of Roman-occupied territory, so Saturninus must have established a base, possibly in the Upper Main area, among the Hermunduri.[5] The base has not yet been found, nor even looked for. The strength of Saturninus' force is also unknown. Tacitus makes Maroboduus say that he was opposed by twelve legions,

Cf. also Pascher, *RLÖ* xix (1949), p. 21. The importance of the amber-route is well brought out by de Navarro, *GJ* lxvi (1925), pp. 481–507.

[1] Wells in the proceedings of the Eighth International Congress of Roman Frontier Studies, 1969 (forthcoming).

[2] Possible sites as listed on p. 159, n. 2, plus Keszthely area and Scarbantia (Sopron), see Szilágyi, *AErt.* lxxvii (1950), pp. 27–8, cf. Alföldy, *Soproni Szemle* xv (1961), p. 352; id., *AArchHung.* xiv (1962), pp. 262–3. On the legionary base at Poetovio, see Mócsy, *AArchHung.* iii (1953), p. 181. Dr. J. C. Mann has brought to my attention evidence suggesting that Savaria was also a legionary base.

[3] Vell. ii. 109. 5. Drusus in his campaign against them also marched through the territory of the Chatti, Dio lv. 1. 2, cf. Strabo vii. 290, Vell. ii. 108. 1, Florus ii. 30, Orosius vi. 21. 5; the Chatti and the Hermunduri were later neighbours, Tac., *Ann.* xiii. 57. Further discussion and refs. in Dobiaš, *Dějiny československého území před vystoupením Slovanů*, pp. 87–8, n. 33.

[4] The 'key fortress' (Westwood, *The Thirty Years' War*, p. 317) of Eger was prominent in the wars of the seventeenth and eighteenth centuries.

[5] Cf. Wells in *Roman Frontier Studies, 1967*, p. 4.

and although it has been suggested that this merely refers to the total number of legions in Germany, Raetia, and Illyricum at this time, we know too little about the numbers which might be assembled for a particular campaign to be sure.[1]

Now Maroboduus was indeed a formidable opponent, a ruler of a kind previously unknown in Germany, substituting autocratic power for the personal influence on which other German chieftains relied to secure what obedience they could.[2] He could however scarcely without exaggeration be said to pose a threat to Rome or Rome's possessions. His Marcomanni had migrated to Bohemia to avoid the Romans, they showed no sign of hostility, and even when the outbreak of revolution in Illyricum forced the Romans to give up their plans for attacking Bohemia and strained their resources to the utmost, Maroboduus, despite the Roman provocation, was content to accept peace. The attack on Bohemia was not a defensive measure, but another act of shameless aggression. If successful, it would have given the Romans a dominating position in Central Europe, including control of the headwaters of the Elbe, and there is no reason to think that it would not have been followed by further advances.[3] The prohibition against crossing the Elbe, whenever it was put in force, was in any case only a matter of temporary expedience. Manifest destiny would soon have called the Romans to cross. But the conquest of Bohemia never occurred. Illyricum had been imperfectly subdued, and was left insufficiently garrisoned. It exploded. The period of confident expansion was over.

6. I. HOLSTERHAUSEN

A Roman camp has been found at Holsterhausen on the north bank of the Lippe some 36 km. from Vetera and 18 km. from Haltern. Although extensive excavation was impossible, limited excavations were carried out by Stieren,[4] who suggests that this

---

[1] Tac., *Ann.* ii. 46.

[2] Thompson, *Acta Univ. Carolinae Phil. et Hist.* i (1963) (Graecolatina Pragensia ii), pp. 203–10; cf. also Dobiaš, *Klio* xxxviii (1960), pp. 155–66, and contrast his position with that of Ariovistus, cf. Nierhaus, *Das swebische Gräberfeld von Diersheim* pp. 217–19, with further refs. On the extent of his territory, Swoboda, *Carnuntum*, p. 234, with further refs.

[3] See above, p. 6.

[4] Stieren, *Germania* xxxii (1954), pp. 165–70. [ADD.]

is a temporary camp for two legions. The evidence bears him out. The camp is roughly rectangular, with a re-entrant at the south-east corner. The south-west corner could not be excavated. The total area of the camp is apparently about 50 ha., large enough for two legions with auxiliaries.[1] The defences comprised a single V-shaped ditch, 4 m. across and 2 m. deep; no trace of a rampart was found, despite a close search in the north-east corner. The Lippe now flows some 500 m. south of the camp, though formerly right alongside. The site resembles that of the marching-camp and legionary base at Haltern: the defences take in a small hillock in the north-east corner, from which the ground slopes away gently on all sides, and the surrounding country is fairly flat.

A certain amount of pottery was found, including amphorae of the same type as those found at Haltern and Oberaden. About 1930, before the existence of the camp was suspected, two *aurei* were found in the area, one roughly 100 m. north and the other 500 m. west of the north and west gates respectively of the camp. Stieren, noting that Augustan gold coins are not common in Westphalia, wishes to associate them with the camp. One is an issue of Lugdunum of 15–12 B.C., the other the well-known 'C. and L. Caesares' type current from 2 B.C. to A.D. 14. If we could be sure that the coins were dropped by troops occupying the camp, this would suffice to date it to after 2 B.C. Stieren indeed does so. But the Roman use of the Lippe valley as a regular route right through to the period of Germanicus' campaigns vitiates this conclusion. Coins might have been dropped at any time.

The Romans commonly established permanent forts at places where they began by pitching temporary camps. Haltern is a clear example, with the legionary base succeeding the marching-camp there. We might expect the same at Holsterhausen. Stieren points out how well it would fit into a series of posts along the Lippe, 18 km. apart. A search for the permanent fort, probably of auxiliary size, might well be profitable. Such a fort might well have been occupied as long as the Haltern base was, and we could more readily bring the gold pieces, if they are not quite fortuitous, into association with this fort than with the temporary marching-camp which is all that is known so far.

[1] The area of the marching-camp at Haltern is approximately 36 ha.

6. 2. HALTERN

A. *General Survey*

Haltern is about 54 km. from Vetera on the north bank of the
Lippe at the point where it is joined by the Stever and where
the valley narrows between the hills of the Hohe Mark and the
Borkenberge to the north and the Haard to the south. Here the
Romans had an important base, just west of the modern town,
which is steadily encroaching upon the Roman sites. The
Roman remains which have been excavated comprise (fig. 8):[1]

(i) a legionary base, known to German scholars as the 'Haupt-
lager', but originally called by its first discoverers the 'grosses
Lager', by comparison with the other sites already known ((iii)
and (v) below);

(ii) a marching-camp for two legions, partly underlying the
base, known as the 'Feldlager'; it was discovered after the base,
and even when it was realized that the camp was bigger than
the base, the name 'grosses Lager' stuck to the latter, while the
camp was at first termed 'ältestes Lager';

(iii) what may possibly be an annexe to the base or a stores-
compound, the so-called 'Anlegeplatz', just south of the base and
the camp, in an area known as the Wiegel, on the edge of an
old bed of the Lippe;

(iv) four successive superimposed forts, also on the old river
bank, east of the stores-compound and south-east of the base,
in an area known as the Hofestatt; these forts are known collectively to scholars as the 'Uferkastell', since the excavators
thought they were built on the very edge of the bank, running
down to the water, with no defences on the river side; I believe,
however, as I have argued below, that this apparent phenomenon is due to subsequent erosion by the river, the forts having
originally had a full circuit of defences;

(v) a fort, some 1·4 km. south-west of the base, measured from
its nearest point, on the Annaberg, a steep height commanding
the valley below.

[1] Each site is discussed separately below. Most excavation took place before the
First World War, and reports appeared in *MAKW* i (1899), ii (1901), iii (1903),
iv (1905), v (1909), vi (1912), and vii (1922); *MAKW* is cited throughout this
chapter by volume number alone, e.g. ii, p. 75, meaning *MAKW* ii (1901), p. 75.

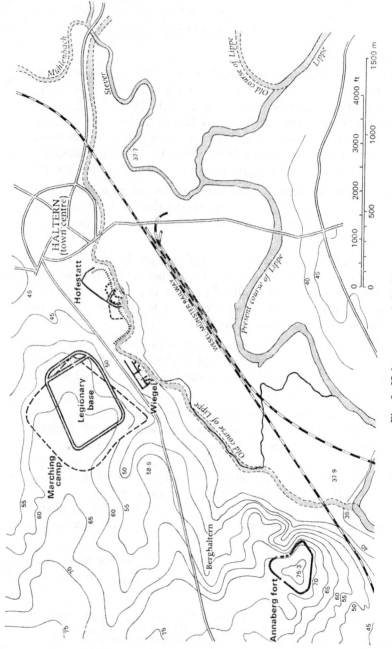

Fig. 8. Haltern: map of the Roman sites

In addition to these sites west of the town, there is also a bridge to the east, which may very well be Roman, though this cannot be proved in the absence of specific finds.[1] It lies 2 km. from Haltern on the road to Hullern and Seppenrade, and was built of three parallel rows, 50 m. long and 2 m. apart, of heavy, square posts rammed over 4 m. deep in the earth at intervals of 5 m. The bridge was approached at each end by an artificial causeway 8 m. wide, revetted with piles and wattle. Massive timber abutments took the thrust of the embankment. Alongside the bridge was a semicircular quay, also made of piles and wattle-work. The whole construction is, as Stieren suggested, more characteristic of the Romans than of the medieval inhabitants of the area. If it is Roman, it shows that the Romans had a regular route eastwards from Haltern along the north side of the Lippe, whether or not they also had a bridge over to the south bank at Haltern.

Other Roman remains in the area must lie there still undiscovered. In particular, the cemeteries belonging to the base and other sites are unknown. A cemetery beneath the eastern slope of the Annaberg cannot on the basis of our present knowledge of finds from the area be assigned to any one of the Roman sites, and indeed it contains post-Augustan material, which leads Stieren to ask whether it was in fact Roman or post-Roman. Support for its Roman origin comes from its situation on the direct line from the east gate of the Annaberg fort to the west gate of the base, and so probably on a road linking the two. The area is unfortunately much disturbed, and the problem may never be solved.[2]

The Annaberg fort was the first of the Roman sites to be the subject of planned excavation, in 1899, after which attention shifted to the stores-compound. Then excavations began in the Hofestatt forts and the base, and the marching-camp was discovered beneath the base. The historical importance of the base was recognized at once, and it came to engross all the money, labour, and skilled personnel available. Every year from 1905 to 1910 excavations were confined to the base and the marching-camp. There were no excavations at all in 1911; further excavation on a restricted scale took place in 1912 and 1913,

[1] Stieren, *Bod. Westf.* i (1929), pp. 20–1, with photograph p. 21.
[2] Ibid., p. 12; id. vi (1943), p. 12.

again in the base, and then came the war. The excavators have never gone back to the other sites, and now it is too late, for tipping and filling and building have changed the configuration of the ground and obliterated the Roman remains.

The Wiegel was used for building even before 1914, the Hofestatt was built up with earth brought from the area of the base and turned into a sports ground between the wars, while the Annaberg had been much disturbed in the last century.[1]

The early excavators learned their trade at Haltern. In Stieren's words: 'Das Grabungsgelände wurde eine Archäologenschule.'[2] The reports in *MAKW* before the First World War are of an enormous length. Volume v (1909) cost so much to produce that later excavations had to be restricted for lack of funds.[3] The reason is that the excavators were at pains to explain in detail their methods, set out their theories, and record their problems, even if the theory later proved wrong or the problem illusory. This does not make for easy reading, but it enables us to see how rapidly their understanding and techniques improved. At the start they were extremely limited. When we see it suggested that the soldiers in a permanent post slept in the open in the holes which they used as hearths for cooking,[4] or when we puzzle over the excavation plans for the stores-compound, we can only wonder at the perseverance and intelligence which produced so enormous an accretion of knowledge in the next few years. Nevertheless it should be remembered that our knowledge of the Annaberg and Hofestatt forts and the stores-compound depends upon only five years' work in all, and those the first five. It is not to be wondered at, if the excavators failed to find all that modern techniques and more thorough excavation would have revealed, or if at times we are forced to conclude that, what they did find, they failed to understand.

I have argued below in their respective sections that the base was finally destroyed by the Germans in A.D. 9, while the Hofestatt fort was possibly reoccupied under Germanicus. The end-date of the stores-compound cannot be determined. The dates at which the various sites were first occupied can be estimated,

---

[1] Stieren, *Bod. Westf.* vi (1943), pp. 8, 12.
[2] Ibid. i (1929), p. 13.
[3] *RGKbl.* ii (1909), p. 85.   [4] ii, p. 75.

if at all, only by comparing the finds. The first attempt to establish a relative chronology was made by Loeschcke in his introduction to his study of the pottery finds from the excavations down to 1907.[1] Subsequent finds have not altered the picture. He sees the Annaberg fort and the stores-compound as the earliest sites. As far as the Annaberg fort is concerned, not only the finds, which were few, but the fact that the rampart was revetted at the front only and the singular design of the towers (if the excavators were not mistaken) support this early dating. The only other known example from the Augustan period of a rampart of this type is in periods B and C at Neuss, where B is to be dated before 12 B.C. The stores-compound excavations were incomplete. The majority of the stores-compound finds come in fact from the area of the so-called 'triangle', probably the site of *horrea* or warehouses of some sort. Some of the sherds from here resemble sherds found in the marching-camp; others, of so-called Belgic ware and of the everyday ware made at Vetera,[2] resemble the Annaberg finds and differ strongly from other forms of the same types of pottery in the base. Sigillata on the other hand, almost lacking on the Annaberg (Belgic ware is extremely rare there too),[3] is found in the area of the 'triangle' in greater quantity than anywhere else in any of the Haltern sites except around the *principia* of the base. If we follow Loeschcke in arguing that the similarity of much of the stores-compound pottery to that of the Annaberg fort shows them to have been occupied at about the same time, we must suppose that the compound went on being occupied much longer.[4] An amphora sherd with a graffito referring to the year 7 B.C. does no more than provide a *terminus post quem*,[5] but some of the sigillata is comparatively late,[6] and the fact that five distinct periods of occupation can be traced in the stores-compound area is

---

[1] Loeschcke, v, pp. 115–17.

[2] On which see Loeschcke, v, pp. 107–11, cf. Hähnle, vi, p. 35.

[3] Cf. Ritterling, ii, pp. 109–10.

[4] Loeschcke, v, p. 120, n. 2, observes that a Lugdunum coin was found on the west slope of the Annaberg, whereas such coins are absent from Oberaden. But this coin is not necessarily connected with the occupation of the fort and does not prove that the Annaberg continued to be occupied after the Lugdunum coins began to reach the area.

[5] Ritterling, ii, p. 167, illustrated pl. xxxi, no. 35: it appears to read '[Ti. Claudio Ne]rone II', no doubt the date when the contents were made or bottled.

[6] Oxé, *Bod. Westf.* vi (1943), p. 70, on a round stamp HERTO.

conclusive. It may have gone on being occupied as long as the base itself. If it was an annexe, as seems most likely and as Koepp first suggested, citing as a parallel a description from the *Periplus Ponti Euxini*,[1] it will have been dependent upon the base and so perhaps founded and given up at the same time as that was.

The base itself is clearly later than the marching-camp. The pottery from the base is partly identical with that from the other sites, partly very different. The latest pottery from any of the sites comes from the base and the Hofestatt. Loeschcke insists that he cannot distinguish between the latest pottery from the two and so concludes that both were given up together. Again we come up against the deficiencies of the evidence. The amount of pottery from the Hofestatt is so small by comparison with that from the base that we cannot be certain that the absence of later pieces excludes the possibility of later occupation. Conversely, we know that the earliest period (the 'yellow' period) of the Hofestatt sites yielded no finds at all, since almost all the fort of that period was destroyed by erosion. We cannot therefore be certain that this earliest Hofestatt fort was not as early as the beginning of the stores-compound. Comparison between different sites, especially between the base and the Hofestatt, is made even more difficult because, as Dragendorff so strongly emphasized, the chronological difference between the earliest and latest pottery finds from each individual site is less than the qualitative difference between those from one site and another.[2] The extreme scarcity of the sigillata from the Hofestatt makes accurate dating there especially hazardous.

Summing up, we may conclude that the Annaberg fort was the first site in the area to be occupied and was probably occupied for a few years only; that the stores-compound was also early, probably continuing to be occupied for a considerable time; that the base therefore, with which the compound was probably associated, was also founded early. I have given reasons below for rejecting the belief that the marching-camp was occupied after 2 B.C.[3] Its date is unknown. We know only

---

[1] Koepp, ii, p. 103, citing *Peripl. Pont. Eux.* ix. 3–4.
[2] Dragendorff, iii, p. 54; cf. Krüger, iv, p. 84, in the final report on the Hofestatt finds, that sigillata is still 'spärlich genug'.
[3] See below, p. 176.

that it preceded the base and probably lasted no more than one
summer. The base, along with the stores-compound, may go
back as far as 8 or 7 B.C., immediately after Drusus' death, when
the Oberaden base was given up, perhaps replaced by Haltern.[1]
The date at which the earliest fort on the Hofestatt was founded
is totally irrecoverable, since all finds from it have perished.
The base went up in flames in A.D. 9. The stores-compound may
have been destroyed at the same time, though that is purely
conjectural, based on the supposed associations of the two sites.
The Hofestatt site may also have ceased to be occupied in that
year, though conjecturally we might also suppose a reoccupation under Germanicus. The homogeneity of the Hofestatt finds
of all periods and the scarcity of sigillata and other fine pottery
susceptible of accurate dating make it impossible to be certain
whether the last fort on the site came to an end in 9 or whether
it was a post-Varian foundation. The evidence is not enough to
decide.

There is evidence that all the Haltern sites were occupied by
post-Roman settlers, and the excavators in the early years seem
to have tried to fit various post-Roman phenomena into the
Roman pattern. I have noted cases of this sort, where I think
they have occurred, under each of the individual sites. The most
important is the medieval pilework along the river-bank in
front of the Hofestatt, which Koepp wrongly took as evidence
for the river's having flowed here in Roman times.[2] If we put
together all the indications of German and Frankish settlement,
we find they are considerable. Loeschcke observed that Germanic sherds had come to light on all four sites.[3] No German
occupation layers had been found, but there were some German
graves, such as those on the Annaberg and the impressive one
found within the *principia* of the base.[4] Roman pottery of the
late second century on the Annaberg and elsewhere can only
have been brought here by Germans.[5] Frankish pits and post-
holes, dated by their pottery contents, are common in the *via*

---

[1] See below, p. 216.   [2] See below, pp. 206–11.
[3] Loeschcke, v, pp. 305–11, cf. also (emphatically) Ritterling, ii, pp. 110–11.
[4] On the Annaberg graves, see below, p. 172; the *principia* grave shown in photograph, v, p. 74, fig. 13; seen by Koepp as Roman, v, pp. 74–5, but this is implausible; identified as a German grave by Dragendorff, rightly.
[5] i, pp. 63–4; iv, pp. 109–10; *Bod. Westf.* vi (1943), p. 12; cf. ibid., p. 79 (a
'Falschmünzerform' of Antoninus Pius); cf. Ritterling, ii, p. 110.

principalis of the base,[1] and Carolingian pottery was found in
the base, the Hofestatt forts and annexe, and the old river-bed.[2]
Two pits in the latest, 'blue' period of the Hofestatt were
especially rich in finds; they also contained Roman sherds, and
would doubtless have been hailed as Roman if they had contained nothing else,[3] like other similar post-Roman pits here and
in the stores-compound,[4] where the excavators did in fact recognize various post-Roman remains.[5] It seems clear that the whole
area was considerably disturbed by post-Roman occupation,
and that this may have destroyed Roman traces or greatly confused the archaeological picture, especially in the Hofestatt and
stores-compound areas.

B. *The Annaberg*

The fort on the Annaberg was the first of the Roman sites at
Haltern to be recognized. A Prussian staff-officer, Major
Schmidt, visited and reported on it in 1838,[6] stating that from
1830 onwards the Annaberg had been used for quarrying stone
for road-building, so that it was now pitted and disturbed, but
that in the course of the quarrying large quantities of Roman
material had come to light. He lists coins, weapons of various
sorts, tools, pottery, bronze vessels, millstones, weights. Four
years later, he was to write that the work of destruction was now
practically complete.[7] But in 1838 he was still able with the
help of the workmen to trace the defences of the fort. He described it as an irregular quadrilateral (later writers prefer to call
it a triangle; its irregularity defies precise geometrical defini-
tion); the north-west side, which is the longest, was the best
preserved, the east side the worst. This side curves inwards to
follow the contour of the hill. The north or north-east corner of
the fort therefore projects to form a vulnerable salient, and
according to Schmidt it was specially protected by three rows of

---

[1] v, p. 116, n. 2.

[2] iv, pp. 56–9, 113–20; v, pp. 316–18; and see n. 22.

[3] Koepp, iv, pp. 53–4; Krüger, iv, p. 113; the pits are marked as V and W on
iv, plate 4.

[4] e.g. those described in iv, p. 79 (pits H, J, K, and perhaps T and Z in plate 4).

[5] Koepp, ii, pp. 76, 77 (with n. 2), 81, 89, 92.

[6] Report published in the *Ztschr. für Westfalischen Geschichte* 1859, pp. 261–8,
reprinted verbatim in i (1899), pp. 61–70.

[7] Letter cited ibid., p. 69, n. 3.

pits, so-called 'Wolfsgruben', in front of it.[1] The circumference
of the fort, which was correctly estimated by Schmidt, is approximately 1050 m. The only trace of any building inside the
fort which he reported was a well about 12 ft. deep and 4½ ft.
across, going down to a layer of clay, which retained the water
and fed the well. Its walls were of cement below and stone
above. The workmen had dug it out, but filled it in again before Schmidt's visit, after a number of animals had fallen into
it. No finds are reported from it, and we cannot be as certain
as Schmidt was that the well is Roman, though on this site it is
probable.

Among the finds which Schmidt records from the area of the
fort as a whole is a remarkable quantity of weapons and missiles. These came from two particular areas. One was close
behind the middle portion of the north-west side; the other was
the area inside the east side of the fort and outside it at the
north-east corner among the 'Wolfsgruben', where *glandes*,
leaden sling-bullets, were scattered about in such numbers that
25 lb. weight of them were picked up and sold for scrap in Haltern. Schmidt took these finds to prove that the fort had been
taken by storm and not freely evacuated by the Romans, but
this inference is not warranted. The finds on the north-west side
might have come from barracks or an armoury or even a rubbish-
pit. We are not told how large the area was from which they
came; the description of them lying all mixed up together
might suggest that they had been placed here together, rather
than lost haphazard in battle. A similar conglomeration of
weapons, though only of missiles, was found behind the east
front of the base, in the remains of an armoury.[2] The sling-
bullets might suggest fighting, but they do not tell us who won.
Against the supposition that the fort was sacked by the Germans
is the absence of skeletons or of human remains of any sort. The
description of Germanicus' visit to the scene of Varus' defeat
suggests that the Germans were not scrupulous about burying
Roman dead. They might have been collected and buried by

---

[1] Schuchhardt, commenting on Schmidt's report, in i, pp. 70 ff., notes that the
ground here is now nothing but pits as the result of quarrying, so that the 'Wolfsgruben' can no longer be identified. What Schmidt took to be the *vallum* of a
Roman road west of the fort was still visible in 1899, but was now judged to be
a natural feature and is marked as a 'Sand-dune' on the plan in ii, plate 39.

[2] See below, p. 186.

the Romans later, but this is purely fictional. We have in fact no reason whatsoever to suppose the fort taken by storm.

Schmidt records the discovery at points where the quarrying had cut through the Roman defences of pile shoes 15·2–20·3 cm. long, 7·4–7·6 cm. across at the top, presumably resembling the finely preserved, considerably larger (38·5 cm. long, approx. 12 cm. across) specimen from Oberhausen. The piles at Oberhausen belong to a construction on the river bank, where probably the piles had been driven into the wet ground, rather than set in previously dug holes, and pile shoes are also reported from Neuss, where it is suggested that they come from a bridge or embankment carrying the road across marshy ground.[1] It is odd to find them on the dry, stony Annaberg.

Among the coins, gold, silver, and bronze, 'consular' issues (including *denarii* of Caesar and Antony) and Augustan were well represented, but no coin of Tiberius was among those which Schmidt inspected. Unfortunately he omits to say how many there were altogether. So many Republican issues (if this is what we are to understand by 'consular') are surprising at an Augustan site. Numismatic science was not far advanced in 1838, and we shall do well not to accept Schmidt's identifications as necessarily correct. Finally Schmidt records that on the west and north-west of the fort many urns containing bones and ashes were found by the workmen and broken up. He thought that these were the remains of the Roman dead, buried within the fort, lest otherwise the Germans should desecrate the graves. Such a proceeding is however unparalleled. It seems more likely that these were native burials. The Haltern area was occupied to a considerable extent in post-Roman times, as I have shown already,[2] and these burial urns are probably to be seen as evidence for post-Roman occupation of the Annaberg, a thing which is extremely likely, in view of the defensive strength of the site.

The first planned excavation on the Annaberg took place in June, 1899.[3] A series of trial trenches eventually cut a section through the defences of the fort on the north-west, but most of

[1] See above, p. 134, and on Augsburg-Oberhausen (Chapter 4. 7).
[2] See above, pp. 169–70.
[3] Schuchhardt, i, pp. 70–6; id., *Sitzber. Kön. Preuss. Akad.* 1900, pp. 303–16; only on the east side was there a gap where the defences could not be traced.

the trenches were, as it later turned out, within the fort, and the most notable feature of this campaign was how very few finds of any sort were made. Digging restarted in October the same year and the rest of the defences were traced, but already the first finds had been made down below the Annaberg in the area of what was to be revealed as the stores-compound, and these, since they promised to be more spectacular than anything to be expected from the Annaberg, were already attracting attention away from the fort.[1] There were further excavations in the area of the fort from Christmas 1900 to mid January 1901 and again in May of that year, by which time the excavators had gathered all the knowledge that has yet been gathered about the site.[2] Excavations planned for 1904 were cancelled to allow concentration of all resources on digging in the legionary base,[3] while limited excavations that were carried out in 1912 and 1931 added nothing.[4]

The 1899–1901 excavations confirmed the accuracy of Schmidt's observations, as far as they went and as far as they could be checked. Schuchhardt relates that the defences were found to comprise a single V-shaped ditch, backed by an earth rampart revetted with timber on the front only, and furnished with towers every 100 Roman feet built in such a way as to project in front of the rampart into the ditch itself.[5] Such projecting towers are not found again in Augustan fortifications, perhaps because, as Koepp later suggested, they were unstable, with their foundations in the sloping ditch, and were liable to be fired.[6] But one wonders whether perhaps the excavators on such a difficult site at so early a date really found what they thought they had found. Two gates were found and excavated, and two periods distinguished therein, but Schuchhardt emphasizes the excavators' difficulties, so that perhaps a pinch of salt is permissible.[7]

Schmidt had spoken as if in his time there were considerable quantities of finds. If so, few survived. A list of Roman material

[1] Schuchhardt, ibid., pp. 307–10.
[2] Full report by Schuchhardt, ii, pp. 175–98, with plan, pl. 39.
[3] iv, p. 2.
[4] Stieren, Bod. Westf. vi (1943), p. 12; cf. Koepp, Bod. Westf. ii (1931), p. 233.
[5] Schuchhardt, op. cit.; id., Sitzber. Preuss. Akad. 1931, pp. 617–20.
[6] Koepp, loc. cit., n. 3.
[7] Schuchhardt, ii, p. 190, referring to the gates as 'diese eigenartigen und in verzweifelt wirrem Zerstörungs-Zustande überlieferten Bauten'.

in the Münster museum catalogued as coming from Haltern or from the Annaberg, which may include pieces found there in the 1830s and 1840s, has only an amphora, a small bronze pot, a spear-point, four hand-mills, and some sling-bullets specifically noted as coming from the Annaberg, and some at least of the pottery in the list dates from the second or third century.[1] Such late finds, like others of that date elsewhere in the area, must come from native occupants of the site, perhaps in this case the same ones who were responsible for the burial urns. The 1899–1901 excavations yielded very little material. Ritterling suggested that the paucity of finds was due not only to the activities of the quarrymen, who would not have taken, even though they disturbed, pottery sherds, but also to the fewness of the Roman garrison and the brevity of their occupation of the fort. If Schuchhardt is right in distinguishing two periods in the gates of the fort, the occupation cannot have been so brief, though we have seen that there is some reason to doubt his observation. The quarrymen do however from Schmidt's account appear to have taken away a great deal, and if pottery sherds were unattractive, they are also fragile and many may have been destroyed in the quarrying. The fort was probably not long occupied, but the evidence is poor, and we should certainly allow for some years' occupation.

c. *The Marching-Camp*

The existence of an older fortification underlying the legionary base was first recognized in October 1903, when a section of its ditch was discovered in between the two east fronts of the base.[2] Early in 1905 another length of ditch was found well to the west of the base by workmen quarrying sand for road-building, and it was immediately hailed as belonging to the same work.[3] Subsequent excavation proved this false, but led to the discovery of the real west front and thereafter of the whole circuit of the ditch, linking up with the stretch first discovered between the east fronts of the base.[4] This new fortification was referred

[1] Philippi, i, pp. 63–4, with illustration, Plate III, p. 65.
[2] iv, p. 5.
[3] *Westd. Ztschr.* xxiv (1905), *Kblt.*, cols. 41–2.
[4] Excavation reports containing data on this fortification, together with data on the base, by Koepp in v, pp. 1–85, and vi, pp. 1–32.

to either as the 'ältestes Lager' or more usually 'Feldlager'. It appears to have been only a temporary marching-camp. What the section of ditch was that was first found west of the base could not be ascertained, since the area was so disturbed by the quarrying of sand.[1] It suggests the possibility that there exist other short-lived and still undiscovered Roman camps in the vicinity. Was there perhaps a building-camp for the men who built the base?

The marching-camp had a single V-shaped ditch, not so deep or so wide as the ditches of the base, but very steep, its profile closely resembling that of the ditch of the annexe to the Hofestatt fort (the so-called 'unfertige Anlage').[2] It was open for only a relatively short time.[3] The area of the camp was about 36 ha., or twice the size of the base in its original form.[4] Although the ditch was found half-filled and overlaid by traces of the *canabae* of the base both on the west and more especially on the north, a strip 3 m. wide along the inner edge of the ditch was quite clear of finds.[5] Koepp rightly suggested that this was where the rampart still stood when the squatters took up occupation in the abandoned ditch. No trace of wooden revetment was found and there was no berm, which indicates that the rampart consisted of a turf wall, the turves for which were probably cut nearby, since in this area the layer of humus which in the base underlies the Roman occupation layers is totally absent.[6]

Inside the rampart no traces of buildings belonging to the marching-camp were found, though there were numerous pits; but in the area where the base also stood, it is hard to tell whether pits belong to the camp or the base.[7] Wells belonging to the camp were found, together with the drain of its *via praetoria*.[8] The absence of buildings, the turf wall, and the

---

[1] Koepp, v, p. 3.

[2] Ibid., p. 89; cf. Dahm, iv, p. 5, n. 1; photograph, v, p. 6, with note p. 7; cf. photographs of base ditches, pp. 14, 15, and annexe ditch, iv, plate 10. 1.

[3] Koepp, v, p. 7, n. 1.

[4] The camp is roughly 600 m. square. The area is wrongly given as 30 ha. in *Westd. Ztschr.* xxiv (1905), *Kbll.*, col. 171.

[5] Koepp, v, pp. 3–5; this later occupation is contemporary with the base and is dealt with in the previous section (6. 2, fin.). [ADD.]

[6] Ibid., pp. 5–6.

[7] So Koepp, v, p. 57; vi, p. 8; the pits of the camp in general contained less finds than those of the base, vi, pp. 3, 6, and are generally shallower (Loeschcke, v, p. 116, n. 2).

[8] Koepp, vi, p. 7; cf. pp. 29–31, with plate 3.

absence of wooden gate-buildings (the position of all the gates except the west one is known) denote that this is a marching-camp like Holsterhausen, a camp, that is to say, intended to shelter a campaigning force, two legions strong, and perhaps at most to provide it with a temporary base during the campaigning season. The same defensive circuit might have been re-occupied in a following year, since there was nothing for the enemy to destroy, short of overturning the turf wall into the ditch, a laborious job without the compensating joy of plunder and swift destruction attendant upon the firing of a wooden fort. But it is impossible that this camp would have been occupied throughout a winter, without any effort having been made to render its defences stronger and more permanent or its interior more habitable. Oberaden shows what the Roman army could construct for itself as winter quarters.

The only evidence which is alleged to bear upon the dating of the marching-camp is the discovery of a silver coin of the 'C. and L. Caesares' issue of 2 B.C. in a pit beneath the *via principalis* of the base.[1] Koepp argued that this pit could have nothing to do with the base itself: it must date from before the marking out of the *via principalis* and so from the period of the marching-camp, which Koepp was prepared to see as somewhat more permanent than is suggested in the preceding paragraph.[2] Loeschcke uttered a *caveat* on the grounds that this particular area was disturbed by post-Roman occupation which may have dislodged the coin from a higher to a lower layer.[3] Koepp dismissed this as an unlikely theory.[4] Wolff thought it not so improbable.[5] Nobody challenged the view that a pit beneath the *via principalis* must antedate it, yet not even this is certain: rubbish may be buried in the road, or used as fill. Excavations in 1964, still unpublished, have for instance revealed sigillata moulds deliberately buried along with debris from the kilns in the *via praetoria*.[6] Koepp's basic premiss therefore falls, and with it the argument for dating the camp to after 2 B.C. We can say

[1] Koepp, v, p. 51; the pit in question is that numbered 43 (v, plate 3).
[2] Koepp, v, pp. 6–7.
[3] Loeschcke, v, p. 116, n. 2.   [4] Koepp, v, p. 402.
[5] Wolff, *RGKbl.* ii (1909), pp. 59–62; but apparently misunderstanding Koepp's comments in v, p. 402.
[6] I am extremely grateful to Dr. Aschemeyer for communicating this information to me. Cf. also below, p. 189, n. 6.

no more than that the camp antecedes the base, and that it therefore dates from the earliest years of Drusus' campaigns in Germany.

D. *The Legionary Base*

The legionary base at Haltern (fig. 9) was first mentioned by Koepp in 1901.[1] The first report on excavations in the base appeared in 1904,[2] and thereafter the base and the partially underlying marching-camp practically monopolized the attention of the excavators,[3] to the detriment of our knowledge of the other Haltern sites. Excavations, which were halted by the First World War, were resumed in 1925, when the site began gradually to disappear beneath a housing estate.[4] There were planned excavations again in 1929–31,[5] while building operations continued and brought to light chance finds of Roman objects,[6] at the same time destroying the archaeological record. After the hiatus of the Second World War excavations began again in 1953,[7] in an attempt, as far as is still possible, to complete the picture of the interior of the base before the site is completely built over.

The base is roughly quadrilateral, measuring about 370 × 485 m. in its original form, with an area of 18 ha. It was later extended by a further 50 m. at the east end and in its second form had an area of about 20 ha.[8] The defences were the first concern of the excavators, and by the end of the 1907 campaign the whole outline had been traced and the four gates were known. Thereafter the excavators turned to exploring the interior. The defences comprised two ditches, estimated to have

---

[1] Then known as the 'grosses Lager', cf. above, p. 163, on the nomenclature of the Haltern sites.

[2] Dragendorff, Koepp, Krüger, Schuchhardt, iv, pp. 1–29.

[3] Reports on excavations and finds 1905–14 by Koepp and others in v (1909), vi (1912), and vii (1922), except for the finds from 1912–13, first published by Albrecht in *Bod. Westf.* vi (1943); of particular importance is the article by Loeschcke on the pottery in v, pp. 101–322.

[4] Von Salis, *Germania* ix (1925), pp. 97–8; Stieren, *Germania* xiii (1928), pp. 70–6; summary of state of knowledge to date in *Bod. Westf.* i (1929), pp. 12–21.

[5] Stieren, *Germania* xvi (1932), pp. 36–45; full account of excavations and finds between the wars by Stieren and others, *Bod. Westf.* vi (1943).

[6] e.g. the pottery ovens described by Stieren, *Germania* xvi (1932), pp. 112–15.

[7] Aschemeyer, *Germania* xxxvii (1959), pp. 287–91; further reports not yet published, but to appear in *Germania* in due course. [ADD.]

[8] iv, pp. 4–6.

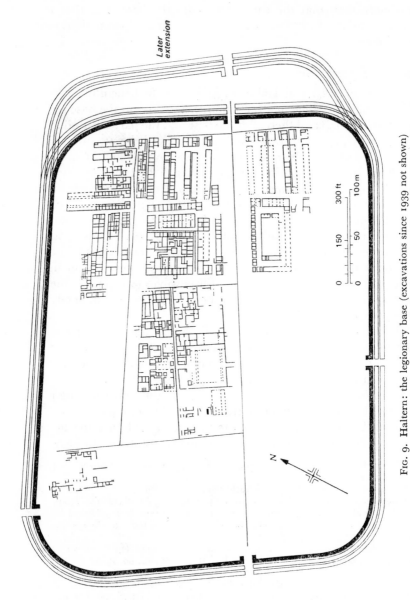

FIG. 9. Haltern: the legionary base (excavations since 1939 not shown)

From *Bodenaltertümer Westfalens VI: Die Funde von Haltern seit 1925* by August Stieren, published on behalf of the Altertumskommission im Provinzial-institut für westfälische Landes-und Volkskunde und des Landesmuseums für Vor- und Frühgeschichte

been originally between 2·5 and 3 m. deep, with a wood-and-earth rampart just under 3 m. wide separated from the inner lip of the ditches by a 1·3 m.-wide berm.[1] There were no towers, although they were at first very carefully sought by the excavators, having in mind the Annaberg defences. All the gates were excavated, at least in part, and since the findings here are supremely important for the history of the base, it is necessary to set them out in some detail.[2]

The first gates to be excavated were those of the two successive east fronts, that of the outer, later front (erroneously supposed at the time to be the earlier of the two) being excavated with particular care and completeness. Then came the turn of the south gate. Here the excavators expected to find evidence of two completely different periods, corresponding to the two periods represented by the inner and outer east fronts, which their working hypothesis assigned to a pre-Varian occupation and a reoccupation after the abandonment and destruction of the base in A.D. 9. This evidence was lacking. Only one gate-tower could be excavated at the south gate, the other lying in a belt of woodland, but the post-holes of this one, like those of the east gates, showed no sign of rebuilding. North and west gates presented the same picture. The north gate-towers showed some irregularities in their ground-plan, in the form of extra, smaller post-holes and sleeper-trenches, apparently to be interpreted as special supports or repairs. Three of its posts had at some time been replaced, no doubt by way of repair, because the timber had warped or rotted. At no single one of the gates had the towers ever been completely rebuilt. This is the one inescapable fact which forbids us to suppose that the base was ever abandoned, destroyed, and reoccupied, despite indications elsewhere that might otherwise be taken for signs of such reoccupation.[3] The rampart as a whole, like the gates, showed no sign of complete rebuilding, despite local repairs and peculiarities due probably to the earlier marching-camp, as for instance to the north of the west gate, where the posts of the rampart were set into older pits that had been packed with stone.[4]

[1] Measurements taken at north-east corner, v, p. 90; on defences in general, v, pp. 89–100.

[2] Reports by Schuchhardt, iv, pp. 22–7 (east), and Koepp, v, pp. 7–13 (south), 18–19 (west), 21–6 (north).

[3] Ibid., p. 401; see further, p. 186.   [4] Ibid., p. 19.

In two of the gateways, those of the outer east front and the south front, the roadway had been roughly paved or patched with stones. Beneath the layer of stones in the east gate were wheel-ruts, not recognized as such until a similar stone layer was found in the south gate.[1] What was originally taken for stone fill in the north gateway was later judged to be more probably a natural feature. There was no sign of stones in the west gate. Beneath the stone fill in the east and south gates was found a burnt layer: that in the east gate is specifically described as charcoal. Since the actual gate-towers had not been burnt down and rebuilt we cannot attribute this burnt layer to any widespread conflagration. One possible explanation is that it consisted of material used to fill the worn places in the gateway before the stone fill was put down.[2] So today we commonly use ashes for this purpose, especially to patch muddy places, and the south gate of the base, low-lying as it is, must have got very muddy at times, before the stones were laid down. That the remaking of the road through these gates with stone was an exceptional measure is clear from the total absence of any form of paving on the roads inside the base.[3]

When they were first excavated, the ruts in the east gate roadway, not recognized as such, were thought to have something to do with a curious and equally puzzling sleeper-trench running across the road between the heads of the outer ditch. This trench, like the ruts and the drain of the *via principalis*, which ran out through the centre of the gateway, was also filled with charcoal. Did this lead the excavators to associate all four? Or did they already associate the three mysterious depressions with one another (the drain was recognized for what it was) and so assume too readily that the filling of all was homogeneous? For if it is, then the layer of stone fill is later than not only the ruts, but the sleeper-trench as well, and the sleeper-trench, as I shall show in the next paragraph, almost certainly belongs to a barricade erected in the gateway at a time of emergency. If that emergency was the emergency of A.D. 9, as seems most

[1] v, p. 31; the stones described as forming 'ein dichtes, gestampftes Pflaster, eine Schotterung' (iv, p. 25).

[2] Cf. Koepp, ii, p. 91, noting that 'man auch heute vielbetretene Wege in dieser Sandgegend durch Aufschüttung von Formsand befestigt'.

[3] Stieren, *Bod. Westf.* i (1929), pp. 19–20: 'weder gepflastert noch sonst befestigt'.

likely, then this line of reasoning leads us to ascribe a post-Varian date to the stone fill, having already shown that the evidence of the gate-towers makes a post-Varian rebuilding of the base impossible. It is possible that the excavation report is misleading, that the charcoal in the ruts came from fill, perhaps half-burnt wood amongst the ash, while the charcoal in the sleeper-trench is the remains of the wooden barricade. On the other hand, the stones in these gateways might be genuinely post-Varian and the burnt layer beneath them might come from the conflagration which destroyed the base, the stones having been laid down and the gateways patched without the rebuilding and reoccupation of the base itself. For if the Romans did reoccupy the Hofestatt site but not the base after A.D. 9, as I have suggested below,[1] they might have mended the roadways to enable them more easily to go in and out of the base, perhaps with wagons to salvage anything that remained (including perhaps the bodies of those who died defending the base in 9 and who could then not be buried in due form outside it). Or again later inhabitants of the area may have made a road through the base, in at one side and out at the other, cutting off the corner, in the way we find at Dorchester-on-Thames,[2] and elsewhere.

Not only the outer east gate, but also the south and north gates had been barricaded. At the south gate two, and at the north gate three, bedding-trenches ran across the roadway, though at the north gate they did not appear to extend the whole width of the road. The trenches at the south gate still contained traces of the posts that had formed the barricade; here the outer ditch actually extended beyond the roadway on the west into the filling of the outer ditch (the ditch east of the roadway could not be excavated). Evidently the ditch near the gate had for some reason been filled before the construction of the barricade. Was an extended barricade thought to protect the gateway better than a ditch? Or was it the attackers who started to fill the ditch up?[3] The barricade at the east gate differs from the other two in having only one trench and that carrying a sleeper-beam, and in having had three posts driven into the head of the outer ditch as if to form a barrier, perhaps because

---

[1] See below, p. 206.
[2] Frere, *Arch. Journ.* xcix (1962), p. 115, fig. 1.
[3] Cf., e.g., Caesar, *BG* v. 51. 3.

here, as at the south gate, the attackers used the ditch to out-
flank the barricade.[1] Differences in construction at the different
gates should not surprise us, since all the barricades must have
been erected, if not under enemy attack, at least in haste and
under immediate apprehension of it. That barricades were part
of normal Roman drill is clear from Caesar's reference to a turf
wall blocking the gates, albeit only by way of ruse,[2] and to the
Pompeians' so-called 'hedgehog', which suggests a barrier set
with spikes: 'erat obiectus portis ericius; his paulisper est pugna-
tum . . . sed tamen nostri virtute vicerunt excisoque ericio . . .
irruperunt.'[3] It is only conjecture that associates the barricades
here at Haltern with the Roman disasters of A.D. 9, but I think
a reasonable conjecture, since we know that all Roman military
stations were attacked as soon as the army with Varus had
perished,[4] and the only other occasion in the late Augustan or
early Tiberian period when we hear of a Lippe fort being
seriously endangered was in 16,[5] when the base no longer stood.

It is therefore certain that if the base fell to the Germans in 9,
the Romans never subsequently reoccupied it. If on the other
hand we wish to argue that it was occupied during the period of
Germanicus' campaigns, we must conclude that it did not suffer
the common fate of all other Roman stations beyond the Rhine
in 9, but remained intact and fully garrisoned throughout the
aftermath of Varus' defeat and the years of Rome's discomfiture
thereafter. This I take to be precluded by the literary evidence.[6]
A number of finds from within the base have been supposed to
favour a post-Varian occupation, unnecessarily, as I have shown
below, though Stieren, relying on them, was willing to discount
the literary evidence.[7] Having to choose between the enormous
improbability that the Romans never gave up the base between

---

[1] Koepp, even after the finds at the south and north gates, denied that the remains
at the east gate were those of a barricade (v, p. 13); this was first asserted by
Loeschcke (v, p. 126, n. 1) and thereafter accepted by Koepp (v, p. 401). Loeschcke
however argued rather oddly that the barricades were erected instead of gates by
the men who reoccupied and rebuilt the base after A.D. 9.

[2] Caesar, *BG* v. 50–1.   [3] Ibid. iii. 67.

[4] Dio lvi. 22. 2a.   [5] Tac., *Ann*. ii. 7.

[6] Dio, loc. cit., states that the Germans took all the Roman forts but one, and
goes on to relate how this one too eventually fell; cf. Vell. ii. 120. 4. Note that
Tiberius in A.D. 10 did not cross the Rhine, but merely guarded the left bank (Dio
lvi. 24. 6), as if the whole area east of the river was now lost to the Romans.

[7] Stieren, *Bod. Westf*. vi (1943), pp. 13–14.

9 and 16 and the possibility that the dating of a small number of artefacts should be set back by a few years,[1] I have little hesitation in preferring the latter.

Two other possibilities should be mentioned; let him harbour them who will. One is that the base was in fact given up by the Romans in 9, left unharmed by the victorious and vengeful Germans, and reoccupied with gates and defences intact by Germanicus' troops some years later, and this despite the Germans' eagerness for plunder and rapine, attested by Dio,[2] whether the place of which he speaks is Haltern or not, a passage which makes it clear that the Germans had no scruple, religious or otherwise, about entering an abandoned fort. The second suggestion is even more fanciful: the base was not merely occupied but actually founded and built under Germanicus.[3] The whole history of the fortress is confined to three years, 14–16. In this time it was built, its east front was demolished and extended, its gate-towers were repaired, the roads through the gates were perhaps mended, and its interior underwent considerable repair and rebuilding (ovens and a tribune's house were built out into the *via quintana*, the *principia* was twice extensively reconstructed, and so on, all discussed below). The fortress at Inchtuthil on the other hand, probably begun in 83 or 84 by Agricola himself, abandoned not before 87 (a coin of that year in good condition was found 'in a well-marked demolition layer'),[4] having therefore had as long a life as the Haltern base would have had on this theory, was never even finished. And this is to ignore the evidence of the pottery, which Müller, the begetter of the theory, dismisses in a very cavalier manner, that the base was already occupied during or very soon after the period of Drusus' campaigns.[5]

We must now consider briefly the interior of the base, and thereafter the finds; briefly, because this does not set out to be a comprehensive monograph on the site, badly though such a work is needed. The *principia* was found and excavated early in

---

[1] The argument centres round a sigillata stamp *in planta pedis*, see below, Appendix I, p. 262.

[2] Dio lvi. 22. 3.

[3] Müller, *BJ* cl (1950), pp. 81–6, and again *PZ* xxxviii (1960), pp. 309–13; *contra*, brief but cogent, Kraft, *BJ* clv/clvi (1955/6), p. 98, n. 4.

[4] Richmond, *JRS* clv (1955), p. 123.

[5] See above, pp. 166–9.

the history of the archaeological exploration of the site; it is in-
variably referred to in the early reports as the *praetorium*, following the normal practice of the time.[1] The true *praetorium*, the
legate's house behind the *principia*, was found later.[2] Three
periods were clearly to be distinguished in the *principia*, as if the
building had twice been partially reconstructed. How the remains are to be allocated among the three periods is not entirely
certain, and some of Loeschcke's criticisms of Koepp's reconstruction are cogent,[3] but the fact of the reconstructions is not
in doubt, nor can it be doubted that we are dealing with altera-
tions to an existing building, not completely new buildings on
the same site. The same is true of the legate's house, which presented a most complicated picture of old pits and trenches, some
of them undoubtedly going back to the earlier marching-camp.
Koepp's remarks about the difficulty of attributing such pits and
the finds they contain to the right period,[4] though not intended
to apply to the legate's house, are nevertheless extremely relevant, and it seems clear that both in the *principia* and in the
legate's house and elsewhere he has at times misconceived the
purpose of the pits he found.

This problem again he has discussed in general terms.[5] Some
pits were undoubtedly cellars, used for storing amphorae and
other bulky objects,[6] others rubbish pits. The larger pits with
their walls lined with planks probably come into the former
category, rather than functioning as dug-outs of the sort Koepp
supposes: 'Wohngruben', 'Schlupfwinkel, in dem man Schutz
vor der Kälte suchte', a luxury for the officers' quarters, the
more comfortable the smaller they were, where a man might
creep and huddle up for warmth, forgetting he was in a hole
in the ground because of the panelled walls. This cannot be
right. No army's morale could stand that sort of thing. It
reminds one of Major Hound in Evelyn Waugh's *Officers and
Gentlemen* going to earth in his culvert. True that none of the

---

[1] Koepp, v, pp. 60–77, *et passim*; on nomenclature, conclusively Fellmann,
JGPV 1957/8, pp. 75–89.

[2] Koepp, vi, pp. 9–19; further, Stieren, *Germania* xvi (1932), p. 36 (plan, p. 38).

[3] Loeschcke, v, p. 124.

[4] Koepp, v, p. 57.

[5] Ibid., pp. 58–9.

[6] The two rectangular cellars added at one of the reconstructions of the *principia*
at the rear of the building are undoubtedly strong-room basements, of the sort
familiar from later forts and fortresses.

buildings had central heating (nor did they at Inchtuthil, apart from the senior centurion's quarters), but they must have had adequate fires. This would be no problem among the German forests, and it was an absolute necessity in the German winter. I too have been a soldier in the Haltern area: *experto crede*. Frontinus tells how the Aliso garrison pretended to be short of firewood when they were not.[1] They must have used vast quantities. The fires also served for cooking. Many the pit that the excavators label 'Kochloch', often, it seems, in despair.[2]

Water-tanks too are sometimes suggested on insufficient evidence. The supposed *impluvium* with two overflow tanks (why have overflow tanks? why not dig the main tanks deeper?) in the legate's house is very doubtful. It is in a most odd place for an *impluvium* and not aligned with the walls, while Koepp's explanation of why one of the tanks cuts into the foundations of the wall is unconvincing. In a different part of the base, inside the north gate, a supposed series of five cisterns, with diameters of from 1·2 to 1·7 m., cannot be considered certain, the alleged evidence being quite insufficient,[3] whereas a water-tank 3·0 × 1·6 m., by the south gate is authentic, and was intended to catch the rain-water from the roof of the gate-tower.[4]

How the base was supplied with water is unknown. This water-tank by the south gate is the only well-authenticated water receptacle yet found, although wells which from their position must belong to the old marching-camp are known.[5] It seems likely that when the base was established, an adequate water-supply was ensured, although we do not know how. But it would not have been difficult to bring down water from the nearby hills, and it is inconceivable that so large and well-appointed a post should have depended on rain-water and on fetching its water up from the river.[6]

The tribunes' houses, like the legate's, show signs of partial

---

[1] Front., *Strat.* iv. vii. 8; perhaps his other story about troops besieged after the Varian Disaster also applies to Haltern (ibid. iii. xv. 4).

[2] Of the pits in the legate's house (vi, plate 1), the 'Kochloch' IV, for instance, may go with pits nos. 22 and 23 (the latter is itself called a 'Kochloch', vi, p. 31); nos. 17, 17a, 17b apparently belong together, and so do nos. 5, 6, 7, and the two unnumbered pits to the north of this row.

[3] Koepp, v, p. 33.

[4] Ibid., p. 11; similar structures are found at Housesteads and elsewhere on Hadrian's Wall.

[5] Ibid. vi, p. 7.   [6] See above on Mainz, p. 144.

internal reconstruction only, one of them indeed showing no signs of reconstruction at all.[1] It was not part of the original plan, actually being built in the *via quintana* where it runs into the *intervallum* of the old east front, so reducing its width from 15 to 6 m. Pottery ovens were also built in the *via quintana*.[2] The barracks on the other hand, of both legionary and cavalry type, near the original east gate showed no sign of reconstructions on the scale of those in the *principia* and the officers' houses. Stieren is drawing on his own experience in excavating, as well as on Koepp's earlier reports, when he states so emphatically in what is his last word on the subject that the base was never destroyed and rebuilt.[3] Were anyone still tempted to doubt this, the unanimous conviction of Koepp, Stieren, and Aschemeyer,[4] the three men most experienced in directing excavations in the base, has an authority greater even than the cumulative weight of the evidence from published accounts of individual structures. The reconstruction of *principia* and officers' houses suggests that each new officer could and did have his quarters (and for the legate his headquarters) rebuilt to his own plan. At Inchtuthil, Richmond notes 'striking differences' in the plan of different houses,[5] readily explicable if the individual officer had a say in the design of his own quarters.

What appears to be an *armamentarium*, not at first recognized as such, was built over the filling of the old east front, by the old gate, when the base was extended; it yielded not only some sixty or so arrow-heads and perhaps some *pilum*-heads, but also thousands of *ballista*-bolts or lance-heads, probably the former, stored here for use by *ballistae* mounted at the new east gate.[6]

---

[1] Stieren, *Bod. Westf.* i (1929), pp. 16–17; id., *Germania* xvi (1932), pp. 38–43; id., *Bod. Westf.* vi (1943), p. 9; Aschemeyer, *Germania* xxxvii (1959), pp. 287–90; these accounts supplement and correct that by Koepp, vii, pp. 3–6.

[2] Stieren, *Germania* xvi (1932), pp. 44–5, 112–15.

[3] Stieren, *Bod. Westf.* vi (1943), pp. 13–14; cf. id., *PZ* xxv (1933), p. 312; the extent of internal reconstruction is however greater than Stieren's phrase, 'hier und da kleine Umbauten' (p. 13), might suggest.

[4] Aschemeyer in conversation, discussing still unpublished excavations of recent years.

[5] Richmond, *PBA* xli (1955), p. 313.

[6] The find itself described by Koepp, iv, p. 10, cf. Loeschcke, v, p. 125; on the nature of the missiles, Dahm, iii, pp. 63–7, with note by Dragendorff, p. 67; further Schramm, iv, pp. 121–4, who notes that they are 'anscheinend ungebraucht', and suggests, with the experienced cynicism of the serving soldier, that they were a type newly designed by the civilian 'experts' and found unusable; but then he thought

The buildings between the old and new fronts were at first dismissed as mere shacks, 'kümmerliche, kleine Bauten' in Stieren's phrase, but recent unpublished excavations in the area have shown that there were substantial buildings here.[1] The new east front has always been recognized as comparatively rich in actual finds, whence Loeschcke argued that its occupation was not to be confined to what he thought of as the post-Varian period of the base,[2] or, as we might say, to merely a brief period of a year or two.

After all that has been said, we need not consider the remainder of the base in great detail. The front of the *principia* was lined with shops or store-rooms facing out on to the *via principalis*.[3] The cellars beneath them were particularly rich in finds, one cellar (number 8 on the plan)[4] containing more than thirty pots in comparatively good condition. They had clearly been stored in the cellar and had not just fallen into it when the building above was destroyed. There was a widespread layer of grey ash throughout the area, and other signs of burning; two cellars (nos. 18 and 19) contained debris which had fallen in from the north side, that is to say, debris from the wall of the *principia*, while in another (no. 9) the layer of ash was overlaid by another destruction layer, which may have come from the same source. This cellar caused some excitement, since the burnt debris was covered by a layer of clean sand in which was a pit, which Loeschcke hailed as evidence for a post-Varian occupation.[5] More probably it is post-Roman. Isolated artefacts of Roman date in post-Roman layers need cause no surprise on a site so thickly strewn with such artefacts. More surprisingly at first sight, a fragment of sigillata from cellar no. 9 fitted a second fragment found in the adjacent cellar no. 8. This is explicable if both came from a vessel broken before the destruction of the buildings, whose fragments were already scattered about the area.

Apart from these cellars, excavations in the area south and

they were merely dumped in a pit, the *armamentarium* not being recognized as such, cf. Dahm, iv, p. 11; on the *armamentarium* itself, Dragendorff, iv, pp. 14–17.

[1] Stieren, *Bod. Westf.* i (1929), p. 20. Unpublished information from Aschemeyer.
[2] Loeschcke, v, p. 126.
[3] Report by Koepp, v, pp. 44–8, who, however, thought the cellars were dugouts belonging to officers' quarters, see above, p. 184; the tribunes' houses had not yet been unearthed.   [4] v, plate 3.   [5] Loeschcke, v, p. 123.

south-east of the *principia*, in the roadway and on either side of
it, produced no clear groundplan of buildings, though numerous pits.[1] Several of these pits revealed more than one layer of
occupation, but it is extremely difficult in the absence of any
over-all groundplan to know which layers belong to the period
of the marching-camp. One of these pits (no. 52 on the plan)
appeared to Loeschcke to be, like that mentioned in the previous paragraph, clear evidence for post-Varian occupation:[2]
here again, the widespread layer of ash was overlaid by a layer
containing Roman material. Were we to consider this one pit
in isolation, we might accept Loeschcke's explanation, and
Koepp, answering Loeschcke, admits that signs are not lacking
which could be used to support Loeschcke's theory, but rightly
emphasizes how little such slight indications weigh against the
overwhelming mass of evidence that the base was never rebuilt.[3]

It remains then to discuss the finds. The coin evidence is discussed below in Appendix II. The latest datable pieces are four
coins with the countermark of Varus.[4] The total absence of
Lugdunum II is no inconsiderable argument for Haltern's abandonment in 9, considering the ubiquity of that issue at Rhineland and Raetian sites, soon after its issue. The countermark
SI . . (?) (*sic*) reported on a Lugdunum coin, 'schlecht erhalten',
from the outer east gate is not otherwise known and need not
refer to Silius, as has been suggested.[5]

As for the pottery, it is Haltern which dates the pots, not the
pots Haltern. Loeschcke's study and classification of the pottery
finds from all the Haltern sites to date, which appeared in 1909,[6]
is one of the works on which the whole modern study of pottery
typology and chronology is based. Loeschcke, as we have seen,
believed that there was evidence for a reoccupation of the base
under Germanicus after its destruction in 9, but he believed this

[1] Report by Koepp, vi, pp. 19–23, with plan, plate 2.

[2] Loeschcke, v, p. 123, before the definitive publication by Koepp; Loeschcke
provisionally gave the pit the no. 126, and refers to it thus in his text and shows it
as 126 in his plan, v, plate 2; this pit also seen as post-Varian by Dragendorff,
RGKbl. i (1908), pp. 76–7.   [3] Koepp, v, p. 401.

[4] Kraft, *JNG* ii (1950/1), pp. 28–9, on countermarks. [ADD.]

[5] iv, p. 86, n. 4, cf. Kraft, op. cit., p. 28, n. 29. It was not illustrated; the late
Sir Ian Richmond suggested to me that it might be TIB, upside-down.

[6] Loeschcke, v, pp. 101–322; the pottery finds from the excavations of 1908–10
were published by Hähnle, vi, pp. 33–66, an article written in Loeschcke's shadow.
See below, Appendix I, pp. 257–60.

entirely on archaeological grounds. No piece of pottery found so far, he thought, could be dated with certainty to the time of Germanicus.[1] Oxé, also one of the leading authorities on early sigillata (and it is on the sigillata that we depend for these fine shades of dating), followed Loeschcke in assuming that there had been a post-Varian occupation and therefore spoke quite wrongly of 'die beiden jüngsten Kulturschichten', meaning the supposed destruction layer of 9 and the later occupation layer of 14–16, which he believed enabled us 'mit einer gewissen Sicherheit' to ascribe at least some of the sigillata to 14–16.[2] Whereupon he naturally proceeded to ascribe the latest pieces of Haltern sigillata to this period. About the comparative dating there is no question, but his absolute dating depends upon a circular argument. To Kraft belongs the credit of first demonstrating it.[3] The latest pieces are probably two fragments with stamps, one *in planta pedis* and one in a *tabula ansata*, both unique at Haltern.[4] The *planta pedis* stamp particularly is commonly seen as introduced only in the early years of Tiberius' reign. Its appearance in the base at Haltern shows that it came into use earlier, probably just before A.D. 9.[5] In 1964 moulds used in making sigillata were found in the base: the implications of this discovery are dealt with below.[6]

Apart from coins and pottery, there is one other object which at first might appear to offer vital information about the date when the base was given up. This is the lead stopper of a medicine jar with the inscription EX RADICE BRITANICA (*sic*), found in the building east of the so-called *praetorium* (this so-called *praetorium* is of course the *principia*).[7] No further details of the circumstances of the find are given, which is unfortunate, as it would greatly help to know whether it was in a clearly marked

[1] Loeschcke, v, p. 122.

[2] Oxé, *Bod. Westf.* vi (1943), p. 68, in an article discussing the pottery finds since 1925.

[3] Kraft, *BJ* clv/clvi (1955/6), pp. 95–111.

[4] v, p. 166, cf. pp. 186–7, and *Bod. Westf.* vi (1943), p. 173, respectively; on forms of stamps at Haltern see Loeschcke, v, pp. 165–6.

[5] Cf. below, pp. 258–60.

[6] Information from Dr. H. Aschemeyer, now also referred to by Schönberger, *JRS* lix (1969), p. 149; see below, p. 256. [ADD.]

[7] Stieren, *Germania* xii (1928), p. 175; illustrated p. 70, fig. 1, and again more clearly *Bod. Westf.* vi (1943), Pl. 30a, cf. p. 118. The piece is happily still preserved and displayed in the Haltern museum, although so much of the Haltern material was lost in the wartime bombing.

occupation layer. Dragendorff established the meaning of the inscription by referring it to Pliny's description of the *herba Britannica* as a remedy for scurvy, pointed out to the Romans by Frisians after Germanicus' establishment of forts in their territory.[1] If Pliny is right, the presence of this medicine in the base seems to show conclusively that it was still in Roman occupation under Germanicus. This conclusion has however been challenged by Kraft.[2] His arguments are threefold: firstly, that the stopper need not betoken occupation of the base, but might have been dropped by a Roman soldier of Germanicus' army visiting the abandoned site; secondly, if the use of the *herba Britannica* was not known to the Romans until the establishment of Germanicus' forts in Frisian territory, which Kraft dates to the summer of 15, then there was not enough time for it to be tested, prepared, put up in doses, sent to Haltern and lost before Germanicus' recall at the end of the following summer; and thirdly, as the name and as Pliny's other reference to the plant[3] suggest, it must have been known to the Romans, though perhaps not as an antiscorbutic,[4] from Britain through the Gauls and especially through the Druids, expert healers, independently of and prior to whatever they may have learnt about it from the Frisians.

Now it is certainly possible that the stopper was dropped by a casual visitor to the abandoned site, since we have no information on the stratigraphy of the find, although a medicine-jar stopper is an odd thing to drop. The argument that there would have been too little time for the medicine to be in use seems less strong; it would not be impossible, especially if we consider that Germanicus might have established forts in Frisian territory before 15, which is the date Kraft suggests.[5] But the argument

---

[1] Pliny, *NH* xxv. 20–1; Drexel, *Germania* xiii (1928), pp. 172–3; Drexel identifies the plant as a sort of dock, probably *Rumex obtusifolius*, whereas the Encyclopedia Britannica (11th edn.), s.v. 'dock', thinks it is *Rumex hydrolapathum*.

[2] Kraft, in *Aus Bayerns Frühzeit*, pp. 142–5, defending his view, based originally on numismatic grounds, that Haltern was given up in 9; his first article setting out this view, *BJ* clv/clvi (1955/6), loc. cit., did not mention the EX RADICE BRITANICA stopper.

[3] Pliny, *NH* xxvii. 2.

[4] Kraft, in *Aus Bayerns Frühzeit*, n. 16, justly points out its use in the ancient pharmacopoeia against other ills than scurvy.

[5] What did Germanicus do in 13? A fort is found already in existence among the Chauci in 14 (Tac., *Ann.* i. 38), and if there, why not among the Frisians?

that Pliny may have got his facts slightly wrong is the strongest of all. His botanical information was not infallible; he credits the Romans, for instance, with introducing the cherry to Britain, when archaeological evidence shows that it was known long before they came.[1] In the case of the *herba Britannica*, Pliny may have confused the son with the father; Germanicus among the Frisians was treading in his father's footsteps, since Drusus too had campaigned, built his canal, and founded forts in those parts.[2] In this case, Roman knowledge of the herb's antiscorbutic properties would go back to the days before the Haltern base was even founded. We may observe that Pliny, relating the story of how the Romans learnt of the plant from the Frisians, adds, 'mirorque nominis causam', which implies that he is aware of the incongruity, that a plant known as *herba Britannica* should first have turned up among the Frisians. We should not base a whole theory of an occupation of the base under Germanicus on so flimsy a piece of evidence as Pliny's unsupported statement, when it goes counter to the whole thrust of the basic archaeological evidence.

So much then for the date of the abandonment of the base. It was lost with Varus' army and never reoccupied. The date of its foundation permits of no such certainty and is closely involved with the history of the other Haltern sites, so that I have considered the chronology of them all together at the start of this section, concluding that the base may well date from around 8 B.C.[3]

To complete this account of the base, we must consider remains which appear to be those of its *canabae*. Clear signs of Roman occupation were observed above the half-filled ditch of the marching-camp. The occupation layer extends beyond the ditch, and is also found within the rampart. It was most obvious over a 90 m. stretch on the west side of the road running north from the north gate of the base.[4] It seems likely that the occupiers built their shacks (since there is no evidence of anything more substantial) in the ditch and behind the rampart for shelter against bad weather. No doubt Koepp is right to see

[1] Pliny, *NH* xv. 102; cf. Godwin, *History of the British Flora*, p. 110 (*Prunus avium, Prunus cerasus, Prunus padus*); cf. p. 337. I am grateful to S. Applebaum (Tel Aviv) for bringing this parallel to my attention.

[2] Above, p. 111. [3] Above, pp. 166–9. [4] Koepp, v, pp. 3–5.

them as camp-followers of the base, *canabae*-dwellers, if we do
not use this word in its later developed sense.[1] The finds here were
in a burnt layer, the *canabae* having evidently been destroyed
by fire. The fact that the rampart of the marching-camp was
allowed to stand (for the occupation layer was broken by the
rampart) and the *canabae* to grow up along it suggests that the
country passed for semi-pacified, or at least that the Romans
were confident that the base would not be attacked. The
Haltern base shelters its civilian dependents no less than Neuss
or Mainz at the same period. The *canabae* cannot have survived
the German attack in 9. Perhaps their inhabitants had time to
take refuge in the base, forming the mass of women and children
who cumbered the garrison's escape, if indeed it is Haltern that
Dio's story relates to.[2] Loeschcke pointed to the absence of any
complete or nearly complete pots or other useful objects in the
remains of the *canabae* as indicating that they were evacuated
peacefully. I do not think it too fanciful to suppose that news
of Varus' defeat and the impending German onslaught reached
the garrison at Haltern in time for them to prepare, as Tacitus
describes Vetera preparing to receive Civilis: 'legati legionum
vallum murosque firmabant, subversa longae pacis opera, haud
procul castris in modum municipii exstructa, ne hostibus usui
forent.'[3] Is not this what the Haltern *canabae* suggest, 'longae
pacis opera'? Not surprising, if, as I have suggested, the base
stood for 16 or 17 years.

E. *The Wiegel*

Schuchhardt describes with evident excitement how the excavators in their first season's work at Haltern, while they were
engaged on the Annaberg, had their attention directed to
Roman finds from an area known as the Wiegel, on the lower
ground between the Annaberg and the town of Haltern, an area
where no Roman remains were previously known.[4] After trial
digs in the autumn of 1899, full-scale excavation here began the
following year.[5] The site was an extremely complicated one

---

[1] See above, pp. 98–9.   [2] Dio lvi. 22. 2.
[3] Tac., *Hist.* iv. 22.
[4] Schuchhardt, *Sitzber. Kön. Preuss. Akad.* 1900, pp. 307–10.
[5] Reports by Koepp, ii, pp. 55–105 (the excavations); Ritterling, ii, pp. 107–
74 (the finds); with comments on some points of interpretation by Loeschcke, ii,
pp. 217–24, and Dahm, ii, pp. 225–8.

which the excavators identified as an 'Anlegeplatz', a place for boats to tie up and unload; it was mistakenly supposed that the river had washed right into the site in Roman times.[1] The excavations of 1900 were the only ones ever carried out in this area, since interest then shifted to the Hofestatt forts and the marching-camp and base. Now further excavations are impossible. Building and tipping have destroyed or deeply buried everything. This is unfortunate, since it is quite clear that the excavators at so early a stage of the Haltern investigations lacked the technique and the experience necessary to find all that might have been found or to understand what they did find. A comparison of the plans published in the report on the 1900 excavations[2] with those from later volumes of *MAKW* reveals at a glance how quickly the excavators learned their trade in the next ten years.

The two most striking features of the site are the numerous ditches which criss-cross it and the so-called 'triangle' ('Dreieck') with its surrounding excavations, the so-called 'Westgraben', 'Nordgraben', and 'Ostgraben'.[3] Apart from these the excavators recovered the groundplan of one complete Roman house, which is labelled on the plan 'Verwaltungsgebäude'; a well; four so-called 'Ufereinschnitten' (supposed to be ramps or flights of steps down to the river); and a large number of pits and holes, variously described as 'Wohngruben', 'Vorratsgruben', and 'Kochgruben'. Many of these are undoubtedly post-Roman.[4] There was one stretch of ditch which the excavators recognized as medieval, significantly in the same area as a very complicated feature which the excavators signally and confessedly failed to understand (the so-called 'Durchgang' through the long east–west 'Palissadengraben'),[5] whose irregular depressions and pits and variously-sized post-holes do not appear to be Roman, although the excavators seem to have assumed that they were. They are undoubtedly the remains of

---

[1] ii, pp. 84–5; see below, pp. 206–11.

[2] ii, plates 7 (1:1,000), 7, 8 (1:5,000); the 1:1,000 plan is said to be unreliable (Koepp, ii, p. 104), and comparison with the 1:5,000 plans shows how unreliable.

[3] See plan, where the triangle itself is marked 'Kornspeicher'.

[4] Various traces in the ground were recognized as post-Roman, cf. ii, pp. 76, 77, 81, 89, 92. Post-Roman pottery was not uncommon in the whole area and post-Roman remains were recognized in the other Roman sites; cf. also the roof-tiles reported, surely not Augustan, pp. 85, n. 1, 91; see also above, p. 143. [ADD.]

[5] ii, pp. 90–4.

post-Roman occupation, as are probably other features which the excavators sought to fit into the Roman pattern, for instance the so-called 'Kochgruben' containing sherds and animal bones overlying the 'Verwaltungsgebäude'.[1]

This building, though labelled 'Verwaltungsgebäude' on the plan, is in the text generally referred to as a 'Kaserne', while elsewhere it is suggested that it might be an officer's house. It belongs to a fairly early period of occupation, since a later ditch ('Spitzgraben A') runs right across it.[2] In the light of what is said below about the possibility that the Wiegel remains are those of a stores-compound, we may perhaps compare this building to the administration building and commandant's quarters of the Rödgen supply-depot (below, Chapter 6. 8).[3]

Now ditch A referred to in the previous paragraph is interrupted by the 'Nordgraben' of the triangle, continuing on the other side of it as ditch B.[4] A long so-called 'Palissadengraben', which we may refer to as P[1], was continued in the filling of the 'Westgraben' of the triangle, and the 'Westgraben' and 'Nordgraben' are really one single ditch.[5] We have then in this area four periods: the house is earlier than the ditch AB, which is earlier than the 'Nord-' and 'Westgraben', which are earlier than P[1]. P[1] however is itself intersected elsewhere by the later ditch X,[6] so that there are at least five periods of Roman occupation of this site. X is also later than ditch F, which is said to be a continuation of C,[7] though, if so, the plan is badly drawn,[8] and also later than C, which is parallel to P[1]. The purpose of these ditches was not established. Koepp denies that they can be drainage ditches, and suggests that enlightenment must come from further excavation.[9] Unfortunately this has never taken place. The only ditches whose function he claimed to know were

---

[1] ii, pp. 73–4, where they are called storage pits, but cooking pits on the plan, pl. 7; it is also suggested that the absence of other buildings was due to the soldiers sleeping in the cooking pits.

[2] ii, p. 95, retracting the conjecture on p. 75, that the ditch is earlier.

[3] ii, p. 75, cf. Schönberger, *Germania* xlv (1967), p. 90, with plan, fig. 2.

[4] ii, pp. 74, 88; but Koepp contradicts himself on p. 95.

[5] ii, p. 78; Koepp tries to deny this, unconvincingly, pp. 78–80, see Loeschcke, pp. 221–3, with photo., p. 223; cf. plate 17. 1.

[6] ii, pp. 81–2, 95.

[7] ii, p. 90.

[8] It does not show CF as being in the same line, but rather F as in almost the same line as AB.

[9] ii, p. 89.

the two 'Palissadengräben', P¹ and P², though he admitted that they contained no trace of a palisade.¹ In view of what we said above about the Roman house requiring to be within a regular fortification, the question naturally arises whether some of the ditches may not be V-shaped ditches of the type normally used in the defences of Augustan military posts.

The photographs indeed show a number of ditch profiles of this characteristic shape, none more characteristic than those of P¹. This surely cannot be a palisade trench. In plates 17. 1 and 17. 2 it has very clearly the profile of a V-shaped ditch of this defensive type, one which has lain open for some time and silted up naturally. In plate 18. 1 the profile is quite different—we almost wonder whether it can really be the same ditch—but nearly identical with that of the ditch of the marching-camp.² There is no photograph of P², but it is described as being of the same form as P¹.³ P¹ and P² cannot be contemporary, but it is impossible to assign to either one the priority. The ditch X is also a V-shaped ditch of this sort, as is clear from plates 19. 2 and 20. 1, although it is not described on the plan as a 'Spitzgräben'. Ditches A–G on the other hand are all specifically called 'Spitzgräben'. But whether or not all or any of them are part of the defences of a series of forts cannot be decided.

The problem is of course complicated by the washing away of the whole southern part of the site, and by the fact that the two big north–south ditches, P² and X, were not traced northwards beyond the modern road. This erosion also prevents us from saying what the so-called 'Ufereinschnitten' were. Koepp, believing that the Roman river washed the foot of the bank which now terminates the site to the south, thought they were flights of steps or ramps down to the water, despite the fact that, as he points out, there was no trace whatsoever of either steps or ramps.⁴ The two out of the four such structures on which Koepp chiefly relies for his interpretation, A and B, are illustrated on plates 20. 2 and 21, but unfortunately without an accompanying description in the text.⁵ The work is extremely rough, and the photographs give no clue to what the structures really were. There were no finds associated with them, so that

---

¹ ii, pp. 76–7, cf. p. 89.
² Cf. photograph of marching-camp ditch, v, p. 6.
³ ii, p. 80.   ⁴ ii, p. 86.   ⁵ Cf. ii, pp. 85–6.

there is no proof that they are Roman. They might for instance be associated with the post-Roman course of the river along this bank.

It remains only to discuss the triangle, which is the most important of all the structures found during the 1900 excavations, not only in itself, but for the sigillata which it yielded. When anyone discusses the date of the so-called 'Anlegeplatz', he really means of the triangle area, from which all the evidence comes. The triangle gets its name from the shape of the piece of ground enclosed by the three wide 'Gräben'. This piece of ground has an area of about 170 sq. m.[1] It contained no trace of buildings or other constructions. Of its surrounding ditches, the west is about 7 m. broad, the north 6 m., and the east, which forms the hypotenuse of the triangle, about 4 m. at its northern end, broadening towards the south.[2] The east ditch is also crooked, and it looks from the plans as if it may have been made by two separate ditches of different periods running together, though this possibility does not seem to have been considered by the excavators.

The west and north ditches are alike in shape and in the nature of their fill.[3] It seems that they were deliberately filled in, for on the photographs clods of earth can be seen, incompatible with natural silting,[4] which is not unlikely, since, as we have already stated, P[1] was dug in the filling of the west ditch. The east ditch is not only different in shape and in the nature of its fill,[5] which we shall discuss further in a moment, but is also separated from the L-shaped west and north ditch at each end.[6] On the strength of two post-holes at one end and one at the other Koepp postulated two gate-buildings, but quite unjustifiably. There were also two rows of post-holes within the northern part of the east ditch, of undetermined purpose.[7]

The filling of the west and north ditches, or ditch, comprised two burnt layers, the upper one distinguished by the presence

[1] ii, p. 60.   [2] Measurements taken from plan.   [3] ii, p. 62.
[4] Photographs of filling of west ditch, ii, plates 12. 1, 12. 2, 13. 1, 16. 2; of the north, plate 11. 2; Koepp notes the presence of what were perhaps turves in the filling, ii, p. 66.
[5] Photograph, ii, plate 14. 2.
[6] Carefully described, ii, p. 60; Koepp thought he traced a road leading towards the gap between east and west ditches, but this is doubtful: p. 61, cf. p. 75.
[7] ii, p. 62.

of thousands of carbonized wheat grains and other scattered finds, the lower by quantities of sigillata.[1] The wheat grains were especially common in the north ditch and the northern part of the west ditch. The layers were separated by a layer of impure sand. The east ditch on the other hand contained stones from the Annaberg, which were absent from the west and north ditches,[2] and what at first seemed to be a homogeneous occupation layer. The excavators later and with difficulty thought they had succeeded in distinguishing two layers in it, though without any intervening layer corresponding to the layer of impure sand in the other ditches.[3] Carbonized wheat grains were found in the more northerly part of the ditch only. It seems clear that the east ditch belongs to a different period from the others, and that the triangle itself, to which Koepp attached great significance, is an accident.

Koepp thought that the triangle was the site of a granary, the ditches being dug to keep it dry, and to guard it against fire. He considers and rejects the possibility that the triangle was a 'Festung'.[4] Loeschcke points out, firstly, that the distribution of the carbonized wheat does not agree with the theory of a granary within the triangle; secondly, that this is not the usual Roman way of keeping a building dry; and thirdly, that the sides of the ditches were so steep that they would have needed to be revetted with timber and wattle, itself a grave fire hazard. He thinks that the triangle is an 'Erdschanze', a stronghold, and that the granary or granaries lay to the north of the north ditch.[5] Dahm agrees with Loeschcke on the location of the granaries, pointing out what a vast quantity of corn would be needed for the Roman army operating in Germany.[6] The carbonized wheat grains are in fact found well to the east of the triangle, in ditch X,[7] so that Dahm suggests that the granaries may have occupied any or all of the area bounded by X, P[1], and C. He alone separates the east ditch from the others, which he explains as being the site of storehouses with cellars sunk into the ground, as portrayed in his sketch.[8] The underground cellar

---

[1] ii, pp. 63–9.   [2] ii, p. 63.
[3] ii, p. 64; it seems clear that they were worried by the apparent absence of two separate layers and very concerned to find evidence for two.
[4] ii, pp. 69–70.
[5] Loeschcke, ii, pp. 217–24.   [6] Dahm, ii, pp. 225–8.
[7] ii, p. 69.   [8] ii, p. 225.

would serve for the storage of liquids, wine, oil, etc., in large amphorae whose bases rested in a layer of sand, now in excavating seen as the layer of impure sand below the lower burnt layer and immediately above virgin soil. In the upper room at ground level were stored military supplies, including pottery, so that, when the building was burnt and collapsed into its foundation trench, the debris, including the pots, lay all over the broad floor of the trench, forming the lower burnt level itself. He points out that only on some such assumption can we account for the presence of pottery evenly distributed throughout this layer, since if the pottery had come into the trench from outside, it would naturally lie thicker on one side of the trench than the other. The upper burnt layer and the intervening layer of impure sand were, he suggests, washed into the old foundation trench, while it still lay open, after a conflagration involving the whole area.

Dahm's theory is certainly the most plausible of the three. It accounts for the ditches or trenches, the 'West-' and 'Nordgräben', as Koepp's and Loeschcke's theories do not. Its weakness is that it involves supposing them to have remained open for a long time after the destruction of the storehouses and then to have silted up gradually, which, as we have seen, was not the case. Or is it possible that the carbonized wheat grains were not washed in but were in the earth which was used as fill? That the west and north ditches are in fact foundation trenches for storehouses seems likely; but this only emphasizes our ignorance of the layout and history of this whole complicated site. It is tempting to see the remains as those of a stores-area, an annexe perhaps to the legionary base, but this is pure hypothesis. We might however note that the quantity of the amphora sherds reminded Ritterling of the harbour area at the Dimesser Ort below Mainz;[1] and for this reason it is perhaps the most plausible hypothesis that the remains are those of a stores-compound.

F. *The Hofestatt*

After the discovery and partial excavation of the stores-compound, if that is what it is, Koepp set himself to seek for further remains of a similar nature higher up the old river's course, and

---

[1] Ritterling, ii, p. 164; on the Dimesser Ort, see above, p. 146.

here in October 1901 he found the first trace of what the excavators came to call the 'Uferkastell', occupying the land known as the Hofestatt on the old river-bank.[1] Excavation the following year and in January 1903 revealed four successive fortifications on the same site.[2] Each of the four periods is shown in a different colour on the published plans (fig. 10),[3] and it is convenient to refer to them by these colours. Thus we shall speak of the yellow fort, the green, the red, and finally the blue. There is no doubt that the blue fort is the latest of the four and the red fort the next youngest, but it should be noted that the defences of the yellow and the green forts do not intersect each other, and that only one slender piece of evidence, discussed below, supports the excavators' hypothesis which assigned priority to the yellow. All four forts, as revealed by the excavations, end abruptly on the edge of an old river-bank, along which no trace of defences was found: hence the name 'Uferkastell' and the assumption that the purpose of the forts was to enclose a length of river-bank, presumably for use as a bridgehead.[4] For it was thought that this old river-bed was that of the river in Roman times, an assumption which we cannot accept.[5] I believe we are dealing with normal rectangular or polygonal forts which have been partly destroyed by the river since Roman times.

The defences of the yellow period enclosed a strip of about 20 m. of the bank; the maximum depth of the enclosure is now about 2 m., although Koepp supposes that in Roman times it was about 10 m.[6] It is hardly surprising then that no remains belonging to the yellow period were found within the defences.[7] It does not seem to have occurred to the excavators that a fort of such limited dimensions must have had a very limited value. The defences comprised a single ditch with a wood-and-earth

[1] Koepp, iii, pp. 3–5.
[2] Reports by Koepp, iii, pp. 1–5, and Koepp, Dragendorff, and Krüger, iv, pp. 33–79.
[3] iv, plate 4 is the final and definitive plan; comparison with iii, plate 3, shows how later discoveries or maturer reflection changed the excavator's interpretation of certain details, not all referred to in the text.
[4] Koepp, iii, p. 39; a corresponding bridge-head was sought on the opposite side of the valley, without success.
[5] See next section (G).
[6] Koepp, iii, pp. 24–5.
[7] Ibid., p. 35; cf. p. 28.

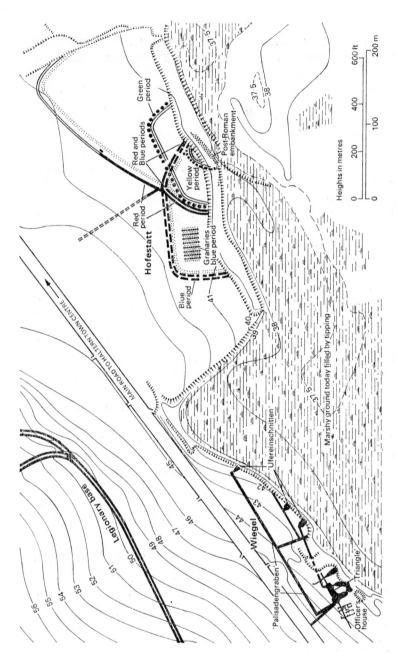

FIG. 10. Haltern: the Hofestatt

Red and
Blue periods

Green
period

Yellow
period

Post-Roman
embankment

Red
period

Granaries
blue period

Blue
period

Hofestatt

41

40

39

38

MAIN ROAD TO HALTERN TOWN CENTRE

37·5

38

37·5

38

Heights in metres

0
100
200
400
600 ft

0
100
200 m

Marshy ground today filled by tipping

Ufereinschnitten

37·5

45

46

47

48

49

50

51

52

53

54

55

56

Legionary base

42

43

44

Wiegel

'Palisadengraben'

Triangle

Officer's
house

rampart; the wooden revetment was supported by posts consisting of half-logs set in individual post-holes and joined by timbers laid in a sleeper-trench.[1] On the east side a second, outer
ditch was added, inexplicable as it stands, but not if the greater
part of the fort has been washed away and the ditch originally
strengthened the defences at the corner. The excavators failed
to find a gate,[2] no doubt because all the gates were destroyed by
the river.

The green fort is considerably larger (or rather, more of it is
preserved), which led the excavators to assume it was also later.
In its present form it is roughly rectangular, 150 × 50 m., its
longer side running along the old river-bank.[3] There is a gate
in the middle of the north side[4] with a corduroy roadway
through it.[5] Its defences, like those of the yellow period, were
formed of a single ditch with a wood-and-earth rampart, whose
posts however were set, not in separate post-holes, but in a continuous bedding-trench.[6] Irregularities at the north-east corner
are unexplained,[7] and what Koepp, following Schuchhardt,
originally took for evidence of an earth bank behind the rampart was later seen to belong to the red period, not the green.[8]
Buildings inside the fort were found, most notably two on either
side of the road leading in from the gate, one of which yielded
more pottery than any other building in the Hofestatt area. No
complete picture of the interior, however, could be formed.[9]

The defences of the red fort, consisting of a double ditch and
a wood-and-earth rampart, can be seen to overlie remains of the
yellow and green periods.[10] At one point the red post-holes
appear from a photograph to be set into pits that must belong
to the green period and both are dug in the filling of the yellow
ditch.[11] The excavators do not however mention this, which, if
my interpretation is correct, is nevertheless the only evidence

---

[1] Koepp, iii, p. 22; photographs of the defences in iii, plates 8. 1, 8. 2 (with
erroneous caption, reprinted in iv, plate 8. 1, with correct caption, see note in iii,
Vorwort, p. iii), 10. 2, 11, 12. 1–3.

[2] Koepp, iii, p. 27.   [3] Ibid., p. 25.   [4] Ibid., p. 20.

[5] Ibid., p. 30; Albrecht cites this as parallel to the corduroy roads in Oberaden,
Das Römerlager in Oberaden i, p. 19.

[6] Koepp, iii, p. 28.   [7] Ibid., p. 29.

[8] Ibid., p. 30, but cf. iv, plate 4, with iii, plate 3.

[9] Ibid., pp. 35–8; Krüger, iv, pp. 68–70.

[10] Photographs, iii, plates 8. 1, 12. 1, 12. 3, 13. 2.

[11] iii, plate 12. 3.

supporting their theory that the yellow fort is earlier than the green. One corner only of the red fort is preserved, the angle between the two sides being about 90°.

When the blue fort was built, it retained the north-east side of the red fort, but instead of turning south-westwards, as the red fort did, the blue defences continued westwards, reducing what had been a right angle to one of about 35°.[1] The red fort may have been rectangular or even roughly triangular; the blue one was certainly polygonal. The need to fill in the red ditches along the north-west side of the fort and extend the ditches of the north-east side westwards caused certain difficulties. It appears that just east of the junction of red and blue ditches the inner ditch had to be re-dug on a new and straighter line. Timbers and posts showing on the lip of the blue ditches are explained by Koepp as intended, in some way that he does not explain, to strengthen the ditches; the actual significance of the finds is not however clear.

More traces of rotted wood were found in the filling of the red ditches, but again it is uncertain what, if anything, this means. South of the junction, where the north-west side of the red fort overlies the north-west corner of the green fort, further peculiarities were found whose significance at the time was not realized, but which the excavators on further reflection decided betokened a tower.[2] This is the only tower found in any of the Hofestatt forts, a fact which, since one tower does not exist in isolation, suggests that others were missed or misunderstood by the excavators.

In the north-east side, which is common to both red and blue forts, a gate was found. This is the only red gate to have survived erosion, but the west gate of the blue fort was also found.[3] Of great importance for the history of the forts, it is clear that the red ditches had been allowed to start silting up before they were deliberately filled to allow the blue defences to go through them.[4] Again at the north-west gate, where the red ditches were re-used for the blue fort, one of the photographs shows that the ditches had been recut. It seems that the red ditches were open

---

[1] Report on excavation of junction of red and blue defences, Koepp, iii, pp. 15–18; photographs, plates 5. 1, 5. 2, 6. 1, 6. 2, 7. 1, 7. 2 (on which see p. 17, n. 2).
[2] Koepp, iv, pp. 63–4.
[3] iv, p. 54.
[4] Koepp, iii, p. 15; see photographs, esp. iv, plate 13. 1.

and neglected for some time before the establishment of the blue fort on the site.

Within the area occupied by both red and blue forts it is a difficult task to determine which remains belong to which period,[1] nor is there any guarantee that the excavators found all that might have been found with modern methods and modern experience. Krüger, describing what he takes for the remains of the red fort,[2] ascribes to it an interior layout quite unparalleled in any known Roman fort (barracks lining the rampart around a semicircle of some 28 m. diameter, with the commander's tent erected over a pit in the middle and cooking-fires all round it), and one which depends upon the false assumption that the red fort is complete as we have it. In fact we know virtually nothing of the real layout.

In the north-west corner of the blue fort, where excavation and observation were easier, since here there was only the blue period of occupation to deal with, a large building or series of buildings was found.[3] Krüger took them for barracks, while leaving open the possibility that they might be boat-houses, although with the reservation that one would expect to find boat-houses at the water's edge, which these are not, nor is there any sign of a slipway. 'Boat-houses' in fact is a wild guess, barracks equally impossible. The structure consists of eight 'fish-bones', parallel trenches, 25 m. long and 6 m. apart, each with cross trenches 1·8 m. apart.[4] The long trenches are just over 0·5 m. wide, the cross trenches on the average 3·25 m. long. Between each fish-bone and the next and outside each end one was a row of post-holes. If we take the trenches as the foundations of walls, the rooms of which the blocks are composed measure only 1·8 m. by less than 1·5 m., impossible dimensions for a barrack-room. What we have in fact is a granary, supported on posts, the fish-bone trenches being sleeper-trenches for the underpinning of the floor. The extreme scarcity of finds

---

[1] Cf. the difficulty of distinguishing remains of the marching-camp from those of the base, Koepp, v, p. 57.

[2] Krüger, iv, pp. 70–2.   [3] Ibid., pp. 75–8.

[4] Only the most westerly 'fish-bone' was completely excavated, and the five most easterly ones are known only from trial trenches; compare the irregularities found in the groundplan where excavated (Krüger calls them 'nicht nur unerklärt, sondern unerklärbar') with the far too tidy and imaginative reconstructed plan given on plate 4.

in the area of these buildings supports this identification. The granary measures some 45·5 × 25 m., or slightly less than the largest of the granaries at Rödgen (47·25 × 29·50 m.), which again exhibits the same basic method of construction with upright posts and extensive underpinning intended both to support the weight of the grain and to keep it dry by raising the floor of the granary and permitting the circulation of air underneath.[1] At Rödgen however the timbers are laid parallel, generally about 1 m. apart, instead of in fish-bone pattern, as here. A ditch surrounding the granary, thought by Krüger to be the bedding-trench for a palisade, is probably a drain.[2]

East of the granaries, remains were found which Krüger identified as those of buildings of the blue fort, lying in part over the filling of the red ditch.[3] The traces were somewhat irregular: Krüger thought of long, low, mud huts with wooden roofs, a type of building not generally found in Roman forts. The post-holes, taken to have been for roof-supports, are uncharacteristically large for Roman post-holes. No evidence connects these remains, whatever they are, with Roman occupation, and they are probably post-Roman.

So far we have not mentioned what the excavators called the 'unfertige Anlage', a ditch with rampart which continues the line of the outer ditch of the west side of the red fort northeastwards when the ditches of the fort turn south-eastwards; it continues to the eastern edge of the Hofestatt, there turns sharply southwards along the edge and is lost to view in the gardens which lie on the bank of the old river-bed.[4] The rampart, of the usual wood-and-earth type, is so far behind the ditch that there would have been room for an inner ditch between the two. The absence of such a ditch and of a gate-building at the point where there is a break in ditch and rampart led the excavators to suppose the work unfinished, and irregular depressions between rampart and ditch were taken by Koepp for various attempts to start digging the inner ditch.[5] They are more probably remains of post-Roman occupation, undoubted traces of which are found in the area of the ditch and

[1] Schönberger, *SJ* xxi (1963/4), p. 102; see below, Rödgen, (Chapter 6. 8).

[2] Krüger, loc. cit.; cf. v, 29–31, where the drain of the *via principalis* of the base was at first mistaken for such a bedding-trench.

[3] Krüger, iv, pp. 72–3.

[4] Koepp, iv, p. 55; cf. iv, plate 1.   [5] Koepp, iii, pp. 33–4.

rampart.[1] The so-called 'unfertige Anlage' is in fact more probably an annexe to the red fort, such as is found, for instance, at Chew Green or Fendoch or Newstead, intended to give temporary shelter to bodies of men or convoys of stores in transit.[2] It may also have contained workshops of the red period, located outside the fort, as in the post-Augustan *canabae*. This however seems rather doubtful and depends only upon the somewhat arbitrary attribution to the red period of pits, post-holes, burning, and slag found near buildings of the green fort but not apparently belonging to them.[3]

The annexe may have been planned with a double ditch like the red fort, and only one ditch built, the other seeming unnecessary in a time of long peace. The gateway will have been provided with some temporary barrier when the annexe was occupied. The annexe may have stood for some time. At one point the post-holes show signs of what might naturally be explained as the replacement of posts which had rotted or warped, an explanation which Koepp rejected as inappropriate because he believed the defences never to have been finished.[4] There is said to be no trace of posts left in the post-holes, as if the Romans had themselves levelled the works.[5]

The annexe may possibly have been joined to the legionary base also by a ditch, or else have had a second annexe attached on the north. A ditch was found running northwards from just outside the annexe ditch, without post-holes or bedding-trenches (though it might have had a turf rampart),[6] and was followed to the modern road, where excavation broke off, though a similar ditch verging more towards the west was found beyond the road. Koepp believed the two to be connected and to link up with the base. Unless it bent back to rejoin the Hofestatt fort defences and so form a second annexe, it seems likely that Koepp is right. This may in fact be the same ditch as that found underlying the outer, later, east front of the base, the so-called 'Anschlussgraben', which puzzled the excavators, but which

---

[1] iv, pp. 56–8.
[2] Newstead had three annexes, Curle, *A Roman Frontier Post and its People*, pp. 86–8; cf. also Collingwood and Richmond, *The Archaeology of Roman Britain*, p. 89.
[3] Krüger, iv, p. 72.
[4] Koepp, iv, pp. 59–60, with plan, p. 58.
[5] Ibid., p. 62.
[6] Ibid., p. 65.

Koepp and Schuchhardt decided linked the earlier east front of the base to the Hofestatt fort.[1]

It is hard to come to any conclusion about the absolute date of the Hofestatt forts, though their dates relative to one another are clear. The earliest of them, the yellow fort, as has already been stated, yielded no finds at all. The interior of the remainder, such of it as the river has left, was not excavated nearly as intensively as the base, and the number of finds is less. Where finds were made in the Hofestatt area, sigillata, the most useful aid to dating, was rare, and much rarer than in the stores-compound or the base.[2] I can find nothing to indicate at what date the green fort replaced the yellow or the red the green. There are however indications that an appreciable period elapsed between the building of the red fort and its replacement by the blue, in that the red ditches had begun, and had been allowed to begin, to silt up before they were either recut or filled in for the building of the new fort. It is possible that the red fort was the one destroyed in A.D. 9 and the blue fort a foundation of Germanicus. The finds, as already stated, are not enough to establish the date of the latest occupation of the site. An occupation under Germanicus is, I hasten to add, pure hypothesis. It enables us, however, to suppose that Haltern is Aliso, Aliso being the name for the place as a whole, not for any single one of the Roman structures there. I have discussed the whole problem of Aliso above.[3] Here I merely observe again that the identification of Aliso with Haltern is tempting and, if the blue period of the Hofestatt fort is post-Varian, possible.

G. *The Course of the Lippe in Augustan Times*

As stated above, both the Wiegel and the Hofestatt remains come right down to the edge of an old bed of the Lippe. This bed runs along the northern edge of the flood plain of the river and the present course of the river along the southern edge. Where did the river run in Roman times? The question was first raised in connection with the remains on the Wiegel, and

---

[1] Schuchhardt, iv, p. 29; Koepp, v, p. 394, n. 4; just beside it on the outer east front was a strange projection, whose purpose I can no more fathom than could the excavators. It was not a tower, nor did it apparently have anything to do with the 'Anschlussgraben' (Schuchhardt, iv, pp. 27–8).

[2] Cf. Loeschcke, v, p. 115.

[3] See above, pp. 152–3.

became acute with the discovery of the 'yellow'-period Hofestatt fort, which had clearly suffered erosion.[1] The old bed was
tested by excavation, and proved to be about 60 m. wide, after
which firm cultivable land began again, stretching across to the
present stream on the other side of the valley.[2] No sign of a
third channel could be detected,[3] although the whole valley is
so low-lying as to be liable to flooding.[4] Three possibilities exist:
either the river in Roman times flowed in the old bed alongside
the Wiegel and the Hofestatt, and changed to its present bed in
medieval times; or the Roman river flowed more or less in the
present bed, changed to the northerly channel, and changed
back again (perhaps more than once) in medieval times; or the
Roman channel lay elsewhere in the valley, between the present
bed and the old one which we see, and has so silted up as to be
no longer visible.[5] Koepp began by asserting rather than arguing for the first explanation, while ignoring the second and
denying the possibility of the third.[6] The whole interpretation
of the Wiegel and Hofestatt finds depended upon this. Critics
suggested that Koepp's view was wrong, that the river had
changed over to the more northerly bed in post-Roman times
and washed away part of the Roman works.[7] Koepp therefore
attempted to prove his case, resting it upon the supposed Roman
origin of a timber embankment found along the edge of the
channel where the Hofestatt forts came down to it.[8]

The embankment was constructed of piles of two main sizes,[9]
with big treetrunks set amongst them in no discernible pattern,
sometimes held in place by piles. The piles of the thicker sort

[1] Koepp, iii, p. 24, cf. p. 3, n. 1: 'denn konnte hinter dem Wall blieben jetzt kaum
noch ein paar Meter Fläche: so konnte diese Befestigung unmöglich ursprünglich
ausgesehen haben.'

[2] Ibid., pp. 24–5; further, iv, 160–3 (n. on plate 17).

[3] iv, p. 163.

[4] Koepp, iii, p. 39; iv, p. 34; cf. von Petrikovits's warning *RE* viiiA, col. 1804:
'Bei der Lokalisierung älterer Flussläufe ist allerdings immer zu berücksichtigen, dass
nicht regulierte Flüsse im Flachland zahlreiche nicht beständige Läufe (Hochwasser-
rinnen) bilden, die vielfach untereinander querverbunden sind. Deshalb kann man
nicht einfach von einem Rhein- oder Lippelauf sprechen.'

[5] The oldest map of the area extant is of the late 16th century, but large-scale
and inaccurate; we have no evidence for the medieval course of the river (ii, p. 5).

[6] Koepp, iii, pp. 24–5; one argument is advanced, iii, p. vi, but recanted, iv,
p. 37.

[7] Koepp, iv, p. 34.   [8] Ibid., pp. 38–45.

[9] The actual piles described and classified by Krüger, iv, pp. 46–53, with photographs, plate 18.

were found only along the stretch of bank enclosed by the yellow fort; the thinner piles extended further along the bank, although in the west they did not go beyond the limits of the blue fort.[1] Only in front of the yellow fort however was full-scale excavation attempted. Beyond that, the embankment is known only from trial trenches. Unfortunately, unsupervised workmen destroyed part of the embankment and the excavators themselves tidied up and restored the remains before photographing them.[2] Krüger points out two ways in which the rows of piles differ from those to be observed in the Roman ramparts; he suggests it is because they are not ramparts, whereas we might rather suggest that it is because they are not Roman: one is that even the thickest piles here are less than 1/3 the section of the piles of the ramparts of the forts, the other that the bedding-trenches of the embankment piles are irregular in width and in direction.[3] The whole embankment in fact appears to have been built just anyhow, with no straight lines, the unshaped tree-trunks which give weight to the structure being scattered apparently haphazard. Not thus did the Romans build their landing-stage at Vetera or construct their building foundations in the wet, low-lying ground at Vechten or Valkenburg.[4] What we miss here at Haltern is the Roman order, precision, and engineering skill.

Koepp himself, while holding that the relationship between the remains of the embankment and the defences of the forts, especially of the yellow fort, proved that they were contemporary (a point to examine below), admitted that finds, especially of pottery, associated with the embankment might seem to cast doubt on this.[5] The piles were laid in a 'Moorschicht', a layer of waterlogged ground identified with the old river-bed, now covered by firm soil washed down from above.[6] In this layer were found sherds of Roman pottery, especially of amphorae and other large vessels, together with later sherds of all dates from the Middle Ages to the 19th century. They included not many Germanic sherds and only one indisputably Carolingian. Moreover, in the very deepest layer, below the

[1] Koepp, iv, pp. 42–3.
[2] Ibid., pp. 39, 41; photographs, plates 8. 2, 9. 1.
[3] Krüger, iv, pp. 49–50.   [4] See above, pp. 108–9.
[5] Koepp, iv, pp. 40–1.
[6] Cf. ibid., pp. 24–5.

Roman sherds, medieval tiles were found. This Koepp seeks
to explain by supposing that the waterlogged layer was not
covered up until the 19th century, that the post-Roman sherds
were washed down by flood-water, and that the fragments of
medieval tiles sank the deepest because they were the heaviest.
He seems to recognize the implausibility of this explanation, for,
repeating this conclusion later, he says he must leave it to
experts to decide why the waterlogged ground lay open for so
many centuries, as the sherds show that it did.[1] That is to say,
Koepp sees that the obvious interpretation of the evidence leads
to another conclusion, that the embankment is a medieval work;
but since he is unwilling to admit this, he casts around for some
explanation, what it is he knows not, consistent with a Roman
date. The fact remains that fragments of medieval tiles were
found below the Roman layers amongst the piles in the layer in
which the bedding-trenches for the piles were dug. Of course
the weight of the tiles would make them sink deeper in swampy
ground than small sherds of finer pottery would, but amphora
sherds are heavy too, and had hundreds of years longer than the
tiles in which to settle. If the fragments of tiles came into the
bedding-trenches when they were dug (how large the trenches
were is not known, since their filling was indistinguishable from
the waterlogged earth),[2] all is clear and simple. We should not
seek for any other explanation unless compelled to do so.

Is then the relationship between the rows of piles and the
Roman forts so clear as to compel us none the less to accept the
Roman origin of the piles? Koepp thought so, arguing that
the piles running along the bank turned inwards to join up with
the western end of the rampart of the yellow fort at the point
where it reached, or at least where the excavators expected it to
reach, the bank.[3] Unfortunately, the defences failed to appear
where expected,[4] and indeed Koepp has to admit that, although
at first the excavators expected the connection between the
embankment and the defences to be easy to establish, further
investigation failed to provide the evidence they were seeking.

[1] Ibid., pp. 42–3.

[2] Ibid., p. 43.

[3] Ibid., p. 41, cf. Krüger, iv, p. 50. No corresponding turn inwards was observed
at the eastern end, but there was a broad depression of unknown significance going
down below the water table.

[4] Koepp, iv, p. 44.

Although the actual piles were not preserved above the water table, two parallel trenches which the excavators took for the bedding-trenches in which they had been set could be seen higher up the bank. These stopped however where the bank got steeper and could not be shown to link up with the defences of the fort.[1] There is in fact no evidence at all to link the trenches with the piles, nor, if there were, would there be anything to connect both with the defences of the yellow fort. And yet rather than give up the theory that the piles met the defences, Koepp, having failed to prove it, pertinaciously assumes that they met elsewhere, at a point which was not excavated. He will not give up the Roman origin of the embankment, for which he has now on his own showing no shred of evidence.

It remains only to consider the argument brought against the medieval origin of the work, that no medieval remains were found immediately above it and no important medieval remains anywhere on the rising ground above the old river-bed, where the Roman occupation traces are so extensive.[2] It is true that of the post-Roman finds reported from here, Germanic and Carolingian appear to outnumber later medieval,[3] a fact which might suggest that had the embankment been Roman and the 'Moorschicht' open to later finds, as Koepp suggested, Germanic and Carolingian should not have been so few there, compared with later ones. But it should be pointed out, first, that all excavation has been directed to elucidating Roman remains, and evidence for post-Roman occupation of any period has come to light fortuitously and at random; and secondly, that occupation evidence may be irrelevant. If the river changed its course and swiftly eroded as much land on the north side of the valley as it did (for it clearly eroded the greater part of the Hofestatt forts), an embankment to protect the good farming land is reasonable. That the town of Haltern was in existence from, at the latest, the beginning of the eleventh century, when it was called Halostron, is incontestable.[4] It is not unlikely that

[1] Koepp, iv, pp. 43–4; his description of the excavations and his arguments are here particularly obscure and ill-expressed; cf. also Krüger, iv, pp. 50–1. These bedding-trenches are those marked X1 and X2 on iv, plate 17. Krüger, p. 50, notes that they were originally taken for the bedding-trenches of the rampart revetment.

[2] Koepp, iv, p. 41.

[3] See above, pp. 169–70.

[4] Cf. Philippi, i, p. 62, n.; east of the town is a medieval fortified site, id. ii, pp. 17–20.

the medieval inhabitants farmed the river banks, even if they did not inhabit them, and were concerned to protect them from the river. The embankment is at a point where it would take and break the full destructive force of the current: this is what it was built for.

6. 3. OBERADEN

Oberaden lies east of Lünen and north-east of Dortmund, about a mile south of the river Lippe. The Roman base (fig. 11) occupied a hill above the village, on which now stand the village school, a new church, and increasingly more and more houses. From the hilltop the land drops away on all sides, on the north-east side alone rising again to further hills; but even on this side it does not begin to rise for about a mile, so that the Oberaden hill commands its surroundings magnificently in every direction. The defences encircle the hilltop, so that the perimeter is considerably lower than the centre of the base. The fall from the spot-height beside the present school-house in the region of the *principia* of the base to the south gate is 14·4 m.; it is here, on the south and south-west, that the defences reach furthest down the hill, but the drop on the other sides is almost as great and generally steeper.

The results of the pre-1914 excavations by Baum and of subsequent observations, together with specialist reports on the finds, were assembled by Albrecht.[1] The base is an irregular heptagon with rounded corners, defended by a single ditch 4–6 m. wide, with a rampart revetted with timber front and rear and surmounted by a breastwork of wattle and mud, with four gates, the whole enclosing an area of approximately 60 ha.[3] This is three times the size of the base at Haltern, and half as big again as the marching-camp there; bigger too than the camp at Holsterhausen.[3] The original excavator, Baum, claimed to have discovered towers every 45 m. between the north and west gates, though he had looked for similar towers on the other

[1] Albrecht, *Das Römerlager in Oberaden*; two volumes were published, of which the second is very rare; a planned vol. iii giving details of excavations in 1937 and 1938 was destroyed by bombing before it could appear, cf. Aschemeyer, *PZ* xli (1963), p. 211.

[2] Albrecht, op. cit. i, p. 17.

[3] Cf. comparative scale drawings in von Petrikovits, *Das römische Rheinland*, p. 25.

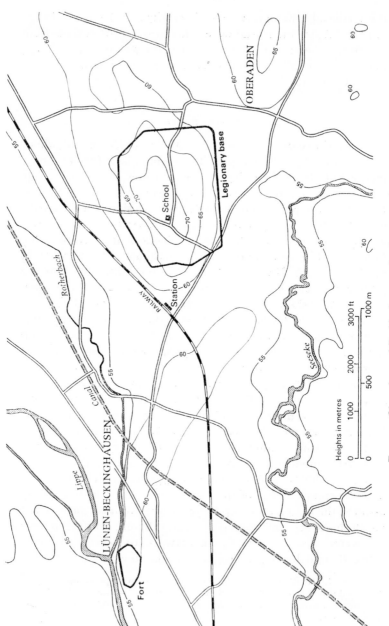

Fig. 11. Oberaden and Beckinghausen: the Augustan sites

sides unsuccessfully, and although Albrecht doubted whether they existed even where Baum claimed to have found them, the accuracy of Baum's observations has now been established by Aschemeyer.[1] The defences of this north-west front were also strengthened by a barrier of sharp wooden stakes, about 300 of which were found in the ditch here, but nowhere else. They were probably set up originally along the inner lip of the ditch or in the bottom of the ditch to present an extra obstacle to attackers.[2] The original identification of them with *pila muralia* cannot be sustained.[3] It appears that for some reason the north-west front of the base was particularly well fortified.

The fact that Oberaden has only a single ditch excited comment when it was first excavated. Kropatschek suggested however that it was sufficiently steep and slippery to form as difficult an obstacle as Haltern's double ditch[4]—slippery, one must assume, if the weather were conveniently wet. He had in mind the nature of the ground, which is hard to dig in, red clay on an equally intractable subsoil, as hard for the excavator as it must have been for the Romans. Aschemeyer, like Kropatschek, is moved to comment on the difficulties.[5] Traces of wooden buildings and other structures are barely decipherable, a fact which suggests that Baum's failure to find towers at points other than on the north-west front is not necessarily conclusive proof that they never existed. The single ditch, however, is no longer surprising. The early bases at Vetera and Neuss offer ready parallels. The gates at Oberaden are indeed bigger and stronger than those at Haltern.[6] There is nothing feeble or makeshift about the Oberaden defences.

The interior was as carefully laid out and constructed as the defences. The *via principalis*, contrary to the practice of later Augustan and post-Augustan times, ran along the long axis, rather than the short. The headquarters buildings lay on top of the hill in what is now the area of the school. The difficulties of

[1] Excavations of 1963, still unpublished. [ADD.]

[2] Albrecht, op. cit. i, p. 15; in greater detail, with bibliography of discussion, Oxé in ibid., pp. 76–81.

[3] *Pila muralia* described by Caesar, *BG* v. 40; that these are not *pila muralia*, however, was shown by Conrads, *Germania* xi (1927), pp. 71–3; similar stakes at Saalburg also wrongly hailed as *pila muralia*, Jacobi, *SJ* vi (1914/24), pp. 156–67.

[4] Kropatschek, *Westd. Ztschr.* xxvi (1907), *Kblt.*, cols. 133–8.

[5] Aschemeyer, op. cit., p. 212; cf. Kropatschek, op. cit., col. 133.

[6] Albrecht, op. cit. i, p. 17.

the ground, to which we have already alluded, prevented the early excavators from recovering the full plan of the buildings here, but subsequent excavations by Albrecht and by Asche-meyer have revealed timber buildings of the normal type of construction.[1] Aschemeyer's still unpublished excavations in 1963 also recovered the groundplan of barracks in the north-west portion of the base. Roads were surfaced with corduroy, or made of rammed clay covered with sand.[2] A striking feature was the very large number of pits found beneath the roads and indeed beneath the buildings.[2] Since pits underlying corduroy road or building foundations cannot have been dug while the road or building was there and in use, many of the pits must date from a period before the base was laid out in this form. The garrison may originally have lived in tents within the defences while laying out their permanent quarters. Absence of observed traces of tents, such as were found at Vindonissa and elsewhere,[3] is scarcely surprising in such difficult soil.

Within the base the excavators found the remarkable total of 28 wells,[4] in addition to three water tanks, two of which, close behind the north-west rampart, were thoroughly excavated,[5] while the third, behind the eastern rampart, though shown in Albrecht's plans, is not mentioned in his text and does not appear on Baum's earlier plan.[6] The tanks that were excavated measured 11·5 × 4·6 m. and 12 × 4 m.[7] They had a very well constructed wooden lining that was still preserved below the water table. One of them was found to contain many sherds, a sort of dagger with a wooden hilt, and an ornamental ladle of gilded bronze with a vertical handle, the top of which was fitted with a small sieve. The other contained the wreckage of what appears to have been a roof, built of timber and clay-daubed wattle, along with sherds, the studded sole of a boot, and a clump of rusted-

---

[1] Aschemeyer, op. cit., pp. 210–12; cf. Albrecht, op. cit. i, p. 20.

[2] Albrecht, op. cit. i, pp. 18–19.

[3] Evidence for tents at Vindonissa, Neuss, Mainz, and Hüfingen assembled by Wiedemer, *JGPV* 1962/3, p. 19, to which add evidence from Valkenburg, Glas-bergen, *42 n. C.—Het eerste jaartal in de geschiedenis van West-Nederland*, p. 9.

[4] Albrecht, op. cit. i., p. 19.

[5] Ibid., p. 14, with photographs, plates 6 and 7, and plans, plates 25, 35, 36; slightly fuller account by Kropatschek, *RGKbl.* ii (1909), pp. 1–2.

[6] *Mannus* v (1913), plate 1.

[7] Kropatschek gives to one the dimensions 12 × 4·5 m. and does not give those of the other; but Albrecht's dimensions are consistent with his plans.

together iron objects, including files, chisels, and spear- and *pilum*-heads. Neither tank had an inlet pipe, so that they must have been filled from springs, by rain-water, or by hand. The excavators supposed that their main task was to supply water for the daily needs of the base, with the secondary function of providing an emergency water supply for fire-fighting at this apparently particularly threatened north-west sector of the defences. Kropatschek saw the weapons in the tanks as evidence for a hard fight at this point.[1] He suggested further that the number of wells and the tanks implied that an adequate water-supply was something of a problem, and that this factor may have led the Romans to give up the base. The latter suggestion is attractive. The tanks however may have been a reserve supply, rather than meant for everyday needs, which would be met by the wells. There are no springs in the vicinity now, and unless the roof, already referred to, was only a partial one, they did not collect rain-water, so that we must conclude that they were filled by hand, specifically for use in reserve if the wells ran dry. We observe similar tanks in the fort at Hod Hill,[2] which was otherwise dependent for its water on the stream at the foot of the hill, outside the defences. The roof may possibly have been meant to afford protection against missiles, rather than against the rain ('zum Schutz gegen ungünstige Witterung' is Albrecht's phrase, reminiscent of an open-air concert announcement). There seems little point in protecting men against the rain just while they were dipping their containers into the tank, when they had to walk there and back exposed to the elements, unless the tank were used for some stationary activity, such as laundry; but this is to enter the realms of purely imaginative 'reconstruction'.

There can be no doubt whatsoever that the base was built for permanent occupation. All parts of the work, defences and interior alike, are extremely well built.[3] Koepp, at the time of the earliest excavations, states that he has observed with his own eyes how well built Oberaden is, how much more carefully the timbers there are cut and shaped than at Haltern.[4] A base of

[1] Kropatschek, op. cit., p. 8.
[2] Richmond, *JRS* xlv (1955), p. 141.
[3] Albrecht, op. cit. i, p. 21: 'scheinen alle fest und solide und nicht für eine vorübergehende Benutzung, sondern für eine lange Dauer gebaut gewesen zu sein.'
[4] Koepp, *MAKW* v (1909), pp. 398–9.

this size was meant for at least two legions plus auxiliaries, if garrisoned at full strength. Even a holding force would have had to be of considerable size to man so large a perimeter. The coin evidence discussed below in Appendix II makes it clear that the site ceased to be occupied by the Romans before the Lugdunum altar-series replaced the Nemausus crocodile-series as the normal currency of the Rhine army, that is to say, within a year or two of 10 B.C., probably about 8/7.[1] There is abundant evidence that the base was destroyed by fire, whence Albrecht concludes that it was taken and burnt by enemy action. This conclusion is invalid, although the same error is commonly found in reports on other sites also. Schleiermacher, reviewing Albrecht's book, pointed out that the burning might just as well have followed a planned withdrawal as its capture by the Germans.[2] We have the clear testimony of Josephus that it was standard Roman practice to put the torch to a camp they were abandoning.[3] And even if they marched out and left the base standing, it is hard to imagine that the Germans would have refrained from burning it once they found it empty. Evidence that a fort or base was burnt can of itself tell us nothing about how or why it was burnt. Burning is merely the quickest way of getting rid of timber buildings.[4]

What then can we deduce about the history of Oberaden? Dio's account of Drusus' expeditions into Germany implies that in his first year, 12 B.C., he established no permanent posts in Germany, and that the following year he established only two, one on the Lippe, the famous Aliso, and the other in the territory of the Chatti.[5] Aliso is not Oberaden.[6] If then Dio's account is accurate, a permanent garrison cannot have been established at Oberaden until 10 B.C., for which year Dio records operations against the Chatti and other tribes, but without details. If we

[1] See below, p. 272.

[2] Schleiermacher, *Germania* xxiii (1939), pp. 195–6.

[3] Josephus, *Bell. Jud.* iii. 5. 4.

[4] This is still so; I append a brief news item from *The Ottawa Citizen* of 19 August 1965, p. 13: 'Nepean fire department burned down an abandoned two-storey frame house on Richmond Road four miles west of the city limits Wednesday night, drawing about 200 spectators . . . National Capital Commission had asked for the blaze as an easy and inexpensive means of demolishing the house.'

[5] Dio liv. 32–3.

[6] Aliso was still occupied in A.D. 9 and again in A.D. 16 (Vell. ii. 120. 4, Tac., *Ann.* ii. 7).

are right in suggesting that the first Roman garrison lived in tents, then this could have been in a temporary occupation in 11 B.C., but the number of pits implies occupation for more than just a night or two. Alternatively, the builders of the permanent wooden buildings of the base might have lived in tents within the defences while building, rather than in a separate building-camp on a different site in the area, such as we find, for instance, at Inchtuthil.[1]

The permanent wooden base must have been designed for winter occupation. In the first place, as we have already noted, it is too carefully constructed to be meant to stand for one summer only, and if it had been abandoned at the end of the summer, it would assuredly not have remained untouched by the Germans throughout the winter for the Romans to march into again next year. Secondly, wooden buildings were scarcely necessary for summer occupation, however essential they might be for a German winter. Thirdly, the labour involved in building the base was considerable, and the Roman army under Drusus did not march into Germany to spend its summers in building. The careful workmanship which so attracted Koepp's attention implies, moreover, that the work was done at leisure, not in the middle of the campaigning season. And fourthly, the fortress at Inchtuthil, though apparently more elaborately laid out and constructed (but smaller), teaches us how long it took to build a legionary headquarters; Inchtuthil, begun probably in 84, was still unfinished when abandoned in or just after 87.

If then Oberaden was to be occupied the whole year round, what was to be its garrison? Its area of about 60 ha. is enough for at least two legions with auxiliaries, or perhaps three, if the auxiliaries were accommodated in a separate camp, as at Haltern. It is possible that the full garrison was not maintained during the winter, and that a holding force was left, while the legions pulled back to their bases beyond the Rhine. If so, when was the base ever used for its full garrison? Every summer from 12 to 8 B.C. was fully occupied with campaigning. Only in 7 does there seem a slackening off, when Dio records a punitive expedition, but 'nothing worth mentioning'.[2] But we cannot suppose that in the years 10–8 the legions, having wintered

---

[1] Cf. Richmond in *Limes-Studien*, pp. 152–4.
[2] Dio lv. 8. 3, 9. 1.

behind the Rhine, marched out for the summer to sit at
Oberaden. Drusus and his successor Tiberius were remarkably
mobile. Drusus' campaign in 9, for instance, took him through
the territory of the Chatti to that of the Suebi, back to the
Cherusci, then across the Weser and ultimately to the Elbe.[1]
Velleius says of Tiberius 'peragratus victor omnes partes Germaniae'.[2] The Romans conquered Germany by marching and
fighting. Only in the winter would the legions have reason or
leisure to occupy the Oberaden base. And if indeed we were to
say that it was their summer base, that they reactivated it in the
spring and campaigned from it, what would be the need of so
large and elaborate a base for at the most a few weeks' occupation each year? The inescapable fact is that Oberaden had to
be defended throughout the winter. The smaller it was, the
easier to defend. Why not a small fort, capable of being used as
a base in the summer, with the legions in spring occupying a
temporary camp close by? For consider the minimum garrison
needed to hold the base. Its perimeter measures over 2·7 km.
The garrison of Aliso under a *praefectus castrorum*, hence at least
the nucleus of a legion, had difficulty in holding out against the
Germans after the destruction of Varus and his army,[3] so that
it does not seem unreasonable to suggest that perhaps an entire
legion would be needed even just to hold Oberaden, which was
three times as large as the normal legionary base.

What prevents us from adopting the simplest solution to
these problems, namely that Oberaden was a permanent base
for at least two legions? That is to say, that in 10 B.C. or at the
latest 9, Drusus moved the *hiberna* of these legions forward well
into Germany. It is not important that none of our sources mentions it. They do not mention the establishment of bases on the
Rhine. Dio's mention of the two forts in 11 B.C. is a fortunate
exception. The only contrary evidence is Velleius' statement
generally taken to mean that Tiberius was the first Roman
general to let his army winter in Germany, in A.D. 4.[4] Velleius'
language is ambiguous, but even if he is claiming primacy in
this respect for Tiberius, he need not necessarily be right. He
gives Tiberius credit for being the first to reach the Elbe, 'quod

[1] Dio lv. 1.   [2] Vell. ii. 97.
[3] Cf. Syme, *Germania* xvi (1932), pp. 109–11.
[4] Vell. ii. 105, but see above, p. 159.

nunquam antea spe conceptum, nedum opere temptatum erat',[1] despite the fact that Drusus had done it 13 years earlier[2] and Domitius Ahenobarbus had actually crossed it in the meantime.[3] It was Caesar's practice in Gaul to winter his legions in newly conquered territory.[4] We should not be surprised that Drusus did the same. No competent commander undertaking the conquest of Germany could ignore the lessons of Caesar's conquest of Gaul. Only forty years separate the fall of Alesia from Drusus' first crossing of the Rhine. I have invoked Inchtuthil to illuminate Oberaden, but it is nearly a century later. We must always remember how much closer the Augustan army is to Caesar's than to that of the Flavian period.

This picture of a Roman army wintering at Oberaden in 10/9 or 9/8 B.C. will appear strange to many. The conventional view is that recently restated by Scullard: 'Roman armies had overrun the country from Rhine to Elbe [i.e. by A.D. 6], but the conquest had not yet been consolidated by the construction of permanent forts or roads, and regular patrolling was still needed.'[5] What sort of conquest is it, when the conquered territory is not even garrisoned? Only familiarity can blind us to the implausibility of this view. Believing, as they did, that Germany was not garrisoned, Oldfather and Canter more logically concluded that 'Augustus had no other purpose in his operations in Germany than to make repeated demonstrations of Rome's power, in order to impress the barbarians. . . . it was not at any time his intention to conquer Germany, and to organize it as a subject province.'[6] Their conclusion fails only because the premiss is false.

Apart from the archaeological evidence from Oberaden, Florus attributes to Drusus the establishment of 'praesidia atque custodias' throughout the newly conquered territory up to the Elbe, and his evidence on this point deserves more attention than it has often received.[7] We have no reason to deny the presence of two legions and auxiliaries in winter-quarters at Oberaden. It seems a reasonable hypothesis that this base was

---

[1] Vell. ii. 106. [2] Dio lv. 1. [3] Dio lv. 10a.
[4] Caesar, *BG* ii. 35, iii. 29, iv. 38, etc.
[5] Scullard, *From the Gracchi to Nero*, pp. 266–7.
[6] Oldfather and Canter, *The Defeat of Varus and the German Frontier Policy of Augustus*, p. 81.
[7] Florus ii. 30; see above, p. 157.

established in 10 B.C., occupied for perhaps only two years, and given up in 8. Kropatschek's suggestion that the difficulties of the water-supply were found to be too great is attractive, or perhaps the base here had simply served its purpose. The decision to abandon it may have been taken by the new commander-in-chief, Tiberius. If it was a permanent base, there can be no question of its having fallen to assault. This would have involved too great a disgrace to be omitted from our sources, and would have been a grave setback to the extension of Roman power. If details then remain conjectural, the main conclusion, that Oberaden was a regular legionary base, is nevertheless inescapable.

The fort at Beckinghausen on the Lippe 2 km. away, discussed in the next section, served not only to link the base with the Rhine by river, and hence to assure its supplies, but also to guard the old river-crossing and enable the Oberaden garrison to operate north of the Lippe as well as south. Whether the fort was given up at the same time as the base is not known. The presumption that the two were interdependent is now strengthened by the finding in 1964 of pottery and coins contemporary with those from fort and base some 150 m. outside the latter and in the direct line between the two.[1] Excavation is needed to show from what sort of occupation site they come. It is possible to think of *canabae*, an auxiliary fort, a marching-camp, but all remains purely conjectural until further excavations can be carried out.

6. 4. BECKINGHAUSEN

There are the remains of a Roman fort on the south bank of the Lippe, where a small stream, the Rotherbach, joins it at the nearest point of its course to the legionary base of Oberaden (fig. 11). It has been assumed ever since the discovery of the fort in 1911 that it was merely an appendage of the base. The excavations carried out in 1912–14,[2] though they traced the

---

[1] Unpublished information from Dr. H. Aschemeyer, the director of the excavations. Cf. Schönberger, *JRS* lix (1969), p. 149.

[2] Albrecht, *Oberaden* i, p. 12 describes the discovery of the fort and the excavations with fuller account of excavations, pp. 21–4, basing himself largely on the only contemporary reports, both very brief, by Kropatschek, *Frankfurter Zeitung*, no. 149, 19 May 1911 (summarized in *RGKbl.* iv (1911), p. 59), and by Baum,

defences, produced little information about the interior and few finds, largely because two-thirds of the area of the fort had been destroyed by sand-pits, leaving only the area immediately in-side the west gate, where 18 pits were found, two of them probably pottery ovens.[1] All the finds too came from this area. The only finds which can be closely dated were in fact two coins, both of the Nemausus crocodile-series, one of them halved.[2] They would support the assumption, as would the other finds, that fort and base were contemporaneous, but in the absence of sufficient evidence we cannot be certain that the fort was in fact abandoned when the base was. If the theory that there were forts every 18 km. is correct, then Beckinghausen will have con-tinued as a link in this chain.

The defences of the fort[3] comprised a triple ditch and a wood-and-earth rampart with towers every 30 m., enclosing an area of 1·56 ha. There were two gates, east and west. On the river side there was a rampart but no ditches, and the rampart ran along the edge of a steep slope about 11 m. high falling at an angle of about 45° to the river. Sherds of German pottery inside and outside the fort showed that this site, like that of the Oberaden base, was occupied by Germans after the Romans left.[4] The fort lies directly above an old ford on a prehistoric trackway known as the Hünenpad,[5] and it is an easy conjecture that it was estab-lished primarily to guard this ford. The Romans themselves must habitually have crossed the Lippe between Haltern and Oberaden, probably between Datteln/Olfen and Oberaden,[6] and may well have used this long-established crossing-place. Kropatschek is credited with the suggestion that the fort may also have served for the loading and unloading of boats.[7] Baum however thinks of a separate landing-place, still to be found.[8] I

Mannus v (1913), pp. 42–3; Albrecht notes the absence of detailed plans, photo-graphs, etc.; there is a photograph of the slope dropping down to the river taken from the opposite bank in Prein, *Aliso bei Oberaden und die Varusschlacht*, pl. 4.

[1] Albrecht, op. cit. i, p. 23.

[2] Regling in Albrecht, op. cit. i, pp. 25 ff., nos. 35, 152.

[3] Baum, op. cit.; Albrecht, op. cit. i, pp. 21–4. Baum's plan, plate 3, differs slightly from Albrecht's, plan 3, in its representation of the ditches at the east of the fort where they cease at the edge of the bank, and is presumably to be preferred.

[4] Albrecht, op. cit. i, p. 23, who assumes the German occupation to precede the Roman.

[5] Albrecht, op. cit. i, p. 12, with map, p. 11, fig. 2.

[6] See above, p. 151. [7] Cf. *RGKbl.*, loc. cit.

[8] Baum, op. cit., p. 43.

agree with him. The height and steepness of the river-bank at
the fort make it unsuitable for berthing and unloading boats,
and there must have been a landing-place to serve the base,
which will have been supplied by water rather than land.[1]

6. 5. ANREPPEN

Anreppen lies on the south bank of the river Lippe, about 10
km. north-west of Paderborn. Here were discovered in the
autumn of 1968 the remains of an Augustan legionary base or
camp.[2] The presence of such a base in the Paderborn area had
long been conjectured, and Anreppen is not far from the Elsen
which Mommsen and others wrongly took to be Aliso.[3] But the
existence of a base on the Anreppen site itself was previously
altogether unknown.

The site is being excavated by Dr. H. Beck (Münster i. W.),
who informs me that the north part has been eroded by the
Lippe, leaving a stretch of about 680 m. of the south front.
This is what we suggested earlier had happened to the forts on
the Hofestatt site at Haltern, where the Lippe had also changed
course since Roman times.[4] That Anreppen is Augustan cannot
be doubted, but no evidence is yet forthcoming that would permit us to date the site more precisely within the Augustan
period.

6. 6. WIESBADEN

Wiesbaden (Aquae Mattiacorum) lies almost due north of
Mainz on the right bank of the Rhine and on the edge of the
Taunus range. Its mineral springs gave it its Roman name,
Aquae Mattiacorum. Simon has recently assembled all the evidence in favour of an Augustan fort here,[5] which is not implausible a priori as a protection for the flank of Roman troops
and supplies using the Mainz–Kastel crossing. Ritterling long

---

[1] Cf. Oxé in Albrecht, op. cit. i, p. 75, on the quantity of amphorae found, and
continuing to be found, in the base.
[2] Schönberger, JRS lix (1969), p. 149. [ADD.]
[3] See above, pp. 151–3.
[4] See above, pp. 206–11.
[5] Simon, Germania xli (1963), pp. 328–38.

ago supposed that there must on strategic grounds have been such a fort, but he could produce no real evidence.[1] Simon discusses finds from two separate and distinct areas, the one on the Heidenberg, described by Ritterling as the natural site for a fortification in the area,[2] the other some 350 m. south of this in the area of the present Mauritiusstrasse. The Heidenberg is the site of a later stone fort, beneath which lie the ditches of three periods of a wood-and-earth fort, on the same site but a different orientation. Simon shows that, contrary to views expressed elsewhere, these ditches are pre-Flavian and at the latest Claudian.[3] That they are pre-Claudian, i.e. Augustan, is possible, but cannot be proved. The Mauritiusstrasse area on the other hand has yielded traces of buildings, as well as Roman finds which begin, as Simon demonstrates, in late Augustan or early Tiberian times. These early Roman finds lay in a clearly distinguishable stratum, traced for some 200 m. in an east–west direction, beneath the occupation layer of the end of the first century. There is also known in this area a section of ditch, probably Flavian.[4] From the absence of any finds of native goods mixed with the Roman ones Simon excludes the possibility that this site was occupied by friendly, part-Romanized natives. It seems clear, indeed, that the area was under Roman occupation in late Augustan or early Tiberian times. Simon will not admit *canabae* at this date,[5] relying on von Petrikovits's arguments, which however show only that official *canabae* in the usual later sense did not exist in Augustan times. It is wrong to conclude that settlement outside the fortifications of a military post did not occur; there is no doubt that it did, as we have seen elsewhere.[6] In the present state of the evidence, I think it is highly probable that the Mauritiusstrasse site is a civilian settlement which grew up under the protection of a late Augustan or early Tiberian fort on the Heidenberg, the Mauritiusstrasse finds serving thus to date the fort. The theory can, however, be proved or disproved only by further excavation.

[1] Ritterling, *ORL* ii B.31, *Kastell Wiesbaden*, (1909), pp. 63, 66–7.
[2] Ibid., p. 63.
[3] Simon, op. cit., pp. 336–7, with refs. to discussion, esp. Schoppa, *Nass. Ann.* lxiii (1962), pp. 1 ff.
[4] Ritterling, op. cit., plate 1; this is the ditch labelled E.
[5] Simon, op. cit., p. 338.
[6] See above, pp. 98–9.

6. 7. HÖCHST-AM-MAIN

The presence of an Augustan fort here is known from the excavations of Wolff and Ritterling in 1896 and 1904 respectively; the definitive work on the site is still Schmidt's volume in the *ORL* series published in 1912.[1] The fort lies beneath the old town, the Altstadt, of Höchst, on a site which Schmidt compares to that of Haltern, since both sites watch over a river confluence, of the Nidda and Main or the Stever and Lippe, and command the whole countryside around.[2] The size of the Höchst fort is not known. The Altstadt which overlies it prevented extensive excavation. Two ditches however were found, side by side, though not parallel, both containing objects of Augustan date resembling finds from Haltern, including Italian sigillata, with stamps of Ateius and Rasinius, and coins, among which the issues of Augustus are most frequent (20 Augustan out of 23 Julio-Claudian, with 10 Republican and 18 coins of the period 69–98).[3] Other excavations at a point which must lie outside the fort revealed traces of Roman buildings.[4] This may be, as at Wiesbaden, a civilian settlement under the protection of the fort. The evidence does not permit us to date any of the remains exactly. The Augustan fort may have been rebuilt, or a later fort have stood on the same site. Later ditches might get Augustan pottery in them once it lay about the site. Were there only one Augustan occupation, we should think of Germanicus rather than earlier; if two, as is more likely, then we do not know when the fort was first established.

6. 8. FRIEDBERG

The hill known as 'die Burg' at Friedberg is a position of great natural strength, which commands the Wetterau and blocks the exit from it to the south.[5] It was a strong-point in medieval

---

[1] Schmidt, *ORL* ii B.28, *Kastell Höchst am Main*, with refs. to earlier reports.
[2] Schmidt, op. cit., pp. 2–3.
[3] Ibid., pp. 7–9. [Add.]   [4] Ibid., p. 8.
[5] Schmidt, *ORL* ii B.26, *Kastell Friedberg*, p. 3: 'Dieser nördliche Teil der Anhöhe, wo heute vielfach der nackte Fels zutage liegt, stürzt auf drei Seiten steil in die Tiefe ab und bietet so einem Verteidiger starken natürlichen Schutz. Wer von Norden kommend auf die trotzige Höhe herüberblickt, dem zeigt sich recht augenfällig, dass dieser Platz der geeignetete Stützpunkt war für jede Macht, die die Wetterau beherrschen wollte.'

times and is still walled, while the top of the hill which the walls enclose is largely occupied by old buildings. For this reason excavations there have been extremely limited, although even before the First World War Augustan finds were to hand, on the basis of which Schmidt concluded not merely that Friedberg was the site of an Augustan fort, which might have been legitimate, but that it was *the* fort which Germanicus established in A.D. 15 'super vestigia paterni praesidii in monte Tauno',[1] which was not.[2] The dominating strategic position of the hill made such a speculation attractive and local patriotism embraced it willingly. There is still a plaque set up in the public garden at the north end of the hill recording the conjecture as fact. Schmidt noted the absence of specifically Claudian finds, such as are so common at Hofheim, and concluded that the Friedberg fort was probably abandoned after Germanicus' recall until Flavian times.

The identification of Friedberg with Germanicus' fort was upheld by Mager and Roth, who were able to conduct extremely limited excavations on the Burg.[3] Their excavations were in fact confined to an area about 9 × 11 m.[4] Here they found overlying the remains of a La Tène house three pits containing pottery and other finds, sealed partly by a Domitianic hypocaust, partly by a layer containing second-century pottery. The contents of the pits were typical of Augustan or early Tiberian sites. One pit yielded only a few fragments of insignificant pottery; the second, fragments of five different types of sigillata and fifteen types of 'Belgic' ware, together with two Lugdunum altar-series coins countermarked VAR; and the third, assorted sherds which, however, included only one fragment of sigillata and none at all of 'Belgic' ware.[5] The handle of a storage jar turned up in one pit, while the other fragments of the jar were found in the other. Because one pit contained almost all sigillata and 'Belgic' ware, and the other practically none, Mager and Roth argued that the pits had not been filled in at the same time and that therefore they represented two distinct periods of occupation, although there was no stratigraphic evidence for more

[1] Tac., *Ann.* i. 56.
[2] Schmidt, op. cit., p. 23.
[3] Mager and Roth, *BerRGK* xxix (1939), pp. 6–30.
[4] Ibid., p. 24, cf. plans, pp. 8, 10.
[5] Contents set out in detail, ibid., pp. 11–24, compared pp. 24–8.

than one pre-Flavian period.[1] Despite the admitted absence of any sherds comparable with those of Oberaden or any evidence for a date earlier than A.D. 6 (the Varus countermarks), Mager and Roth with the eye of faith discerned that the two periods of occupation were one from Drusus to A.D. 9, and one under Germanicus 'super vestigia paterni praesidii'.[2] A more rational interpretation sees evidence of only one period; if it is then necessary to choose between pre- and post-Varian occupation, the latter on the basis of the finds seems more likely. The absence of anything recognizably B.C. or clearly parallel with Oberaden is in sharp contrast to the mass of finds of this period at nearby Rödgen, where there is nothing recognizably A.D.

A further limited excavation was carried out in 1963 by Dr. Jorns (Darmstadt), whose results are not yet published. This excavation was in the same area as that of Mager and Roth. The Roman levels were a very long way down; the finds included a small quantity of Italian sigillata and a coin of Lugdunum II. Only one stratum was found which could be assigned to the Augustan or Tiberian period.[3] The excavation seemed to confirm that the site was first occupied under Germanicus. The implications of this have been fully discussed above.[4]

Elsewhere, a length of V-shaped ditch, turning at a right angle and containing Gaulish sigillata, was once discovered near the Friedberg railway station, below the Burg, and the presence of a Roman camp has also been conjectured in the neighbouring area known as the Liebfrauengarten.[5] There are no finds here of the Augustan period. Nevertheless it reminds us that the top of the Burg is small, and the operations of both Drusus and Germanicus must have produced marching-camps in the area. Perhaps the area of the station will one day yield further finds to the excavator's trowel or the contractor's mechanical digger.

6. 9. RÖDGEN

The village of Rödgen lies on the east bank of the Wetter, which is at this point a stream a few yards wide flowing in a steep-

---

[1] There is a 'schematisches [very!] Bodenprofil', Mager and Roth, BerRGK xxix (1939) p. 9.   [2] Ibid., p. 28. [ADD.]

[3] Cf. Schönberger, SJ xxi (1963/4), p. 108, n. 36.

[4] See above, pp. 20–1.   [5] Schmidt, op. cit., p. 8. [ADD.]

sided, narrow valley. Though Roman forts were known or suspected at Friedberg and at Bad Nauheim close by, no Roman finds had ever been made along the east bank of the Wetter until sherds came to light in June 1960 in the course of excavations to prepare the site for a new school just north of Rödgen, halfway between that village and the next village of Wisselsheim.[1] A mechanical digger was cutting away part of the hill above the Wetter to level a platform for the building of the school, and on the discovery of the Roman sherds, Dr. Simon (Bad Nauheim), visiting the site, was able to recognize the profile of two V-shaped ditches in the exposed face of the hill cut away by the digger. Archaeological excavations were begun the following year under the direction of Dr. Schönberger and continued each year until 1966, when they were judged complete.

The excavations have revealed a fort (fig. 12) of about 3·3 ha. in area, polygonal in shape, with a double ditch and a wood-and-earth rampart.[2] In the east side, facing towards the road which ran north along the high ground, was a large gate flanked by towers, which were not repeated on the other sides of the fort. This wide gate, and the broad main road of the fort behind it, will have been designed to accommodate wagons, for the fort was in fact a supply base, as was shown by the three large granaries that flanked the road, their combined area over 3,450 square metres, far too much to have supplied only the garrison of the fort itself, which cannot have exceeded at most a thousand men. Smaller gates probably existed in the other sides of the fort. Water will have been obtained from the Wetter; there was no trace of wells. Also excavated were the building which appears to have done duty both as *principia* and as *praetorium*, and barrack blocks. Traces of a workshop were also found.

[1] First report by Schönberger, *SJ* xix (1961), pp. 37–58, (hereinafter referred to as Schönberger I) with finds from the 1961 excavation discussed by Simon, ibid., pp. 59–88; subsequently Schönberger, *SJ* xxi (1963/4), pp. 95–108 (hereinafter Schönberger II); and a preliminary report on the complete series of excavations, id., *Germania* xlv (1967), pp. 84–95 (hereinafter Schönberger III); there is also a further brief notice, id., *Die Umschau in Wissenschaft und Technik* vi (1965), pp. 180–1.

[2] Description of defences and interior of fort from Schönberger III, supplementing and in some points correcting the earlier reports, cf. also Schönberger II, esp. p. 107. There is a plan of the fort, III, p. 88, fig. 2. With the identification of the barrack blocks, the theory that the garrison lived in tents has been abandoned.

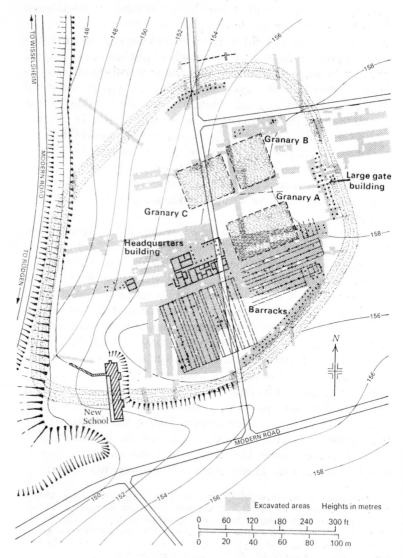

FIG. 12. Rödgen: the supply-base

The finds show clearly that this supply-depot was established in connection with Drusus' operations.[1] As at Oberaden, the Nemausus coins predominate, with 24 out of 25 identifiable bronze coins, the twenty-fifth being a *tresviri as*. No single coin of the Lugdunum altar-series was found.[2] The sigillata closely parallels that from Oberaden, Service I heavily predominating over Service II; detailed publication of the sigillata finds is, however, still awaited. The absence of the Lugdunum II altar-series, supported by the close resemblance of the sigillata from the two sites, shows that Rödgen, like Oberaden, was abandoned before this series took over as the normal currency among the Rhine army, that is to say, within a few years of 10 B.C. The fort clearly dates from around 12 B.C., when Drusus' campaigns began, or perhaps 11.[3] Schönberger compares its site with that of the Annaberg fort at Haltern, but considers and rightly rejects the possibility that Rödgen might be one of the two forts recorded by Dio in connection with the campaigns of 11 B.C., and the Annaberg the other.

Indeed the situation of the two forts is not so similar as Schönberger seems to suggest. The Annaberg fort, as already described, lies on the end of a steep spur with the ground falling away on three sides. It completely commands its surroundings. The Rödgen fort is better described as occupying the edge of a plateau. Only on the west does the ground fall steeply to the Wetter. To the north the fort has an excellent field of view also, to the east only fair. In this direction the plateau rises steadily, though gently. But on the south, the defences of the fort lie in the bottom of a dip formed by a shallow re-entrant, and are overlooked by a hilltop only about 100 m. away; and this hilltop is actually higher than the highest point within the fort's defences. Not only is Rödgen a far weaker site from the defensive point of view than the Annaberg, but it is weaker than

---

[1] Finds from 1961 excavation listed by Simon, *SJ* xix (1961), pp. 59–88, supplemented by brief notices in Schönberger II, p. 107, and Schönberger III, pp. 94–5. Simon is at work on the definitive publication of the finds.

[2] Simon in Schönberger III, p. 94. There are also 2 Republican and 2 Augustan *denarii* of the years 20–16 B.C.

[3] Schönberger II, pp. 107–8, thought a date even before 12 possible, but subsequently, Schönberger III, p. 95, suggests that any date before 11 is precluded by Dio liv. 33. 4; I do not think this is necessarily so, but in fact we have no warrant for putting the fort earlier than 11 B.C. on the basis of the evidence and the parallel with Oberaden.

other possible sites in its own area. In notes made on my first visit to the site in 1963 I wrote: 'It is hard to see why the site should have been chosen in preference to other sites, some higher and/or more isolated, along the edge of the plateau along the Wetter.'

When I wrote this I supposed that the site was chosen, like the Annaberg, primarily for defence. But the Rödgen fort was situated amongst friendly natives, just as Caesar used to set up his supply depots and collect his supplies among his allies, and these natives will doubtless have supplied Rödgen with corn, even if other supplies were sent up from the base depot at Mainz.[1] The extensive La Tène settlement at Bad Nauheim, 2·5 km. away, continued to be inhabited throughout the period when the Romans were occupying Rödgen.[2] The cemetery belonging to this settlement lay on the Goldstein, only 1 km. from the Rödgen fort, facing it across the Wetter valley, and from this cemetery Roman coins are known (three of the Nemausus series, one of the *tresviri* issues from Rome) together with brooches of a type that led Schönberger, before the discovery of the Rödgen fort, to conclude that the cemetery and hence the Bad Nauheim settlement continued in use into the first two decades A.D.[3] Unfortunately, since the absolute chronology of the La Tène period is not fixed, we cannot date the end of the cemetery and settlement precisely. Some at least of the Roman coins and pottery of Augustan date found in the area of the settlement itself and discussed in the next section might have been in use among the native inhabitants, obtained in trade with the Romans, rather than being evidence for an Augustan fort or marching-camp. If so, they support Schönberger's conclusion that the settlement was still occupied in the early years A.D., the *terminus post quem* for its abandonment being A.D. 6, since the latest datable find is a coin with Varus' countermark.

6. 10. BAD NAUHEIM

Bad Nauheim, referred to in the previous chapter as the site of a La Tène settlement continuing into the first decade A.D., may

---

[1] Schönberger I, p. 44; Simon, *SJ* xviii (1959/60), p. 15, n. 34.
[2] Schönberger II, p. 108; see also Chapter 6. 10 below.
[3] Schönberger II, p. 108.

have become under Germanicus the site of a Roman legionary camp, discovered during construction work, followed by planned archaeological excavation, from which within the last few years we have obtained the greater part of our knowledge of Roman and pre-Roman activity at this site, although Roman, Hallstatt, and La Tène finds have been known from here since the last century.[1] It was the site of a Domitianic fort and of a fairly extensive pre-Roman settlement continuing into Late La Tène times, whose inhabitants extracted salt from the mineral springs which make the modern town a *Kurort*.[2] Late Augustan finds have also been made, and have led to the supposition that there was a military post or camp here under Germanicus. In particular, Roman objects resembling those found at Augustan military sites, especially Haltern, came to light during building and excavations in 1958–9, and were discussed by Simon,[3] who saw them as confirming a conjecture made long ago by Schumacher that Bad Nauheim was occupied by Germanicus' forces.[4] They comprise mainly pottery, of which sigillata, as Simon notes, forms an unusually small proportion. There are only five fragments of sigillata, plus one whole cup of Service II, Haltern Type 8a, with the stamp ATEI ZOILI; there are twelve fragments and a cup of imitation sigillata; while 68 vessels of 'Belgic' ware and 36 vessels of various other sorts are known from the same pits as the sigillata, complete or in fragments. There are also eleven coins (three *asses* of the *tresviri* issues, one of which is halved; five Lugdunum I, one of which has the countermark VAR, and one is halved; two bronze coins of the Aduatuci; one unidentified *as*, halved); a brooch; and a tool made from the prong of an antler. This last is included among the Augustan finds because it came from a closed deposit on Schwalheimer Strasse, along with a *tresviri as*, an Aduatucan coin, two fragments of imitation sigillata, ten fragments of Belgic ware, one fragment of a mortar, and one fragment of a storage-jar. Simon singles out this deposit as being well outside the area of Late La Tène deposits, an area which the area of Augustan find-spots overlaps. The two extreme Augustan points are some 300 m. apart.

[1] Simon, *SJ* xviii (1958/60), pp. 5–34, with bibliography of earlier research, p. 5.   [2] Jorns, *Germania* xxxviii (1960), p. 178.
[3] Simon, op. cit., pp. 5–15.   [4] Schumacher, *MZ* vii (1912), p. 72.

The coin with Varus' countermark cannot have reached the site before A.D. 6. The cup with the stamps ATEI ZOILI is also late Augustan. 'Zoilus' appears three times at Haltern—the spelling 'Zoelus' is an earlier form. Loeschcke set the start of Zoelus/Zoilus' production at the end of the first decade A.D.,[1] but now

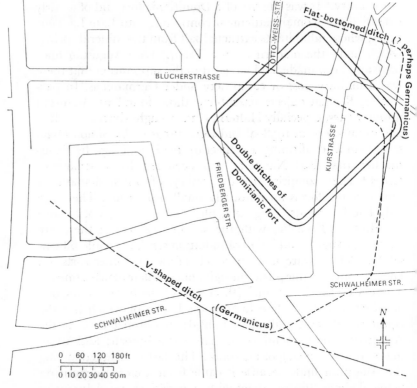

Fig. 13. Bad Nauheim: ditches of early Roman military installations

that we know that Haltern was destroyed in A.D. 9, it is clear that Loeschcke set the start of production too late. It should probably be advanced to the beginning of the century. The Zoilus cup, like the coin with Varus' countermark, will have reached Bad Nauheim in all probability in or after the second lustrum A.D.

[1] Loeschcke, *MAKW* v (1909), pp. 189–90.

These two finds at least forbid us to associate the period in which the Roman objects we are discussing reached the site exclusively with the campaigns of Drusus, and Simon sees the finds as a whole as evidence for Roman occupation of the site under Germanicus, probably during his campaign of 15 B.C. against the Chatti, although he recognizes the presence of earlier forms, such as the two *tresviri asses* of 16/15 B.C. and the sigillata fragments of Service I. Indeed some of the pieces of coarse pottery have their parallels from Oberaden as well as Haltern.[1]

Now we know that Bad Nauheim was the site of a large La Tène settlement, whose cemetery, as mentioned above, has yielded Roman objects of Augustan date, and whose inhabitants were apparently on friendly terms with the Roman garrison of Rödgen. The hypothesis of a Roman military occupation of the Bad Nauheim site under Germanicus implies the abandonment before that time of the native settlement, since the area of Augustan finds overlaps that of the settlement. But if Roman objects occur in the native cemetery, why not in the settlement itself? In other words, does the presence of Roman objects necessarily imply that of Roman troops here? Consider for a moment the closed Augustan deposit on Schwalheimer Strasse described above, comprising in the main Belgic ware and coarse pottery, with a Celtic coin and a tool made from an antler-prong, plus a *tresviri as* (such as is also found in the cemetery) and two fragments of imitation sigillata: nothing here that need depend upon Roman troops, and the tool might more reasonably be associated with natives than with Romans.

On the other hand, however, since Simon's article was published, further excavations have revealed sections of V-shaped ditch separate from the ditches of the Domitianic fort, and apparently belonging to a legionary camp, probably a marching-camp from Germanicus' campaigns (fig. 13).[2] The layout of this camp is not yet clear, nor the length of the period of occupation. Bad Nauheim should however probably be added to the list of Roman sites; but further excavation would be highly desirable.

[1] Simon, op. cit., p. 15.
[2] Schönberger, *SJ* xix (1961), pp. 37–8; fullest account to date by Süss, *Fundber. aus Hessen* v/vi (1965/6), pp. 26–38.

PART III

EPILOGUE

7

REBELLION AND RETRENCHMENT

ILLYRICUM had been stripped of troops to provide an army
for the invasion of Bohemia. Even the legate of the province,
M. Valerius Messalla Messalinus, was with Tiberius at Carnuntum. But Illyricum was less thoroughly pacified than it must
have seemed. It was a fatal miscalculation. For when the Dalmatians were called upon to supply levies for the expedition,
and rebelled, and the uprising spread to other areas, there were
not enough troops available to stop it.[1] The Breuci attacked
Sirmium, a position of some importance, and were prevented
from taking it only by the prompt action of A. Caecina Severus,
legate of Moesia, who brought his army and his Thracian allies
to raise the siege.[2] Other rebels attacked Salonae and ravaged
the Dalmatian coast, until they were brought to battle by the
advance guard of Tiberius' army hurrying back from Carnuntum and defeated, whereupon they retired down the Sava and
joined the Breuci in fortifying the Fruška Gora (Alma mons)
north of Sirmium.[3] There they were attacked by Severus, who
had to disengage after an initial success, because in his absence
from Moesia Dacian and Sarmatian raiders had again crossed
the Danube.[4] Such raids were to be a feature of the next decade
or so;[5] the Illyrican revolt, by draining troops from the neighbouring province, rapidly nullified Lentulus' pacification of the
Lower Danube. Now, although most of Illyricum was lost, the

---

[1] Dio lv. 29. 1–2; the common term 'Pannonian Revolt' is inaccurate, since the
Dalmatians both began the affair and were the last to give in.

[2] Ibid. 29. 3.

[3] Ibid. 30. 1–2; Vell. ii. 112. 1–2; Köstermann, *Hermes* lxxxi (1953), p. 350,
denies Dio's account, on the grounds that a 'semiplena legio', to which Velleius
refers, ought to mean the troops left behind in their base. But why? On p. 353 he
tacitly assumes that *legio XX* was in fact at Carnuntum.

[4] Dio lv. 30. 4.

[5] Festus, *brev.* 8 (A.D. 9); Orosius vi. 22. 2, 'Dacorum commotio' (A.D. 10); Ovid
ex Ponto i. viii. 11–19, iv. ix. 75–86; etc.

Romans still held the important strategic points from which to reconquer it: not only Siscia, where Tiberius and Messalinus took up their position, and Sirmium, but the colonies of the Dalmatian coast and probably the Dalmatian bases of Burnum and Tilurium, 'nobilitata proeliis castella'.[1]

We are comparatively well informed about the events of the next three years. Tiberius based his strategy on the command of the Sava and its Bosnian tributaries.[2] The lost territory was regained bit by bit, and as it was regained it was garrisoned and secured.[3] The end of the fighting in 9 left the country pacified, but with the peace of devastation. The rebellion, 'gravissimum omnium externorum bellorum post Punica',[4] had strained Rome's resources to the utmost. A special war-tax on the sale of slaves was imposed, freedmen were enlisted in the army, reinforcements poured into Illyricum.[5] At one time there were 15 legions there, with the appropriate number of auxiliaries,[6] and Velleius records a concentration of ten legions, the largest army assembled in one place since Actium.[7] Once again, as in 13 B.C., the eastern army was called upon for aid, Plautius Silvanus, legate of Galatia–Pamphylia, bringing two legions 'ex transmarinis provinciis'.[8] The rebellion was crushed, but the cost to Rome was heavy.

The news of disaster in Germany rapidly followed that of success in Illyricum.[9] Varus, betrayed and ambushed, perished with his whole army. Dead, he was made the scapegoat for his superiors' mistakes, damned by his defeat. Velleius has harsh things to say of him, but in his scorn we discern the truth. 'Vir ingenio mitis, moribus quietus . . . otio magis castrorum quam bellicae adsuetus militiae.'[10] He had previously governed Africa and Syria, but had had only limited experience of warfare in

---

[1] Pliny, *NH* iii. 142.

[2] Syme in *CAH* x, pp. 369–73; Köstermann, op. cit., pp. 345–78, esp. 354 ff.; Köstermann's account is especially valuable, and is based on personal experience gained while serving in the German army against the Jugoslav partisans.

[3] Cf. *CIL* 3346, gravestone of cavalry officer, 'bello Batoniano praefuit Iapodiai et Liburn(iai)', cf. Köstermann, op. cit., p. 369, n. 1; such local military commands were continued after the war in wilder areas, cf. *CIL* ix. 2564.

[4] Suet., *Tib.* 16. 1.   [5] Dio lv. 31.

[6] Suet., *Tib.* 16. 2.   [7] Vell. ii. 113. 1.

[8] Vell. ii. 112. 4; Ritterling, *RE* xii, col. 1235; Atkinson *Historia* vii (1958), p. 328.   [9] Vell. ii. 117. 1, 'intra quinque dies'; Dio lvi. 18. 1.

[10] Vell. ii. 117. 2.

either post.[1] His career before he came to Germany is very different from that of any of his predecessors in the German command—Drusus, Tiberius, perhaps Sentius Saturninus, Ahenobarbus, Vinicius, Saturninus, and Tiberius again, *viri militares* all.[2] And now Quintilius Varus. 'Que diable allait-il faire dans cette galère?' 'Mediam ingressus Germaniam velut inter viros pacis gaudentes dulcedine iurisdictionis agendoque pro tribunali ordine trahebat aestiva.'[3] So too Dio, adding that Varus imposed taxation, so Florus, with his usual picturesque detail.[4] And why not? This was what he had been appointed for. Dio notes the presence of Roman garrisons in Germany, the incipient growth of cities, markets, peaceful assemblies, the whole familiar process of Romanization beginning, a process which Varus set out to speed up.[5] He went too fast; hence the revolt. There was an error of judgement either on Varus' part or on the part of those who sent him. But he was appointed to introduce peacetime administration. He had three legions, enough to keep the peace, and in Africa and Syria he had commanded troops, even if not in any major campaign; but in Germany he was not expected to fight a major campaign.

And now these three legions (XVII, XVIII, XIX) ceased to exist, 'exercitus omnium fortissimus, disciplina, manu experientiaque bellorum inter Romanos milites princeps'.[6] All the Roman garrisons in North Germany were wiped out save that at Aliso, which held out for some time and then made its escape through the German lines to the relieving force which was coming up under L. Nonius Asprenas.[7] Asprenas' two legions deterred the Germans from trying to cross the Rhine.[8] Germany however was lost. Tiberius, who assumed command in this

---

[1] Cf. Syme, *The Roman Revolution* (1939), p. 401. Webster, *The Roman Imperial Army*, p. 52, calls him 'a leading lawyer without any military qualities'. [Add.]

[2] On Sentius' possible first governorship, ibid., p. 435, n. 4.

[3] Vell. ii. 117. 4.

[4] Dio lvi. 18. 3–4; Florus ii. 30.

[5] Dio lvi. 18. 2; in 18. 1 Dio appears to say that Roman control over Germany was only partial, but the sentence is obscure. The view that Varus was made a scapegoat for his superiors' error of over-optimism is well set out by Sander, *Archiv für Kulturgesch.* xxxviii (1956), pp. 129–51.

[6] Vell. ii. 119. 4.

[7] Dio lvi. 22. 2a–4, who tells the story of the only garrison to resist, but without names; Vell. ii. 120. 4, on L. Caedicius, *praefectus castrorum* at Aliso, clearly referring to the same incident; cf. Syme, *Germania* xvi (1932), pp. 109–11.

[8] Vell. ii. 120. 3; cf. Dio lvi. 23. 1, 24. 1.

emergency, was so much on the defensive that even the following year, 10, he remained behind the Rhine.[1] In 11 he crossed the river, but did not go far and fought no battle.[2] In 12 Germanicus was in Rome the whole year, in 13 Tiberius apparently in Dalmatia, perhaps in connection with the great road-building programme that was being initiated.[3] In neither year do we hear of anything happening in Germany. Yet in 14, when our information suddenly becomes fuller, we hear of 'in Chaucis . . . praesidium agitantes vexillarii'.[4] It is clear that either a forward movement had been going on which our very inadequate sources do not tell us about, or that the regions along the North Sea coast had never been lost. It is not clear whether in 12 and 13 preparations were already going forward for the campaigns which in fact took place in 14–16, 'abolendae magis infamiae ob amissum cum Quintilio Varo exercitum quam cupidine proferendi imperii aut dignum ob praemium'.[5]

Few events in Roman history have been discussed more fully than the *clades Variana*. It is not my purpose to discuss in detail the attempts to locate the site of the battle. It cannot be done with any certainty. We suffer above all from not knowing what routes the Romans used, apart from the obvious ones, like the Lippe valley. There *were* roads in North Germany, and the Romans improved them or constructed new ones,[6] but we cannot trace them.[7] The most likely site for Varus' defeat is still the Barenau area, proposed by Mommsen and now recently put forward again by Koestermann in his lengthy and valuable article on Germanicus' campaigns.[8] A remarkable concentration

---

[1] Dio lvi. 24. 6 (Zonaras); Vell. ii. 121, 122. 2.

[2] Dio lvi. 25. 2; Vell., loc. cit.

[3] *CIL* iii. 3198–3201, 8512, amended by Abramić, *Vjesnik za Arheologiju i Historiju Dalmatinsku* xlix (1926/7), pp. 147–55, and Alföldy, *Klio* xlvi (1961), pp. 323–7; implications discussed most fully by Pasalić, *Arch. Jug.* iii (1959), pp. 61–74.

[4] Tac., *Ann.* i. 38. 1.

[5] Tac., *Ann.* i. 3. 6.

[6] Cf. the *pontes longi* of Ahenobarbus, Tac., *Ann.* i. 63. 6, corduroy roads such as had been known to the inhabitants of North Germany for centuries, see Forbes, *Notes on the History of Ancient Roads and their Construction*, pp. 38–46; cf. *PZ* xli (1963), pp. 206–9.

[7] Cf. Wormstall, *Bod. Westf.* iv (1935), pp. 267–70, trying dubiously to establish Roman lines of march by plotting scattered, accidental coin finds.

[8] Mommsen, *Ges. Schriften* iv, pp. 200–46; Koestermann, *Historia* vi (1957), pp. 441–3; see also on this question and on Arminius in general von Petrikovits, *BJ* clxvi (1966), pp. 175–93.

of Augustan gold and silver coins has been found here,[1] which *may* have come from the spoils of the Roman baggage train, as well as of individual soldiers, and Mommsen and Koestermann both show how well the Barenau–Wiehengebirge area suits the accounts of Dio and Tacitus.[2] Müller does the best he can for the chief alternative contender, the Paderborn–Teutoburger Wald area, but the case seems less strong.[3]

In 14 when Augustus died the Rhine legions were all on the left bank of the Rhine. The four legions of Lower Germany were in what Tacitus describes as a summer camp among the Ubii; Germanicus, the commander-in-chief, was away in Gaul on business connected with the census.[4] Perhaps Augustus' death was anticipated and the legions were to be ready for possible trouble in Gaul. Although it was already August, they were standing by without obvious duties, 'per otium aut levia munera'. Idleness bred mutiny. The mutiny was suppressed, not without moments of danger, in a way that stands to Germanicus' everlasting discredit, and he resolved upon an improvised campaign to distract the men and reunite them against a common foe. The Marsi were chosen to pay the price for Roman dissensions: 'non sexus, non aetas miserationem attulit.'[5] It was a demonstration of little military value.

Germanicus' serious campaigning was confined to the two years 15 and 16. The topography of these campaigns has been well discussed by Koestermann. In both years Germanicus' strategy centred on the Ems, on which his land and naval forces converged. Although in 16 he crossed the Weser, the Elbe was beyond his reach. Nor did he win a decisive victory, for although he had the better of two successive battles with the forces of Arminius and set up a trophy, 'superbo cum titulo', the result

---

[1] Mommsen, op. cit., pp. 212–28; Koestermann, op. cit., pp. 441–2; Wormstall, op. cit., map, p. 270; Knapke, *AArchKöb*. xiv (1943), p. 58; Wheeler, *Rome Beyond the Imperial Frontiers*, p. 54, also with a clear map; Ritterling's objection, *Nass. Ann.* xiv (1912), p. 118, n. 140, that finds at military sites are mostly bronze is irrelevant, cf. the purses found on the Wall (see below, p. 278, n. 1.).

[2] Mommsen, op. cit., pp. 205, 234–44; Koestermann, loc. cit.; cf. ibid., pp. 443–4, n. 32, refuting the theory of John, *Die Örtlichkeit der Varusschlacht bei Tacitus*, that in Tac., *Ann.* i. 61. 3, 'in medio campi' means 'in the middle of the parade-ground'.

[3] Müller, *PZ* xxxvi (1958), pp. 265–70; id., *Germania* xxxvii (1959), pp. 242–3; cf. Holmes, *The Architect of the Roman Empire* ii, pp. 166–74. [Add.]

[4] Tac., *Ann.* i. 31, 33, 45. This camp may possibly be at Neuss, see above, p. 132.

[5] Ibid. i. 51.

was a withdrawal of all his forces behind the Rhine.¹ Nothing
in Tacitus' account justifies the claim which he attributes to
Germanicus, that one more year would have completed the
reconquest of Germany to the Elbe, a river which Germanicus
after three campaigns had not yet even seen.² Koestermann
believes that Germanicus' judgement was sound, and supposes
that he had been appointed by Augustus to recover the lost
province, a policy which Tiberius did not like, but in which he
continued to acquiesce for a year or two in order not to break
too obviously with Augustus' wishes.³ It is hard to reconcile this
with the 'consilium coercendi intra terminos imperii' which
Augustus is said to have bequeathed to his successor.⁴ The
dream of ever-widening empire had passed, or had been
shelved. Germanicus established or re-established a number of
posts some way beyond the Rhine. We know of a 'castellum
Lupiae flumini adpositum', which may be at Aliso, since Aliso
was joined to the Rhine 'novis limitibus aggeribusque'.⁵ On the
other old invasion route a fort was established 'super vestigia
paterni praesidii in monte Tauno'.⁶ There was the post among
the Chauci mentioned above.⁷ But no attempt was made, so far
as we know, to reoccupy Germany in strength, to cover it with
a network of forts such as Drusus had set up, to rebuild the
important legionary base at Haltern. Germanicus was nowhere
near reconquering the country.

   Germanicus and his chief legates had nothing to complain
about in the awards made to them for their achievements. To
Germanicus himself, a triumph, 'de Cheruscis Chattisque et
Angrivariis quaeque aliae nationes usque ad Albim colunt'.⁸
Coins were issued with the legend GERMANICUS SIGNIS RECEPT(is)
DEVICTIS GERM(anis).⁹ His three legates of consular rank, L.
Apronius, who had been in command of the lines of communi-
cation,¹⁰ A. Caecina, and C. Silius, received the *ornamenta trium-
phalia*, more as an acknowledgement of their seniority than for

----

¹ Tac., *Ann.* ii. 22. 1.   ² Ibid. ii. 26. 4.
³ Koestermann, op. cit., pp. 465–6, cf. n. 80. [ADD.]
⁴ Tac., *Ann.* i. 11. 7.
⁵ Ibid. ii. 7. 1, 7. 5; see above, pp. 152–3.
⁶ Ibid. ii. 56. 1.   ⁷ See p. 240.
⁸ Tac., *Ann.* i. 55. 1, ii. 41. 2–4.
⁹ Sutherland, *Coinage in Roman Imperial Policy*, p. 112.
¹⁰ Tac., *Ann.* i. 56. 1.

any outstanding achievements.[1] Germanicus was promoted to the supreme command over all the eastern provinces and granted a consulship with Tiberius in 18.[2] It was not thought necessary to continue the annual expeditions into Germany. Left to themselves the Germans could be counted on to compass their own destruction.[3]

It is commonly said that the frontier of the Empire was now the Rhine. This view needs to be modified. The Frisii and Batavi right of the Rhine below the Lippe remained faithful to Rome. The Frisii were provoked into rebellion in 28, but only by the rapacity of the tax-collector.[4] South of the Lippe the right bank of the Rhine was kept free from German settlement, forming an empty glacis in front of the river, and this empty glacis, or part of it, was included in the *territoria* of the left-bank bases. It was extended even north of the Lippe under Claudius.[5]

On the Middle Danube after Maroboduus' downfall, the occasion of a speech by Tiberius to the Senate in which he expatiated upon the menace which the king might have been to Rome, had he been so minded,[6] a client kingdom was set up beyond the river in the area east of the river March (Czech Morava).[7] On the Lower Danube, where there was considerable trouble in Thrace, the provinces of Achaea, Macedonia, and Moesia were united under one governor, C. Poppaeus Sabinus, who held office from 15 to 35, having already been appointed to Moesia alone in the last years of Augustus' reign.[8] Tiberius knew better than anyone just what Rome could do. After a youth spent in augmenting the Empire and a middle-age in defending it, he set his face against further expansion. His

---

[1] Ibid. 72. 1; 'The selection appears to be grounded on rank (these three legati alone being consulars); for the personal service of Silius is unmentioned, and that recorded of Apronius (c. 56. 1) trivial. The award ... seems to show that the success was exaggerated at Rome' (Furneaux, ad loc.); this seems more likely than Koestermann, op. cit., p. 431, that they performed notable service which Tacitus omits.

[2] Tac., *Ann.* i. 43. 2, 53. 1.   [3] Cf. ibid. ii. 44.

[4] Ibid. iv. 72.

[5] Kahrstedt in *Congress of Roman Frontier Studies, 1949*, pp. 44–51; von Petrikovits, *Das römische Rheinland*, pp. 69–70; id., *Limes-Studien*, p. 91; on the new Claudian policy, Tac., *Ann.* xi. 19, xiii. 54. 2, 'agros vacuos et militum usui sepositos'.

[6] Tac., *Ann.* ii. 63. 3–4.

[7] Ibid. ii. 63. 7, 'inter flumina Marum et Cusum', cf. *AArchHung.* ii (1952), p. 192; cf. also Klose, *Roms Klientel-Randstaaten*, pp. 95–9.

[8] Tac., *Ann.* i. 80. 1, iv. 46–51, v. 10. 3, vi. 39. 3: 'par negotiis neque supra erat.'

concern was for consolidating what Rome already possessed. No more dangers were to be incurred by pushing ahead to the conquest of a Bohemia while the barbarians behind were not yet fully pacified. In 21 the Aedui and Treveri rose, and although the revolt was soon put down by C. Silius, Germanicus' old legate, with the legions of Upper Germany,[1] it showed what might happen even in a province so long held and so comparatively civilized as Gaul.

What had happened to change Rome's policy? Were the rebellion in Illyricum and the loss of the legions with Varus decisive? Was Rome now exhausted, incapable of raising and training men of the number and calibre required to reconquer Germany, as she had in fact reconquered Illyricum? There were 66 legions in the field after Mutina, though doubtless 'legiones semiplenae', 74 or 75 after the defeat of Sex. Pompeius. Whatever temporary difficulties might have been experienced in raising recruits at a moment's notice on the outbreak of rebellion in A.D. 6, it cannot be argued that it was impossible to replace Roman losses, and even to expand the army to whatever size might be necessary for the reconquest of Germany. That this was not done may argue a failure of nerve, a loss of that will to empire which is so salient a feature of the Augustan period. It is a failing to which imperial peoples and their rulers appear to be prone from time to time. It may however also mean that Tiberius appreciated the changed circumstances in Germany, which, as we have shown in Chapter 2, made its reconquest and subsequent pacification a less easy and less attractive task than in the time of Drusus. The Germans were on the move, and conquering Germany meant not only over-running the country and mastering the present population, but also excluding from it for the future the migrating bands pressing upon north and central Germany, and especially, it would seem, upon the Lippe valley and Wetterau, thrusting along Roman invasion routes from the opposite direction. The new invaders had a virtually inexhaustible reservoir of man power to draw on in their Baltic homeland and their kinsfolk beyond the Elbe. Was this in Augustus' mind when he forbade operations beyond the Elbe for fear of uniting the tribes on both sides in common hostility? Perhaps Tiberius, who knew Germany if any Roman

[1] Ibid. iii. 40–7.

did, realized this and saw the impossibility of recovering the territory lost after the Varian Disaster. Whereas in 12 B.C. the Romans could not have known of the tribes beyond tribes stretching across north Germany, by A.D. 16 it was no doubt painfully obvious to Tiberius, if not to Germanicus, that it was pointless to wage war with the tribes beyond the Rhine, if by defeating and massacring one tribe, you were merely clearing room for seven other tribes of devils, fiercer and even less tractable, from beyond the Elbe. The imperial dream in Germany was over.

8

AUGUSTAN STRATEGY:
CONCLUSIONS

AT the end of this examination of the archaeological and literary evidence for Augustus' campaigns in Germany, it may be found useful briefly to summarize the conclusions to which it leads concerning Augustan strategy:

1. There is no trace at this period of a *limes* such as developed under the Flavians. The Augustan commanders did not have the Maginot Line mentality. They were not thinking about keeping the barbarians out, but of going out themselves to conquer the barbarians.

2. The Augustan legionary bases are commonly set well up towards the front, though not in the front line, commanding such vital lines of advance as the Lippe, the Wetterau, and the Sava. They serve also a defensive purpose; the Rhineland bases, for instance, are available to put down trouble in Gaul. No legion under Augustus is, however, known to have been stationed at a point where its whole function was basically defensive, such as Strasbourg or Vindonissa, which were first occupied by a legion after the Varian Disaster.[1]

3. The sites of known Augustan or early Tiberian legionary bases on the German front, with probable approximate dates of foundation, are as follows:

   (a) founded before 12 B.C.: Vechten, Vetera, Neuss, Mainz, Dangstetten;
   (b) founded between 12 B.C. and A.D. 6: Cologne, Holster-hausen (marching-camp), Haltern (on site of earlier marching-camp), Oberaden (abandoned *c.* 8/7 B.C.), Anreppen, Carnuntum;

---

[1] Unless perhaps we may consider that the Dalmatian bases of Burnum and Tilurium were designed *ab initio* to guard Italy, as in Tac., *Ann.* iv. 5. 5.

(c) founded around or after A.D. 9: Nijmegen, perhaps Mainz-Weisenau, Strasbourg, Bad Nauheim (presumed marching-camp), Vindonissa.

4. Auxiliary and *vexillatio* forts are found at strategic points, set to guard roads, like the line of forts from Basle to Gauting, or river-crossings, like the Lorenzberg and Oberhausen, and perhaps Koblenz and Bingen, or to block possible invasion routes, like the short-lived fort at Zürich; but it was not Augustan strategy to waste troops by splitting them up into penny packets.[1]

5. The sites of known or very probable Augustan forts, with probable approximate dates of foundation, are as follows:

(a) founded before 20 B.C.: Trent (the Dos Trento), Neuss (replaced by legionary base before 12 B.C.), Zürich (with advanced watch-towers along the Walensee; abandoned before 1 B.C.);

(b) founded between 20 and 15 B.C.: Basle (given up before 1 B.C., reoccupied after A.D. 9), Vindonissa (replaced by legionary base after A.D. 9), Oberwinterthur;

(c) founded before 10 B.C.: Nijmegen (Kopse Hof site), Bonn, Strasbourg (replaced by legionary base after A.D. 9), Haltern (the Annaberg), Beckinghausen, Rödgen (given up *c.* 8/7 B.C.), the Lorenzberg;

(d) founded before 1 B.C.: Haltern (the Hofestatt), Chur, Augsburg-Oberhausen;

(e) no evidence for occupation before A.D. 9, but such occupation probable: Bregenz, Kempten (the Burghalde), Gauting, perhaps Salzburg;

(f) no evidence for occupation before A.D. 9: Asberg, Andernach, Urmitz, Koblenz, Bingen, Kastel, Höchst-am-Main, Speyer, the Auerberg, and a post on the summit of the Septimer Pass.

(g) probably founded after A.D. 9: Wiesbaden, Friedberg.

6. The legionary bases and forts which we know of at this period are all built of wood. Stone does not come in on the Rhine and Danube until the reign of Claudius, perhaps then owing to a central initiative from Rome, a recognition that the bases really

[1] On this see Ritterling, *BJ* cxiv/cxv (1906), p. 171.

were permanent.[1] There is a wide variety of design in the
defences of the Augustan military stations: we find them with
either a single or a double ditch, most often with wood-and-
earth ramparts revetted front and rear, though sometimes on the
front only, as on the Annaberg at Haltern or in periods B and
C at Neuss; towers are found at Vechten, Nijmegen, Neuss (D,
E, and F), Oberaden, Beckinghausen, and at Haltern (Annaberg and the red period of Hofestatt); a polygonal outline with
a re-entrant angle is not uncommon.[2] *Canabae* in the strict sense
of the word, with the ovens and workshops of the legion in them,
are not yet found, but settlements of traders and hangers-on are
known outside the bases of Neuss, Haltern, Mainz, and perhaps Oberaden, and the forts of Wiesbaden, Höchst-am-Main,
and Basle. There are in fact ovens within the fortifications at
Vechten, Haltern, Oberaden, Mainz, and Beckinghausen.
Notable features which are rare or unique in our knowledge
are the rather suspect so-called 'Wolfsgruben' on the Annaberg
and at Mainz, the *fossa Punica* at Mainz, the *tutuli* at Vetera and
Mainz, and the barricades in the gateways at Haltern.

7. The Augustan frontier is not identical with the forward line
of military posts. Roman control extended as far as her arm
could reach; and the army was very mobile. The Empire in
Europe had no clearly defined frontier, but it is clear that the
Roman writ ran beyond the Rhine, even after Germanicus'
recall, and beyond the Upper Danube, where the Hermunduri
were clients of Rome. On the Lower Danube a Roman sphere
of influence was established over the Bastarnae and their allies.
Armenia, made a client kingdom in 20 B.C. and subsequently
recalled to her allegiance, proved recalcitrant, and Parthia remained stubbornly independent, but from Syria through Egypt
to the Atlas Mountains only the desert, nomadic tribes, and
client rulers bounded Rome's dominions.

8. Augustus treated client kings as part of the Empire. In his
own estimation, or at least in his public utterances, there was
no difference between a client and a conquered enemy, while
his disposal of client kingdoms and his power of interference in
their affairs (except for the uncooperative Armenians and the

---

[1] Cf. von Petrikovits, *RE* viiiA, col. 1818.
[2] Id., *Das römische Rheinland*, pp. 24–6.

only nominally surrendered Britons) are themselves enough to dispose of any idea that they were independent.[1]

9. No writer before Dio alleges that Augustus intended to call a halt to his conquests at any particular point. The expedition against Arabia is the hardest of all the episodes of the reign to reconcile with the theory that Augustus' policy was basically defensive, but all his campaigns down to the outbreak of the Illyrian Revolt in A.D. 6 were planned well in advance and with the foresight one would expect of Augustus as part of a general policy of universal conquest. Such a policy is the simplest and most natural explanation of the very numerous references in the Augustan poets to Rome's 'manifest destiny' of universal empire, and of Augustus' own emphasis in the *Res Gestae* and elsewhere on his conquests and martial glory.

10. There is in particular no reason whatsoever to suppose that Augustus aimed to establish the frontier on the line of the Elbe and Danube. Apart from lack of any evidence for such an intention, such a frontier would not be easy to defend, and if it were, the Romans in the then state of geographical knowledge would scarcely have known it. Germany was in fact conquered, probably to the Elbe, and Varus was carrying out the job entrusted to him of imposing taxation and regular civil administration when he was killed.

11. The drain on Rome's resources of manpower and morale through the successive rebellions of Illyricum and Germany, plus the realization that Rome was now faced with massive immigration of German tribes into north Germany, led to the decision not to attempt to reconquer the lost province. Germanicus' campaigns, whatever he himself thought of them, were, as Tacitus says, 'abolendae magis infamiae . . . quam cupidine proferendi imperii'.[2] The decision was no doubt accorded little publicity at Rome, and the government preferred that it should be quietly forgotten how close Germany had been by A.D. 9 to becoming properly incorporated in the Empire; hence a tendency in later writers to minimize the completeness of the Augustan conquest.

[1] Cf. Suet., *Aug.* 48: 'reges socii' described as 'membra partesque imperii', and Augustus' close control stressed.
[2] Tac., *Ann.* i. 3. 6.

12. What would have happened had Illyricum not rebelled in A.D. 6 is a matter for speculation (one might speculate rather differently on what would have happened had the rebellion come a month or so later, when Tiberius' army was no longer at Carnuntum, but committed to battle deep in Bohemia). But it seems likely that Bohemia would have fallen to the same sort of pincer movement as conquered the Alps, and that Augustus would have gone on in his career of conquest, whether in Central Europe or now turning his attention to Parthia.

APPENDIXES

APPENDIX I

THE DATING VALUE OF TERRA SIGILLATA

It is the object of this appendix to give some explanation of the research which lies behind the frequent statements in the chapters devoted to individual sites that such-and-such a date is based on the evidence of pottery, or more especially of terra sigillata; for the coarser wares, cooking pots, storage jars, and the like, though they can perhaps be ascribed to Roman or native manufacture, and to the Augustan period rather than the second century, changed too slowly to be of much value for accurate dating.[1] The common red-gloss table-ware of the Roman Empire, however, commonly known as terra sigillata, but in England more often as 'Arretine' or 'Samian' ware, evolved more rapidly. Indeed for the Augustan period, when it was relatively new in the West, we can sometimes fix the date of manufacture of a given piece to within five or ten years. Much work remains to be done. We are not yet able to write a definitive account of the sigillata industry, and among much new evidence still unpublished or undigested, we may note the enormous quantities of sigillata still awaiting publication from Neuss and Vidy; the sigillata from the Magdalensberg in Carinthia, published year by year but not yet the subject of a comprehensive study; the important excavations in progress at Gaulish centres of manufacture; the Oxé–Comfort catalogue of Arretine potters' stamps, published in 1968 after sixty years' preparation; the appearance that same year of Goudineau's study of the sigillata from Bolsena; and the excavations at Cosa, under the Regia at Rome, and elsewhere in Italy. With so much unknown or unfamiliar, it may be another ten years before we can expect a definitive work.[2] It follows then that what appears in

---

[1] Excellent discussion of archaeological value of sigillata, concentrating on Roman Britain, but largely valid for the Augustan period also, by Hartley in Collingwood and Richmond, *The Archaeology of Roman Britain*, pp. 235–6.

[2] Until then, the standard work, though written over thirty years ago, remains the invaluable article by Comfort, *RE* Supp. vii, cols. 1295–1352, s.v. 'Terra sigillata', esp. cols. 1306–24 on Italian, and 1324–42 on Western European, provincial sigillata; for English readers there is a brief history in Charleston, *Roman Pottery*, pp. 5–23, with bibliography of earlier works. On the Magdalensberg, see annual reports in *Carinthia I* cxxxix (1949) onwards; notices of French excavations by Vertet and others most conveniently in *RCRFA* and, briefly, *RCRFComm.*, esp. vii

this Appendix is necessarily tentative; it is also written with some trepidation, for the layman, rather than the pottery specialist. Here and in earlier chapters I have in general erred on the side of conservatism, aware that a more radical reappraisal of many generally accepted theories may yet be thrust upon us in the very near future.

The name 'Samian ware' is derived from the supposed origin of this red-gloss ware on the island of Samos; 'terra sigillata' refers to the practice of making vessels in impressed moulds which left a design in relief upon the exterior of the vessel produced. Most 'terra sigillata' however is undecorated, smooth, and perfectly plain, so that the term is strictly a misnomer, although too well established now to be abandoned. The peculiarly English usage of 'Samian ware' might well be dropped, while 'Arretine' is needed to distinguish the products of Arezzo itself from those of other centres, whether Italian or elsewhere, although even in antiquity Arezzo (Arretium) in Etruria, having been the earliest centre for the manufacture of such pottery in the West, beginning probably around the middle of the first century B.C.,[1] gave its name to the whole type, *vas Arretinum*, wherever made, as we speak of 'china'.[2]

Throughout the Augustan period Arezzo remained the chief centre for sigillata manufacture, despite the development of potteries at Puteoli and in the Po valley. Sigillata was in common use in the legions, even if the officers will probably have used silver, and sigillata in the Arretine style is found on virtually every Augustan military site in Europe, as well as in veteran colonies and civilian settlements.[3] It is common in Italy and Spain. It was exported to

(1966), viii (1967), ix (1968); also Vertet, *Gallia* xx (1962), pp. 351–90; id., *Revue archéologique* 1967, pp. 255–86. Oxé and Comfort, *Corpus Vasorum Arretinorum*, appeared too late for me to make the use of it which otherwise I should have done; Prof. Comfort was however kind enough to allow me to consult various entries earlier, in proof. Goudineau, *Bolsena* iv: *La Céramique arétine lisse*, also came into my possession only after the whole typescript of this book was completed; it too is one of the most important contributions to the study of sigillata in recent years, with a general history of Arretine sigillata, pp. 317–66, and I regret having been unable to incorporate Goudineau's new evidence and conclusions throughout my work. I have added to certain footnotes references in parentheses to Goudineau, where he supplements or modifies what I have written. [ADD.]

[1] The earliest Arretine sigillata was black-gloss; this was gradually superseded by the red, but was apparently still being produced early in Tiberius' reign, Kenner, *Carinthia I* cli (1961), pp. 91–2, cf. cxlvi (1956), pp. 41–2; in general, however, black-gloss sigillata may be regarded as relatively early. Further study is however urgently needed, cf. Schleiermacher, *Gnomon* xxiv (1962), p. 317. (See now Goudineau, op. cit., pp. 322–36; also Schindler, *Die 'schwarze Sigillata' des Magdalensberges*.) [ADD.]

[2] Comfort, *RCRFA* v/vi (1963/4), p. 12; cf. on nomenclature Waagé, *Antiquity* xi (1937), pp. 46–55; also Pliny, *NH* xxxv. 160.

[3] Arretine north of the Alps does not necessarily indicate Roman military

places as far away as Timna' in South Arabia and Arikamedu in South India.[1] Much however of what was once taken to be 'Arretine' sigillata found on military sites in Europe, is now known to have been made north of the Alps, as we shall see below. Late in Augustus' reign, moreover, a new style of sigillata is found, the so-called 'South Gaulish'. At Vindonissa (Chapter 3. 2) the lowest occupation layers have Gaulish-type sigillata inextricably mixed with Italian-type sigillata, the latter still being identical with sigillata from the latter days of the legionary base at Haltern (Chapter 6. 2–6. 8), where no Gaulish-type sigillata was found. It is therefore to be supposed that the foundation of the legionary base at Vindonissa and the start of sigillata production in the Gaulish style follow very closely upon the abandonment of the Haltern base in A.D. 9. This Gaulish sigillata rapidly drove the Italian-type sigillata out of Gaul and the Rhineland (at about the same time the Padanian potteries, aided by geography, captured the market in Noricum and Pannonia from Arezzo); Italian-type sigillata is extremely rare at Hofheim, founded around A.D. 40 (below, p. 261, n. 1).

The relation between the Italian centres such as Arezzo and Puteoli and the earliest centres of production in Gaul is very obscure, and the excavations of Vertet at Lezoux and Lyon have clearly demonstrated that Italian-type sigillata, such as would once unhesitatingly have been classified as Arretine, was in fact made in Gaul, before the genuinely 'Gaulish' sigillata began, so that it is now necessary to use the terms 'Gaulish' and 'Italian' in this context to refer simply to technique, and not necessarily to provenance.[2] The Gaulish technique, as exemplified in the mature work of the Gaulish workshops under Tiberius and thereafter, may in general be clearly

occupation, as was generally assumed by earlier scholars, and as some later ones have continued to assume, despite evidence to the contrary. As an example of sigillata at a civilian site, cf. the Magdalensberg already referred to, or Mont Beuvray (Bibracte), see Déchelette, *Les Fouilles du Mont Beuvray*, pp. 26, 54–5, 65; cf. also pre-conquest imports into Britain, on which, e.g., Hawkes and Hull, *Camulodunum*, p. 180; Comfort, *Hommages Grenier* i, pp. 455–6, with some comments on 'heirlooms'. For silver even on active service, though admittedly under Nero, not Augustus, see Pliny, *NH* xxxiii. 143.

[1] On Timna', Comfort in Bowen, Albright, et al., *Archaeological Discoveries in South Arabia*, pp. 119–207; on Arikamedu, Wheeler, *Ancient India* ii (1946), pp. 34–41; Ohlenroth, *Germania* xxx (1952), pp. 389–92.

[2] Above, p. 253, n. 2, cf. esp. Vertet, *RCRFComm.* vii (1966), p. 2: 'Il apparaît comme certain aussi que Lyon a joué un rôle de relai entre les ateliers de l'Italie et ceux de la Gaule.' Also id., *Revue archéologique* 1967, p. 285: 'On sait que bien des vases attribués aux fabriques arétines n'en sont point . . . et il nous faut croire à l'existence d'officines inconnues, qui ont travaillé, au départ, avec l'esprit et le répertoire arétin, puis lui ont apporté quelques modifications, dans les motifs, comme dans les assemblages.'

distinguished from the Italian, although it will be understood that individual pieces may be very hard to classify.[1] Italian sigillata was also made in the actual military bases, to judge from the discovery at Haltern in 1964 of sigillata moulds and debris from the kilns deliberately buried in the *via praetoria* near the gate.[2]

Even before excavation provided proof, however, it had long been conjectured that Arretine manufacturers, and especially the group of potters centring on the Ateius family, whose products are so extraordinarily common on the Rhine and in military bases in Germany, must have had branches manufacturing there or in Gaul.[3] That the Ateius group also had workshops in Arezzo has been proved by excavation, though only a summary report has so far been published.[4] How their predominance in the Rhineland and in Germany was achieved, however, we cannot tell, not knowing enough about Roman procedures of marketing, shipping, and distribution, or about the Roman army's methods of requisition and supply. A study of the distribution of a number of Ateius-group stamps based on the Oxé–Comfort catalogue has demonstrated how different are the distribution patterns of the products of different members of the group; the group's production appears to begin around 5 B.C., and is at its peak in the first two decades A.D., during which period some members of the group appear to have delivered almost exclusively to Gaul and Germany, which would be readily explicable, if they actually produced there.[5]

In the hope of further elucidating the problem of provenance, attempts have been made to apply modern laboratory techniques, and a comparison of the manganese to sodium quotient for pieces which there are grounds for thinking to be genuine Arretine and other Italian pieces appears to confirm what we already know from other sources, that Italian sigillata identical with that made at Arezzo was also made elsewhere from clays of different chemical

---

[1] Hawkes and Hull, *Camulodunum*, p. 180, define Gaulish ware by 'its hard pinkish instead of soft yellowish paste, its lustrous cherry-red instead of rather friable dark-orange glaze, and its more standardised and metallic finish'.

[2] Unpublished information generously communicated by Dr. H. Aschemeyer (Münster), the excavator, cf. above, p. 189, n. 6.

[3] Oxé, *BJ* ci (1897), pp. 3–18; id., *Bod. Westf.* vi (1943), pp. 47–68. Some 200 pieces with stamps of this group were found at Haltern down to 1939. (Goudineau, op. cit., pp. 37–43, following Oxé, cf. also p. 359, accepts the existence of provincial workshops and asks whether they may not have been more conservative than those of Arezzo itself.)

[4] Maetzke, *RCRFA* ii (1959), pp. 25–7; cf. also, on sigillata in the Arezzo museum, papers by Stenico, *RCRFA* i (1958), pp. 32–7, and ii (1959), pp. 51–61, which whet the appetite for more. Cf. also Stenico, *Revisione critica delle pubblicazioni sulla ceramica arretina.*

[5] Ettlinger, *RCRFA* iv (1962), pp. 27–44; cf. further, Comfort, ibid., pp. 5–25.

composition,[1] but it may be doubted whether laboratory techniques are as yet capable of determining the place of manufacture with the precision we desire.[2]

All signs point however to the supersession of Italian by Gaulish sigillata in Gaul and on the Rhine soon after the date of the destruction of Haltern, in other words in late Augustan or early Tiberian times, and the presence in any quantity of Italian sigillata, whether ascertainably Arretine or of Italian technique but unknown provenance, is therefore a fairly reliable indication of Augustan or early Tiberian occupation in this area. Such is not of course the case in Italy or in the Danube provinces; on the Magdalensberg for instance Italian sigillata is common through to the end of the settlement in Claudian times. Gaulish sigillata on the other hand, where it appears in the earliest levels of a site, will indicate that the site can scarcely have been first occupied before the end of the first decade A.D. at the earliest.

Greater precision in dating can be obtained by studying the typology of the pots. Although by the second century A.D. sigillata became more standardized, in the Augustan period potters were still experimenting. The earlier forms give the impression of being crude and unbalanced, gradually however becoming better-proportioned and more elegant. The typological study of the much commoner undecorated ware is a far more useful tool than the study of the development of decorated moulds and designs, although this latter has more importance in the work of the Gaulish potteries. Since moreover each piece of sigillata is regularly stamped with its maker's name, initials, or mark, we can also trace the activity of individual potters, and the typology of the stamps themselves is a further clue to chronology. The result is that given pieces of sigillata can often be dated to within a few years, to the great assistance of the archaeologist.

The basis of sigillata typology for the Augustan period was laid in the first decade of this century by Loeschcke, who divided the sigillata found at Haltern into 21 'types', or basic shapes, which he arranged in four distinct sets or 'services', all the 'types' of vessel in each particular 'service' sharing certain distinguishing characteristics (figs. 14, 15).[3] Service I, for instance, is distinguished from the

---

[1] Sayre and Dodson, *AJA* lxi (1957), pp. 35–41; Comfort in Bowen, Albright, *et al.*, op. cit., p. 199, n. 3.

[2] Cf. Blanc, *Revue arch. de l'Est et du Centre-Est* xv (1964), pp. 285–93, with further refs.; cf. also the rather inconclusive results of neutron activation and spectroscopic analysis applied to British and second-century East Gaulish sigillata, Emeleus, *Archaeometry* iii (1960), pp. 16–19, and Simpson, ibid., pp. 20–4.

[3] Loeschcke, *MAKW* v (1909), pp. 136–8 (services), 138–63 (types). (Goudineau,

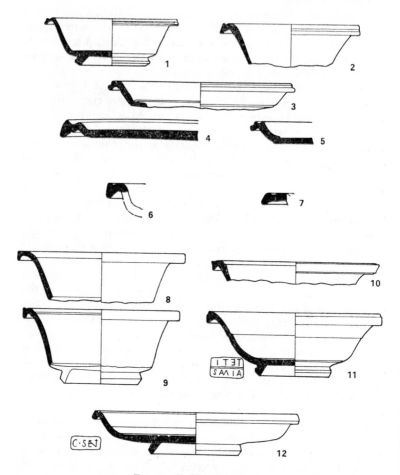

FIG. 14. Sigillata. Service Ia

(Nos. 1–5 from the Palatine, Rome, are the earliest pieces shown; nos. 6 and 7 from Zürich are also early; nos. 8 and 9 from Zürich and 10–12 from Basle belong to the next stage of development.)

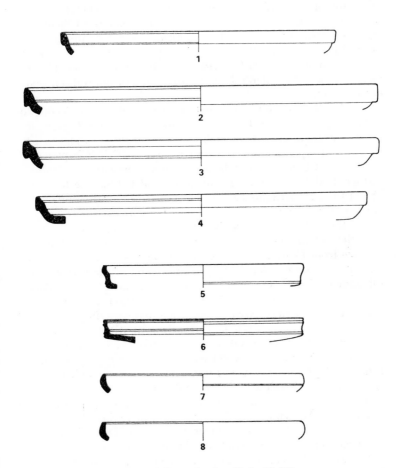

FIG. 15. Sigillata. Services I*b*, I*c*, II, III

(All pieces from the gravel-pit finds at Augsburg-Oberhausen: Services I*b* (nos. 1, 2), I*c* (3, 4), II (5, 6), III (7, 8).)

other services by its so-called 'Hängelippe', the lip of the vessel
turning outwards to form a projecting or overhanging rim. Service
II on the other hand has an almost vertical rim, generally with a
slight concavity in the wall of the vessel on the exterior beneath the
rim, the interior being divided into horizontal bands by thin grooves;
Service III has a smooth, rounded, convex lip, and Service IV the
vertical rim of Service II but without the dividing grooves. The services may also be differentiated by the shape of the wall and base
of the vessel.

Much later Vogt, observing that the vessels with the projecting lip
('Hängelippe'), which Loeschcke defined as Service I, were less
homogeneous than those of each of the other services, and in particular that types of this service occurred at Zürich (Chapter 3. 3)
and Basle (Chapter 3. 1) which were not represented at Haltern,
further subdivided Service I into I*a*, I*b*, and I*c*.[1] Service I*a*, totally
absent from Haltern, appears stylistically to be an early and clumsy
version; the main distinguishing features are that the overhanging
lip is almost disproportionately large, and the angles where the lip
joins the wall and the wall the base of the vessel relatively sharp. Its
absence from Haltern might be due to some peculiarity of supply,
were it not that it is found, though very rare, at the neighbouring
Oberaden (Chapter 6. 9).[2] It is relatively common at Zürich, Augst,
Basle, Vidy, Neuss (Chapter 5. 4), on the Magdalensberg, and on
sites in Gaul and Italy. Archaeological and stylistic criteria alike lead
to the conclusion that I*a* is in fact an early form, which was becoming
rare in 11–10 B.C. when Oberaden was founded and had perhaps
ceased altogether to be produced a year or two later when the
legionary base and the Wiegel site at Haltern, from which most of
the Haltern sigillata comes, were established.

The value for the study of pottery of the Lippe valley sites such
as Oberaden and Haltern is clear, since on general historical grounds
they cannot have been founded before the start of Drusus' campaigns
in 12 B.C. The end of Oberaden is dated by the coin finds from the
site to about 8/7 B.C. and that of Haltern by the archaeological and
literary evidence to A.D. 9, although Loeschcke and Oxé, misinter-
preting the evidence, supposed Haltern to have been finally given
up only in A.D. 16. They therefore ascribe to the period around 16,

op. cit., pp. 233–5 ff., notes the occurrence at Bolsena of new types not found
north of the Alps, and therefore proposes a thoroughgoing revision of Loeschcke's
classification; it remains to be seen whether it will be generally accepted.)

    [1] Vogt, *Der Lindenhof in Zürich*, pp. 150–2; see further the lucid exposition of
Ulbert, *Die römische Keramik aus dem Legionslager Augsburg-Oberhausen*, pp. 9–15; also
Ettlinger, *Die Keramik der Augster Thermen*, pp. 18–22.
    [2] Evidence cited by Ulbert, loc. cit., to whose discussion I am much indebted.

rather than around 9, certain phenomena linked with the date of the abandonment of Haltern, such as the introduction of Gaulish sigillata, referred to above, or of so-called *planta pedis* stamps discussed below. The significance of these sites needs to be emphasized, since on so many sites it is the pottery finds that the archaeologist must use to date the site, and the danger of arguing in a circle is obvious. Indeed Haltern and Hofheim, in the lower valley of the Main, first established around A.D. 40, its sigillata admirably published by Ritterling,[1] have long been among the brightest of the fixed stars in the archaeologist's sky.

At the Helvetian sites referred to above, Zürich, Augst, Basle, and Vidy, as at Neuss, it is therefore the presence of early sigillata, Service I*a*, which marks the sites as early, in contrast to Haltern and Oberaden. But it is significant that they are in fact all sites which on general historical grounds are likely to have been occupied before the Lippe valley sites. Everything then points to the conclusion that during the decade preceding the start of the Roman invasions of Germany in 12 B.C., Service I*a* was apparently in full production and flowing into Helvetia, the Rhineland, and Noricum. And yet the classification I*a* itself includes a considerable variety of forms, so that stylistic grounds lead us to date certain pieces of Service I*a* sigillata from Zürich, Vidy, and Neuss earlier than any of the pieces, also defined as Service I*a*, from Basle or Augst; we thus have no grounds for dating these two sites as early as the three former ones.[2]

We may also draw conclusions as to the date of manufacture of sigillata vessels, and hence of individual sites, from the distribution of potters' stamps. The stamp LSG, for instance, is found seven times at Oberaden, out of 46 stamps in all, at Haltern not at all out of over ten times that number, while it occurs eight times at Vetera (Chapter 5. 3), as well as at Mainz (Chapter 5. 8), Neuss, and Vechten (Chapter 5. 1) on the Rhine, and at Rome, Arezzo, and elsewhere.[3] It appears to belong to the early Augustan period, along with a number of other stamps, among which we may mention those of the potters L. Tetti Samia, C. Sentius, C. Annius, P. Attius, the Titii, and others.[4]

Individual potters may of course also be dated, not only by the distribution of their products at dated sites, but also by the services

---

[1] Ritterling, *Nass. Ann.* xiv (1912), pp. 1–416, esp. on date, pp. 81–4.

[2] See above, p. 41.

[3] Oxé in Albrecht, *Das Römerlager in Oberaden* i, pp. 52–4, 60; cf. Kropatschek, *RGKbl.* ii (1909), p. 7.

[4] Cf. Fellmann, *Basel in römischer Zeit*, pp. 89, 90, 93; Ettlinger, op. cit., pp. 30–1; id. in *Limes-Studien*, pp. 45–9.

their stamps appear on and what form the stamps take. The earliest of all Italian pieces are stamped with the maker's mark, rather than with his name; unlettered stamps of this sort are found at Italian sites and on the Magdalensberg.[1] Then came stamps bearing the maker's name or initials, generally rectangular in shape, occasionally circular. Vessels were normally stamped in the centre of the base; large plates however were originally stamped on the radius, usually four times, sometimes six or two, such radial stamping being a mark of early date.[2] Stamps of fancy shape, where the name is set in a border the shape of the naked foot, referred to as *in planta pedis*, or more rarely in a clover-leaf, a horseshoe, a cross, a *tabula ansata*, or other distinctive shape, are late Augustan, or later. The Haltern base, for instance, has yielded only one *planta pedis* stamp, and these stamps, though common in Italy, are rare north of the Alps.[3]

The general conditions and limitations under which sigillata may be used to date sites were however set out by Sir George Macdonald in his classic article, 'The Dating-Value of Samian Ware'.[4] His warnings against abuse have been generally heeded. It is still true that we cannot tell how long a period of transition there is, when two types were simultaneously in production and (for even longer) in use. We cannot for instance fix a date at which Service II replaced Service I, while Services II and III appear to have come into use simultaneously.[5] Nor do we know how long individual pieces remained in use. Sigillata was valuable enough to be repaired and rivetted when broken, and pieces which appear to be up to 30 years apart in date of manufacture have been found together in the same closed deposit, in circumstances where they had clearly been in use together.[6] This means that too much emphasis should not be placed

---

[1] For Magdalensberg, see reports in *Carinthia I* cxlii (1952), pp. 140–2; cxliii (1953), p. 896; cxlv (1955), p. 30, cxlvi (1956), pp. 42–3; cxlviii (1958), p. 77–8; cxlix (1959), p. 77; cli (1961), pp. 92–3; 26 pieces in all, of which 16 red-gloss and 10 black-gloss, itself an indication of the early date of these unlettered stamps. (On stamps, see now of course Oxé and Comfort, op. cit. (above p. 254, n. 2); also Goudineau, op. cit., esp. pp. 352–7.)

[2] Cf. Loeschcke's statistics for Haltern, *MAKW* v (1909), pp. 165–6.

[3] The *planta pedis* stamp at Haltern in Oxé, *Bod. Westf.* vi (1943), p. 74. One has been found on the Magdalensberg on a piece of Service I, an interesting combination, see *Carinthia I* cli (1961), p. 87.

[4] Macdonald, *JRS* xxv (1935), pp. 187–200, reviewed and echoed by Fabricius, *Germania* xx (1936), pp. 214–16. Macdonald is however concerned primarily with Flavian and Trajanic sigillata, which is more standardized than Augustan and Tiberian, and therefore a more hazardous tool for the archaeologist to use in dating.

[5] Cf. Ulbert, *Die römische Keramik aus dem Legionslager Augsburg-Oberhausen*, p. 15.

[6] Schönberger, *Neuere Grabungen am obergerm. und rät. Limes*, p. 124, n. 296, with examples from Bregenz (see p. 111, n. 224), and Wroxeter (p. 117, n. 273); cf.

on isolated pieces. The chance that six pieces a generation old would all survive to be found is clearly remoter than the chance that one might. On the other hand we should not adopt too readily the hypothesis that some piece is a survival because it does not fit the general pattern, or the preconceived theory.[1] Macdonald also urges our ignorance of the Roman supply system. Was sigillata bought by a central commissariat? Were there large depots, were reserve supplies held in the forts? Did private traders visit outlying forts themselves? Ettlinger's paper, already discussed, on sigillata from early Swiss sites now shows that Vidy was a great entrepôt for the trade, but does not help to show whether that trade was in military or civilian hands. Nor does the find of sigillata moulds at Haltern answer this question. It remains the greatest uncertainty affecting our use of sigillata for dating.

A further problem is to know how long it might take new styles of pottery to spread throughout the Empire, and even beyond. It is certainly possible a priori, though scarcely susceptible of proof, that less sophisticated markets might have been fobbed off with the more old-fashioned lines.[2] If moreover, as we now know, Italian sigillata was also made in Gaul and Germany, how much contact was there between the workshop or workshops supplying Vetera and Haltern and those supplying Basle or Vindonissa? How strong, in the case for instance of the Ateius group, was the influence or control of the head office at Arezzo? Our typological theories may in fact be based on too simplified and schematic an approach. A statement therefore that such-and-such a site is shown by the pottery finds to have been established or abandoned in or about a given date should be read as a working hypothesis, a probability arrived at on the basis of all known facts, but subject to constant revision as new facts come to light.

Hawkes and Hull, Camulodunum, p. 176, noting a Tiberian bowl, form 29, and a platter by Xanthus, repaired and rivetted, found in a stratified context and thus shown to be 'in use up to at least 30 or 40 years after its typological date of manufacture'.

[1] Cf. the splendid controversy over the date of the foundation of the fort at Günzburg between Drexel, BerRGK vii (1912), p. 35, and Knorr, BerRGK viii (1913/15), pp. 72–4, the latter asserting, correctly, in the light of subsequent research, that the fort is Claudian, the former denying this 'on principle' (i.e. because it does not suit his theories) and asserting that all pre-Flavian sherds must have been brought to the new fort 'in Privatbesitz' in early Flavian times; cf. Comfort's words of warning in Hommages Grenier i, pp. 455–6.

[2] So Charlesworth in Studies in Honour of A. C. Johnson, p. 135, suggests that the sigillata found at Arikamedu may have got there later than similar pieces reached European sites, 'since India would offer a safe dumping-ground for out-of-fashion stuff'; but cf. Schönberger, op. cit., pp. 122–6.

It is however no small argument for the over-all validity of modern research into sigillata typology and distribution that dates based upon this research are corroborated, where corroboration is to be had, by other dating techniques. Pottery, coins, and general strategic considerations combine to make the foundation of a legionary base at Vindonissa in the period 10–17 probable, just as the resemblances between the pottery from Oberaden, Rödgen, (Chapter 6. 8) and Bibracte (above, p. 94, n. 2) agree with what coins tell us, that all three sites were abandoned at about the same time, around the middle of the last decade B.C. We are therefore justified in concluding that sigillata such as is found at all three sites is itself to be dated to this period, so that it may therefore in its turn be used to date other sites where it appears.

The emphasis in this chapter has been throughout on sigillata, as being the most valuable type of pottery for dating purposes. There are however two other types of fine ware akin to sigillata in the Augustan–Tiberian period, the one typical of Gaul and the Rhine, the other more widely distributed. The first is commonly known as 'Belgic' ware and includes native imitations of sigillata, the so-called 'terra rubra' and 'terra nigra'. The Roman army produced most of its own pottery for everyday use, sigillata apart. Haltern was supplied from Vetera and Neuss, and also had its own potteries.[1] But the army also used ware made by native potters in a style deriving from La Tène models, sometimes however influenced by Roman types, such as sigillata. Loeschcke called this native ware 'Belgic', since he thought that the chief manufacturing centres were the Belgic settlements at Nijmegen, Trier, and Bibracte.[2] Identical pottery also occurs in Switzerland, however, where the Belgae clearly had nothing to do with its manufacture, so that the name, however sanctified by usage, is a misnomer.[3] 'Belgic' ware comprises both fine and coarse wares, some deriving directly from traditional native styles, others imitating imported Italian pottery, especially sigillata. Loeschcke, while drawing a clear distinction between 'Gefässe in Anschluss an römischen Formen und Techniken' and those in native style, points out that the latter cannot always be sharply divided from supposedly 'Roman', Italian-style, ware. The ordinary, everyday ware differs little in the two traditions, and 'Belgic' and 'Roman' pots were sometimes made by the same man in the same oven.[4] It is with

[1] Loeschcke, op. cit., pp. 107–12; cf. Hähnle, *MAKW* vi (1912), p. 35; see above, p. 189.
[2] Loeschcke, op. cit., pp. 112–13.
[3] Ettlinger, *Die Keramik der Augster Thermen*, p. 18; on the modern use of the name 'Belgic', cf. Simon, *SJ* xviii (1959/60), pp. 7–8.
[4] Loeschcke in Albrecht, *Das Römerlager in Oberaden* ii, p. 115; his account of the

the imitations of sigillata that we are most concerned here, and it is sufficient to say that, from the point of view of dating, the imitation is far more conservative than the original. The earlier styles of Italian sigillata continue to appear in native imitation sigillata long after the Italian potters have abandoned them,[1] so that the imitation sigillata is a far less accurate and useful indicator of date than sigillata proper.

Closely related to sigillata are the drinking vessels commonly known as Aco-beakers, typically in their original form 'hard, thin, brownish-gray ware, mold-made on the exterior and wheel-sponged or the like on the interior', named from their principal manufacturer, Aco, and produced not only in the Po valley or elsewhere in North Italy, but also at Lyons and Lezoux.[2] These vessels are widespread, being found as far afield as south Arabia, as well as in the Rhineland, north Switzerland, and the Voralpenland, although Haltern has yielded only one example, still unpublished, and it has been suggested that import into the Rhineland ceased during the last decade B.C.[3] It is however clear that on the Magdalensberg it continued throughout the Augustan period,[4] and the position remains unclear. Later ware of this type, associated with the potters Sarius and Surus, is often found with a red gloss like that of terra sigillata, and is probably to be dated to late Augustan and early Tiberian times.[5]

Belgic ware from Oberaden, pp. 115–43 (the fine ware illustrated, Plates 38–42), is of the greatest value; cf. further on the Haltern Belgic ware, Loeschcke, *MAKW* v (1909), pp. 258 ff., and on Hofheim, Ritterling, op. cit., pp. 326–58; cf. also Holwerda, *De belgische Waar in Nijmegen.*

[1] Ettlinger, op. cit., pp. 18–22, esp. p. 21, and pp. 28–9, 42–8; Vogt, op. cit., p. 153. The supposed 'sigillata' from the Petrisberg above Trier, thought by Loeschcke to be some of the earliest north of the Alps, may well be imitation sigillata of perhaps considerably later date than Loeschcke suggested, and of no great importance for the history of sigillata in Gaul and Germany: Loeschcke, *TZ* xiv (1939), pp. 93–112; id. in Albrecht, *Das Römerlager in Oberaden* ii, p. 61, n. 3, with pp. 116, 144; cf. Koethe and Kimmig, *TZ* xii (1937), pp. 44 ff.

[2] A fine example and description given by Comfort in Bowen, Albright, *et al.*, op. cit., p. 202, with excellent photographs of exterior and interior, plates 121–2; cf. still Loeschcke, *MAKW* v (1909), pp. 162–3; there is an excellent discussion by Ulbert, *Der Lorenzberg bei Epfach*, pp. 64–8, 85–6; cf. id., *Die römische Keramik aus dem Legionslager Augsburg-Oberhausen*, p. 23. Aco-ware in Gaul, Vertet, *RCRFComm.* vii (1966), p. 2; viii (1967), p. 31. Aco's contemporary, Norbanus, had a workshop at Cremona, Stenico, *RCRFA* v/vi (1963/4), pp. 51–9.

[3] Comfort, loc. cit.; Vogt. op. cit., pp. 153–4. [ADD.]

[4] Kenner, *Carinthia I* cxlix (1959), pp. 63–7; id., *RCRFA* i (1958), p. 16.

[5] Cf. Ulbert, *Der Lorenzberg bei Epfach*, pp. 64–5. [ADD.]

APPENDIX II

THE AUGUSTAN COINAGE IN GAUL AND GERMANY

In considering the use that may be made of coin evidence for dating Augustan sites in Gaul and Germany,[1] we must address ourselves to two questions in particular, corresponding to the two sections into which this appendix is divided. The first question is that of the dates at which the main issues of bronze coinage circulating in Gaul and Germany under Augustus appeared.[2] The second is that of the use that may legitimately be made of statistics based on the relative frequency of finds of different issues at given sites, a question that requires us also to consider exactly how the coinage in fact circulated. The source of all statistical data in this appendix is the comprehensive table (Table I) of coin-find statistics from various sites, unless another reference is given in the notes.

1. The Dates of Issue of the Main Augustan Issues

The vast majority of coins found at the sites which concern us come from one of three mints, namely the senatorial mint in Rome, and the mints at Lugdunum (Lyons) and Nemausus (Nîmes). The dates of the various issues of the first two mints have already been established with some certainty and require no long discussion here. The Nemausus mint will detain us somewhat longer.

At the senatorial mint in Rome six colleges of mint-masters (IIIviri A.A.A.F.F.) in the early and middle years of Augustus' principate coined in bronze and signed their issues with their names

---

[1] For general principles governing the use of coins as historical evidence, see Richmond and Collingwood, *The Archaeology of Roman Britain*, pp. 224–32, esp. emphasizing the importance of condition; see also Kraft, *JNG* vii (1956), on the 'wechselnde Intensität des Geldausstosses' (pp. 42–5), on differences between finds from occupation layers and from hoards (pp. 39–42), and on the 'Verzögerungsfactor' or 'coin drift', (p. 67).

[2] Under Augustus the base-metal coinage was struck from bronze, pure copper, or the alloy of copper and zinc known as *oricalchum*; English numismatists generally refer to it as *aes* coinage, see *RIC*, p. 25, cf. Grant, *From Imperium to Auctoritas* (hereinafter referrred to as Grant, *FITA*), p. ix, n. 1; but the Germans call it bronze or sometimes copper coinage, and I have used the term 'bronze coinage' as being more immediately comprehensible to the non-numismatist than *aes*.

(excluding colleges whose bronze issues were limited to *quadrantes*, which are rarely found north of the Alps). They are as follows:

I*a*	C. Marcius Censorinus	I*b*	P. Licinius Stolo
	T. Quinctius Crispinus		M. Sanquinius
	Q. Aelius Lamia		Ti. Sempronius Gracchus
II*a*	C. Asinius Gallus	II*b*	C. Plotius Rufus
	C. Cassius Celer		Cn. Calpurnius Piso
	C. Gallius Lupercus		L. Naevius Surdinus
IV*a*	A. Licinius Nerva Silianus	IV*b*	P. Lurius Agrippa
	Sex. Nonius Quinctilianus		M. Salvius Otho
	Volusus Valerius Messalla		M. Maecilius Tullus

Kraft, calculating from the dates, where known, of these men's later consulships, has overthrown previous numismatists' theories and shown that the *tresviri* issues I and II date from the period 19–15 B.C., and IV from about 3–2 B.C.[1] Nothing further need be said.

The Lugdunum altar-series on the other hand can scarcely begin before 10 B.C., the year in which the Lugdunum altar portrayed on the reverse, with the legend ROM(A) ET AVG(VSTVS), was dedicated. Suetonius gives the date of the dedication as 1 August 10 B.C., the day on which the future emperor Claudius was born, direct testimony not to be refuted by appealing to Dio.[2] In 10 Tiberius certainly went back to Gaul after dealing with the Illyrian troubles, while Drusus' campaigns may perhaps have been cut short to allow him to attend; it is hard to believe, as some have argued, that 'Claudius natus est Iullo Antonio Fabio Africano coss. Kal. Aug. Lugduni eo ipse die quo primum ara ibi Augusto dedicata est' means only that the altar was dedicated on 1 August in some other year, a coincidence so slight as to be scarcely worth mentioning, although it is not unlikely that there was already in existence a yearly festival, to which Dio refers, which the altar and the rites pertaining thereto were grafted on to.[3] The altar-series therefore begins in or just after 10 B.C.; for it is unlikely to be much later than this event which it commemorates.

The altar-series has four different obverse types, the earliest of which

[1] Kraft, *MZ* xlvi/xlvii (1951/2), pp. 28–35; Kraft reserves the numbers III and V for colleges striking only *quadrantes*, op. cit., p. 29; Kraay, *Die Münzfunde von Vindonissa*, p. 30, renumbers these six colleges from I–VI; I have however retained Kraft's numbering throughout. The old exploded dating is exemplified in *RIC* (I*a*, *b* = *RIC* 85–94, 136–46; II*a*, *b* = *RIC* 63–84, hence supposed to be the earliest of these issues; IV*a*, *b* = *RIC* 186–97). Later issues of the senatorial mint no longer bear the mint-master's name. That these issues were valid throughout the Empire, and not only in Italy or the senatorial provinces, has been amply demonstrated by Grant, *FITA*, pp. 91–8.

[2] Suet., *Claud.* 2; Dio liv. 32. 1.

[3] Dio liv. 36, *pace* Holmes, *The Architect of the Roman Empire* ii, pp. 157–8.

TABLE I. Table of bronze coin finds

A = Total
B = No. of 1's and ½'s

	Magdalensberg[b]		Bibracte[c]		Neuss, Sels[d]		Oberaden[e]		Haltern[f]		Mainz, base area[g]		Augsburg-Oberhausen[h]		Vindonissa[i]		Kempten, Lindenberg[j]	
	A	B	A	B	A	B	A	B	A	B	A	B	A	B	A	B	A	B
Republican/triumviral	9	1	5	0	2	1	1	1	4	1	4	1	9	8	517	318	23	17
Local Gallic issues[p]	2	1	4 (approx. 800)	1	73	49	3	2	3 (?)						47	26		
'Celtic' issues	13	0			660	0	2	0	403	0	15	0	6	0	30	0		
Nemausus I							111[s]	20	5	7	4	1	10	4	65	24	1	1
II			3	0							3	2	12	7	44	28	5	2
III			1	1							1	0			26	19	1	1
I or II			349	?							6	4	4	3	41	38	1	0
uncertain	3	0			199[r]	44	32	17	33	12	26	0					5	3
Nemausus TOTAL	3	0	38	?	199	44	143[s]	37	38	19	40	7	26	14	176	109	13	7
Lugdunum (altar-series) I	2 or 3	0			91	4					20	1	123	28	476	156	26	3
IIa					8	0					5	0	3	1	69	13	10	1
IIb											1	0			47	6	5	0
IIc											7	0			274	25	10	1
IIb or c	1	1			5	0					5	1	1	0	259	70	9	1
uncertain	1	1	3	0	135	13			328[t]	80	107	11			200	90	11	2
Lugdunum TOTAL	3 or 4	1	3	0	239	17			328	80	145	13	127	29	1,316	360	71	8
Tresviri Ia,b	2	0			3	0	1	0	10	0	2	0	6	0	14	0	4	0
IIa,b	17	0			10	0			29	0	12	0	42	10	185	9	16	1
IVa,b	20	4			25	0			9	0	33	1	32	11	488	26	22	1
uncertain	4	0	1	0	96	5	1	0			29	0	26	2	301	26	19	1
Tresviri TOTAL	43	4	1	0	134	5	2	0	48	0	76	1	106	23	988	61	61	3
SC issues, A.D. 10-21	3	0			3	0					6	0	1	0	134	11	29	0
Spanish, African, Eastern	7	0			10	0	5	2			2	0	3	0	15	4	1	0
Other Augustan, incl. unidentifiable	23	6	438	?	96	5	65	at least 16			8	2	41	at least 28	35	0	4	0
TOTALS: Augustus + Tiberius to A.D. 21[u] or 78	77 or 78	12	484	?	744	120	213	at least 55	418	102 (?)	275	23	301	at least 94	2,696	567	178	18
Tiberius A.D. 21-37	28	0			42	0					88	0			1,017	22	212	0
Gaius	22	0			20	0					46	0			438	2	59	0
Claudius	34	0			18	0					42	0	1	0	267	6	119	0
Nero	0	0			19	0					26	0	1	0	197	15	41	0
Later reigns	1	0			14	0					etc.		5	0	554	5	etc.	

TABLE I (continued)

	Aislingen[k]		Augsburg[l]		Bingen[m]		Mainz-Weisenau[n]		Neuss, Claudian fortress[o]	
	A	B	A	B	A	B	A	B	A	B
Republican/triumviral	3	0			1	0	2	2	5	0
Local Gallic issues										
'Celtic' issues	1		1	0	1	0	4	0	5	0
Nemausus I					6		7			
II			2		1		1			
III			1							
I or II			2		1					
uncertain	2		2		5		4		6	3
Nemausus TOTAL	2	0	7	0	13	0	13	0	6	3
Lugdunum (altar-series) I	6	0			3					
IIa	1		2		5					
IIb										
IIc	4				2					
IIb or c			1							
uncertain									2	0
Lugdunum TOTAL	11	0	3	0	10	0			6	0
Tresviri Ia,b	5	0	6	0	3	0	2	0	4	0
IIa,b	11	0	9	0	5	0	7	0	8	1
IVa,b										
uncertain	1	0			2	0	4	0	16	0
Tresviri TOTAL	17	0	15	0	10	0	13	0	28	1
SC issues, A.D. 10–21	10	0	2	0			1	0	4	0
Other Augustan, incl. unidentifiable	1	0					3	0	21	7
TOTALS: Augustus+Tiberius to A.D. 21[u]	87	0	27	0	29	0	30	0	65	10
Tiberius A.D. 21–37	37	0	26	0	20	0	15	0	19	0
Gaius	13	0	15	0	12	0	3	0	10	0
Claudius	14	0	16	0	0	0	2	0	61	0
Nero	6	0	14	0	16	0	4	0	106	0
Later reigns	18	0	etc.		etc.		etc.		etc.	

a. The sources used sometimes contradict themselves; 'hybrids' and 'forgeries', where reported, are ignored in this Table; in older reports Nem. and Lugd. issues are often not distinguished and halved coins are not accurately reported. cf. Kraft, BJ clv/vi (1955/56), 100, n. 22, 104, n. 31.

b. Compiled from annual reports in Carinthia I, 1949–64.

c. Dechelette. Les Fouilles du Mont Beuvray; 13, 22, 31–2, 54, 85 ff. (temple area excluded)

d. BJ cxi/ii (1904), 444 ff.

e. Albrecht, Das Römerlager in Oberaden, i. 25 ff.

f. Kraft, BJ clv/vi (1955/56), 95–111: 'Celtic' coin statistics compiled from reports in MAKW and Bod. Westf.; an up-to-date list is now in preparation for FMRD.

g. FMRD iv. 1, 205 ff.

h. FMRD i. 7, 81 ff.

i. Kraay, Die Münzfunde von Vindonissa. 53ff., 63ff.

j. FMRD i. 7, 238 ff.

k. FMRD i. 7, 114 ff.

l. FMRD i. 7, 26 ff.

m. FMRD iv. 1, 104 ff., incl. 118–121.

n. FMRD iv. 1, 389 ff.

o. BJ cxi/ii (1904), 253 ff.

p. Incl.Vienna, Arausio, and Lugdunum (pre-altar-series).

q. Many are said to be Nem. I; another 30 or so coins are said to be possibly Nemausan.

r. Very few are Nem. III (op. cit., p.452,n.2).

s. Incl. 2 from Beckinghausen

t. About five-sixths are now lost. The remainder are all Lugd. I.

u. Excluding 'Celtic; Spanish, African and Eastern issues

is commonly known as I and the other three collectively as II. We may define them as follows:

I.   Head of Augustus facing right; legend in bold letters either side of head CAESAR | PONT. MAX.

IIa.   Head of Augustus facing right; legend running right round the coin, in smaller letters than the legend on I, CAESAR AVGVSTVS DIVI F. PATER PATRIAE.

IIb.   Head of Tiberius, facing right or left; legend, in the same form as that of IIa, TI. CAESAR AVGVST(I) F. IMPERAT(OR) V (the unabbreviated version is found only on *sestertii*).

IIc.   As IIb, but with IMPERAT(OR) VII.[1]

Of these, I was a very large issue, as was IIc, while IIa and IIb are relatively small. At Vindonissa the number of coins of the various issues is as follows: I 476, IIa 69, IIb 47, IIc 274, IIb or IIc (the number of imperatorial salutations being indecipherable) 250. IIa and IIb therefore were probably confined to a relatively short period. IIa cannot have been issued before Augustus received the title 'pater patriae' in 2 B.C., but that it was issued as early as that is most improbable, in view of the relative size of issues I and IIa. Kraay argues convincingly that IIa and IIb are contemporary and date from about 10–11 A.D., while the much larger issue IIc replaces them at the very beginning of Tiberius' reign and goes on being issued for some years.

In ascribing IIc to the beginning of Tiberius' reign rather than to the last years of Augustus, Kraay notes that we do not expect to find Tiberius honoured independently of Augustus with a special issue of his own on the scale of IIc in Augustus' lifetime, nor an issue as large as IIc confined to a single year. Yet it would be natural for Augustus, the revered 'pater patriae', and Tiberius, 'Augusti filius' and 'imperator V', the destined heir and commander-in-chief, to be honoured jointly on the Lugdunum coinage (issues IIa and IIb) at a time when Tiberius was in Gaul and when it was of great importance to restore confidence in the government after the Varian Disaster and to smooth the way for Tiberius' succession. On Augustus' death the coins with Tiberius' portrait continue, bearing the same legend now brought up to date. Not until 18 did Tiberius become 'imperator VIII'. The emphasis is not on the new ruler's assumption of power, but on the continuity of the dynasty.

The dating of the Nemausus crocodile-series is more difficult and controversial. Here we have to deal with three different issues, all

---

[1] Coins with IMPERAT VI are recorded, *BMC*, p. 95, no. 578, and *NC* xix (1939), p. 217, but as Mattingly observes (*BMC*, loc. cit.): 'Reading uncertain . . . it is doubtful if IMP VI ever really occurs.'

with the same reverse type of a crocodile chained to a palm-tree and the legend COL(ONIA) NEM(AVSVS), and bearing on the obverse heads of Agrippa (left) and Augustus (right), looking outwards, with the following variations:

I. Augustus bare-headed; legend IMP. DIVI F.
II. Augustus wearing an oak wreath;[1] same legend.
III. Augustus wearing a laurel wreath; legend IMP. DIVI F. P.P.

Of these issues I may be subdivided. On a comparatively few examples Agrippa is portrayed with a beard (I*a*), on most he is beardless (I*b*). Kraft distinguishes further I*c*, where he is not only beardless, but also somewhat shorter in the chin.[2] I*a*, which is very rare, is noticeably heavier than I*b* and I*c*.[3]

Different scholars have suggested widely differing dates for the Nemausus crocodile-series issues. Willers dated the entire series within the years 29–20 B.C.[4] Grant on the other hand would continue it down to A.D. 69, arguing that I*a* is a local issue of *c.* 29/27–*c.* 15 B.C., whose type is continued in the 'at least 100 times larger' 'official' issue I*b* for general circulation 'not long after 15'.[5] II, he suggests, may begin in Tiberius' reign, but is primarily Claudian, as is shown by the way in which the heads of Agrippa and Augustus have become assimilated to those of 'prominent Julio-Claudian personalities', and III is dated, again on iconographic grounds, to Nero's reign, continuing down to A.D. 69. Other considerations are brought in to support this iconographic evidence, but it is on the latter that Grant chiefly relies.

Grant's arguments however cannot be sustained against the

---

[1] Willers, *Num. Ztschr.* xxxiv (1902), pp. 123–4, confidently identifies this as an oak wreath, the *corona civica*; so too others, e.g. Macdonald, *Catalogue of Greek Coins in the Hunterian Collection* iii (1905), p. 705, n. 8; and again Kraft, *BJ* clv/clvi (1955/6), p. 108, n. 46; others describe it as a laurel wreath, as in III (e.g. *RIC*, p. 44; Grant *FITA*, p. 70; Kraay, op. cit., pp. 24, 71; etc.); oak and laurel are notoriously hard to tell apart, especially if the coin is at all worn, cf. *BMC*, p. lxiv; Grant, *The Six Main Aes Coinages of Augustus* (hereinafter referrred to as Grant, *SMACA*), p. 10; Schulz, *Die Rechtstitel und Regierungsprogramme auf römischen Kaisermünzen*, p. 8, n. 19, and p. 13; in this case, however, oak is correct; a decisive piece is a coin in the British Museum, from the collection of the Duc de Blacas, acquisition no. 1867–1–1–2247, which I have examined, where the oak leaf can be seen too clearly to leave any further doubt.

[2] Kraft, op. cit., p. 95, cf. Grant, *FITA*, p. 70.

[3] Grant, *FITA*, pp. 73–4, cf. pp. 114–15; cf. id., *SMACA*, pp. 116–27.

[4] Willers, *Num. Ztschr.* xxxiv (1902), pp. 128–9.

[5] Grant, *FITA*, pp. 73–8, 114–15; id., *SMACA*, pp. 116–22; the date of *c.* 15 is based on Grant's theory that portraits on bronze coinage are copied from those on gold and silver coinage, the latter being drawn direct from officially circulated *imagines*; this is unproved and unlikely, cf. Sutherland, *JRS* xliii (1953), p. 201, reviewing *SMACA*.

weight of evidence from archaeological finds marshalled against them by Kraft and Kraay.[1] The latter argues that the series must have been produced as an official coinage on a large scale at least as early as the late twenties B.C.; he supports this by two arguments, one archaeological (which I shall discuss later) and one typological, namely 'the close relation of the obverse type to those of Lugdunum and Vienna (to be dated to the thirties B.C.) and the reminiscence of the *Aegypto capta* types (28–26 B.C.) to be found in the crocodile of the reverse'. This typological argument appears to support a date of around 28–27 for the first issue of the series better than it does Kraay's late 20s.[2] If so, is this the date at which the series was launched as a small local issue, to be reissued later as a large official one? Or was the series issued on a large scale for general circulation throughout Gaul from the start? Kraay, appealing to the archaeological evidence, sees 'the very large numbers that were circulating at Oberaden by 12 B.C.' as evidence that the large official issue began in the twenties.[3] The Oberaden finds show that in the period when Oberaden was occupied, from about 11–8 B.C., the Nemausus coinage was the only one in common use among Drusus' troops. It need not however have been in common use long; it is quite possible to suppose that it was first struck in quantity specially to pay the legions assembled for Drusus' campaigns, which would account for its frequent occurrence at Oberaden, and this is supported by the fact that the state of wear of the surviving Nemausus coins from Oberaden, where this can be determined, is consistent with a relatively short period of circulation, rather than the reverse.[4]

[1] Kraft, op. cit., pp. 108–10; Kraay, *NC* xv (1955), pp. 75–87.

[2] Hirschfeld, *Wiener Studien* iii (1883), p. 319, argued from the absence of the name Augustus on the coinage that it began before 27; but this name is not used on Lugdunum I either.

[3] Kraay, op. cit., p. 85.

[4] I am extremely grateful to Dr. Clemens Weissgerber, Director of the Dortmund Geschichtliches Museum, where the Oberaden finds are lodged, who at my request very kindly examined all the surviving Nemausus coins from that site with a view to establishing their condition at the time when they were lost. His conclusions are set out in a letter of 17 March 1965, the relevant part of which is as follows: 'Wie ich dem Regling-Aufsatz in Band I Oberaden entnehme, handelte es sich ehedem um 230 Münzen . . .

'Was nun die Oberadener Münzen anbetrifft, dürfte der weitaus überwiegende Teil derselben durch Kriegs- bzw. Nachkriegseinwirkungen verlorengegangen sein. Der heutige für mich fassbare Rest beträgt kaum mehr als 50 Nominale, von denen wiederum nur ein geringer Teil erkennbar und bestimmbar ist.

'Unter diesem Rest sind gerade einige Nemausus-Dupondien besser erhalten, wogegen die meisten der übrigen Münzen einen durchoxydierten Kern haben, über dem das Material völlig bröckelig ist. Wenn Sie von mir gern bestätigt hätten, dass unter den Nemausus-Münzen solche sind, deren Zustand auf eine längere Umlaufzeit schliessen lässt, muss ich Ihnen leider in Ihrem Wunsche nach einer

We have already noticed the distinction between the small I*a* issue and the larger I*b* and I*c*.[1] It seems likely then that the Nemausus series begins about 28 B.C. with I*a*, but only as a local issue, like those of other colonies in Gaul, such as Orange, Vienne, and (at this time) Lugdunum. Only later, probably after 19 B.C., when the end of the war in Spain brought more legions to Gaul, was the Nemausus mint set to coin for their needs; this is probably when I*b* replaced I*a*, the lighter coin for the large issue. I*c* appears to be contemporary with I*b* and of no particular significance. Henceforth, until the coming of the Lugdunum altar-series, Nemausus was without a serious rival on military sites in Germany. At Oberaden, for instance, out of 148 identifiable Augustan coins, 143 are of Nemausus, whereas at the neighbouring Haltern out of 418 only 38 are of Nemausus and 328 of Lugdunum, and at Vindonissa the Lugdunum coins outnumber those of Nemausus by 1,316 to 176. The inference is clear: before the appearance of the Lugdunum altar-series on the Rhine, the Nemausus issues had it all their own way there, but when the altar-series came along, the importance of the Nemausus mint declined, and its issues henceforth circulated chiefly in southern Gaul, while Lugdunum supplied the Rhine legions.

This is corroborated by the relative scarcity of the latest Nemausus issue, Nemausus III, at sites in this area. The Selssche Ziegelei

früheren Datierung der Nemausus-Serie eine Enttäuschung bereiten. Die Dupondien sind, in so schlechtem Zustand sie sich auch befinden, im Relief sowohl der Agrippa-Augustus-Köpfe auf dem Avers, als auch dem des Revers mit Krokodil, Palme, Perlkreis usw. gut *erhaben* und relativ scharfkonturig. Beweis für eine nur kurze Umlaufzeit ist weiter die Prägnanz der radförmigen Einstempelung zwischen den Köpfen (gelegentlich auch am Halse des Augustus) der Vorderseite. Allein zwei bis drei Münzen scheinen im Grade ihrer Abnutzung auf Vernutzung durch sehr langen Gebrauch schliessen lassen zu wollen. Leider erkenne ich auf diesen Münzen Spuren gewaltsamer mechanischer Reinigung, die Abnutzung ist unwahrscheinlich unregelmässig, die Aufschrift teilweise breit *verwischt*, sodass für mich ausser Zweifel steht, dass die Stücke irgendwann unsachgemäss bearbeitet wurden und heute nur älter erscheinen, ohne es zu sein.

'Ich fasse zusammen: Soweit die einzelnen Münzen überhaupt noch imstande sind, zur Beantwortung Ihrer Frage und zur Klärung des Datierungsproblems herangezogen zu werden, ist selbst auf den stark korrodierten Stücken die Prägung besser *fühlbar* als sichtbar, also nicht abgegriffen. Nur einige Ausnahmen, die aufgrund ihres besseren Erhaltungs-zustandes einer mechanischen Reinigung standhielten, haben eine gewaltsame Oberflächenveränderung erfahren, sind so heute ohne Aussage geschweige Beweiskraft bezüglich der Festsetzung ihrer Umlaufzeit und scheiden damit als Datierungskriterien aus. Um dennoch zu einen Facit zu kommen, würde ich nach gründlicher Untersuchung des Restes der Oberadener Nemausus-Münzen eher auf eine verhältnismassig kurze Umlaufzeit schliessen, als auf das Gegenteil.' [ADD.]

[1] Kraft, op. cit., p. 108, n. 45, notes that of 86 Nemausus I coins which he saw in the Dortmund Museum, only one belonged to I*a*; his argument that I*b* and I*c* must be earlier than the *tresviri* I and II issues has been discussed and rejected above.

site at Neuss, for instance, yielded 199 coins of Nemausus to 239 of the altar-series; although the issues of the Nemausus series are not clearly differentiated, it is reported that very few were Nemausus III. At Vindonissa, out of the 176 coins of the Nemausus series, figures for the separate issues are as follows: I 65, II 44, I or II 41, III 26. Now the legionary base at Vindonissa, from all indications, was established after A.D. 9; the Selssche Ziegelei site continued to be occupied throughout the Julio-Claudian period (it yielded 42 coins of Tiberius (from A.D. 21), 20 Caligula, 18 Claudius, 19 Nero). Yet Nemausus III is rarer than its predecessors at both places, and at Vindonissa—whether this is also true of the Ziegelei we do not know —Nemausus I is half as common again as II. The figures from the area of the legionary base at Mainz, while the number of coins involved is too small to count beside the Ziegelei and Vindonissa, do nevertheless tend to corroborate the figures from those sites: of 40 Nemausus coins, only 14 can be assigned more closely, of which only 1 is Nemausus III; I has 4 examples, II 3, I or II 6. We might explain this by supposing that each successive issue was smaller than its predecessor, except that Grant observes that III forms 'rather over 33 per cent of all Nemausan coins in museums of Southern France'.[1] Hence we see that on its home ground III at least holds its own with I and II. Its comparative rarity on the Rhine and at Vindonissa can be explained only by supposing that it was kept out of that area by the now predominant Lugdunum altar-series. And this process of exclusion, to judge from the Vindonissa figures, had already begun during the period of peak circulation of Nemausus II.

On the basis of the archaeological evidence Kraay has argued that III should be dated to around A.D. 10, contemporary with Lugdunum IIa and IIb, which we may accept, while II he would date to 'the very early years of the first century A.D.', citing as evidence the statistics of finds, especially those from Port-Haliguen-en-Quiberon (Morbihan) and Oberhausen.[2] A hoard from the former place contained 358 coins of Lugdunum I without a single one of Lugdunum II, but in addition to 42 coins of Nemausus I it had 9 of Nemausus II. At Oberhausen the figures for Lugdunum are: I 123, II 4; for Nemausus: I 10, II 12. The conclusion is inescapable that Nemausus II came into circulation at least several years before Lugdunum II, i.e. before about A.D. 10.[3] Yet at Oberaden

---

[1] Grant, *FITA*, p. 77, n. 5.

[2] Kraay, op. cit., pp. 84–5, where PP on III is rightly interpreted as standing for *pater patriae*; for other interpretations, see Mattingly, *NC* vi (1946), p. 132; Grant, *FITA*, p. 78, n. 11; id., *SMACA*, p. 57.

[3] So too Kraft, op. cit., pp. 108–9.

no Nemausus II have been found, as against 111 Nemausus I, with 32 Nemausus coins not identifiable as belonging to a particular issue. This suggests the date of the abandonment of Oberaden as a *terminus post quem* for the issue of Nemausus II and tells strongly against Kraft's suggestion that Nemausus II originated about 15 B.C.[1] Kraft bases this theory on the presence of the oak wreath, the *corona civica*, on II, observing that Augustus on issues from 11 B.C. onwards is always shown as laurelled or bare-headed. The *corona civica* is however rare at any time. Why this should be, we do not know. But there is no reason why it should not appear after 11 B.C., just as readily as before. Nemausus, with Agrippa wearing the naval crown and with the whole motif of crocodile and palm-tree, is not afraid to recall past glories and does not conform to the types of Lugdunum and Rome.

The Port-Haliguen and Oberhausen evidence would however support a date in the last decade B.C. for Nemausus II more readily than Kraay's early A.D. This is not too long before A.D. 10 to allow for 9 coins of the issue to turn up in the Port-Haliguen hoard, when it has only 51 Nemausus pieces altogether and seven times that number of Lugdunum coins, since presumably the onset of Lugdunum I reduced the flow of Nemausus issues to Brittany, so that Nemausus II is likely to have percolated thither more slowly than Nemausus I, which did not have to face the competition of Lugdunum. The Oberhausen evidence still more strongly supports a B.C. date for Nemausus II. The figures for the occurrence of the Nemausus issues at Oberhausen may be tabulated as follows, alongside those from Vindonissa:

	I	II	I or II	III	Total
Oberhausen	10	12	4	nil	26
Vindonissa	65	44	41	26	176

Now Vindonissa, where Nemausus I outweighs II and II outweighs III, continued to be occupied throughout the first century A.D. into a period when the Nemausus issues had passed their peak of circulation and become old-fashioned rarities. Late Tiberian Aislingen on the Upper Danube, for instance, yields only two Nemausus coins, Claudian Günzburg none; on the Rhine, Weisenau yields none, the Claudian fortress at Neuss only six. It is therefore surprising that at Oberhausen, still further away from Gaul than Vindonissa is, and where the coin-sequence ends soon after A.D. 14, apart from a few isolated later coins, Nemausus II should outweigh

[1] Kraft, op. cit., p. 108, n. 46.

Nemausus I.[1] Chance might here play a bigger part than at Vindonissa, the total number of coins being so much less. But the evidence does suggest that we should allow Nemausus II as long as possible to reach Oberhausen, and so set its beginning B.C. rather than A.D. And the evidence from Mont Beuvray confirms this, where of 38 certainly attested Nemausus coins only four are identified as belonging to a particular issue, one of which however belongs to Nemausus II; yet Lugdunum provides only three coins at this site.[2] It might be possible to argue that Lugdunum at first issued only to the army; but this is unlikely, especially in view of the Port-Haliguen find. It is simpler to suppose that Nemausus II appeared at a time when Lugdunum I was already circulating, but not yet in any great quantity. Since we agreed that the date of the abandonment of Oberaden was a *terminus post quem* for the issue of Nemausus II, we shall consequently set the date of this issue very soon thereafter, towards the middle of the last decade B.C.

Let us then summarize our conclusions concerning the dates of issue of the various issues of this series. It seems that I*a* begins around 28 B.C., as a small issue, probably of little more than local significance; that at a later date, perhaps around 20 B.C., perhaps some years later, the Nemausus mint began to coin on a larger scale for the whole of Gaul and particularly for the army that was being assembled for the campaigns of 15 B.C. onwards against Raetia and Germany (I*b*); and that Nemausus II began probably towards the middle of the last decade B.C., and Nemausus III about A.D. 10, by which time Nemausus was again coining only for local needs.

We may then sum up our conclusions on the probable approximate dates of issue of the main Augustan bronze issues as follows:

28 B.C.:	Nemausus I*a* (small local issue only)
20 or soon after:	Nemausus I*b*
19–15:	*Tresviri* I, II
10:	Lugdunum I
8 or soon after:	Nemausus II
3–2:	*Tresviri* IV
A.D. 10–11:	Lugdunum II*a*, II*b*: Nemausus III
14:	Lugdunum II*c*

---

[1] Cf. Kraay, op. cit., p. 86, noting that Vindonissa is better placed than any other military station in the Rhine area for trade with the area where the Nemausus issues were strongest.

[2] Déchelette, *Les Fouilles du Mont Beuvray*, pp. 85–126. Here and in the Selssche Ziegelei site at Neuss, native 'Celtic' issues far outnumber any others. It looks as if the native Gauls went on using their own coinage well into the Augustan period. The large number of 'Celtic' coins at Haltern however is very strange. Can they all come from auxiliaries? Or what is the explanation?

Lugdunum IIc does not in fact appear to be an Augustan issue at all, and Nemausus III probably continues into Tiberian times, but it is impossible to treat Augustan issues as an entity distinct from those of the early years of Tiberius' reign. The next major issue was one in honour of Divus Augustus, with the legend SC and PROVIDENT(IA) on the reverse, struck not only in Italy, but also, despite the legend, in the provinces, and dating from about A.D. 20; intervening issues from the senatorial mint, bearing now the emperor's name instead of the mint-master's and with various pictorial types (an eagle, a thunderbolt, a seated woman who may be Livia), are all comparatively small.[1] But with none of these need we concern ourselves here.

2. The Circulation of the Coinage and the Validity of Inferences from Statistics Concerning Circulation and Finds

Numismatists concentrating on when coins were 'issued' have not always sufficiently considered just how they are then put into circulation and how they pass from hand to hand and place to place. Kraay suggests that the time needed for an issue of a mint to reach a given site varies according to the distance from the mint: the less the distance, the shorter the time.[2] The case of Nemausus however shows that it is not only distance that affects the speed with which an issue reaches a site, but the intervention or non-intervention of another mint. Kraay himself, enunciating his principle, applies it to a comparison of Lugdunum II and *tresviri* IVb issue at Vindonissa; the former, though issued much later than the latter, probably reached Vindonissa much more quickly. This is true, not because the distance to Vindonissa from Lugdunum is less than that from Rome, but because the territory north of the Alps was already flooded with the issues of Nemausus and Lugdunum, especially with Lugdunum I, when the *tresviri* IVb issue was made. It failed to penetrate the Alps rapidly or in great quantity primarily because it was not needed there. It was a large issue—compare the figures for IVb with those for the other *tresviri* issues at Vindonissa—but it was meant for and absorbed by those areas which were served by the senatorial mint.

Now when we apeak of an issue from the mint at Lugdunum, or the mint at Rome, we should not think of the issue as spreading outwards from that point like the ripples from a stone dropped into a pond. The issue is struck at the mint, taken into the strong-room there and distributed thence as required. When pay day comes round, the paymaster at Vindonissa, for instance, must draw the

---

[1] Cf. Kraay, *Die Münzfunde von Vindonissa*, p. 34.   [2] Ibid., p. 9.

money which he requires from the department of the provincial procuarator, or a branch thereof. This authority will issue the necessary sum from the coins in the vaults. This stock of coins will be composed largely of the money collected by the department from taxes, duties, and other sources of revenue.[1] This is money already in circulation. If there is not enough in the bank, more money, or more coins of whatever denomination may be in particularly short supply, will be taken out of store, or indented for to the mint. The convoy of coin for the legion's pay sent out to Vindonissa will therefore comprise coins already in circulation, and quite probably new coins freshly issued from the mint.[2] It is clear that such new coins, though in one sense issued at Lugdunum, are only in fact put into circulation when they are paid out across the table at Vindonissa. We may reasonably suppose that, the more remote and unproductive a region, the less money the local officials of the procurator's department will collect and the more they will have to draw from the mint to meet their outgoings.

Coin in circulation passes from hand to hand in trade, or travels from place to place, perhaps over long distances, in a traveller's purse, and in this way spreads outwards from the actual point of issue, which is the paymaster's table in barracks or in the field, or wherever else the government's financial agents must disburse money in the course of their business. The points of issue are many. The subsequent dissemination of the issued coins is like the spreading of ripples, not from a stone, but from a handful of gravel. The ripples meet, overlap, intermingle, until the whole surface of the water is covered. But, in the same image, we may imagine the Alps as a log lying across the pond, and there are two handfuls of gravel, one dropped on one side of the log (the issues of the Gallic mints), the other on the other side (senatorial issues). The ripples wash up against the log, and wash back. Only a little water, only comparatively few coins, cross the barrier.

This picture of coins flowing outwards from centres of issue is of course excessively simplified. It fails, for instance, to allow for the long-distance traveller. The merchant goes from Rome or Arezzo to

---

[1] Richmond points out that under Hadrian the proportion of new coins to old in the soldiers' purses found on Hadrian's Wall (*Trans. Cumb. and West. A. and A. Soc.*, N.S. liv (1954), pp. 56–60) is only 3 per cent or less, yet all this money is what they had been paid with; the 97 per cent of coin already in circulation will have been collected by the procurator in taxes and reissued in pay; cf. the story of Licinus, Dio liv. 21, for the procurator's function in this respect.

[2] How did such large sums travel? How many wagons or pack animals would be required to carry pay for a legion thrice a year? Lugdunum's facilities for waterborne transport may suggest why it took over from Nemausus as the mint supplying the Rhine army.

Gaul and takes with him a purse full of Italian money. The same thing happens on a larger scale with troop movements from one province to another. Grant has pointed out that Gallic and Italian issues alike are found at sites throughout Illyricum, the issues of the *tresviri* being reported rather more often than those of Lugdunum or Nemausus.[1] Of the fifteen legions and auxiliaries assembled in Illyricum to deal with the great rebellion in A.D. 6–9, any which were drafted in from Germany or Raetia will have brought with them in their purses the Gallic money in which they had always been paid. In Illyricum payment was in the coinage of the senatorial mint; and legions moving to Germany after the rebellion was over took the issues of the *tresviri* with them.

Table II shows how many coins issuing from mints in (*a*) Gaul and (*b*) Italy, in the Augustan and early Tiberian period, have been found at various sites north of the Alps. This table does not take into account gold and silver coinage, issues of other provinces (most commonly found are those of Spain, but also Africa, Macedonia, Eastern provinces, etc.), or barbarous imitations and hybrids. By including the first years of Tiberius' reign, it includes not only the whole Lugdunum series, but also the minor issues of the senatorial mint from the second decade A.D. referred to above. The real change in the coinage comes, not with Augustus' death, but after A.D. 20, with the closing of the Lugdunum series and the introduction of the 'Providentia' *asses* and other new types struck both at Rome and in the provinces, Roman and provincial issues differing no longer in type, but only in execution. My table therefore includes all issues of the senatorial mint and of mints in Gaul down to about A.D. 20, including the so-called 'Celtic' or native issues of Gallic provenance. These are also listed separately, as well as being included along with the issues of Vienna, Nemausus, Arausio, and Lugdunum in the Gallic total; the table is based on the more detailed statistical analysis given above in Table I, and the dates ascribed to the sites of Groups A and B are those established in the relevant chapters of this work where those sites are discussed. The dates of the sites in Group C are discussed below.

It is clear from Table II that the proportion of Italian coins to Gallic ones depends both upon the geographical location of the site and upon the date at which it was occupied and/or abandoned. If we compare the Rhineland sites, we see that at the Selssche Ziegelei, a site probably lying outside the area of the Augustan–Tiberian legionary base and partially abandoned on the building of the Claudian fortress east of the earlier base, Italian issues account for

---

[1] Grant, *SMACA*, pp. 14–21.

TABLE II. Distribution of Republican, Augustan and early Tiberian bronze issues.

		Number of Coins issued in		Italian issues as percentage of total
		(a) Gaul	(b) Italy	
A Augustan and early Tiberian Foundations				
Lippe valley	Oberaden	148 (2)	3	2·0
	Haltern	773 (403)	48	5·8
Middle and Lower Rhine	Neuss (Sels. Zieg.)	1,171 (660)	137	10·6
	Mainz (base area)	200 (15)	86	30·1
North Switzerland and Raetia	Augsburg-Oberhausen	159 (6)	116	42·2
	Vindonissa	1,569 (30)	1,639	51·1
	Kempten (Lindenberg)	84 (nil)	113	57·3
B Late Tiberian and Claudian Foundations				
Middle and Lower Rhine	Neuss (Claudian fortress)	17 (5)	32	65·3
Raetia	Aislingen	13 (nil)	30	69·8
	Augsburg (Domkirche hill)	11 (1)	17	67·8
C Date uncertain				
Middle and Lower Rhine	Bingen	20 (1)	11	35·5
	Mainz-Weisenau	17 (4)	16	48·5

Figures in brackets show the number of Celtic coins included in the totals for Gaul.

10·6 per cent of the total Augustan, pre-Augustan, and early Tiberian coinage. At Mainz from the area within and immediately beside the legionary base the percentage of Italian issues is 30·1. This site, like the Selssche Ziegelei, was first occupied when the legions moved up to the Rhine in preparation for Drusus' campaigns. Unlike the Ziegelei however it continued to be intensively occupied throughout the first century and beyond. The Claudian fortress at Neuss, on the other hand, has yielded 65·3 per cent of Italian coins, or 32 Italian to 17 Gallic. Add to these a further 21 coins of Augustus which could not be assigned to any definite issue, and the total of pre-20 A.D. coins is still only 70, compared with 61 of the reign of Claudius, 106 of Nero, 77 of Vespasian, and so forth. In other words, at this Claudian foundation, the Augustan and early Tiberian issues form only a comparatively small part of the total coin finds, but amongst these early issues, the Italian productions predominate by nearly 2:1; whereas at the Augustan foundation of Mainz the Augustan issues greatly outweigh those of any other reign, but among the Augustan and early Tiberian issues those of Gaul are more than twice as common as those of Italy. Both sites continued to be occupied into a period when these early issues had ceased to be a significant proportion of the coinage in circulation, so that the date of their abandonment does not affect the balance between Italian and Gallic issues. At the Ziegelei, where Gallic issues of this early period are nearly ten times as common as Italian, the early issues as a whole account for over 90 per cent of all identifiable coins from the site. At all three of these sites the total number of coins found is large enough to give us a worthwhile and, we may hope, valid sample. And the evidence of these sites leads us to suppose that on the middle Rhine in the Augustan and early Tiberian period the coinage in circulation was preponderantly of Gallic issues, but that after this period, perhaps because of the closing of the Lugdunum mint, the Italian issues of the period continued to flow into the Rhineland until in the early part of the second half of the century they outweighed the Gallic issues.

Three sites are not enough to prove a rule, but they do suffice to suggest a hypothesis. And the evidence of other sites enables us to check and to develop this hypothesis. It is not perhaps surprising that at Oberaden Italian issues amount to only 2·0 per cent of the total, in fact 3 coins, 1 Republican and 2 Augustan. But Oberaden was not founded until 11/10 B.C., and though it was soon given up, there was a period of some years during which the *tresviri* I–II issues might have got there. Yet only two were found. At least it is clear that Italian issues at this period did not percolate very rapidly to the Lippe valley. At Haltern the proportion of Italian coins had risen to

5·8 per cent. The *tresviri* issues amount to 48, only nine of which are *tresviri* IV*a*, *b*. Yet when Haltern was abandoned in A.D. 9, these issues had already been in circulation for some ten years. The *tresviri* IV*b* issue was very large, as we have already observed; yet Lugdunum had in only some seven or eight years longer provided 328 coins to be found at Haltern. Again we see that Italian issues showed no great alacrity in reaching North Germany.

When we turn our attention to the Augustan and early Tiberian sites nearer Italy, in north Switzerland and the Voralpenland, we find a significantly higher percentage of Italian issues than at the sites further north. At Oberhausen, for instance, where the coin-sequence goes on to after A.D. 14, the Italian coins account for 42·2 per cent of the whole, whereas at Haltern, abandoned in 9, they are 5·8 per cent. The total number of coins recovered at Oberhausen is less than at Haltern, but the *tresviri* IV issue amounts to at least 32, probably about 40 pieces, whereas at Haltern it numbers only 9. Yet it had twelve years in which to reach Haltern, and probably only nineteen or twenty in which to reach Oberhausen, evidence of the greater ease and speed with which the *tresviri* issues reached the Raetian site. Oberhausen has a higher proportion of Italian issues than even Mainz has. Despite its long occupation, Mainz never became so exposed to the influx of Italian coinage as did Oberhausen, so favourably situated for trade with Italy along what was to become the Via Claudia Augusta.

It is of course dangerous to argue from the Oberhausen statistics, when the nature of the deposit is unknown. Nevertheless the legionary base at Vindonissa and the civil settlement on the Lindenberg at Kempten, early Tiberian foundations both, show a consistent picture—51·1 per cent and 57·3 per cent respectively of Italian issues. Later than Oberhausen, from their foundation they were recipients of a currency in which the Italian element was now stronger than in Augustan days, and getting stronger. The late Tiberian foundations of Augsburg and Aislingen show 67·8 per cent and 69·8 per cent respectively. The trend continues. Both are however still slightly ahead of the Claudian fortress at Neuss, no doubt because of their geographical position. But the difference is slight. It looks as if, by about the middle of the first century, the Italian issues of the Augustan and early Tiberian period are thoroughly at home north of the Alps, whether on the Upper Danube or on the Rhine. At any earlier period the Italian issues are more strongly represented in the areas where intercourse with Italy is easiest, and what is true for Italian issues as a whole will *a fortiori* be true of the more recent of those issues.

What then follows from this? We should like to know to what

extent the traffic was two-way, whether the Gallic issues spread *pari passu* into Italy. But it seems likely that the Italian issues were larger than the Gallic. We might wish that we could extend our investigation to later issues. Here however the study to assign individual specimens to individual mints is not sufficiently far advanced, and the whole question of provenance is too obscure. If our conclusions have any validity, one possibility which does follow is that of reversing the process adopted so far in this paper, and using the percentage of Italian issues at a site as a guide to help us determine the date of its first occupation. Bingen has been conjectured as the site of an Augustan fort, set to guard the crossing of the Nahe where it flows into the Rhine.[1] Italian issues account for 35·5 per cent of the coins of our period there, compared with 30·1 per cent for the Mainz fortress. This would agree with an Augustan, or better, early Tiberian date for the establishment of the fort, perhaps as part of the reorganization of the Rhine frontier after Germanicus' recall.

Harder to interpret, Weisenau yields 48·5 per cent of Italian coins —16:17, with one Augustan coin of unidentifiable type. Perhaps, as at Bingen, this is too few coins to give any valid conclusion. But for what it is worth, it would seem to indicate a foundation between the Augustan base at Mainz (30·1 per cent) and the Claudian fortress at Neuss (65·3 per cent)—and excavation has revealed traces of a base at Weisenau, short-lived but apparently founded under Caligula.[2] This fits nicely. Unfortunately pottery finds suggest that the site was under Roman occupation from the time of Augustus, and was a native settlement before that. The whole area is greatly disturbed by quarrying activities. No technique of statistical analysis can hope to disentangle the traces of successive occupations of different types by different—widely different—numbers of men, especially when the material is so scanty and most probably unrepresentative to boot. The apparent connection between our percentage of Italian coins and the Caligulan occupation is no doubt purely fortuitous, and no conclusion whatsoever may safely be drawn from it.

More sophisticated techniques of statistical analysis have been proposed. Kraft, in an attempt to determine the date at which the legionary base at Haltern was given up, calculated what proportion *tresviri* IV*a* and IV*b* issues formed of all *tresviri* issues at Haltern, Oberhausen, and Vindonissa.[3] At Haltern they are 18·8 per cent, at Oberaden 40·0 per cent, and at Vindonissa 70·8 per cent. The difference, Kraft suggested, is due to the different dates at which the

---

[1] *FMRD* iv. 1, pp. 100–17.
[2] Cf. on Weisenau area, above, p. 146.
[3] Kraft (*BJ* clv/vi 1955/6), pp. 101–2, cf. p. 106.

different sites were first occupied and afterwards given up. And he defined four factors as liable to affect the proportions of various issues occurring at different sites:

(i) the different dates at which the sites in question were first occupied;

(ii) the different dates at which they were given up;

(iii) a change in the size of the garrison at one or other of the sites (i.e. a hypothetical site which was occupied for twenty years by a single legion and thereafter for twenty years by two legions would show a higher proportion of later coins to earlier ones than another site occupied by either one legion or two legions throughout the same period);

(iv) the location of the sites in relation to the mint or mints supplying them.[1]

Now in view of what has already been said about the factors affecting the circulation of coins from different mints, it is clear that the fourth of Kraft's variables is conceived of too simply. Kraft's own observations on his method scarcely touch on the practical difficulties involved in trying to measure and allow for the immeasurable complications governing circulation.[2] He refers casually to the possibility of 'unexpected' differences (mere 'Befürchtungen', he calls them) between the pattern of circulation in Lower Germany on the one hand and Upper Germany and Raetia on the other, and advises that, 'where possible', sites in the same area should be compared.[3] In the case of Haltern and Oberhausen, which are conspicuously not in the same area, he claims to compensate for this by not comparing the issues of one mint at one site with those of another mint at the other site. When he urges that the *tresviri* IV issues form only 18·8 per cent of all *tresviri* issues at Haltern, but 40·0 per cent at Oberhausen, this he regards as a fair comparison, since IV will have had no more and no less chance of getting to Haltern or alternatively to Oberhausen than the earlier issues from the same mint. And therefore, since the effect of the different location of the two sites in relation to the mint is cancelled out, Kraft concludes that the lower proportion of the later issue at Haltern can only be explained by supposing that Haltern was abandoned first. For with regard to the other two variables set out above, he assumes that Oberhausen was founded as a legionary base in 15 B.C. and that any change in

[1] Kraft, op. cit., esp. p. 106.

[2] Id., *JNG* vii (1956), pp. 9–71, conceived as an introductory article to *FMRD*, on the use of coins for dating (cf. esp. pp. 45–58 on his own method of statistical analysis).   [3] Id., op. cit., p. 57, n. 77.

garrison at either site can only have been a reduction in the size of the garrison at Oberhausen, and therefore both these factors would tend to *increase* the proportion of *earlier* issues there, so making the priority of the abandonment of Haltern even more certain. We have seen, however, that whatever the nature of the Roman occupation of the Oberhausen area, there is no reason to suppose there was a legionary base here, and considerable reason to think, on the evidence of the pottery, that the deposit does not begin any earlier than the base at Haltern. To argue from the evidence of Oberhausen towards the end-date of Haltern is to seek *obscurum per obscurius*.

The peculiarities of Oberhausen, while invalidating the comparison between the Oberhausen finds and those of Haltern, do not tell against the method as such. But the number of factors affecting circulation is so much greater than Kraft allowed for that I think the method itself cannot provide reliable conclusions.[1] Kraft does not wholly refrain from comparing proportions of issues of different mints at different sites in different areas, despite his awareness of the risks involved. He argues that, because at Oberaden there are only two coins of the *tresviri* I and II issues to over 130 Nemausus I*b* and I*c*, therefore Nemausus I*b* and I*c* must have appeared before *tresviri* I and II.[2] He argues that, because the proportion of *tresviri* IV issues to Lugdunum I increases from Haltern to Oberhausen to Vindonissa, therefore this proves that the three sites were given up in this order.[3] I hope that I have shown that, while chronological factors have a lot to do with it, so do geographical factors and the law of supply and demand. The issues of the senatorial mint percolated slowly into the Lippe valley, while those of Nemausus in the years 12–8 B.C. or thereabouts and of Lugdunum thereafter flowed in a strong current from official sources to pay the troops. Kraft lays great emphasis on the 'Hauptprägezeit' and the 'Umlaufshöhepunkt' of the various issues, developing at some length the argument that the only issues which can achieve full circulation at any given site are those which are first issued after the date of occupation of that site and which have come into full circulation before the date of its abandonment.[4] But there is no independent check on what constitutes the 'Umlaufshöhepunkt' or full circulation. The danger of circular argument is very real. And the evidence of different sites presents some odd discrepancies. At Oberhausen Nemausus II

[1] Metcalf, *JNG* ix (1958), pp. 187–96, discusses the validity of this and similar methods from the point of view of statistical theory and concludes (p. 192) that it is virtually impossible to fulfil all the conditions for getting reliable results.

[2] Kraft, *BJ* clv/vi (1955/6), p. 108.

[3] Kraft, op. cit., pp. 104–5.

[4] Id., *JNG* vii (1956), loc. cit., esp. p. 49, cf. id., *BJ* clv/vi (1955/6), p. 106.

outnumbers Nemausus I: Kraft concludes that it has therefore reached its 'Umlaufshöhepunkt'. The *tresviri* IV issues form 40·0 per cent of identifiable *tresviri* issues at Oberhausen, 70·8 per cent at Vindonissa: therefore they have not reached their 'Umlaufshöhepunkt' by the time Oberhausen was abandoned. Therefore, concludes Kraft, the Nemausus II issue has its 'Umlaufshöhepunkt' and consequently its 'Hauptprägezeit' earlier than *tresviri* IV, i.e. before 3 B.C.[1] I pass over the uncertainties inherent in such a comparison of the issues of different mints. But I observe that at Vindonissa the figures for the Nemausus I and II issues are: I 65, II 44. Therefore, by parity of reasoning, Nemausus II has *not* reached its 'Umlaufshöhepunkt' at Vindonissa. This is, I suggest, the *reductio ad absurdum* of the method.

The attempt to use the evidence of halved coins for dating sites is also fraught with uncertainties. Kraft observes that at Vindonissa 36 per cent of Nemausus I coins are halved, 63 per cent of Nemausus II, 76 per cent of Nemausus III; the number of coins has increased since then, and the proportions should now read 36·9 per cent, 63·5 per cent, and 73·1 per cent respectively.[2] In addition, another 41 coins, 39 of them halved (92·7 per cent), belonged to either I or II (it is obviously harder to distinguish halved than whole coins). As for the Lugdunum I issue, out of 328 at Haltern 24·3 per cent are halved; out of 476 at Vindonissa 32·8 per cent (when Kraft wrote, this was 30·0 per cent out of 433). Kraft therefore argues that the practice of halving coins was commonest at the end of Augustus' reign and under Tiberius.[3] Unfortuntely, as he himself realized, the statistics for Lugdunum I at Oberhausen spoil the tidy pattern: out of 123 coins of this issue only 22·7 per cent are halved, a lower percentage than at Haltern. Perhaps, he suggests, many of the halved pieces at Haltern were broken accidentally (how does one break a coin accidentally?), so that the percentage of deliberately halved coins here should go down below that of Oberhausen, thus restoring the desired pattern. Some may regard this as an attempt to accommodate facts to theory, instead of vice versa. But the argument from the Nemausus statistics at Vindonissa is no happier. For if we

---

[1] Id., op. cit., p. 109; the Vindonissa figure is now 7·10, see Table I.

[2] The new figures from Kraay, op. cit.; observe that the proportion of halved coins in III is reduced by almost three per cent. This makes no difference to Kraft's argument, but does emphasize the dangers of relying overmuch on statistics which can change so quickly. Kraft warns against giving weight to statistics based on too few examples, where chance may falsify the picture, (op. cit., p. 106, cf. p. 104, n. 31), but how few are too few? Kellner in Krämer, *Cambodunumforschungen 1953* i, pp. 54–9, applies Kraft's method to the *tresviri* issues at Kempten, where there are only nine coins from all *tresviri* issues put together.

[3] Kraft, op. cit., p. 104.

allocate those three whole and 38 halved coins belonging to either I or II to those issues in proportion to the numbers of certainly assured whole or halved coins belonging to them, we shall have to give Nemausus II one whole and 20 halves, which would bring the percentage of halved coins in this issue to 73·8 per cent, fractionally higher than the figure for III. This is of course only an approximation, but we cannot leave these ambiguous coins out of account. Kraft with his fondness for the 'Umlaufshöhepunkt' points out that the percentage of halved coins in the Lugdunum II*c* issue at Vindonissa is only 9·9 per cent (now 9·1 per cent), compared with the figure of 76 per cent (now 73·1 per cent) for Nemausus III. This he takes to prove that the practice of halving coins reached its peak during the period of peak circulation of Nemausus III, but before Lugdunum II*c* had reached its peak. Another explanation is possible. We observe that not only at Vindonissa, but at all sites for which adequate statistics are available, of whatever period—Haltern, Oberhausen, Kempten, the Selssche Ziegelei site and that of the Claudian fortress at Neuss, and the area of the legionary base at Mainz—at all these sites the Nemausus issues show a higher percentage of halved coins than those of any other mint. There is but one class of exceptions, a significant one: at both Vindonissa and the Selssche Ziegelei the issues of the other Gallic mints, excluding the Lugdunum altar-series, outdo them. Of the issues of Orange and Vienne and the copia, the eagle, and the bull issues of Lugdunum 75 per cent are halved at Vindonissa and 70 per cent at the Ziegelei. No other site in our list has enough coins of these issues to give a significant percentage. It looks however as if halving may be a Gallic phenomenon, geographical, instead of or as well as chronological. Similarly Kraay notes that the senatorial issues are halved less often than any others at Vindonissa, and offers as one of the possible explanations the suggestion that perhaps halving was not in vogue in Italy, although Buttrey's studies cast doubt upon this theory.[1]

Halving in fact is something we know little about. Where was the bisection carried out? By whose authority? What is its history? Is there any truth in the suggestion that the double heads on the Nemausus series were deliberately designed to facilitate halving?[2] If so, we should expect to find that coins of this series were usually split in such a way as to leave one head on each half. Are they? None

---

[1] Kraay, op. cit., p. 8; Buttrey, *AJA* lxxi (1967), p. 184. A fuller publication of Buttrey's research, based largely on the finds from Morgantina, may well upset a number of theories and answer a number of questions in this field. He sees halving as an officially sponsored phenomenon, dating from the 20s B.C.

[2] Grant, *FITA*, p. 74, n. 9, actually records a Nemausus coin from Bonn, halved, which the position of the lettering is said to show to have been struck as a half.

of these questions can yet be answered, although a study of a large number of halved coins would settle the last one, and by inference the one before that. Kraay has brought the phenomenon of halving into connection with the sudden increase in the number of *semisses* issued early in Tiberius' reign, noting that at Vindonissa there are 37 coins of this denomination (including 1 halved) in the Lugdunum IIc issue and another 45 belonging to either II*b* or II*c*, as against only 8 of II*a* and II*b* together and none at all among the 476 coins of Lugdunum I. This goes contrary to Buttrey's theories, but would agree with Kraft's suggestion that the peak period of halving came in the late Augustan and Tiberian period. And yet, if this is so, it would still seem that halving was also much more common in some areas than others. We should be chary of drawing unwarranted chronological inferences from statistics of 'Halbierungshäufigheit'.

The problem is further complicated by its connection with the unexplained reappearance of Republican *asses*, which are totally lacking at Haltern, are rare at all other Augustan sites, and yet occur probably 517 times at Vindonissa and 23 times, out of a much smaller number of coins, in the Tiberian settlement at Kempten. 61·5 per cent of the Republican coins at Vindonissa are halved, 17 out of the 23 at Kempten, 8 out of 9 at Oberhausen. Yet only 4 Republican *asses* are known from the fortress area at Mainz, only 2 from the Selssche Ziegelei, none from the Claudian fortress at Neuss. Is there again some geographical factor at work? It is easier to pose the question than to answer it. It is clear that the occurrence of a Republican *as* on a site is not an indication of early Augustan occupation, as is sometimes supposed. But the circumstances in which the Republican bronze coinage returned to circulation remain obscure. Where so many problems await answers, it is unwise to seek to impose too rigid a sytematization on the subtle and insufficiently understood pattern of coin circulation.

BIBLIOGRAPHY

THE first part of this bibliography contains all books referred to in the text or footnotes, together with all articles of general interest. Articles devoted only to one specific site are omitted, unless also of outstanding general importance. They can be traced by looking up the site in question in the Index, and complete bibliographies are usually to be found for each site in G. Forni's article 'limes' in the *Dizionario Epigrafico*. The second part lists all periodicals cited, with their full title and place of publication, to help English-speaking readers identify and track down the more unfamiliar items. Many general works which were consulted but found to contain nothing new do not appear; of the making of books on such well-worn topics as the site of the Varian Disaster or the geography of Germanicus' campaigns, there is truly no end. Nor was it thought necessary to refer to earlier works whose interest is now only for *Forschungsgeschichte*. A number of works which appeared too late to be used in writing this book are listed in the Addenda at the end of the Bibliography.

PART I. BOOKS AND ARTICLES

ABRAMIĆ, M., 'O novim miljokazima i rimskim cestama Dalmacije', *VAHD* xlix (1926/7), 139–55.

ALBRECHT, CHR., *Frühgeschichtliche Funde aus Westfalen im Städtischen Kunst- und Gewerbemuseum Dortmund* (Veröffentlichungen aus dem Städtischen Kunst- und Gewerbemuseum, Dortmund), Dortmund, 1936.

—— *Das Römerlager in Oberaden und das Uferkastell in Beckinghausen an der Lippe* (Veröffentlichungen aus dem Städt. Mus. für Vor- und Frühgeschichte Dortmund ii. 1, ii. 2), 2 vols., Dortmund, 1938, 1942.

ALFÖLDI, A., 'Rhein und Donau in der Römerzeit', *JGPV* 1948/9, 5–21.

—— 'The Moral Barrier on Rhine and Danube', in *Congress of Roman Frontier Studies, 1949*, 1–16.

ALFÖLDY, G., 'Eine Strassenbauinschrift aus Salona', *Klio* xlvi (1965), 323–7.

—— 'Taurisci und Norici', *Historia* xv (1966), 224–41.

—— *Die Hilfstruppen der römischen Provinz Germania Inferior* (Epigraphische Studien vi), Düsseldorf, 1968.

Analecta Archaeologica: Festschrift Fritz Fremersdorf, Cologne, 1960.

ANDERSON, J. G. C., (ed.), *Cornelii Taciti de origine et situ Germanorum*, Oxford, 1938.

Aspects of archaeology in Britain and beyond: essays presented to O. G. S. Crawford, ed. W. F. Grimes, London, 1951.

ATKINSON, K. M. T., 'The Governors of the Province Asia in the Reign of Augustus', *Historia* vii (1958), 300–30.

Atti del 1º Convegno Preistorico Italo-Svizzero, Locarno–Varese–Como, 29 giugno– 2 luglio 1947, Como, 1949.

Aus Bayerns Frühzeit: Friedrich Wagner zum 75. Geburtstag (Schriftenreihe zur Bayer. Landesgesch. lxii), ed. J. Werner, Munich, 1962.

BAATZ, D., *Mogontiacum: neue Untersuchungen am römischen Legionslager in Mainz* (Limesforschungen iv), Berlin, 1962.

——— 'Zur Frage augusteischer Canabae Legionis', *Germania* xlii (1964), 260–5.

BADIAN, E., *Roman imperialism in the late Republic*, 2nd edn., Oxford, 1968.

BALSDON, J. P. V. D., 'Gaius and the Grand Cameo of Paris', *JRS* xxvi (1936), 152–60.

——— review of Sattler, *Augustus und der Senat*, in *Gnomon* xxxiii (1961), 393–6.

BALTY, J. C., 'COL(onia) NEM(ausus): notes d'archéologie et d'histoire augustéenne', *RBPh.* xxxviii (1960), 59–73.

BAROCELLI, P., *Forma Italiae, Regio XI Transpadana* i: *Augusta Praetoria* (Unione Accademica Nazionale), Rome, 1948.

——— *La romanizzazione della Valle d'Aosta* (Biblioteca Storica Universitaria ii. 4), Milan, 1954.

BAUMAN, R. A., 'Tiberius and Murena', *Historia* xv (1966), 420–32.

BEHRENS, G., *Denkmäler des Wangionengebietes* (Germanische Denkmäler der Frühzeit i), Frankfurt a. M., 1923.

BENADÍK, B., VLČEK, E., and AMBROS, C., *Keltski pohrebiská na juhozápadnom Slovensku* (Keltische Gräberfelder der Südwestslovakei) (Archaeologica Slovaca Fontes i), Bratislava, 1957.

BENARIO, J. M., 'Book 4 of Horace's Odes: Augustan Propaganda', *TAPA* xci (1960), 339–52.

BERCHEM, D. VAN, 'Aspects de la domination romaine en Suisse', *SZG* v (1955), 145–75.

——— 'Du portage au péage: le rôle des cols transalpins dans l'histoire du Valais celtique', *MH* xiii (1956), 199–208.

——— 'Zur römischen Kolonisation in der Schweiz', *JSGU* xlvi (1957), 13–23.

——— 'Conquête et organisation par Rome des districts alpins', *REL* xl (1962), 228–35.

BERETTA, I., 'Incorporazione de "Salassi incolae" nella colonia di Augusta Praetoria', *Acme* v (1952), 493–508.

BERGER, L., *Die Ausgrabungen am Petersberg in Basel: ein Beitrag zur Frühgeschichte Basels*, Basle, 1963.

——— 'Die Gründung der Colonia Raurica und die Bedeutung der Mittelland-Hauenstein-Strasse', in *Provincialia: Festschrift Laur-Belart*, 15–24.

BIRLEY, E., *Roman Britain and the Roman army: collected papers*, Kendal, 1953.

BITTEL, K., *Die Kelten in Württemburg* (Römisch-germanische Forschungen viii), Berlin and Leipzig, 1934.

BLANC, A., 'Les Études de laboratoire sur la céramique antique', *Revuearch. de l'Est et du Centre-Est* xv (1964), 285–93.

BLONDEL, L., 'La route romaine du Mont-Joux: étude topographique', *Hommages Grenier* i, 308–16.

BONA, I., 'Beiträge zur Geschichte der Quaden', *AArchHung.* xv (1963), 239–307.

BONNARD, G., *see* Gibbon, E.

BOUFFARD, P., 'La route romaine du Grand St-Bernard', *Ur-Schweiz* x (1946), 49–52.

BOWEN, R. LE B., JR., ALBRIGHT, F. B., and others, *Archaeological discoveries in South Arabia* (Publications of the American Foundation for the Study of Man ii), Baltimore, 1958.

BRUHL, A., 'Le souvenir d'Alexandre le Grand et les Romains', *MEFR* xlvii (1930), 202–21.

BRUNSTING, H., *Het grafveld onder Hees bij Nijmegen: een bijdrage tot de kennis van Ulpia Noviomagus* (Allard Pierson Stichting, Archaeologisch-historische Bijdragen iv), Amsterdam, 1937.

—— *400 Jaar Romeinse bezetting: Noviomagus Batavorum*, Leiden, 1961.

BRUNT, P. A., review and discussion of Meyer, *Die Aussenpolitik des Augustus*, in *JRS* liii (1963), 170–6.

—— 'Reflections on British and Roman Imperialism', *Comparative Studies in Society and History* vii (1965), 267–88.

—— and MOORE, J. M., *Res Gestae Divi Augusti: the Achievements of the Divine Augustus*, London, 1967.

BRYCE, LORD, *The ancient Roman empire and the British empire in India; the diffusion of Roman and English law throughout the world*, Oxford, 1914.

BUTTREY, T. V., 'Halved Coins of the Late First Century B.C.' (summary), *AJA* lxxi (1967), 184.

BYVANCK, A. W., *Nederland in den Romeinschen tijd*, 2 vols., Leiden, 1945.

—— *Excerpta Romana: de bronnen der Romeinsche geschiedenis van Nederland* (Rijks geschiedkundige publicatiën lxxiii, lxxxi, lxxxix), 3 vols., The Hague, 1931–47.

CAGNAT, R., *L'Armée romaine d'Afrique et l'occupation militaire de l'Afrique sous les empereurs*, 2nd edn., Paris, 1913.

Carnuntina: Ergebnisse der Forschung über die Grenzprovinzen des römischen Reiches: Vorträge beim internationalen Kongress der Altertumsforscher, Carnuntum 1955 (Römische Forschungen in Niederösterreich iii), ed. E. Swoboda, Graz and Cologne, 1956.

CAROE, SIR OLAF, *The Pathans, 550 B.C.–A.D. 1957*, London, 1958.

CARY, M., *The geographic background of Greek and Roman history*, Oxford, 1949.

CASIMIR, P., *Le Trophée d'Auguste à la Turbie*, Marseilles, 1932.

Celticum xii: *Actes du IVe Congrès International d'Études Gauloises, Celtiques et Protoceltiques, Sarrebruck (Sarre), 4–9 septembre 1964* (Supplément à *Ogam — Tradition Celtique* xcviii), Rennes, 1965.

CHARLESTON, R. J., *Roman pottery* (Faber Monographs on Pottery and Porcelain), London, 1955.

CHILVER, G. E. F., *Cisalpine Gaul: social and economic history from 49 B.C. to the death of Trajan*, Oxford, 1941.

CHRIST, K., 'Die Militärgeschichte der Schweiz in römischer Zeit', *SZG* v (1955), 452–93.

—— 'Ergebnisse und Probleme der keltischen Numismatik und Geldgeschichte', *Historia* vi (1957), 213–53.

—— 'Zür römischen Okkupation der Zentralalpen und des nördlichen Alpenvorlandes', *Historia* vi (1957), 416–28.

CHURCHILL, SIR WINSTON, *My early life: a roving commission*, London, 1930.

—— *The river war: an account of the reconquest of the Soudan* (first publ. 1899), London, 1933.

COLLINGWOOD, R. G., and MYRES, J. N. L., *Roman Britain and the English settlements* (The Oxford History of England), 2nd edn., Oxford, 1937.

—— and WRIGHT, R. P., *The Roman inscriptions of Britain* i: *inscriptions on stone*, Oxford, 1965.

—— and RICHMOND, I. A., *The archaeology of Roman Britain*, London, 1969.

COLLINS, J. H., 'Propaganda, ethics and psychological assumptions in Caesar's writings', dissertation, Frankfurt a. M., 1952.

COMFORT, H., 'Terra sigillata', *RE* Supp. vii, 1295–1352.

—— 'An Italian Sigillata Crater in Britain', in *Hommages Grenier* i, 448–56.

—— 'Late Ateius Signatures', *RCRFA* iv (1962), 5–25.

—— 'Puteolan Sigillata at the Louvre', *RCRFA* v/vi (1963/4), 7–28.

Congress of Roman Frontier Studies, 1949, ed. E. Birley, Durham, 1952.

CONRADS, A., 'Pila muralia und ihre Verwendung', *Germania* xi (1927), 71–3.

Corolla Memoriae Erich Swoboda Dedicata (Römische Forschungen in Niederösterreich v), Graz and Cologne, 1966.

CREASY, SIR EDWARD, *The fifteen decisive battles of the world* (first publ. 1851), Everyman's Library, London, 1960.

CURLE, J., *A Roman frontier post and its people: the fort of Newstead in the parish of Melrose*, Glasgow, 1911.

CURZON, LORD, *Frontiers* (The Romanes Lecture, 1907), Oxford, 1907.

DANIËLS, M. P. M., *Noviomagus: Romeins Nijmegen*, Nijmegen, 1955.

DÉCHELETTE, J., *Les Fouilles du Mont Beuvray de 1897 à 1901*, Paris and Autun, 1904.

—— *Manuel d'archéologie préhistorique, celtique et gallo-romaine* iv, 2nd edn., Paris, 1927.

DEHN, W., 'Die gallischen "Oppida" bei Cäsar', *SJ* x (1951), 36–49.

DEHN, W., 'Einige Bemerkungen zum Murus Gallicus', *Germania* xxxviii (1960), 43–55.

DION, R., 'Explication d'un passage (26) des "Res Gestae divi Augusti"', in *Mélanges Carcopino*, 249–69.

DOBIÁŠ, J., 'King Maroboduus as a Politician', *Klio* xxxviii (1960), 155–66.

—— *Dějiny československého území před vystoupením Slovanů* (The history of the Czechoslovak territory before the appearance of the Slavs) (Nakladatelství Československé Akademie Věd), Prague, 1964.

—— 'Rom und die Völker jenseits der mittleren Donau', in *Corolla Swoboda*, 115–25.

EGGERS, H. J., *Der römische Import im freien Germanien* (Atlas der Urgeschichte i), Hamburg, 1951.

—— *Einführung in die Vorgeschichte* (Sammlung Piper), Munich, 1959.

—— WILL, E., JOFFROY, R., and HOLMQUIST, W., *Kelten und Germanen in heidnischer Zeit* (Kunst der Welt), Baden-Baden, 1964.

EMELEUS, V. M., 'Neutron Activation Analysis of Samian Ware Sherds', *Archaeometry* iii (1960), 16–19.

ERTL, F., *Topographia Norici: die römischen Siedlungen, Strassen und Kastelle im Ostalpenraum*, Kremsmünster, 1965.

ETTLINGER, E., *Die Keramik der Augster Thermen (Insula XVIII): Ausgrabung 1937–8* (Monographien zur Ur- und Frühgeschichte der Schweiz vi), Basle, 1949.

—— 'Frühaugusteische Arretina in der Schweiz', in *Limes-Studien*, 45–8.

—— 'Vorbemerkungen zu einer Diskussion des Ateius-Problems', *RCRFA* iv (1962), 27–44.

—— 'Frühe Arretina aus Neuss', in *Studien zu den Militärgrenzen Roms*, 77–85.

—— 'Vindonissa', *RE* ixA, 82–105.

EVANS, D. E., *Gaulish personal names: a study of some continental Celtic formations*, Oxford, 1967.

FABRICIUS, E., review of Macdonald, 'The Dating Value of Samian Ware', in *Germania* xx (1936), 214–16.

FEIST, S., *Germanen und Kelten in der antiken Überlieferung*, Halle (Saale), 1927.

FELLMANN, R., *Basel in römischer Zeit* (Monographien zur Ur- und Frühgeschichte der Schweiz x), Basle, 1955.

—— 'Die Principia des Legionslagers Vindonissa und die Zentralgebäude der römischen Lager und Kastelle', *JGPV* 1957/8, 75–89.

Festschrift zu Ehren Hermann Wopfners i: *Beiträge zur Geschichte und Heimatkunde Tirols* (Schlernschriften lii), Innsbruck, 1947.

Festschrift für Rudolf Egger: Beiträge zur Alteren europäischen Kulturgeschichte, ed. G. Moro, 3 vols., Klagenfurt, 1952/4.

FILIP, F., *Keltové ve střední Evropě* (Die Kelten in Mitteleuropa) (Monumenta Archaeologica: Acta Praehistorica, Protohistorica et Historica Instituti

Archaeologici Academiae Scientiarum Bohemoslovenicae v), Prague, 1956.

FILTZINGER, P., 'Bemerkungen zur römischen Okkupationsgeschichte Südwestdeutschlands', *BJ* clvii (1957), 181–212.

FISCHER, F., 'Beiträge zur Kenntnis von Tarodunum', *Bad. Fundber.* xxii (1962), 37–49.

FORBES, R. J., *Notes on the history of ancient roads and their construction* (Allard Pierson Stichting, Archaeologisch-Historische Bijdragen iii), Amsterdam, 1934.

FORMIGÉ, J., 'Le trophée des Alpes: la Turbie', *Gallia*, Supp. ii, Paris, 1949.

FORNI, G., 'Limes', *Diz. epig.* iv, 1074 ff. (still incomplete).

FORRER, R., *Strasbourg-Argentorate, préhistorique, gallo-romain et mérovingien*, 2 vols., Strasbourg, 1927.

—— *L'Alsace romaine*, Paris, 1935.

FOX, SIR CYRIL, *A find of the early Iron Age from Llyn Cerrig Bach, Anglesey* (National Museum of Wales), Cardiff, 1946.

FRESHFIELD, D. W., *Hannibal once more*, London, 1914.

—— 'The Great Passes of the Western and Central Alps', *GJ* xlix (1917), 2–26.

FUCHS, H., *Augustin und der antike Friedensgedanke: Untersuchungen zum neunzehnten Buch der Civitas Dei* (Neue philolog. Untersuchungen iii), Berlin, 1926.

FURNEAUX, H., *The Annals of Tacitus*, vol. I, books i–vi, 2nd edn., Oxford, 1896.

GARCÍA Y BELLIDO, A., 'El "exercitus Hispanicus" desde Augusto a Vespasiano', *AEA* xxxiv (1961), 114–60.

GARDTHAUSEN, V., *Augustus und seine Zeit*, 2 vols. in 5, Leipzig, 1891.

GELZER, M., *Caesar, politician and statesman*, tr. P. Needham, Oxford, 1968.

Γέρας: *Studies presented to G. Thomson on the occasion of his 60th birthday*, ed. L. Varel and R. F. Willetts (Acta Univ. Carolinae Phil. et Hist. i) (Graecolatina Pragensia ii), Prague, 1963.

GIBBON, E., *The history of the decline and fall of the Roman Empire*, ed. J. B. Bury, 7 vols., London, 1896.

—— *Le Journal de Gibbon à Lausanne, 17 août 1763—19 avril 1764*, ed. Georges Bonnard (Université de Lausanne, Publ. de la Faculté des Lettres viii), Lausanne, 1945.

GLASBERGEN, W., *42 n. C.—het eerste jaartal in de geschiedenis van West-Nederland* (Koninklijke Nederlandse Akademie van Wetenschappen, I.P.P. Publicatie xc), Amsterdam, 1966.

GLÜSING, P., 'Frühe Germanen südlich der Donau: zur ethnischen Deutung der spätlatènezeitlichen Grabfunde von Uttenhofen und Kronwinkl in Niederbayern', *Offa* xxi/xxii (1964/5), 7–20.

GODWIN, H., *The history of the British Flora: a factual basis for phytogeography*, Cambridge, 1956.

GOESSLER, P., 'Poeninus (2)', *RE* xxi, 1156–62.

GOUDINEAU, C., *Fouillles de l'École française de Rome à Bolsena (Poggio Moscini) 1962–1967* iv: *la Céramique arétine lisse (MEFR,* Supp. vi), Paris, 1968.

GRANT, M., *From Imperium to Auctoritas: a historical study of aes coinage in the Roman Empire 49 B.C.–A.D. 14,* Cambridge, 1946.

—— *The six main aes coinages of Augustus: controversial studies,* Edinburgh, 1953.

GROAG, E., 'P. Sulpicius Quirinus, cos. 12 v. Chr.', *RE* ivA, 822–43.

HACHMANN, R., review of Melin, *Die Heimat der Kimbern,* in *Gnomon* xxxiv (1962), 56–65.

—— KOSSACK, G., and KUHN, H., *Völker zwischen Germanen und Kelten: Schriftquellen, Bodenfunde und Namengut zur Geschichte des nördlichen Westdeutschlands um Christi Geburt,* Neumünster, 1962.

HAGEN, J., *Römerstrassen der Rheinprovinz* (Erläuterungen zum Geschichtlichen Atlas der Rheinprovinz viii), 2nd edn., Bonn, 1931.

HAMMOND, M., 'The Sincerity of Augustus', *HSCP* lxix (1965), 139–62.

HANSLIK, R., 'M. Vinicius, cos. suff. 19 v. Chr.', *RE* ixA, 112–16.

HAVERFIELD, F., *Some Roman conceptions of empire* (Occasional Publications of the Classical Association iv), Cambridge, *c.* 1916.

HAWKES, C. F. C., 'Celtes, Gaulois, Germains, Belges', in *Celticum* xii, 1–7.

—— 'The Celts: Report on the Study of their Culture and their Mediterranean Relations, 1942–1962', in *Le Rayonnement des civilisations grecque et romaine,* 61–79.

—— and HULL, M. R., *Camulodunum: first report on the excavations at Colchester 1930–1939* (Reports of the Research Committee of the Society of Antiquaries xiv), Oxford, 1947.

HAYEN, H., 'Grosse Bohlenwege im Randmoor westlich der Unterweser', *PZ* xli (1963), 206–9.

Helvetia Antiqua: Festschrift Emil Vogt, ed. R. Degen, W. Drack, R. Nyss, Zürich, 1966.

HETTEMA, H., JR., *De Nederlandse wateren en plaatsen in de Romeinse tijd,* 2nd edn., The Hague, 1951.

HEUBERGER, R., *Rätien in Altertum und Frühmittelalter* i (Schlernschriften xx), Innsbruck, 1932.

—— *Das Burggrafenamt im Alttertum* (Schlernschriften xxviii) Innsbruck, 1935.

—— 'Wann wurde Rätien Provinz?', *Klio* xxxiv (1942), 290–2.

—— 'Der Eintritt des mittleren Alpenraumes in Erdkunde und Geschichte', in *Festschrift Wopfner* i (1947), 69–118.

—— 'Vindelici', *RE* ixA, 1–17.

HEURGON, J., 'Encore un problème de Boulogne: le pont de Drusus', *REA* li (1949), 324–6.

HIRSCHFELD, O., 'Die Crocodilmünzen von Nemausus', *Wiener Studien* v (1883), 319–22.

HOFMEISTER, H., *Die Chatten* i: *Mattium, die Altenburg bei Niedenstein* (Germanische Denkmäler der Frühzeit ii), Frankfurt a. M., 1930.

HOLMES, T. RICE, *The architect of the Roman Empire*, 2 vols., Oxford, 1928–31.

HOLWERDA, J. H., *De Belgische Waar in Nijmegen* (Beschrijving van de ver-zameling van het Museum G. M. Kam te Nijmegen), Nijmegen, 1941.

Hommages à Albert Grenier (Collection Latomus lviii), ed. M. Renard, 3 vols., Brussels and Berchem, 1962.

HOWALD, E., and MEYER, E., *Die römische Schweiz: Texte und Inschriften mit Übersetzung*, Zürich, 1940.

HÜBENER, W., 'Römische Wehranlagen an Rhein und Donau als militär-geschichtliche Quelle', *Militärgeschichtliche Mitt.* ii (1968), 7–34.

HYDE, W. W., *Roman Alpine routes* (Memoirs of the American Philosophical Society ii), Philadelphia, 1935.

JACOBY, F., *Die Fragmente der griechischen Historiker*, 2 vols., Berlin, 1923–6.

JAMESON, S., 'Chronology of the Campaigns of Aelius Gallus and C. Petro-nius', *JRS* lviii (1968), 71–84.

JANKUHN, H., 'Terra . . . silvis horrida (zu Tacitus, *Germania* cap. 5)', *Archaeologia Geographica* x/xi (1961/3), 19–38.

JOHN, W., *Die Örtlichkeit der Varusschlacht bei Tacitus*, Göttingen, 1950.

JULLIAN, C., *Histoire de la Gaule*, 8 vols., Paris, 1914–26.

KÄHLER, H., 'Die Ara Pacis und die augusteische Friedensidee', *JDAI* lxix (1954), 67–100.

KAHRSTEDT, U., 'The Roman Frontier on the Lower Rhine in the Early Imperial Period', in *Congress of Roman Frontier Studies, 1949*, 41–54.

—— 'Grundsätzliches zu historischen und archäologischen Grenzen', in *Ur- und Frühgeschichte als historische Wissenschaft*, 60–2.

—— 'Methodisches zur Geschichte des Mittel- und Niederrheins zwischen Caesar und Vespasian', *BJ* cl/cli (1950/1), 63–80.

KAM, W. H., *De versterking op het Kopseplateau te Nijmegen: bewoning en Romeinse vondsten*, Nijmegen, 1965.

KIENAST, D., 'Augustus und Alexander', *Gymnasium* lxxvi (1969), 430–56.

KIMMIG, W., and HELL, H., *Vorzeit am Rhein und Donau*, Lindau and Constance, 1958.

KIRWAN, L. P., 'Rome beyond the Southern Egyptian Frontier', *GJ* cxxiii (1957), 13–19.

KLEISS, W., *Die öffentlichen Bauten von Cambodunum* (Materialhefte zur Bayerischen Vorgeschichte xviii), Kallmünz, 1962.

KLINDT-JENSEN, O., *Denmark before the Vikings* (Ancient Peoples and Places iv), London, 1957.

KLOSE, J., *Roms Klientel-Randstaaten am Rhein und an der Donau: Beiträge zu ihrer Geschichte und rechtlichen Stellung im 1. und 2. Jhdt. n. Chr.* (Historische Untersuchungen xiv), Breslau, 1934.

KLOTZ, A., 'Die geographischen Commentarii des Agrippa und ihre Überreste', *Klio* xxiv (1931), 38–58, 386–466.

KNAPKE, W., 'Aurei- und Solidi-Vorkommen am Mare Balticum und deren westliche Zusammenhänge', *AArchKöb.* xiv (1943), 55–66.

Kölner Untersuchungen: Festgabe zur 1900-Jahrfeier der Stadtgründung (Die Kunstdenkmäler in Landesteil Nordrhein, Beiheft ii), ed. W. Zimmerman, Ratingen, 1950; also published under the title *Untersuchungen zur frühen Kölner Stadt-, Kunst- und Kirchengeschichte* (Die Kunstdenkmäler des Rheinlands, Beiheft ii), Essen, 1950.

KOEPP, F., *Die Römerlager bei Haltern: Führer durch das Ausgrabungsgelände Haltern 1921/22*, Münster i. W., 1922.

—— review of Feist, 'Germanen und Kelten in der antiken Überlieferung', in *Göttingische Gelehrte Anzeigen* cxc (1928), 201–17.

—— *Varusschlacht und Aliso: Vorträge und Nachreden aus drei Jahrzehnten*, new edition with bibliography by Erich Thurmann of works published since 1909, Münster i. W., 1940.

KOESTERMANN, E., 'Die pannonisch-dalmatinische Krieg 6–9 n. Chr.', *Hermes* lxxxi (1953), 345–78.

—— 'Die Feldzüge des Germanicus 14–16 n. Chr.', *Historia* vi (1957), 429–79.

KRAAY, C. M., 'The Chronology of the Coinage of Colonia Nemausus', *NC* 6th ser. xv (1958), 75–87.

—— *Die Münzfunde von Vindonissa bis Trajan* (Veröffentlichungen der Gesellschaft Pro Vindonissa v), Basle, 1962.

KRAFT, K., 'Zu den Schlagmarken des Tiberius und Germanicus: ein Beitrag zur Datierung der Legionslager Vindonissa und Oberhausen', *JNG* ii (1950/1), 21–35.

—— 'Zur Datierung der Münzmeisterprägung unter Augustus', *MZ* xlvi/xlvii (1951/2), 28–35.

—— 'Das Enddatum des Legionslagers Haltern', *BJ* clv/vi (1955/6), 95–111.

—— 'Bemerkungen zur kritischen Neuaufnahme der Fundmünzen der römischen Zeit in Deutschland ("Antiker Münzfundkatalog")', *JNG* vii (1956), 9–71.

—— 'Die Rolle der Colonia Julia Equestris und die römische Auxiliar-Rekrutierung', *JRGZ* iv (1957), 81–107.

—— review of Hachmann, Kossack, and Kuhn, *Völker zwischen Germanen und Kelten*, in *Germania* xlii (1964), 313–20.

KRAHE, H., 'Alteuropäische Flussnamen', *Beitr. zur Namenforsch.* i (1949), 24–51.

KRÄMER, W., *Cambodunumforschungen 1953* (Materialhefte zur bayerischen Vorgeschichte ix, x), 2 vols., Kallmünz, 1957.

KRANER, F., and DITTENBERGER, W., *C. Iulii Caesaris Commentarii de Bello Gallico*, 19th edn., revised by H. Meusel, Berlin, 1961.

KUNKEL, O., *Ausgrabungen in der Keltenstadt bei Manching an der Donau: Ausstellung der Prähistorischen Staatssammlung München 1960 und 1961*, Munich, 1961.

LAET, S. J. DE, review of Hachmann, Kossack, and Kuhn, *Völker zwischen Germanen und Kelten*, in *Helinium* iv (1964), 265–71.

LA PENNA, A., *Orazio e l'ideologia del principato* (Saggi no. 332), Turin, 1963.

LAUR-BELART, R., *Vindonissa: Lager und Vicus* (Römisch-germanische Forschungen x), Berlin, 1935.

—— 'Fortschritte in der Erforschung des Legionslagers Vindonissa', in *Carnuntina*, 91–4.

—— *Über die Colonia Raurica und den Ursprung von Basel*, 2nd edn., Basle, 1959.

LAWRENCE, T. E., *Seven pillars of wisdom: a triumph* (privately printed 1926), London, 1935.

LEHNER, H., *Vetera: die Ergebnisse der Ausgrabungen des Bonner Provinzial-museums bis 1929* (Römisch-germanische Forschungen iv), Berlin and Leipzig, 1930.

LEVI, M. A., *Il tempo di Augusto* (Storici antichi e moderni, N.S. vii), Florence, 1951.

Limes-Studien: Vorträge des 3. Internationalen Limes-Kongress in Rheinfelden/Basel 1957 (Schriften des Instituts für Ur- und Frühgeschichte der Schweiz xiv), Basle, 1959.

LOESCHCKE, S., 'Keramische Funde in Haltern: ein Beitrag zur Geschichte der augusteischen Kultur in Deutschland', *MAKW* v (1909), 101–322.

LUNZER, D. VON, 'M. Valerius Messalla Messallinus, cos. 3 v. Chr.', *RE* viiiA, 159–62.

MACDONALD, SIR GEORGE, *Catalogue of Greek coins in the Hunterian Collection, University of Glasgow* iii, Glasgow, 1905.

—— 'The Dating-Value of Samian Ware: a Rejoinder', *JRS* xxv (1935), 187–200.

MAGIE, D., *Roman rule in Asia Minor to the end of the third century after Christ*, 2 vols., Princeton, 1950.

MAJOR, E., *Gallische Ansiedlung mit Gräberfeld bei Basel*, Basle, 1940.

MARCKS, J. F., 'Die römische Flottenexpedition zum Kimbernlande und die Heimat der Kimbern', *Jb. Altfr. Rh.* xcv (1894), 29–45.

MARX, F. A., 'Die Quellen der Germanenkriege bei Tacitus und Dio', *Klio* xxvi (1933), 323–9.

—— 'Die Überlieferung der Germanenkriege besonders der augusteischen Zeit (Velleius und Dio)', *Klio* xxix (1936), 202–18.

—— 'Aufidius Bassus', *Klio* xxix (1936), 94–101.

MARY, G. T., *Novaesium* i: *die südgallische Terra Sigillata aus Neuss* (Limes-forschungen vi), Berlin, 1967.

MATTINGLY, H., review of Grant, *From Imperium to Auctoritas*, in *NC* 6th ser. vi, (1946), 129–33.

Mélanges d'archéologie, d'épigraphie et d'histoire offerts à Jérôme Carcopino, Paris, 1966.

MELIN, B., *Die Heimat der Kimbern* (Uppsala Universitets Årsskrift 1960: 5), Uppsala, 1960.

METCALF, M., 'Statistische Analyse bei der Auswertung von Münzfund-materialien', *JNG* ix (1958), 187–96.

MEYER, E., 'Neuer Forschungsergebnisse über die Schweiz in römischer Zeit', *MH* xix (1962), 141–55.

—— 'Nach einmal Hannibals Alpenübergang', *MH* xxi (1964), 99–102.

MEYER, H. D., *Die Aussenpolitik des Augustus und die augusteische Dichtung* (Kölner historische Abhandlungen v), Cologne and Graz, 1961.

MILTNER, F., 'Augustus' Kampf um die Donaugrenze', *Klio* xxx (1937), 200–26.

—— *Römerzeit in österreichischen Landen* (Vierring-Reihe ii), Brixlegg and Innsbruck, 1948.

MÓCSY, A., 'Das Territorium Legionis und die Canabae in Pannonien', *AArchHung.* iii (1953), 179–200.

—— 'Die vertuschte Dakerkrieg des M. Licinius Crassus', *Historia* xv (1966), 511–14.

—— 'Pannonia', *RE* Supp. ix, 516–776.

MOMIGLIANO, A., '*Panegyricum Messalae* and "Panegyricum Vespasiani" ', *JRS* xl (1950), 39–42.

MOMMSEN, T., 'Die Örtlichkeit der Varusschlacht' (orig. publ. in *Sitzber. Kön. preuss. Akad.* 1885, 63–92), *Gesammelte Schriften* iv: *Historische Schriften* i, Berlin, 1906, 200–46.

MOREAU, J., *Die Welt der Kelten* (Grosse Kulturen der Frühzeit, N.F.), Stuttgart, 1958.

MORRIS, JAMES, *Pax Britannica: the climax of an empire*, London, 1968.

MOTYKOVÁ-ŠNEIDROVÁ, K., *Die Anfänge der römischen Kaiserzeit in Böhmen* (Fontes Archaeologici Pragenses vi), Prague, 1963.

MUCH, R., review of Feist's art. 'Germanen' in Ebert's *Reallexicon der Vorgeschichte*, in *Wiener präh. Ztschr.* xv (1928), 1–19.

—— 'Waren die Germanen Kelten?', *Ztschr. für deutsches Altertum und deutsche Litteratur* lxv (1928), 1–50.

—— *Die Germania des Tacitus*, 3rd edn., revised by H. Jankuhn and W. Lange, Heidelberg, 1967.

MÜLLER, W., 'Klarstellungen und Beiträge zur Teutoburgfrage', *PZ* xxxvi (1958), 265–70.

—— 'Augusteische Sigillata bei Heidenoldendorf nahe der Grotenburg und andere bemerkenswerte Funde im Umkreis', *Germania* xxxvii (1959), 242–3.

NAVARRO, J. M. DE, 'Prehistoric Routes between Northern Europe and Italy defined by the Amber Trade', *GJ* lxvi (1925), 481–507.

NECKEL, G., *Germanen und Kelten: Historisch-linguistisch-rassenkundliche Forschungen und Gedanken zur Geisteskrisis* (Kultur und Sprache vi), Heidelberg, 1929.

NESSELHAUF, H., 'Umriss einer Geschichte des obergermanischen Heeres', *JRGZ* vii (1960), 151–79.

NESTLE, W., *Der Friedensgedanke in der antiken Welt* (*Philologus* Supp. xxxi), Leipzig, 1938.

Neue Ausgrabungen in Deutschland (Römisch-germanische Kommission des Deutsch. archäol. Inst.) ed. W. Krämer, Berlin, 1958.

NEUSTUPNÝ, E. and J., *Czechoslovakia before the Slavs* (Ancient Peoples and Places xxii), London, 1961.

NIERHAUS, R., 'Die Westgrenze von Noricum und die Routenführung der Via Claudia Augusta', in *Ur- und Frühgesch. als hist. Wissenschaft* (1950), 177–88.

—— 'Zu den ethnographischen Angaben in Lukans Gallien-Exkurs', *BJ* cliii (1953), 46–62.

—— *Das swebische Gräberfeld von Diersheim: Studien zur Geschichte der Germanen am Oberrhein vom gallischen Krieg bis zur alamannischen Landnahme* (Römisch-germanische Forschungen xxviii), Berlin, 1966.

NOHEJLOVÁ-PRATOVÁ, E., (ed.), *Nálezy mincí v Čechach, na Moravě a ve Slezsku* (Corpus of Coins in Bohemia, Moravia, Silesia) (Československá Akademie Věd, Numismatická Komise), Part I, *Celtic coins*, by Pavel Radoměrský, and *Ancient coins*, by Eugen Pochitonov, Prague, 1955.

NOLL, R., 'Römische Siedlungen und Strassen im Limesgebiet zwischen Inn und Enns (Oberösterreich)', *RLÖ* xxi (1958).

NORDEN, E., *Die germanische Urgeschichte in Tacitus Germania*, 2nd edn., Leipzig and Berlin, 1922.

NUBER, H. U., 'Zur Entstellung der Raeterkohorten', in *Studien zu den Militärgrenzen Roms*, 90–3.

OBERZINER, G., *Le guerre di Augusto contro i popoli alpini*, Rome, 1900.

OLDFATHER, W. A., and CANTER, H. V., *The defeat of Varus and the German frontier policy of Augustus* (U. of Illinois Studies in the Social Sciences iv. 2), Urbana, 1915.

ONDROUCH, V., *Nálezy keltských, antických a byzantských mincí na Slovensku* (Československá Akadémia Vied, Numizmatická Komisia), Bratislava, 1964.

OSWALD, F., and PRYCE, T. D., *An introduction to the study of terra sigillata treated from a chronological standpoint*, London, 1920.

OXÉ, A., 'Die Halterner Sigillatafunde seit 1925', *Bod. Westf.* vi (1943), 15–76.

—— and COMFORT, H., *Corpus vasorum arretinorum: a catalogue of the signatures, shapes and chronology of Italian sigillata* (*Antiquitas*, Reihe 3: Abhandlungen zur Vor- und Frühgeschichte, zur klassischen und provinzial-römischen Archäologie iv), Bonn, 1968.

PARET, O., 'Die spätkeltischen Viereckschanzen', in *Ur- und Frühgesch. als hist. Wissenschaft*, 154–62.

PASALIĆ, E., 'Römische Strassen in Bosnien und der Herzegowina', *Arch. Jug.* iii (1959), 61–74.

PASCHER, G., 'Römische Siedlungen und Strassen in Limesgebiet zwischen Enns und Leitha', *RLÖ* xix (1949).

PATSCH, C., 'Burnum', *RE* iiiA, 1068–70.

PELICHET, E., 'Le problème de la frontière ouest des Helvètes au début du Ier siècle avant J.-C.', in *Atti del 1º Convegno Preistorico Italo-Svizzero*, 96–103.

—— 'Autour de la fondation de la colonie équestre du Nyon', *Revue historique vaudoise* lxvi (1958), 49–60.

PESCHECK, C., 'Zum Bevölkerungswechsel von Kelten und Germanen in Unterfranken', *Bay. Vorgbl.* xv (1960), 75–99.

—— 'Zur historischen Aussage prähistorischer Funde: Möglichkeiten und Grenzen', *Ber. des Hist. Ver. des ehem. Fürstbistums Bamberg* cii (1966), 7–23.

PETRIKOVITS, H. VON, *Novaesium: das römische Neuss* (Führer des Rheinischen Landesmuseums in Bonn iii), Cologne and Graz, 1957.

—— 'Das niedergermanische Limes', in *Limes-Studien*, 88–95.

—— *Das römische Rheinland: archäologische Forschungen seit 1945* (Arbeitsgemeinschaft für Forschung des Landes Nordrhein-Westfalen, Geisteswissenschaften lxxxvi) (*BJ* Beiheft viii), Cologne and Opladen, 1960.

—— 'Arminius', *BJ* clxvi (1966), 175–93.

—— 'Vetera', *RE* viiiA, 1801–34.

PFLAUM, H.-G., *Les Carrières procuratoriennes équestres sous le Haut-Empire romain* (Institut français de Beyrouth, Bibliothèque archéologique et historique lvii), 4 vols., Paris, 1960–1.

PHILIPP, H., 'Segusio', *RE* iiA, 1107.

PIGGOTT, S., *Ancient Europe from the beginnings of agriculture to classical antiquity: a survey*, Edinburgh, 1965.

POLASCHEK, E., 'Noricum', *RE* xvii, 971–1084.

POWELL, T. G. E., *The Celts* (Ancient Peoples and Places vi), London, 1958.

PREIDEL, H., *Die vor- und frühgeschichtlichen Siedlungsräume in Böhmen und Mähren* (Südosteuropäische Arbeiten xl), Munich, 1953.

PREIN, O., *Aliso bei Oberaden und die Varusschlacht*, Münster i. W., 1930.

PREMERSTEIN, A. VON, 'Der Daker- und Germanensieger M. Vinicius und sein Enkel', *JÖAI* xxviii (1933), 140–63, and xxix (1934), 60–81.

Provincialia: Festschrift für Rudolf Laur-Belart, ed. E. Schmid, L. Berger, P. Bürgin, Basle and Stuttgart, 1968.

Quintus Congressus Internationalis Limitis Romani Studiosorum (Acta et Dissertationes Archaeologicae iii), Zagreb, 1963.

RADNÓTI, A., 'Ein Legionarshelm aus Burlafingen, Landkreis Neu-Ulm', in *Aus Bayerns Frühzeit*, 157–73.

RAMBAUD, M., *L'Art de la déformation historique dans les Commentaires de César*, 2nd edn., Paris, 1966.

Rayonnement des civilisations grecque et romaine sur les cultures périphériques (8e Congrès international d'archéologie classique, Paris, 1963), Paris, 1965.

REINECKE, P., *Kleine Schriften zur vor- und frühgeschichtlichen Topographie Bayerns*, 1st edn., cyclostyled and privately circulated by Bayerisches Landesamt für Denkmalpflege, Munich, 1951.

REMOUCHAMPS, A. E., *Opgravingen te Vechten*, Utrecht, 1928.

RICHMOND, I. A., 'The Birdoswald Hoard and its composition', *Trans. Cumb. and West. A. and A. Soc.*, N.S. liv (1954), 56–60.

—— *Roman Britain* (Pelican History of England i), Harmondsworth, 1955.

RITTERLING, E., 'Zur Geschichte des römischen Heeres in Gallien unter Augustus', *BJ* cxiv/cxv (1906), 159–88.

—— 'Kastell Wiesbaden', *ORL* ii B.31, 1909.

—— 'Das frührömische Lager bei Hofheim im Taunus', *Nass. Ann.* xl (1912), 1–416.

—— 'Die Alpes maritimae als Rekrutierungsbezirk für Truppenteile des römischen Kaiserheeres', *Klio* xxi (1927), 82–91.

—— *Fasti des römischen Deutschland unter dem Prinzipat* (Beiträge zur Verwaltungs- und Heeresgesch. von Gallien und Germanien ii), Vienna, 1932.

—— 'Legio', *RE* xii, 1186–1829.

Roman frontier studies, 1967 (Proceedings of the 7th International Congress of Roman Frontier Studies), ed. S. Applebaum, Tel Aviv, (forthcoming).

Romana Neerlandica (Archaeologica Traiectina iii), Groningen, 1959.

ROMANELLI, P., *Storia delle province romane dell'Africa* (Studi pubblicati dall'Istituto Italiano per la Storia Antica xiv), Rome, 1959.

ROWLETT, R. M., 'The Iron Age North of the Alps', *Science* clxi (1968), 123–34.

RÜGER, C. B., *Germania Inferior: Untersuchungen zur Territorial- und Verwaltungsgeschichte Niedergermaniens in der Prinzipatszeit* (*BJ* Beiheft xxx), Cologne and Graz, 1968.

SADDINGTON, D. B., 'Roman attitudes to the "externae gentes" of the North', *Acta Classica* iv (1961), 90–102.

SALMON, E. T., *A history of the Roman world 30 B.C. to A.D. 138* (Methuen's History of the Greek and Roman World vi), 6th edn., London, 1968.

SANDER, E., 'Zur Varusschlacht', *Archiv für Kulturgeschichte* xxxviii (1956), 129–51.

SATTLER, P., *Augustus und der Senat: Untersuchungen zur römischen Innenpolitik zwischen 30 und 17 v. Chr.*, Göttingen, 1960.

SAYRE, E. V., and DODSON, R. W., 'Neutron Activation Study of Mediterranean Potsherds', *AJA* lxi (1957), 35–41.

SCHELLER, H., 'Die Entstehung der Bislicher Insel', *BJ* clvii (1957), 272–93.

SCHINDLER, M., *Die "schwarze Sigillata" des Magdalensberges* (Archäologische Forschungen zu den Grabungen auf dem Magdalensberg i) (Kärntner Museumschriften xliii), Klagenfurt, 1967.

SCHLEIERMACHER, W., 'Praefectus Raetis, Vindolicis, vallis Poeninae et levis armaturae', *Germania* xxxi (1953), 200–1.

—— 'Die Besetzung Germaniens durch Drusus', in *Analecta Archaeologica* (1960), 231–4.

SCHMIDT, E., 'Kastell Höchst am Main', *ORL* ii B.28, 1912.

—— 'Kastel bei Mainz', *ORL* ii B.30, 1912.

—— 'Kastell Friedberg', *ORL* ii B.26, 1913.

SCHMIDT, L., *Geschichte der deutschen Stämme bis zum Ausgang der Völkerwanderung*, i *Die Ostgermanen*, ii. 1 and ii. 2. i *Die Westgermanen*, 2nd edn., Munich, 1934–40.

SCHMITTHENNER, W., 'Octavians militärische Unternehmungen in den Jahren 35–33 v. Chr.', *Historia* vii (1958), 189–236.

—— 'Augustus' spanischer Feldzug und der Kampf um den Prinzipat', *Historia* xi (1962), 29–85.

SCHMITZ, H., 'Die Übersiedlung der Ubier auf das linke Rheinufer', *Klio* xxxiv (1942), 239–63.

—— *Stadt und Imperium: Köln in römischer Zeit* i, Cologne, 1948.

—— *Colonia Claudia Ara Agrippinensium* (Veröffentlichungen des Kölnischen Geschichtsvereins e. V. xviii), Cologne, 1956.

SCHÖNBERGER, H., 'Die Spätlatènezeit in der Wetterau', *SJ* xi (1952), 21–130.

—— *Neuere Grabungen am obergermanischen und rätischen Limes* (Limesforschungen ii), Berlin, 1962.

—— 'The Roman Frontier in Germany: an Archaeological Survey', *JRS* lix (1969), 144–97.

—— SIMON, H.-G., and VEGAS, M., *Novaesium* ii: *Die mittelkaiserzeitliche Terra Sigillata von Neuss* (Schönberger and Simon); *Die römischen Lampen von Neuss* (Vegas) (Limesforschungen vii), Berlin, 1966.

SCHUCHHARDT, C., 'Die Römer als Nachahmer im Landwehr- und Lagerbau', *Sitzungsberichte der Preuss. Akad. der Wissenschaften* 1931, Phil.-hist. Klasse, 608–34.

SCHULTEN, A., *Numantia: die Ergebnisse der Ausgrabungen 1905–1912*, 4 vols., Munich, 1914–29.

SCHULZ, O. T., *Die Rechtstitel und Regierungsprogramme auf römischen Kaisermünzen* (Studien zur Geschichte und Kultur des Altertums xiii. 4), Paderborn, 1925.

SCHUMACHER, K., *Siedlungs- und Kulturgeschichte der Rheinlande von der Urzeit bis in das Mittelalter* (Handbuch des Römisch-germanischen Centralmuseums ii) ii, *Die römische Period*, Mainz, 1923.

SCHWARZ, K., *Atlas der spätkeltischer Viereckschanzen Bayerns*, Munich, 1959.

—— 'Spätlatènezeitliche Viereckschanzen keltische Kultplätze', in *Neue Ausgrabungen in Deutschland*, pp. 205–14.

—— 'Zum Stand der Ausgrabungen in der spätkeltischen Viereckschanze von Holzhausen', *Jber. Bay. Bodendenkmalpflege* 1962, 22–73.

SCOLLAR, I., *Archäologie aus der Luft: Arbeitsergebnisse der Flugjahre 1960 und 1961 im Rheinland* (Schriften des Rheinischen Landesmuseums Bonn i), Düsseldorf, 1965.

SCULLARD, H. H., *From the Gracchi to Nero: a history of Rome from 133 B.C. to A.D. 68*, London, 1959.

SHERWIN-WHITE, A. N., *The Roman citizenship*, Oxford, 1939.

—— *Roman society and Roman law in the New Testament* (The Sarum Lectures 1960–1), Oxford, 1963.

SIMPSON, G., 'Notes on Gaulish Samian Pottery and its Analysis by Neutron Activation', *Archaeometry* iii (1960), 20–4.

STÄHELIN, F., *Die Schweiz in römischer Zeit*, 3rd edn., Basle, 1948.

STEIN, E., *Die kaiserlichen Beamten und Truppenkörper im römischen Deutschland unter dem Prinzipat*, Vienna, 1932.

STEINHAUSEN, J., *Archäologische Siedlungskunde des Trierer Landes*, Trier, 1936.

STENICO, A., *Revisione critica delle pubblicazioni sulla ceramica aretina*, Milan, 1960.

—— 'Localizzata a Cremona una produzione di vasellame "tipo Aco" ', *RCRFA* v/vi (1963/4), 51–9.

STEVENS, C. E., review of Drioux, *Cultes indigènes des Lingons*, in *JRS* xxvi (1936), 125–6.

—— 'Britain Between the Invasions (B.C. 54–A.D. 43): a Study of Ancient Diplomacy', in *Aspects of archaeology*, 332–44.

STRASBURGER, H., *Caesar im Urteil seiner Zeitgenossen*, Darmstadt, 1968 (revised and expanded version of art. in *Hist. Ztschr.* clxxv (1953), 225–64).

STUART, P., *Gewoon aardewerk uit de Romeinse legerplaats en de bijbehorende grafvelden te Nijmegen* (*OMRL* Suppl. xliii), Leiden, 1962.

Studien zu den Militärgrenzen Roms: Vorträge des 6. Internationalen Limeskongresses in Süddeutschland (*BJ* Beiheft xix), Cologne and Graz, 1967.

Studies in Roman economic and social history in honour of A. C. Johnson, ed. P. R. Coleman-Norton, F. C. Bourne, J. V. A. Fine, Princeton, 1951.

SUTHERLAND, C. H. V., *Coinage in Roman imperial policy, 31 B.C.–A.D. 68*, London, 1951.

—— review of Grant, *Six main aes coinages of Augustus*, in *JRS* xliii (1953), 199–201.

SWOBODA, E., 'Zur Occupation Noricums', *Klio* xxviii (1935), 180–6.

—— 'Der pannonische Limes und sein Vorland', *Carn. Jb.* 1959, 17–30.

—— *Carnuntum: seine Geschichte und seine Denkmäler* (Römische Forschungen in Niederösterreich i), 4th edn., Graz and Cologne, 1964.

SYME, R., 'Die Zahl der praefecti castrorum im Heere des Varus', *Germania* xvi (1932), 109–11.

—— review of Stein, *Die kaiserlichen Beamten und Truppenkörper im römischen Deutschland unter dem Prinzipat*, in *JRS* xxiii (1933), 94–8.

—— 'Some notes on the Legions under Augustus', *JRS* xxiii (1933), 14–33.

—— 'M. Vicinius (cos. 19 B.C.)', *CQ* xxvii (1933), 142–8.

—— 'Galatia and Pamphylia under Augustus: the Governorships of Piso, Quirinius and Silvanus', *Klio* xxvii (1934), 122–48.

—— 'Lentulus and the Origin of Moesia', *JRS* xxiv (1934), 113–37.

—— 'The Northern Frontiers under Augustus', in *CAH* x, 340–81.

—— review of Forrer, *L'Alsace romaine*, in *JRS* xxvi (1936), 124–5.

—— review of Hyde, *Roman Alpine routes*, in *JRS* xxvi (1936), 113–14.

—— *The Roman revolution*, Oxford, 1939.

SZILÁGYI, J., 'Roman Garrisons Stationed at the Northern Pannonian-Quad Frontier-Sectors of the Empire', *AArchHung.* ii (1952), 189–220.

TACKENBERG, K., *Fundkarten zur Vorgeschichte der Rheinprovinz (BJ* Beiheft ii), Bonn, 1954.

Tetelbierg, site archéologique, catalogue of exhibition held at the Musée d'Histoire et d'Art, 3 April–2 May 1965, Luxembourg, 1965.

THOMPSON, E. A., 'Maroboduus', in Γέρας: *studies presented to G. Thomson*, 203–10.

—— *The early Germans*, Oxford, 1965.

ULBERT, G., *Die römischen Donaukastelle Aislingen und Burghöfe* (Limesforschungen i), Berlin, 1959.

—— *Die römische Keramik aus dem Legionslager Augsburg-Oberhausen* (Materialhefte zur bayerischen Vorgeschichte xiv), Kallmünz, 1960.

—— *Der Lorenzberg bei Epfach: Die frührömische Militärstation* (Münchner Beiträge zur Vor- und Frühgeschichte ix) (Veröffentlichung der Komm. zur archäol. Erforschung d. spätröm. Raetien iii), Munich, 1965.

Ur- und Frühgeschichte als historische Wissenschaft: Festschrif tzum 60. Geburtstag von Ernest Wahle, ed. H. Kirchner, Heidelberg, 1950.

USLAR, R. VON, *Westgermanische Bodenfunde* (Germanische Denkmäler der Frühzeit iii), Berlin, 1938.

—— 'Germanische Bodenaltertümer um Christi Geburt als Interpretationsbeispiel', *JRGZ* viii (1961), 38–65.

—— *Studien zu frühgeschichtlichen Befestigungen zwischen Nordsee und Alpen (BJ* Beiheft xi), Cologne and Graz, 1964.

—— 'Stämme und Fundgruppen: Bemerkungen zu "Stammesbildung und Verfassung" von R. Wenskus', *Germania* xliii (1965), 138–48.

VERMEULEN, W. G. J. R., *Een Romeinsch grafveld op den Hunnerberg te Nijmegen* (Bouwsteenen voor een geschiedenis van Nijmegen ii), Amsterdam, 1932.

VETTERS, H., 'Zur Frage der keltischen Oppida', *Carinthia I* cxli (1951), 677–716.

—— 'Virunum', *RE* ixA, 244–309.

VOGT, E., *Der Lindenhof in Zürich: zwölf jahrhunderte Stadtgeschichte auf Grund der Ausgrabungen 1937/38*, Zürich, 1948.

VOGT, J., *Orbis Romanus zur Terminologie des römischen Imperialismus* (Philosophie und Geschichte xxii), Tübingen, 1929.

VOIGT, T., 'Bemerkungen zu latènezeitlicher Problematik im Elb-Saale-Gebiet und in Mitteleuropa', *Alt-Thüringen* vi (1962/3), 383–402.

VULPE, R., 'Les Gètes de la rive gauche du Bas-Danube et les Romains', *Dacia* N.S. iv (1960), 309–32.

WAAGÉ, F. O., 'Vasa Samia', *Antiquity* xi (1937), 46–55.

WAELE, F. J. DE, *Noviomagus Batavorum* (*Romeinsch Nijmegen*) (Bouwsteenen voor een geschiedenis van Nijmegen i), Nijmegen and Utrecht, 1931.

—— 'Noviomagus (10) = Nijmegen', *RE* xvii, 1204–13.

WAGNER, F., *Die Römer in Bayern*, Munich, 1924.

—— *Denkmäler und Fundstätte der Vorzeit Münchens und seiner Umgebung* (Kataloge der Prähistorischen Staatssammlung München ii), Kallmünz, 1958.

WAGNER, W., 'Zur ala Pansiana, eine epigraphische Nachlese', *Germania* xli (1963), 317–27.

WAHLE, E., *Zur ethnischen Deutung frühgeschichtlicher Kulturprovinzen* (Grenzen der frühgeschichtlichen Erkenntnis i) (Sitzber. Heidelberg. Akad., Phil.-hist. Kl., Abd. ii), Heidelberg, 1941.

WALLER, K., 'Zur Archäologie der Kimbern', *Hammaburg* vii (1961), 67–92.

WALSER, G., *Caesar und die Germanen: Studien zur politischen Tendenz römischer Feldzugsberichte* (*Historia* Einzelschriften i), Wiesbaden, 1956.

—— *Die römischen Strassen in der Schweiz* i (Itinera Romana: Beiträge zur Strassengeschichte des Römischen Reiches i), Berne, 1967.

WEBSTER, G., *The Roman imperial army of the first and second centuries A.D.*, London, 1969.

WEILER, I., 'Orbis Romanus und Barbaricum', *Carn. Jb.* 1963/4, 34–9.

WELLS, C. M., review of Ulbert, *Der Lorenzberg bei Epfach*, in *Phoenix* xxi (1967), 65–7.

—— review of Brunt and Moore, *Res Gestae Divi Augusti*, in *Phoenix* xxiii (1969), 322–5.

—— review of Nierhaus, *Das swebische Gräberfeld von Diersheim*, in *JRS* lix (1969), 303–5.

—— 'The Supposed Augustan Base at Augsburg-Oberhausen: A New Look at the Evidence', *SJ* xxvii (1970), 62–73.

—— 'The Augustan Penetration of Germany: Dates and Destinations', in *Roman frontier studies, 1967*, 1–6.

—— 'Emona and Carnuntum: Evidence for the Start of Roman Occupation', in the transactions of the 8th International Congress of Roman Frontier Studies, Cardiff, 1969 (forthcoming).

WENSKUS, R., *Stammesbildung und Verfassung: das Werden der frühmittelalterlichen gentes*, Cologne and Graz, 1961.

WERNER, J., 'Zur Besiedlungsgeschichte Mitteldeutschlands in der Spätlatène- und Frühkaiserzeit', *Germania* xxvi (1942), 148–54.

WESTWOOD, C. V., *The Thirty Years' War* (first publ. 1938), Penguin edn., Harmondsworth, 1956.

WHEELER, R. E. M., *Rome beyond the imperial frontiers*, London, 1954.

—— and RICHARDSON, K. M., *Hill forts of Northern France* (Reports of the Research Committee of the Society of Antiquaries of London xix), Oxford, 1957.

WIEDEMER, H. R., 'Ur- und Frühgeschichte der Winterthurer Gegend', dissertation, Zürich, 1960.

—— 'Menschliche Skelettreste aus Spätlatène- Siedlungen in Alpenvorland: zum Problem der römischen Landnahme in der Schweiz und Süddeutschland', *Germania* xli (1963), 269–80.

WILD, J. P., 'Die Frauentracht der Ubier', *Germania* xlvi (1968), 67–73.

WILKES, J. J., 'Studies in the Roman province of Dalmatia', dissertation, Durham, 1962.

—— 'The military achievement of Augustus in Europe, with special reference to Illyricum', *Univ. of Birmingham Hist. Journal* x (1965), 1–27.

WILLERS, H., 'Die Münzen der römischen Kolonien Lugdunum, Vienna, Cabellio und Nemausus', *Num. Ztschr.* xxxiv (1902), 79–138.

WOLFF, G., 'Kastell und die Erdlager von Heddernheim', *ORL* ii B.27, 1915.

—— 'Kastell Frankfurt am Main', *ORL* ii B.27a, 1915.

WORMSTALL, A., 'Augusteische Münzfunde im Raume Westfalen und römische Marschrichtungen', *Bod. Westf.* iv (1935), 267–70.

PART II. LIST OF PERIODICALS CITED

Acme. Annali della Facoltà di Filosofia e Lettere dell'Università Statale di Milano, Milan.

Acta Archaeologica, Copenhagen. (*AArchKöb.*)

Acta Archaeologica Academiae Scientiarum Hungaricae, Budapest. (*AArchHung.*)

Acta Classica. Proceedings of the Classical Association of South Africa, Cape Town.

Alt-Thüringen, Weimar.

American Journal of Archaeology, Princeton. (*AJA*)

American Journal of Philology, Baltimore. (*AJP*)

Ancient India. Bulletin of the Archaeological Survey of India, New Delhi.

Annalen des Vereins für nassauische Altertumskunde und Geschichtsforschung [subsequently *Nassauische Annalen*], Wiesbaden. (*Nass. Ann.*)

Année épigraphique, L'. Revue des publications épigraphiques relatives à l'antiquité romaine, Paris. (*AE*)

Antiquaries Journal, The. Being the Journal of the Society of Antiquaries of London, O.U.P. (*Ant. Journ.*)

Antiquité Classique, L', Louvain.

Antiquity. A Quarterly Review of Archaeology, Newbury, Berks.

Archaeologia geographica, Hamburg. (*Arch. geogr.*)

Archaeologia Jugoslavica, Belgrade. (*Arch. Jug.*)

Archaeologiai Értesítö, Budapest. (*AErt.*)

Archaeological Journal, The, London. (*Arch. Journ.*)

Archaeometry, Oxford.

Archiv für Kulturgeschichte, Münster i. W.

Archivo Español de Arqueología, Madrid. (*AEA*)

Badische Fundberichte, Freiburg i. Br. (*Bad. Fundber.*)

Basler Zeitschrift für Geschichte und Altertumskunde, Basle.

Bayerische Vorgeschichtsblätter, Munich. (*Bay. Vorgbl.*)

Beiträge zur Anthropologie und Urgeschichte Bayerns, Munich.

Beiträge zur Namenforschung, Heidelberg. (*Beitr. zur Namenforsch.*)

Bericht der Römisch-germanischen Kommission des Deutschen archäologischen Instituts, Berlin. (*BerRGK*)

Bericht des Historischen Vereins des ehemaligen Fürstbistums Bamberg.

Berichten van de Rijkdienst voor het Oudheidkundig Bodemonderzoek in Nederland, The Hague.

Bodenaltertümer Westfalens, Münster i. W. (*Bod. Westf.*)

Bonner Jahrbücher des Rheinischen Landesmuseums in Bonn und des Vereins von Altertumsfreunden im Rheinlande, Kevelaer. (*BJ*)

Cahiers d'archéologie et d'histoire d'Alsace [later *Cahiers alsaciens d'archéologie et d'histoire*], Strasbourg.

Carinthia I. Mitteilungen des Geschichtsvereins für Kärnten, Klagenfurt.

Carnuntum-Jahrbuch (*Römische Forschungen in Niederösterreich*, Beiheft), Vienna. (*Carn. Jb.*)

Classical Quarterly, O.U.P. (*CQ*)

Comparative Studies in Society and History. An International Quarterly, C.U.P.

Dacia. Revue d'archéologie et d'histoire ancienne, Bucharest.

Duisburger Forschungen. Schriftenreihe für Geschichte und Heimatkunde Duisburgs, Duisburg–Ruhrort.

Ephemeris Epigraphica. Corpus Inscriptionum Latinarum supplementum. (*EE*)

Eranos. Acta Philologica Suecana, Uppsala.

Forschungen zur deutschen Landes- und Volkskunde, Stuttgart.

Fundberichte aus Hessen, Bonn.

Gallia. Fouilles et Monuments archéologiques en France métropolitaine, Paris.

Geographical Journal, The, London. (*GJ*)

Germania. Anzeiger der Römisch-germanischen Kommission des Deutschen archäologischen Instituts, Berlin.

Gnomon. Kritische Zeitschrift für die gesamte klassische Altertumswissenschaft, Munich.

Göttingische Gelehrte Anzeigen, Göttingen.

Gymnasium. Zeitschrift für Kultur der Antike und humanistische Bildung, Heidelberg.

Hammaburg. Vor- und frühgeschichtliche Forschungen aus dem niederelbischen Raum, Hamburg.

Harvard Studies in Classical Philology, Cambridge, Mass. (*HSCP*)

Helinium. Revue consacrée à l'archéologie des Pays-Bas, de la Belgique, et du Grand-Duché de Luxembourg, Wetteren.

Hermes. Zeitschrift für klassische Philologie, Wiesbaden.

Historia. Zeitschrift für Alte Geschichte, Wiesbaden.

Jaarverslag van de Vereeniging voor Terpenonderzoek, Groningen.

Jaarverslag van het Provinciaal Utrechtsch Genootschap van Kunsten en Wetenschappen, Utrecht.

Jahrbuch der Schweizerischen Gesellschaft für Urgeschichte, Basle. (*JSGU*)

Jahrbuch des Bernischen historischen Museums, Bern.

Jahrbuch des Deutschen archäologischen Instituts, Berlin. (*JDAI*)

Jahrbuch des Römisch-germanischen Zentralmuseums, Mainz. (*JRGZ*)

Jahrbuch für Numismatik und Geldgeschichte, Kallmünz. (*JNG*)

Jahrbücher des Vereins von Alterthumsfreunden im Rheinlande (predecessor of *Bonner Jahrbücher*). (*Jb. Altfr. Rh.*)

Jahresbericht der Bayerischen Bodendenkmalpflege, Munich.

Jahresberichte der Gesellschaft Pro Vindonissa, Brugg. (*JGPV*)

Jahreshefte des Österreichischen archäologischen Instituts, Vienna. (*JÖAI*)

Journal of Roman Studies, London. (*JRS*)

Klio. Beiträge zur Alten Geschichte, Berlin.

Kölner Jahrbuch für Vor- und Frühgeschichte, Berlin.

Mainzer Zeitschrift. Mittelrheinisches Jahrbuch für Archäologie, Kunst und Geschichte, Mainz. (*MZ*)

Mannus. Zeitschrift für Vorgeschichte, Leipzig.

Mededelingen der Koninklijke Nederlandse Akademie van Wetenschappen, Amsterdam.

Mélanges d'archéologie et d'histoire de l'École française de Rome, Paris. (*MEFR*)

Memorie della Regia Accademia delle Scienze di Torino, Turin.

Militärgeschichtliche Mitteilungen, Freiburg i. Br.

Mitteilungen der Altertumskommission für Westfalen, Münster i. W. (*MAKW*)

Museum Helveticum. Schweizerische Zeitschrift für klassishe Altertumswissenschaft, Basle. (*MH*)

Nassauische Annalen (*Nass. Ann.*): see *Annalen* . . .

Nassauische Heimatblätter, Wiesbaden.

Neujahrsblatt der Hülfsgesellschaft Winterthur, Winterthur.

Neujahrsblatt der Stadtbibliothek Winterthur, Winterthur.

Nieuws-bulletin van de Koninklijke Nederlandse Oudheidkundige Bond.

Numaga. Tijdschrift gewijd aan heden an verleden van Nijmegen en omgeving, Nijmegen.

Numismatic Chronicle and Journal of the Numismatic Society, London. (*NC*)

Numismatische Zeitschrift, Vienna. (*Num. Ztschr.*)

Offa. Berichte und Mitteilungen, Neumünster in Holstein.

Oudheidkundige mededelingen uit het Rijksmuseum van Oudheden te Leiden, Leiden. (*OMRL*)

Phoenix, The. Journal of the Classical Association of Canada, Toronto.

Prähistorische Zeitschrift, Leipzig and Berlin. (*PZ*)

Pro Alesia. Revue mensuelle des fouilles d'Alise et des questions relatives à Alésia, Paris.

Proceedings of the British Academy, O.U.P. (*PBA*)

Rei Cretariae Romanae Fautorum Acta, Zürich. (*RCRFA*)

Rei Cretariae Romanae Fautorum Communicationes, Zürich. (*RCRFComm.*)

Revue archéologique, Paris.

Revue archéologique de l'Est et du Centre-Est, Dijon.

Revue belge de philologie et d'histoire, Brussels. (*RBPh.*)

Revue des études anciennes. Annales de la Faculté des Lettres de Bordeaux, Bordeaux. (*REA*)

Revue des études latines, Paris. (*REL*)

Revue historique vaudoise, Lausanne.

Rheinisches Museum, Frankfurt a. M. (*Rh. Mus.*)

Römische Limes in Österreich, Der, Vienna. (*RLÖ*)

Römisch-germanisches Korrespondenzblatt (successor to *Westd. Ztschr., Kbl.*), Trier. (*RGKbl.*)

Saalburg-Jahrbuch. Bericht des Saalburgmuseums, Berlin. (*SJ*)

Saeculum. Jahrbuch für Universalgeschichte, Freiburg.

Schwäbische Museum, Das, Ulm.

Schweizerische Zeitschrift für Geschichte, Zürich. (*SZG*)

Science. American Association for the Advancement of Science, Washington.

Sitzungsberichte der (Königlichen) Preussischen Akademie der Wissenschaften, Berlin.

Soproni Szemle. Soproni Szemle Kiadványainak Uj Sorozata, Sopron.

Thurgauische Beiträge zur vaterländischen Geschichte, Frauenfeld.

Tijdschrift van het Koninklijk Nederlandsch Aadrijkskundig Genootschap, Amsterdam. (*TKNAG*)

Transactions and Proceedings of the American Philological Association, Cleveland. (*TAPA*)

Transactions of the Cumberland and Westmorland Antiquarian and Archaeological Society, Kendal.

Trierer Zeitschrift für Geschichte und Kunst des Trierer Landes und seiner Nachbargebiet, Trier (*TZ*)

Umschau in Wissenschaft und Technik, Die, Frankfurt a. M.

University of Birmingham Historical Journal, Birmingham.

Ur-Schweiz (Suisse primitive). Mitteilungen zur Ur- und Frühgeschichte der Schweiz, Basle.

Vjesnik za arheologiju i historiju dalmatinsku (Bulletin d'archéologie et d'histoire dalmate), Split. (*VAHD*)

Vorzeit am Bodensee. Mitteilungen zur Vor- und Frühgeschichte und Heimatkunde des Bodenseeraumes, Überlingen.

Westdeutsche Zeitschrift für Geschichte und Kunst, Trier. (*Westd. Ztschr.*)

Wiener Studien. Zeitschrift für klassische Philologie, Vienna.

Ztschr. für deutsches Altertum und deutsche Litteratur, Frankfurt a. M.

ADDENDA

It was not at first intended to print addenda, but now nearly two years have elapsed since the manuscript was closed, the delay being due largely to difficulties over the figures and to postal strikes in both Canada and Great Britain. As a result, I am grateful to the Clarendon Press for agreeing to these extra pages, and to German and Swiss colleagues who have kindly brought to my attention new material, much of it unpublished, which I might otherwise have missed. A brief visit to the Haverfield Library has enabled me to consult a number of other recent works, but it has not been possible to make a systematic search for all new material published in these past two years, and I must offer my apologies for any omissions.

Oxford, July 1971. C. M. W.

p. 6, n. 6. Further discussion of Agrippa's map by Tierney, *Proc. Royal Irish Acad.* lxiii C.4 (1963), pp. 151–66.

p. 14, n. 1. It has been suggested to me that Caesar, when he speaks of 'Germani qui trans Rhenum incolunt', merely wishes to distinguish these transrhenan Germans from the other Germans this side of the river, and that so far from implying that all Germans live beyond the Rhine, he is in fact tacitly admitting from the start that there are some who do and some who do not. I cannot accept this interpretation. In *BG* i. 1 and i. 2 Caesar gives the impression that he is being extremely careful to define the geography of the peoples he is dealing with. The divisions of Gaul are precisely set out (i. 1), as are, more particularly, the boundaries of the Helvetii (i. 2), whose neighbours are the Germans, the Sequani, and the Roman province. The reader naturally gets the impression that the German territory, again said to be across the Rhine, is a distinct and definable geographical entity, like those of the Sequani, the province, and the Helvetii themselves. We are not prepared to hear that there are in fact other Germans elsewhere. So again in i. 27 Helvetian fugitives make off 'ad Rhenum finisque Germanorum': the same impression.

The presence of Germans west of the Rhine is not mentioned until i. 31, in the speech of Diviciacus, where it is a question only of the Germans of Ariovistus, who, it is emphasized, *crossed* the Rhine ('Rhenum transisse'), and do not belong in Gaul. Caesar is urged to interfere on the grounds that 'futurum esse paucis annis uti omnes ex Galliae finibus pellerentur atque omnes Germani Rhenum transirent'. The implication is clearly that 'omnes Germani', except those with Ariovistus, are now beyond the Rhine. So too in i. 33, 'paulatim Germanos consuescere Rhenum transire', where the implication is the same. In i. 37 there is again question of Germans crossing the Rhine ('pagos centum Sueborum ad ripas Rheni consedisse, qui Rhenum transire conarentur'). In i. 43 Caesar's demand to Ariovistus carries the same emphasis: 'si nullam partem Germanorum domum remittere posset, at ne quos amplius Rhenum transire pateretur'. Here the far side of the Rhine is openly equated with the Germans' home, and Ariovistus' reply (i. 44) accepts this. When battle is joined, the defeated Germans naturally try to get back across the Rhine to safety (i. 53). It would be impossible for any reader of this book, unless he had prior knowledge of facts which Caesar does not choose to reveal, to guess that there were other Germans actually *settled* west of the Rhine, until they surprisingly make their appearance in ii. 3 (cf. above, p. 25).

Caesar of course knew that there were Germans on both sides of the river, but he continues to write as if the Rhine were the natural boundary. Even when we hear of 'Germani cisrhenani' in northern Gaul, it is emphasized that they came originally from beyond the Rhine, and that there are more Germans where they came from who would still like to cross (see above, pp. 25–6). The Roman reader, therefore, having got the impression from *BG* i that all Germans except those with Ariovistus were beyond the Rhine, would learn at the start of *BG* ii that this was not quite true, but he would continue to assume from Caesar's whole account that the Rhine was the natural frontier, and that beyond the Rhine was where the Germans naturally belonged.

p. 16, n. 2. A new edition of Kimmig and Hell's book has now appeared, virtually unchanged, but with a new title, *Schätze der Vorzeit: Funde aus Deutschland, Frankreich and der Schweiz*, Stuttgart, 1965.

p. 20, n. 2. On the Hunsrück–Eifel culture see now, exhaustively, Joachim, *Die Hunsrück-Eifel-Kultur am Mittelrhein*. On the La Tène culture which succeeded it, Mahr, *Die jüngere Latènekultur des Trierer Landes*. Also, more briefly, Wightman, *Roman Trier and the Treveri*, pp. 16–32, discussing the development of the La Tène culture in the Treveran region and its conquest by Caesar, and reaching the same conclusion as I have done, namely that 'the Treveri were a people of mixed origins, who at some point largely adopted a Celtic language, and whose material culture over a period of four or five centuries exhibits, with local variations, many of the features normally associated with other Celtic-speaking peoples' (p. 20).

On the question of the Celtic and German languages, their development, and their use as a criterion of whether a given people is to be considered 'Celtic' or 'German', see further below, addendum to p. 29, n. 3.

p. 21, n. 3. Last, in his article on the Altenburg in the new second edition of Hoops, *Reallexicon der germanischen Altertumskunde* i. 205–9, adds little and declines to commit himself ('So bleibt doch beim gegenwärtigen Forschungsstand die Mischung germanischer und keltischer Komponenten im Fundgut der Altenstein noch ungeklärt und verbietet die sichere Zuordnung zu einem Ethnikum.')

On the other hand, Mildenberger, *Fundber. aus Hessen*, Beih. i (1969), pp. 122–34, reviewing the Altenburg finds, concludes that the *oppidum* was destroyed around the middle of the last century B.C., perhaps by German tribes on the move, and was thereafter abandoned. He links this event with the aggressive behaviour of the Suebi after Ariovistus' downfall, and notes that in any case the Altenburg cannot be Mattium, since the finds prove that it was certainly not still occupied at the time of the destruction of the latter by Germanicus. This identification should therefore be abandoned.

Mildenberger's analysis brings out the similarities between many of the Altenburg finds and those from La Tène *oppida* further south (e.g. horse-gear, p. 124; brooches and other metal objects, pp. 125–6), but his discussion of the pottery (pp. 127–34) supports the hypothesis that the inhabitants of the settlement were 'a border people who . . . assimilated the La Tène culture of their Celtic neighbours' (see above, p. 23). His discussion, op. cit., p. 128, n. 54, on the wheel-made pottery, shows that the influence of La Tène types increased during the life of the Altenburg settlement.

p. 24, n. 3. The phrase 'there can however be no doubt that two separate linguistic groups exist' should be qualified for the earlier period, especially in the light of considerations raised by Weisgerber and discussed in the next item, below.

p. 29, n. 3. Weisgerber, *Die Namen der Ubier*, analyses in detail names from the territory of the Ubii and those recorded elsewhere of men coming from this territory. Since his study covers the entire Roman period, it is not perhaps surprising that over three-quarters of all recorded personal names of civilians are Roman or of Mediterranean origin, as against just over 6 per cent Celtic, and nearly 4½ per cent German, the latter including Frankish names from the late Empire. The proportion of German names is, however, so small that Weisgerber asks (p. 165) whether it is in fact possible to speak of a German stratum in the population, although he answers the question affirmatively. The German names are themselves assignable to different chronological strata (p. 167: 'Nicht nur das die späten frankischen Namen sich deutlich abheben von den "übischen" im engeren Sinne, also den mit den umgesiedelten *Ubii* ins Land gekommenen Elementen. Auch diese selbst scheinen in einer Auseinandersetzung mit den bereits damals vorgefundenen Verhältnissen gestanden zu haben').

In this connection, raising the question of a possible pre-Ubian German stratum, and referring to the Germani Cisrhenani, he considers the possibility of 'German' settlers moving into the area at a period before the occurrence of the characteristic phonological change, the first German 'sound-shift', which made the German language recognizably distinct from Celtic (pp. 169–71). By what criterion, however, could we describe such settlers as 'German'? Kuhn, for instance, in Hachmann, Kossack, and Kuhn, *Völker zwischen Germanen und Kelten*, p. 116, asks whether the Germans in the traditional sense of the word can be considered as having formed an entity before this sound-shift, and goes on: 'Wörter und Namen, in denen unsere Lautverschiebung nicht oder nur teilweise durchgeführt ist, sind nicht germanisch im strengen Sinn'.

The older scholarship saw Celts and Germans as clearly distinct from a much earlier period, cf. Wahle, *Deutsche Vorzeit*, pp. 111–19, and explained linguistic similarities in terms of 'Keltisierung' and 'Germanisierung'. But Krahe, for instance, *Sprache und Vorzeit*, p. 142, concludes that the linguistic evidence, especially that of names, shows the Celts and Germans throughout the last centuries B.C. to have been neighbours with close linguistic and cultural ties; it was during this period that the sound-shift took place, with the greater part of the common Celtic and German vocabulary going back to an earlier period.

Are there then two separate entities, Celt and German, in any meaningful sense before the first century B.C.? *Can* we speak of 'Germans' before there is a German language, distinct from neighbouring languages but having sufficient unity to be regarded as a separate entity? Where we find traces of the German sound-shift on the left bank of the Rhine, does this betoken an influx of German-speaking settlers from beyond the Elbe, or did this linguistic phenomenon take place among peoples already settled on both banks? If the sound-shift took place at a period when Celts and Germans were in contact, as Krahe, for instance, suggests, we should expect a zone of transition, where it took place less completely; as at the present day one finds along the Dutch–German or French–Italian border a zone in which the peasants speak a language which it is sometimes hard to define as being wholly one thing or the other. So perhaps the Ubii may be a people of whom one cannot say that they were wholly Celtic or wholly German, even in their speech, but who spoke a language exhibiting features of both (cf. Weisgerber, op. cit., esp. pp. 397–404, 410–36). It should in any case be clear that we are not at this period, before the Roman frontier was established, dealing with two totally separate and distinct linguistic and cultural groups, but with a tribal spectrum which in the middle may be extremely blurred.

p. 39, n. 3. Preliminary report by Bögli and Sitterding, *Rev. hist. vaudoise* lxxi (1963), pp. 97–186; report on the coins by Martin, ibid. lxxiii (1965), pp. 113–85; further report by Bögli, ibid. lxxv (1967), pp. 179–86. Fuller accounts now by Martin et al., *Lousonna*, including an account of the Italian sigillata by Laufer, pp. 194–226, which confirms that the oldest pieces from Vidy find their parallels at Zürich and on the Magdalensberg, cf. p. 200, commenting on pl. 19, no. 1 ('la réplique des tasses du Lindenhof de Zürich . . . une des pièces les plus anciennes de T. S. italique trouvées en Suisse'); also pl. 20, nos. 9, 10, 18–20; pl. 25, no. 8. There are 133 stamps reported, of which 64 belong to the Ateius group.

p. 40, n. 2. Add now further information, including two new sites, Avenches and Studenberg–Petinesca, in Ettlinger, *JSGU* liv (1968/9), p. 72.

p. 41, n. 1. To this list of sites now add Tongres in Belgium and Pollentia in Majorca. On Tongres, Vanvinckenroye, *Opgravingen te Tongeren in 1963–1964*, esp. p. 33, fig. 1, and Vanderhoeven, *De Terra Sigillata te*

Tongeren iii: *de italische Terra Sigillata*, esp. p. 52, fig. 3, 1–3. The first part of Vanderhoeven's work was also published as an article in *Helinium* vii (1967), pp. 32–64. Cf. also below, addendum to p. 94, n. 5. Unpublished pieces from Pollentia in the Alcudia Museum, Majorca, reported by Ettlinger, *JSGU* liv (1968/9), p. 69. In the same article, pp. 71–2, Ettlinger assembles a list of all Swiss sites known to have yielded Service I sigillata; they include, in addition to sites mentioned elsewhere in our present chapter, three others in north Switzerland (Bennwil, Gelterkinden, and Dietikon). Cf. also above, p. 40, n. 2 and p. 66, n. 3.

p. 46, n. 3. This appears to be untrue. Recent excavations, still unpublished, in the courtyard of the Natural History Museum west of the Münsterplatz have revealed a quantity of pottery, some late La Tène, some Augustan. This has not yet, however, been fully studied and the implications are not clear (information from Professor E. Ettlinger).

p. 52, n. 1. The latest excavations have revealed further early Augustan sigillata stamps from within the area of the base, and Wiedemer sees these as strengthening the probability that there was an earlier fort on the site, perhaps one of those which, he suggests, must have guarded the supply lines of the newly discovered base at Dangstetten (Wiedemer, *JGPV* 1968, p. 5). It thus becomes increasingly urgent to re-examine all the early sigillata finds from Vindonissa to see exactly whereabouts in the base they come from.

As an alternative to the early fort theory, one might suggest that there was after all a short-lived legionary base here in the early Augustan period, as there was at Dangstetten, a base for the conquest of the Alps and Voralpenland, given up, like Dangstetten, around 8 B.C. and only reoccupied twenty-five years later. This would account for the failure to find any trace of the defences of the hypothetical early fort, since an early legionary base would have had the same defences as the later, permanent one.

p. 57, n. 3. I am now grateful for having been allowed to read in proof Fingerlin's own preliminary report on the first four years' excavations, to be published in *Arch. Nachrichten aus Baden* vi (1971), pp. 11–20. The southeastern corner of the base has been excavated, including the east gate. The south side curves inward, reminding one of the re-entrant angles at other Augustan bases. Fingerlin's plan shows that to date the excavated area stretches for about 250 m. in an east–west direction and about 350 m. from north to south. The position of the other sides is still unknown.

In the area excavated are remains of buildings, identified as the *principia*, barrack blocks, and workshops. There were also traces of buildings and of a smithy outside the east gate, which Fingerlin suggests may indicate the presence of native labour, perhaps impressed from the nearby *oppidum* of Altenburg–Rheinau. There were also Celtic finds within the base. Other finds include coins and pottery, as already mentioned in our text above, consistent with an occupation from 15 B.C. to soon after 10 B.C.; a complete millefiori goblet, something of a rarity; and a model of a hand with fingers raised in blessing, identified with the eastern cult of Sabazios, the earliest cult-object of this religion to be found in Western Europe. This and other finds seem to attest the presence of eastern archers in the garrison of the base, which also appears to have included Treveran cavalry.

Further excavation is planned, and this, together with fuller publication of the finds, will doubtless elucidate many of the questions that remain unanswered. Of these, the size of the base is perhaps the most urgent, and it is also desirable to have more precise information on the dating. At the moment Dangstetten appears, like Oberaden and Rödgen, to have been given up at or around the time of Drusus' death, perhaps, as suggested above (pp. 157, 220), because all belonged to the phase of the earliest offensive, which was now over, and were not needed in the period of consolidation which followed. This does not betoken Roman weakness, but rather Roman strength.

Dangstetten then will have been an essential base for the operations of the year 15 B.C. and will have been retained for some years thereafter, but abandoned once Raetia had settled down to its peaceful payment of taxation (above, p. 72), and the legions had moved on to further conquests. It is significant that, although the Wutach valley, which Dangstetten commands, was a natural route from Helvetia northwards, ultimately linking up with the Neckar valley, nevertheless Hüfingen, where this route crosses the line of the Danube, was not occupied by the Romans until Claudian times (above, p. 69), which suggests that the Wutach valley route had little importance for them in the intervening period.

p. 66, n. 3. Further beakers are reported from two sites in the Ticino south of the Alps, at Giubiasco and Solduno, published long ago but known to me only through the reference in Ettlinger, *JSGU* liv (1968/9), p. 72.

p. 94, n. 2. On the Titelberg, see now Wightman, *Roman Trier and the Treveri*, pp. 31–2.

p. 94, n. 5. On the road network, and on the site of the early fort at Trier, see Wightman, *Roman Trier and the Treveri*, pp. 36, 71–2, suggesting that the original Roman fort occupied the site of the later town-centre. On Tongres, Vanderhoeven, op. cit. (see above, addendum to p. 41, n. 1), pp. 76–8, argues on the evidence of the sigillata finds that it was the site of one of Drusus' bases for the invasion of Germany, established around 15 B.C. On the date he is clearly right, and indeed perhaps overly conservative. The sigillata might support a date as early as 20 B.C., cf. Comfort, *Helinium* ix (1969), pp. 189–91. But the sigillata need not come exclusively from Roman troops, and there do not appear to be distinctively military finds or traces of distinctively military construction, as one might expect if Tongres were a base on the scale Vanderhoeven implies. Perhaps here, as at Trier, there was an early fort, but also a civil settlement with, as Comfort puts it, 'enough Roman admixture, whether military, administrative, or commercial, to account for the Italian pottery, but . . . the basic population of Tongres [was] essentially civilian, tribal and Belgian from the very beginning'.

Vanderhoeven also summarizes the evidence for finds of Italian sigillata elsewhere in modern Belgium (op. cit., pp. 79–89). To those sites already named in my p. 94, n. 5, add now Harmignies, Tavier, Braives, Velzeke, Asse, Elewijt, Arlon, Namen. Most of the places named seem to be strung out along two roads, one from Bavai and the other further north from the coast, both of which meet at Tongres and continue to the Rhine at Cologne. The importance of Bavai and of Tongres as road-junctions is made clear by Vanderhoeven's map, op. cit., p. 88, fig. 12.

p. 97, n. 2. An earlier fort now appears to be known also at Asberg, still unpublished (information from Dr. C. B. Rüger).

p. 98, n. 4. On Burnum and Ivoševci, see now Wilkes, *Dalmatia*, pp. 100, 217, where, however, Wilkes equates Ivoševci with the *canabae*, despite its distance from the base.

p. 128, n. 1. Now also Chantraine, *Novaesium* iii: *Die antike Fundmünzen der Ausgrabungen in Neuss*.

p. 135, n. 2. Further Italian sigillata from Cologne published by Camps and Filtzinger, *Kölner Jb. für. Vor- und Frühgeschichte* x (1969), pp. 47–55. Also a hoard of counterfeit *denarii*, to be dated to the first half of the first century A.D., before the foundation of the colony, Nuber and La Baume, ibid., pp. 37–46, arguing further for the location of the *oppidum Ubiorum* south of the legionary base, between the base itself and the Tiberian site on the Alteburg just over 3 km. away, identified with the headquarters of the Rhine fleet (publication of the Alteburg remains by Filtzinger forthcoming).

p. 135, n. 3. I am informed by Dr. C. B. Rüger that this piece has now been published in *Rom am Dom*, the catalogue of the town excavation exhibition of 1970, which, however, I have not yet seen. A graffito of the same legion is also known on a pig of lead from Haltern, now at Münster, to be the subject of an article in a forthcoming issue of *Germania* by Dr. von Schnurbein. Another record of this legion comes from Dangstetten (above, p. 57).

p. 142, n. 2. Cf. Richmond, *Hod Hill* ii, pp. 68–9, in more detail on the Punic ditch at Hod Hill and its tactical use.

p. 148, n. 4. Nierhaus, *Bad. Fundber.* xxiii (1967), p. 121, rightly emphasizes how little interest the Romans had in the Black Forest region, 'das siedlungsleere, also vom Standpunkt der Sicherheit aus betrachtet: harmlose und dazu wirtschaftlich uninteressante Waldgebirge'.

p. 156, n. 5. I do not feel that Timpe, *Rh. Mus.* cx (1967), pp. 289–306, proves his theory of conflicting counsels in the Roman high command on this point, although his article contains much that is of value. He also still holds, wrongly in my opinion, that Oberaden was taken and destroyed by the enemy, see above, p. 216.

p. 158, n. 5. Timpe, *Saeculum* xviii (1967), pp. 278–93, discussing the history of the lost years between Tiberius' two governorships, argues that there is a confusion in the sources, and that Ahenobarbus was in fact already governor of Germany at the time of the Elbe crossing. His arguments do not seem conclusive. Timpe rightly emphasizes the unsuitability of the Elbe as a frontier, although accepting the conventional view that Augustus intended to use it as such, a plan which he sees as based on 'eine geopolitisch falsche Konzeption'. Cf. also above, p. 6.

p. 161, n. 4. A further limited excavation was carried out at Holsterhausen in the autumn of 1970 by Dr. H. Aschemeyer, who has kindly let me have a copy of his still unpublished report. A further stretch of the ditch was uncovered, revealing a particularly pointed profile, like that of the Haltern marching-camp. The absence of a wood-and-earth rampart was confirmed, as was that of wooden buildings in the interior. There can be no doubt that Holsterhausen was, as Stieren concluded, merely a short-lived temporary camp. It remains to be seen whether it was succeeded by a permanent base, as was the similar marching-camp at Haltern, but for the moment at least there is no evidence at all for such a base, and if there was one, it did not occupy the area covered by the 1970 excavations.

p. 175, n. 5. There were further limited excavations in 1967 which confirmed that remains outside the base but associated with it overlay the levelled defences of the marching camp (K. Wilhelmi, *Westfälische Forsch.* xx (1967), p. 115).

p. 177, n. 7. Brief notices by various hands have since appeared in *Westfälische Forsch.* xix (1966), pp. 127, 130, 132, 134; xx (1967), pp. 111, 115–16; xxi (1968), pp. 183–4, covering the excavations from 1960–8. These excavations have greatly increased our knowledge of the road system in the base, especially in its western part, and of the barracks layout. The plan of the legionary base reproduced in this present work (Fig. 9), which shows the state of our knowledge as it was in 1939, is thus out of date.

Among the finds in these years were pottery, including an amphora 87 cm. high, about 100 coins, brooches, lamps, weapons, including two helmets and a *pilum*, roof-tiles, moulds for making decorated sigillata, and remains of pottery ovens and smithies. The existence of the latter inside the base is normal at this period, instead of in the *canabae*, as was the case later (cf. above, pp. 98–9). The importance of the sigillata moulds has already been pointed out (above, p. 256). The roof-tiles (xix (1966), p. 127) are surprising. A fragment of tile was also found at Anreppen (below, addendum to p. 222, n. 2), whereas it was previously the accepted view that roof-tiles on the Rhine come in only with Claudius (cf. above, p. 143, and my scepticism, which I now recant, about an earlier report of roof-tiles on the Wiegel, p. 193, n. 4).

The existence of a pig of lead from Haltern, bearing a graffito of *leg. XIX*, still unpublished, has been recorded above in the addendum to p. 135, n. 3.

p. 188, n. 4. Dr. Aschemeyer kindly informs me (letter of 21 April 1971) that the surviving coins from Haltern have now been re-examined by Herr Korzus, whose research confirms the A.D. 9 date for the end of the base.

p. 189, n. 6. The discovery of the moulds now recorded by Aschemeyer, *Westfälische Forsch.* xix (1966), p. 132; cf. also above, p. 256.

p. 193, n. 4. The report of roof-tiles should not be treated so sceptically now that they have been found in the base at Haltern and at Anreppen (above, addendum to p. 177, n. 7, and below to p. 222, n. 2).

p. 213, n. 1. Brief notes in *Westfälische Forsch.* xix (1966), pp. 127, 130.

p. 222, n. 2. There is a brief account of the first year's excavations by Beck in *Westfälische Forsch.* xxi (1968), pp. 183-4, and an account of both the 1968 and 1969 excavations, also by Beck, in *Germania* xlviii (1970), pp. 60-4. A stretch of 200 m. of the east side was traced; north of that point it had been eroded by the Lippe. The south side was traced for a length of 680 m. There was a double ditch, the outer ditch being deeper than the inner one, and a wood-and-earth rampart, possibly with towers, since a tower and a ramp leading up to it were found at one point. A short disconnected stretch of ditch on a different orientation led to the conjecture that there might have been more than one period of occupation.

The finds included pottery, coins, brooches, and weapons, together with a piece of roof-tile. The coins include those of the Lugdunum altar-series and are said to indicate a relatively late date. The only sigillata stamp yet found is one of Ateius, which would go well with an occupation in the last years before A.D. 9. The base appears to have been erected on the site of a native settlement, but the finds have not yet been studied and published in detail.

The actual size of the base remains unknown. If, as seems likely, the Lippe in Roman times flowed further north than it now does, Anreppen could have been a base for two legions. On the other hand, air photographs and studies of the ground show that there have been periods when the Lippe flowed to the south of the legionary site, instead of to the north. Future finds may elucidate the question.

Anreppen fits well into the supposed series of bases at 18-km. intervals (above, p. 151). In this case there would be three others still to be found within the stretch from Oberaden to Anreppen. It should, however, be pointed out that on the present evidence Oberaden and Anreppen were not occupied simultaneously, and since Holsterhausen, another of the supposed series, was only a short-lived marching-camp (above, addendum to p. 161, n. 4), this hypothesis cannot be considered absolutely certain.

A further article by Beck is to appear in the new second edition of Hoops, *Reallexikon der germanischen Altertumskunde*, and a report on the 1970 excavations will be published in *Westfälische Forsch.* xxiii (1970).

p. 224, n. 3. The Augustan and Tiberian finds from Höchst are now newly catalogued by Kubon and Schauer, *Fundber. aus Hessen* ix/x (1969/70), pp. 77–85.

p. 226, n. 2. Schönberger, *Wetterauer Geschichtsbl.* xv (1966), pp. 21–5, discussing Friedberg in Augustan times, is also sceptical of the claim that the Mager and Roth excavation showed two periods of occupation, and points out that the earliest finds to date, whether from this excavation or the later one in 1963, cannot be dated to the period B.C.

p. 226, n. 5. Schönberger's map, op. cit., p. 23, fig. 2, shows where other lengths of possible fortification are reported to have been found in the area, including the one by the railway station referred to in the final paragraph of our Chapter 6. 8, which, however, Schönberger, p. 25, believes from the scanty finds to date from the period of Domitian.

p. 239, n. 1. Varus was related to Augustus by his marriage to Claudia Pulchra, but his position of influence within the regime is now further emphasized by the discovery that he was also Agrippa's son-in-law by an earlier marriage, see Koenen, *Ztschr. für Papyrologie und Epigraphik* v (1970), pp. 257–68, on the implications of a newly published papyrus fragment of the Greek translation of Augustus' funeral oration for Agrippa. Also on Varus' early career and the date of his proconsulship in Africa see Thomasson, *Eranos* lxvii (1969), pp. 175–9.

p. 241, n. 3. The famous Hildesheim treasure, a large hoard of Roman silver found in 1967 and sometimes alleged to be part of the table service of a Roman officer, perhaps even of Varus himself or one of his lieutenants, is nothing of the sort. An exhaustive reappraisal of the nature and date of the pieces composing the treasure by Nierhaus, *Die Kunde* xx (1969), pp. 52–61, with references to earlier literature, leads to the conclusion that they are of mixed quality, including some that appear unlikely to have been owned by a high Roman officer, and that the hoard cannot have been buried before the second half of the first century A.D.

There is a fuller description of the pieces, with excellent photographs, in another recent publication, Gehrig, *Hildesheimer Silberfund.* Lindemann, *Der Hildesheimer Silberfund*, still maintains the connection with the Augustan period. Nierhaus is, however, to my mind conclusive against this.

p. 242, n. 3. Similarly Timpe, *Der Triumph des Germanicus*, reviewing the history of Germanicus' campaigns, argues that the campaign of 15 had Tiberius' full backing and was seriously intended as a first step towards the reconquest of Germany, but that Tiberius abandoned this plan at the end of that year, the campaign of 16 being carried out by Germanicus in defiance of Tiberius' wishes.

p. 253, n. 2. Reference should also be made to the articles 'Aretini, Vasi', by Stenico, *Enciclopedia dell'Arte antica* i, pp. 608–16, and 'Terra sigillata' by Comfort, ibid. vii, pp. 726–9. An expanded version of Comfort's article was also published separately, together with Stenico's article and articles by Del Chiaro on 'Megaresi, Vasi', and by Paribeni on 'Otricolensi, Vasi'. I have not, however, been able to consult this separate publication.

p. 254, n. 1. Professor E. Ettlinger informs me that in her opinion this supposedly Tiberian black-gloss sigillata, which she has now seen, is in fact 'good, ordinary terra sigillata, but secondarily burnt' (letter of 18 April 1971). If this is so, the apparent exception to the rule that black-gloss sigillata is all relatively early disappears.

p. 265, n. 3. This statement regarding Haltern is inaccurate, see Asche-meyer, *Germania* xxxvii (1959), p. 291, on a very fine Aco-type beaker by the potter Acastus. Another fragment of an Aco-beaker is described by Oxé, *Bod. Westf.* vi (1943), pp. 34–5, 44–5. These remain the only two pieces of Aco-ware from Haltern. On the question of the widespread distribution of this ware, Professor H. Comfort has drawn my attention to the evidence assembled by Iliffe, *Quart. Dept. Ant. Palestine* vi (1936/7), pp. 19–24, for imports of western pottery into Palestine, including Italian and South Gaulish sigillata and Aco-ware.

p. 265, n. 5. Cf. also the discussion of Augustan beakers by Vegas, *RCRFA* v/vi (1963/4), pp. 61–83.

p. 272, n. 4. As a result of reorganization, Dr. Weissgerber's official title is now Head of the Division of Prehistory and Archaeology of the Museum für Kunst and Kulturgeschichte, Dortmund.

ADDENDA TO BIBLIOGRAPHY

CHANTRAINE, H., *Novaesium* iii: *Die antiken Fundmünzen der Ausgrabungen in Neuss* (Limesforschungen viii), Berlin, 1968.

COMFORT, H., review of Vanderhoeven, *De terra sigillata te Tongeren* iii, in *Helinium* ix (1969), 189–91.

—— 'Terra sigillata', in *Enc. dell'Arte antica* vii, 726–9.

DECKER, K.-V., 'Die jüngere Latènezeit im Neuwieder Becken', *Jb. für Gesch. und Kunst des Mittelrheins*, Beih. i (1968), 81 ff.

Enciclopedia dell'Arte antica, classica e orientale (Istituto della Enciclopedia Italiana), 7 vols., Rome, 1958–66.

ETTLINGER, E., 'Keramik-Datierung der frühen Kaiserzeit', *JSGU* liv (1968/9), 69–72.

FINGERLIN, G., 'Rheinheim–Dangstetten: ein Legionslager aus frührömischer Zeit am Hochrhein', *Arch. Nachrichten aus Baden* vi (1971), 11–20.

GEHRIG, V., *Hildesheimer Silberfund in der Antikenabteilung Berlin* (Bilderhefte der Staatlichen Museen Berlin iv), Berlin, 1967.

HOOPS, J., *Reallexicon der germanischen Altertumskunde*, 2nd edn. revised and enlarged, edited by H. Jankuhn, H. Kuhn, K. Ranke, R. Wenskus, Berlin, 1967–   .

ILIFFE, J. H., 'Sigillata wares in the Near East: a list of potters' stamps', *Quart. of the Dept. of Antiquities in Palestine* vi (1936/7), 4–53.

JOACHIM, H.-E., *Die Hunsrück-Eifel-Kultur am Mittelrhein* (*BJ*, Beiheft xxix), Cologne and Graz, 1968.

KOENEN, L., 'Die "laudatio funebris" des Augustus für Agrippa', *Ztschr. für Papyrologie und Epigraphik* v (1970), 217–83.

KRAHE, H., *Sprache und Vorzeit: europäische Vorgeschichte nach dem Zeugnis der Sprache*, Heidelberg, 1954.

LAST, M., 'Altenburg bei Niedenstein', in Hoops, *Reallexicon der germanischen Altertumskunde* i², 205–9.

LINDEMANN, K., *Der Hildesheimer Silberfund: Varus und Germanicus*, Hildesheim, 1967.

MAHR, G., *Die jüngere Latènekultur des Trierer Landes: eine stilkundliche und chronologische Untersuchung auf Grund der Keramik und des Bestattungswesens* (Berliner Beiträge zur Vor und Frühgeschichte xii), Berlin, 1967.

MARTIN, C., et al., *Lousonna* (Bibliothèque historique vaudoise xlii), Lausanne, 1969.

MILDENBERGER, G., 'Das Ende der Altenburg bei Niedenstein', *Fundber. aus Hessen*, Beiheft i (1969) (Marburger Beiträge zur Archäologie der Kelten: Festchrift für Wolfgang Dehn zum 60. Geburtstag am 6. Juli 1969), Bonn, 1969, 122–34.

NIERHAUS, R., 'Römische Strassenverbindungen durch den Schwarzwald', *Bad. Fundber.* xxiii (1967), 117–57.

—— 'Der Silberschatz von Hildesheim: seine Zusammensetzung und der Zeitpunkt seiner Vergrabung', *Die Kunde* xx (1969), 52–61.

RICHMOND, SIR IAN, et al., *Hod Hill* ii: *excavations carried out between 1951 and 1958 for the Trustees of the British Museum*, London, 1968.

SCHÖNBERGER, H., 'Friedberg in römischer und fränkischer Zeit', *Wetterauer Geschichtsbl.* xv (1966), 21 ff.

STENICO, A., 'Aretini o Arretini, Vasi', in *Enc. dell'Arte Antica* i, 608–16.

THOMASSON, P. E., 'Verschiedenes zu den *Proconsules Africae*', *Eranos* lxvii (1969), 175–91.

TIERNEY, J. J., 'The Map of Agrippa', *Proc. Royal Irish Academy* lxiii C. 4 (1963), 151–66.

TIMPE, D., 'Drusus' Umkehr an der Elbe', *Rh. Mus.* cx (1967), 289–306.

TIMPE, D., 'Zur Geschichte und Überlieferung der Okkupation Germaniens unter Augustus', *Saeculum* xviii (1967), 278–93.

—— *Der Triumph des Germanicus: Untersuchungen zu den Feldzügen der Jahre 14–16 n. Chr.* (Antiquitas i, 16), Bonn, 1968.

VANDERHOEVEN, M., *De terra sigillata te Tongeren* iii: *de italische terra sigillata* (Publikaties van het Provinciaal Gallo-Romeins Museum te Tongeren xii), Tongres, 1968.

VANVINCKENROYE, W., *Opgravingen te Tongeren in 1963–1964 door het Provinciaal Gallo-Romeins Museum* (Publikaties van het Provinciaal Gallo-Romeins Museum te Tongeren viii), Tongres, 1965.

VEGAS, M., 'Difusión de algunas formas de vasitos de paredes finas', *RCRFA* v/vi (1963/4), 61–83.

WAHLE, E., *Deutsche Vorzeit*, 2nd edn., Basle, 1952 (1st edn. 1932).

WEISGERBER, J. L., *Die Namen der Ubier* (Wiss. Abhandlungen der Arbeitsgemeinschaft für Forschung des Landes Nordrhein-Westfalen xxxiv), Cologne and Opladen, 1968.

WIGHTMAN, E. M., *Roman Trier and the Treveri*, London, 1970.

WILKES, J. J., *Dalmatia* (History of the Provinces of the Roman Empire), London, 1969.

ADDENDA TO LIST OF PERIODICALS CITED

Archäologische Nachrichten aus Baden, Freiburg i. Br.

Historische Zeitschrift, Munich (*Hist. Ztschr.*)

Kunde, Die. Niedersächsischer Landesverein für Urgeschichte, Hanover.

Philologus. Zeitschrift für das klassische Altertum, Berlin.

Quarterly of the Department of Antiquities of Palestine, Jerusalem and London. (*Quart. Dept. Antiq. Pal.*)

Westfälische Forschungen. Mitteilungen des Provinzialinstituts für Westfälische Landes- und Volkskunde, Munster i. W.

Wetterauer Geschichtsblätter. Beiträge zur Geschichte und Landeskunde, Friedberg.

Wiener Prähistorische Zeitschrift, Vienna. (*Wiener Präh. Ztschr.*)

Zeitschrift für Papyrologie und Epigraphik, Bonn.

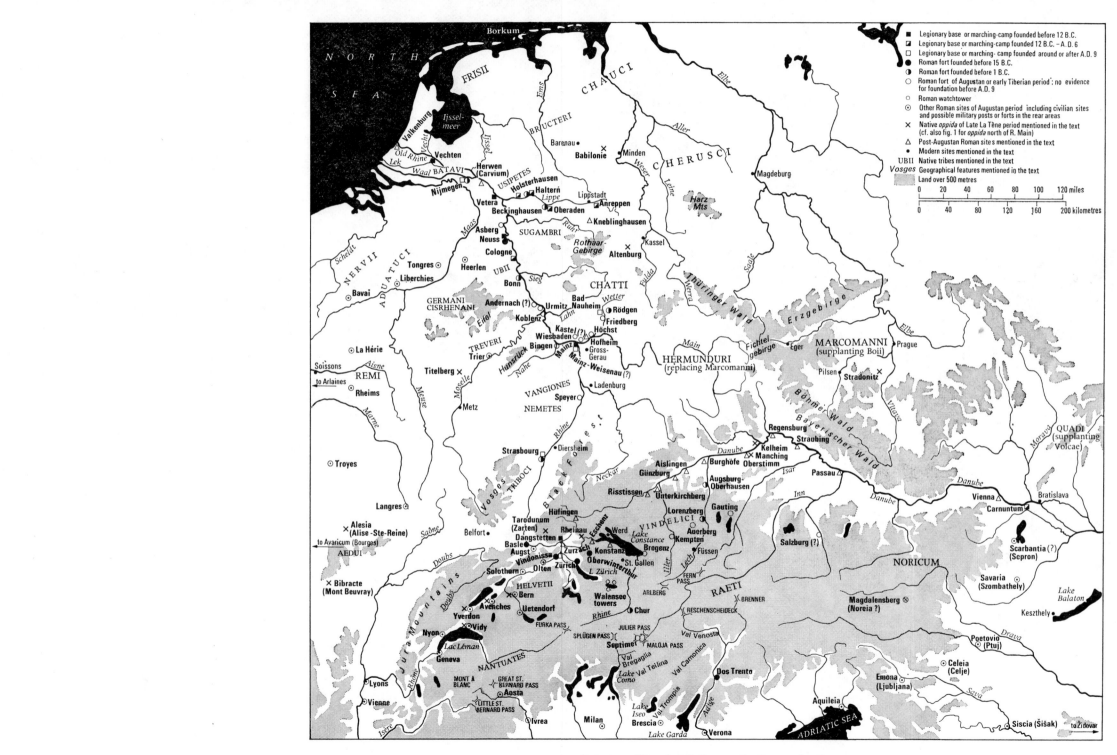

Augustan military installations on the German frontier

INDEX

An entry in **bold type** indicates the principal discussion of the site or subject in question; an entry in *italics* is a reference to a text-figure or table. Roman citizens are listed under their *gentilicia*, except for writers and members of the imperial house, who appear under the names by which they are most commonly known.